RAF Bomber Command Squadron Profiles

300 (Masovian) Squadron

RAF Bomber Command Squadron Profiles

300 (Masovian) Squadron

by Chris Ward

and Grzegorz Korcz

Bomber Command Books

from

MENTION
THE WAR
PUBLICATIONS

This edition first published 2016 by Mention the War Ltd., 32 Croft Street, Farsley, Yorkshire, LS28 5HA.

Cover design: Topics - The Creative Partnership www.topicsdesign.co.uk

A CIP catalogue reference for this book is available from the British Library.

ISBN 978-1-911255-14-7

Contents

Other Bomber Command books from Mention the War

Striking Through Clouds – The War Diary of 514 Squadron RAF
(Simon Hepworth and Andrew Porrelli)
Nothing Can Stop Us – The Definitive History of 514 Squadron RAF
(Simon Hepworth, Andrew Porrelli and Harry Dison)
Lancasters at Waterbeach – Some of the Story of 514 Squadron
(Harry Dison)

A Short War – The History of 623 Squadron RAF
A Stirling Effort – Short Stirling Operations at RAF Downham Market 1942-1944
(Steve Smith)

RAF Bomber Command Profiles:
103 Squadron (with David Fell)
106 Squadron (with Herman Bijlard)
617 Squadron

A Special Duty – A Crew's Secret War with 148 (SD) Squadron
(Jennifer Elkin)
148 Squadron at War 1918 – 1945
(Oliver Clutton-Brock) December 2016

Skid Row to Buckingham Palace
(Ed Greenburgh)
The Boy and the Bomber
(Francois Ydier)
The Pendulum and the Scythe
(Ken Marshall)

The above books are available through Amazon worldwide, as well as from the publisher. For further details or to purchase a signed and dedicated copy, please contact *bombercommandbooks@gmail.com* or visit www.bombercommandbooks.com

Introduction

RAF Bomber Command Squadron Profiles first appeared in the late nineties, and proved to be very popular with enthusiasts of RAF Bomber Command during the Second World War. They became a useful research tool, particularly for those whose family members had served and were no longer around. The original purpose was to provide a point of reference for all of the gallant men and women who had fought the war, either in the air, or on the ground in a support capacity, and for whom no written history of their unit or station existed. I wanted to provide them with something they could hold up, point to and say, "This was my unit, this is what I did in the war". Many veterans were reticent to talk about their time on bombers, partly because of modesty, but perhaps mostly because the majority of those with whom they came into contact had no notion of what it was to be a "Bomber Boy", to face the prospect of death every time they took to the air, whether during training or on operations. Only those who shared the experience really understood what it was to go to war in bombers, which is why reunions were so important. As they approached the end of their lives, many veterans began to speak openly for the first time about their life in wartime Bomber Command, and most were hurt by the callous treatment they received at the hands of successive governments with regard to the lack of recognition of their contribution to victory. It is sad that this recognition in the form of a national memorial and the granting of a campaign medal came too late for the majority. Now this inspirational, noble generation, the like of which will probably never grace this earth again, has all but departed from us, and the world will be a poorer place as a result.

RAF Bomber Command Squadron Profiles are back, the basic format remaining, but, where needed, additional information has been provided. Squadron Profiles do not claim to be comprehensive histories, but rather detailed overviews of the activities of the squadron. There is insufficient space to mention as many names as one would like, but all aircraft losses are accompanied by the name of the pilot. Fundamentally, the narrative section is an account of Bomber Command's war from the perspective of the bomber group under which the individual squadron served, and the deeds of the squadron are interwoven into this story. Information has been drawn from official records, such as group, squadron and station ORBs, and from the many, like myself, amateur enthusiasts, who dedicate much of their time to researching individual units, and become unrivalled authorities on them. I am grateful for their generous contributions, and their names will appear in the appropriate Profiles. The statistics quoted in this series are taken from The Bomber Command War Diaries, that indispensable tome written by Martin Middlebrook and Chris Everitt, and I am indebted to Martin for his kind permission to use them.

Finally, let me apologise in advance for the inevitable errors, for no matter how hard I and other authors try to write "nothing but the truth", there is no such thing as a definitive account of history, and there will always be room for disagreement and debate. Official records are notoriously unreliable tools, and yet we have little choice but to put our faith in them. It is not my intention to misrepresent any person or RAF unit, and I ask my readers to understand the enormity of the task I have undertaken. It is relatively easy to become an authority on single units or even a bomber group, but I chose to write about them all, idiot that I am, which means 128 squadrons serving operationally in Bomber Command at some time between the 3rd of September 1939 and the 8th of May 1945. I am dealing with eight bomber groups, in which some

120,000 airmen served, and I am juggling around 28,000 aircraft serial numbers, code letters and details of provenance and fate. I ask not for your sympathy, it was, after all, my choice, but rather your understanding if you should find something with which you disagree. My thanks to you, my readers, for making the original series of RAF Bomber Command Squadron Profiles so popular, and I hope you receive this new incarnation equally enthusiastically. My thanks also to Simon Hepworth of Mention The War Publications for seeing the potential of bringing them back, and for investing so much effort and time in the project.

There has been little written in the English language about the Polish squadrons of Bomber Command, whose commitment to victory over Nazi Germany was second to none. As always when writing about a particular squadron, I seek out someone who has devoted much of their life to researching it, and ask for their input. Greg Korcz first offered his assistance when I was writing 1 Group Bomber Command, and we quickly became good friends via the internet, exchanging information and planning a wartime history of the Polish bomber units. Greg is an aviation historian living in Gdansk, and knows more about Poland's contribution to Bomber Command that anyone else on the planet. I extend my gratitude to Greg for the time and effort he has expended on this project, and to him and all others who have kindly donated photographs from their collections for publication in this work.

Chris Ward. Lutterworth. August 2016.

1940

Following the defeat of Poland in the September campaign of 1939, many of its airmen escaped via the neighbouring countries of Hungary, Romania, Lithuania and Latvia, and ultimately made their way to France. Here they were gathered on a station at Lyon-Bron, where they were organised into mainly fighter training groups. Meanwhile, in November 1939, British and Polish authorities signed an agreement, which became the foundation of future close cooperation between the Royal Air Force and a forming Polish Air Force. According to this document, Great Britain agreed to accept 2,300 Polish airmen, and arrange them into four bomber squadrons, two operational and two in reserve. The bomber crews eventually found themselves in Africa, mostly at Blida in Algeria, and it was from there that they arrived in December 1939 at Eastchurch on the south coast of England, at a camp established for Polish airmen. All aircrew satisfying the requirements for operational duties had to complete elementary training covering the basics of the King's Regulations and the English language, the latter essential to being effective contributors to the war effort. This was to be the start of a strong association between 1 Group RAF Bomber Command and Polish airmen, which would continue to the end of the war.

The two first COs of 300 Squadron: British – W/C Lewis (left) and Polish – W/C Makowski (right). (PISM London)

On the 4th of June a new RAF station was officially opened at Bramcote, a village about four miles to the south-east of the mining town of Nuneaton in Warwickshire. On the 15th W/C Evan Christopher Lewis arrived to assume joint command of the soon-to-be-formed first Polish squadron in Bomber Command, and act as the British adviser and intermediary between Polish airmen and British officialdom. Two days later W/C Waclaw Makowski paid a visit to the station, in advance of becoming W/C Lewis's Polish counterpart. W/C Makowski was born in Russia in 1897, and graduated from primary flying training in 1919. Thereafter he was involved in a number of aviation roles, including test pilot, and from 1930, until being called up once more for military duty, he served as the head of the Polish airline LOT. He arrived in the UK in December 1939, and initially organised a training school at Upavon in Wiltshire.

The first batch of Fairey Battles was flown into Bramcote from a maintenance unit at Benson in Oxfordshire on the 26th of June, the day on which F/L Cwynar was appointed as the new squadron's A Flight commander. Two days later W/C Makowski returned to Bramcote in preparation to take command of the unit on its official formation as 300 Squadron on the 1st of July, when a ceremonial parade was held in the morning. The last of its complement of Battles arrived on the 3rd of July to bring the squadron up to its full strength of sixteen. In a somewhat confusing development, S/L Kenneth Purdon Lewis was

Bramcote, 7th August 1940. Gen. Sikorski saluting Polish aircrews. (PISM via W. Matusiak)

Bramcote, 20th August 1940. The first visit of King George VI to Bramcote. From left: 1st W/C Rudkowski CO of 301 Squadron, 2nd Gen. Sikorski, 4th G/C Davidson CO of RAF Station Bramcote. (PISM via WM)

posted in on the 4th of July as the British commander of the squadron, and W/C E.C. Lewis was appointed Wing Commander Flying. Also on this day F/L Pronaszko became B Flight commander. The first night flying exercises by Polish pilots took place on the 11th, when two aircraft were involved, and three were used on the 13th. Thereafter, for the remainder of the month, both day and night exercises were mounted, which included cross-countries, dive-bombing and communications. By month's end the squadron boasted a cadre of fifteen commissioned pilots and eight non-commissioned. While this had been on-going, a second Polish squadron, 301, was officially formed at Bramcote on the 24th under W/C Rudkowski.

On the 7th of August, Polish Prime Minister General Sikorski paid a visit to Bramcote to inspect the Polish squadrons in the company of many senior RAF and Polish dignitaries. They enjoyed a march-past and a dive-bombing demonstration, and, as both Polish squadrons were initially attached to the then 6 Group, its A-O-C, Air Commodore W McNeece Foster, flew in the back of the lead Battle to demonstrate his faith in the ability of Polish pilots. Five days later a message was received by the Secretary of State for Air from General Sikorski, which read; "I feel I must send you this line at once to tell you how extremely satisfied I was with my visit to my airmen yesterday. Everywhere we were received with the utmost courtesy and goodwill, and everywhere I found my men in splendid form. My visit has only endorsed what I already knew, namely, that the RAF is giving Polish airmen a really good and fair deal. I trust it will not be long before my men will be able to prove their value over German soil." General Sikorski returned to Bramcote by air on the morning of the 20th with the Polish Ambassador and senior Polish officers. He inspected Polish troops and presented a Polish Cross for Valour to a G/C Alexander P Davidson. His Majesty King George VI arrived later by car from Nuneaton to inspect the British and Polish Guards of Honour and watch a demonstration of low-level bombing, before lunching in the officers mess and departing again for Nuneaton at 14.40.

Meanwhile, a few miles to the south-west of Lincoln, a new RAF station was stirring into life under the control of 1 Group. Swinderby, Lincolnshire, like its Nottinghamshire neighbours, Newton and Syerston, nestled alongside the A46, the main road linking Leicester and Lincoln, before continuing on in a north-easterly direction to the coast at Grimsby. Swinderby opened on the 1st of August, and, although it was by no means ready to launch operations, it did contain plenty of accommodation. It was to be home to 300 and 301 Squadrons, and W/C E.C. Lewis was appointed as its first station commander on the 17th, by which time many of the permanent staff had moved in to prepare to welcome the first arrivals. The advance party of 300 Squadron moved in on the 22nd, and later in the day, W/C Makowski, eighteen officers and twenty-five airmen landed in a dozen Battles, one Battle trainer and an Anson, at which point the squadron officially joined 1 Group. Apparently, a telephone call was put through to friends in 301 Squadron at Bramcote to announce that there was an airfield and little else, no water, no Officers Mess, no beds and no chairs in the rooms. This was not welcome news to the 301 Squadron people, who would, themselves, soon be passing through the Swinderby main gates. The move by 300 Squadron was completed on the 23rd with the arrival by road of the rear party under S/L K. P. Lewis, who was accompanied by nineteen officers and 146 airmen.

1 Group had been disbanded in September 1939, when its squadrons were formed into the Advanced Air Striking Force (AASF), and were posted to France on the 2nd of September, the day after Germany invaded Poland, and the day before Britain and France declared war on Germany. The German advance into the Low Countries on the 10th of May 1940 brought an end to the shadow boxing of what the American press had dubbed the "Phoney War", during which time neither side bombed the other for fear of reprisals. Before committing themselves to the attack, the British and French waited until the enemy had established defensive positions, and within days the AASF's Fairey Battles had been shot out of the sky in large numbers. They endured for a further month, until the battered remnant was withdrawn to England in mid-June.

On the 22nd of June a newly-constituted 1 Group had come into being with headquarters at Hucknall in Nottinghamshire, and five days later Air Commodore J. J. Breen was installed as the Air-Officer-Commanding. Curiously, the recording of the group's activities in an operations record book would not begin until the 1st of August. Its strength at this time consisted of 103 and 150 Squadrons at Newton in Nottinghamshire, and 12 and 142 Squadrons at Binbrook in Yorkshire. They had all retained their Battles for the time-being, and the Binbrook units had carried out the first 1 Group operation on the night of the 31st of July. They were attached temporarily to Coastal Command during August, while the Newton squadrons continued training. The arrival of 300 Squadron was a boost, and before month's end, the second Polish squadron, 301, had also taken up residence at Swinderby. Whenever the weather allowed, the crews took to the air, but there were days, as the 301 Squadron commanding officer, W/C Rudkowski, commented, that even the seagulls had to go about on foot to avoid mid-air collisions!

As the Battle of Britain raged overhead, invasion fever gripped the nation, and, until it receded, 1 Group would employ its Battles against the fleets of invasion barges being assembled in the Channel ports of France, Belgium and Holland. 301 Squadron began to move into Swinderby on the 28th of August, and this left two other Polish squadrons, 304 and 305, under training at Bramcote, until they, too, joined 1 Group on moving into Syerston later in the year. Training for 300 Squadron continued into September as the Battle of Britain approached its crescendo, and 142 and 12 Squadrons returned to Binbrook on the 6th and 7th of September respectively. On the evening of the 7th six aircraft each from 103 and 150 Squadrons were dispatched from Newton to Calais to attack invasion barges, and although all returned safely, searchlights and conditions generally had impeded the accuracy and assessment of the bombing. A further six Battles from Newton carried out a repeat operation on the evening of the 9th, and one from 103 Squadron failed to return and was lost without trace. Calais had been the intended target for a further assault on the late evening of the 10th, but it was changed during the day to Boulogne, and all six participants returned safely from what was another indeterminate operation.

By this time W/C Lewis, who never seemed to remain long in a post, had been succeeded as station commander at Swinderby on the 4th by G/C Lawrence Pendred. The Polish airmen were eager to begin operations, and were about to take off on the evening of the 12th when the operation was scrubbed. They had to wait a further two days to get their chance, when, on the evening of the 14th, invasion barges at Boulogne were the target for three aircraft each from 300 and 301 Squadrons. F/O Sulinski[1] had the honour of leading the 300 Squadron element away at 18.55 in L5317, and he was followed over the succeeding ten minutes by F/O Antonowicz in L5427 and P/O Jasinski in L5353. F/O Sulinski's observer was F/O Bujalski, who had just 140 hours flying time in England, and no night flying experience. As the first operation to be launched from Swinderby it was a major occasion, and it seemed that everyone wanted to wave them off. A large crowd gathered, which included representatives of every non-flying section on the station, and squadron colleagues, who were envious of those selected to carry the war to the hated enemy.

Swinderby, summer 1940. Fairey Battle L5427 BH-E about to take-off on a training flight. This aircraft was one of the first three Battles sent by Polish crews on a bombing operation on 14/15th Sept. 1940. (PISM via WM)

Although titled observer in these early days of the war, F/O Bujalski was the navigator and bomb-aimer, and as the French coast hove into view, his confidence began to ebb from him. Would he be able to plot the correct course and not miss the target, and would his aim be true as he released the bombs? It was quite dark as they neared the target, but he was able to pick out the harbour basins before crawling to his position to fuse the bombs. Cones of searchlights sprang up, and then the red, white and green tracer was curling up at them but falling short. He had the aiming point in his bomb sight, when a searchlight beam flicked across his vision and dazzled him, and he was forced to ask Sulinski to take them round again. This time the defenders knew where the attack was coming from, and an even more dense forest of

[1] *In RAF squadrons the pilot was crew captain, irrespective of his rank in relation to the others on board, but the Polish Air Force designated the highest ranking officer as crew captain, whatever his trade. For the purpose of this book, however, crews will be referred to by the name of the pilot.*

searchlights probed the sky, making Sulinski weave in and out as he lined up for the bombing run. The four 250lb bombs fell away from 10,000 feet at 20.43, and Bujalski had the satisfaction of observing the orange flashes as they detonated. Unfortunately, the intense searchlight activity prevented observation of the results. The w/op-gunner, Sgt Biezunski, shot up a searchlight station near the target, and although it was immediately extinguished, others sprang up and a flak shell exploded close by. The Battle bucked and fell away in a nose-dive, much to the consternation of Bujalski, who questioned his pilot but received no response. He fastened his parachute as quickly as he could, and continued to try to communicate with his pilot. He wanted to check on Sulinski, but the design of the Battle prevented access, and all the time the aircraft was losing altitude in a kind of falling leaf manoeuvre. They were down to 4,500 feet when the pilot suddenly came over the intercom to say, "I'll tell you in a minute". It turned out that Sulinski had decided to emulate his gunner, and strafe the ground, but dived a little too steeply, and was too busy avoiding the searchlights to talk to his crew. All three aircraft returned safely and were back on the ground by 23.15.

It had now been decided at group that 300 and 301 Squadrons would operate alternately, and the two squadron commanders threw dice to decide which would take the next opportunity. Having won the right, W/C Makowski led the way on the following night as six 300 Squadron Battles returned to Boulogne. They took off between 18.55 and 19.10, and reached the target at around 20.45. W/C Makowski chose to deliver his bombs in a shallow dive, while F/O Gebicki dived-bombed, releasing his 250 pounders in two salvoes, before strafing the harbour searchlights from 3,000 feet. F/L Krynski and F/O Kaluza opted for a straight-and-level run at 8,000 and 9,000 feet respectively, P/O Kula shallow-dived, and Sgt Kuflik made some kind of error that prevented him from bombing at all. No results were observed, and all returned safely.

As Krynski and Kuflik had brought some bombs home, the former because of a hang-up, they joined a 301 Squadron attack on the same target on the morning of the 18th, departing Swinderby at 03.00 and 03.15 respectively. Kuflik dive-bombed from 11,000 to 8,000 feet, and saw his bombs straddle basins 2 and 6 before exploding. That evening six fresh crews from 300 Squadron went back yet again to Boulogne, and five bombed the harbour, although only one observed any detonations. The squadron continued to blood new crews, and sent five aircraft to Boulogne in the early hours of the 24th, while a sixth attacked the docks at Calais. There was another early start for nine crews on the 26th, as F/O Sulinski led nine Battles off the ground between 02.45 and 03.30 with the docks at Ostend as their destination. They delivered their bombs from between 5,000 and 12,000 feet, but were again unable to determine the results. A note in the 1 Group ORB for September stated "the Polish squadrons have given a very good account of themselves, both by their enthusiasm and their ability to learn and put into practice the British procedure in all of its ramifications." 300 Squadron's first month of operations ended with a tally of thirty-two sorties from six operations and no losses.

Battle of Britain skirmishes continued into October, but the threat of invasion had diminished sufficiently by then to effectively end the operational career of the Fairey Battle in Bomber Command service by mid-month. As an example of its limited employment, 12 Squadron, since its return from France, had logged just eight operations and thirty-six sorties. During the same period Hampdens, Whitleys and Wellingtons from the other groups had been much more active, playing their part in the defence of the country by also attacking marine craft, but mostly by targeting Ruhr industry and communications. It was not until the evening of the 10th of October that 300 squadron went into battle again, this time with eight aircraft against the harbour at le Havre. P/O Kula led them off at 18.21, and they bombed the target from a variety of altitudes between 6,000 and 10,000 feet. All returned safely, five of them with claims of strikes in the docks area on Nos 6 and 2 basins.

On the 13th six 300 Squadron Battles were led into the air at 17.40 by F/O Gebicki bound for the docks at Calais. They reached the target area at around 19.50, and released their bombs from between 8,000 and 12,000 feet, observing detonations across basins 2 to 7. On return to home airspace they found conditions had deteriorated, and only two managed to land at Swinderby. L5499 crashed at Oxton, eight miles north-east of Nottingham, killing F/O Gebicki and his crew. L5427 force-landed at Sherwood Lodge, also in Nottinghamshire, on return, and Sgt Koczwarski and his crew walked away unscathed. This was the final operation for the Fairey Battle with 300 Squadron and 1 Group hands as bad weather prevented further activity, and this was also the end for the time being of 1 Group's contribution to the war effort. October's operational record showed fourteen sorties from two operations for the loss of one aircraft and crew.

S/L Stanislaw Cwynar followed W/C Makowski as CO of 300 Squadron. From Sept. 1940 to Dec. 1941 he took part in 20 operations. Later he became Chief Flying Instructor in 18 OTU at Bramcote and then CO of 16 (P) SFTS at Newton. (W. Zmyslony)

300 Squadron took its first dual-control Wellington on charge on the 18th of October in the form of L7789, which was flown in during the afternoon by a Polish pilot in the Air Transport Auxiliary (ATA), P/O Janas, and attached to A Flight. Soon afterwards, P/O Kirby DFC arrived to provide instruction for the more advanced Polish pilots, so that they in turn could instruct others. The squadron would not be fully equipped until December, and Battles remained on charge for training purposes in the meantime. L5356 was engaged in a dive-bombing exercise on the 29th, when a wing failed and it crashed at Sutton-on-Trent in Nottinghamshire, killing Sgt Goebel and his crew. They were buried with full military honours at Newark on the 1st of November. The rest of November passed with no operations and no major incidents as training continued at Swinderby, Binbrook and Newton. At Swinderby the Battles were gradually being ferried out to maintenance units and replaced by Wellingtons, and familiarization flights took place whenever the weather allowed. After just five months as A-O-C 1 Group, Air Commodore Breen was posted to the Air Ministry on the 27th, and was succeeded by Air Commodore Robert Oxland.

A third Polish unit joined 1 Group on the 2nd of December and took up residence at Syerston. 304 Squadron had been formed at Bramcote on the 22nd of August, and had been equipped with Battles until taking on its first Wellingtons on the 1st of November while still at Bramcote. The final Polish addition to 1 Group, 305 Squadron, moved into Syerston on the 4th, having been formed at Bramcote on the 29th of August, and like the other Polish units, equipping with Battles before converting to Wellingtons, the first of which had been taken on charge on the 5th of November. On the 18th of December the group declared that it had twelve Wellingtons and crews available for operations, six each from Newton and Swinderby. On the 20th the figure was amended to eighteen, and that night the first six sorties by 1 Group Wellingtons were launched from Newton against Ostend. Swinderby's turn came shortly afterwards, for which three crews from each squadron were called to briefing in the afternoon of the 21st, to learn they were to attack oil storage facilities at Antwerp. Take off was planned for the early hours of the 22nd, and it was F/O Sulinski who was first away of the 300 Squadron trio at 04.16 in R1178. He was followed by P/O Kula and P/O Kaluza at 04.22 and 04.27 respectively, and it was approaching 07.00 when the first two reached the target area.

Fairey Battle N2241 BH-G during preparations for a training flight at Swinderby in summer 1940. (PISM via WM)

Situation board of No. 1 Group Squadrons in Group HQ at Hucknall showing operations scheduled for 19/20th Sept. 1940. (PISM)

Sulinski made his first run across the target at 06.50, releasing a stick of bombs from 10,000 feet, and observing four bursts on the southern bank of the River Scheldt, which produced purple, red and orange flashes. On his second run he delivered incendiaries, but was unable to determine the results. P/O Kula made two similar runs from the same altitude with a similar outcome before turning for home. Meanwhile, P/O Kaluza had by this time already attacked an alternative target, a railway station, after being thrown off course by unfavourable weather conditions over Orfordness.

The Christmas period was allowed to pass without operations, but it was back to business for Newton and Swinderby on the night of the 28/29th, when ports were the targets. S/L Cwynar took part in his first operation on this night, but it was the recently promoted F/L Krynski who led the six 300 Squadron Wellingtons away from Swinderby at 16.25. S/L Cwynar took off at 16.41, and at 18.36 dropped his five 500lb bombs on a searchlight concentration believed to be in the target area. Despite being at only 5,000 feet he was unable to observe any detonations. Sgt Nowakowski delivered his bombs and incendiaries from 12,000 feet, and observed two bursts. Returning from this operation R1035 crashed and burst into flames a mile short of Swinderby while trying to land, and P/O Krynski was killed outright, while one of his crew succumbed to his injuries later in station sick quarters. They were buried on the morning of the 31st. During the course of the month the squadron operated on two occasions, and dispatched nine sorties for the loss of a single aircraft.

Northolt, 1st November 1940. Sir Archibald Sinclair, Secretary of State for Air speaking with F/L Krynski, "A" Flight Commander during official Polish Air Forces parade. Gen. Sikorski and W/C Rudkowski - CO of 301 Squadron are standing behind them on the right. (PISM)

January 1941

As the New Year dawned, Bremen found itself the object of the Command's attention during the first three nights, while other small scale operations were carried out against a variety of targets in Germany and the occupied countries. Newton and Swinderby each dispatched six crews on the night of the 1/2nd, but 300 Squadron was not involved. It turned into a disaster for Swinderby's 301 Squadron, which had two of its Wellingtons crash near Digby on return, and only a single gunner survived from the twelve occupants.

The weather conditions were difficult at the start of the year, and planned operations for four 300 Squadron crews on the consecutive nights of the 3rd, 4th and 5th were cancelled as a result. In the meantime, the battleship Tirpitz was believed to be at berth in Wilhelmshaven, and six operations of varying sizes were launched against the port during the course of January, beginning on the night of the 8/9th. 1 Group's contribution to this first operation was cancelled because of doubtful weather conditions, but ten aircraft were made ready at Newton for the following night, for what would prove to be the largest operation of the month. The target was not the Tirpitz, but the oil town of Gelsenkirchen in the Ruhr, for which a new record force of 135 aircraft was detailed.

A "freshman" target was laid on for Swinderby on this night, which turned out to be clear, and the four crews who had been standing-by since the 3rd would finally get their chance. They were assigned to attack oil storage tanks in Rotterdam, and were led away from Swinderby by W/C Makowski at 16.45. He arrived over the centre of the target at 19.05, and delivered a stick of bombs and incendiaries in a pass from south-east to north-west from 13,000 feet, without observing any result. Sgt Kuflik made two runs across the target in the same direction, and observed bursts and flames. F/O Kaluza and Sgt Dziekonski chose a south-west to north-east attack, and each saw bomb-bursts, flames and smoke before returning safely home. The Gelsenkirchen operation set a trend that would be repeated time and again over the Ruhr in the ensuing two years, as bombs were sprayed liberally around the region, without any indication as to where they fell.

On the 15th the commander-in-chief of Bomber Command, Sir Richard Peirse, who had been in post since succeeding Sir Charles Portal in October, received a new directive from the Air Ministry setting out the latest bombing policy. It was believed that Germany's oil situation was approaching a critical period, and that attacks on its synthetic oil production over the next six months would impact heavily upon its war effort. Accordingly, a list of seventeen targets had been prepared, the top nine of which represented around 80% of output. These plants were at Leuna, Politz, Gelsenkirchen, Zeitz, Scholven-Buer, Ruhland, Böhlen, Magdeburg and Lützkendorf, and they represented the sole, primary aim for Peirse's forces until further notice. Peirse would wait until February before beginning the campaign, and would continue with his policy of one large-scale attack per month against a major industrial city. There were to be no further operations during the month for 300 Squadron, as generally unfavourable weather conditions prevented all but occasional training flights from Swinderby.

The first of two attacks on the Tirpitz at Wilhelmshaven on the nights of the 15/16th and 16/17th caused significant damage to the town and buildings in the docks area, but there was no mention of Tirpitz. Of the ten Wellingtons dispatched by 1 Group from Newton, six reached and bombed the primary target and there were no losses. The second half of the month found 1 Group stations under snow for most of the time, and they were declared unserviceable as far as operations were concerned. French ports had been of interest during January, and this would continue into February with attacks on the likes of Boulogne,

Brest, le Havre, Lorient, and Dunkerque, while mines were laid in the sea lanes around them. The highlight of the month for Swinderby was an official visit by Their Majesties King George VI and Queen Elizabeth on the 27th, when both Polish squadrons were presented to them. The squadron undertook just one operation during the month, and launched four sorties without loss.

Swinderby, 27th Jan. 1941. King George VI visiting Polish squadrons. W/C Makowski is assisting the King. Below: Queen Elizabeth receiving flowers from Polish airmen. (PISM via WM)

February 1941

Swinderby was largely unserviceable at the start of February because of snow and rain, and occasional training flights were all that was possible. This was still the case on the night of the 10/11th, which was devoted to the month's large-scale effort, for which Hanover was selected. 222 aircraft, the largest force yet sent to a single target, took off for the city, and 183 returning crews claimed to have attacked their assigned aiming points. Two crews each from 300 and 301 Squadrons were briefed at 17.00 on the 10th for an early departure on the following morning. They were to attack the docks and shipping at Boulogne, and flew over to Newton to launch their effort from there. F/L Sulinski took off at 04.55 in R1178, and he was followed five minutes later by Sgt Kazimierczak in T2836. Two hours later F/L Sulinski delivered a stick of bombs and incendiaries across No 5 basin in a south-to-north pass from 11,000 feet, and observed two bursts. Sgt Kazimierczak ran across Nos 4 and 5 basins from south-west to north-east, saw three bursts, and watched a fire burning for a few minutes as he left the target area for a safe return to the satellite airfield at Winthorpe. While these operations were in progress, more than forty other aircraft attacked oil storage tanks at Rotterdam, and among them were three Short Stirlings from 3 Group on the type's operational debut.

103 Squadron would spend the 11th to the 22nd at Lindholme, after the heavy February rains made Newton unfit for operations. During mid month, indeed, all of 1 Group's stations were declared unserviceable, and its squadrons sat out the start of the oil campaign, which began in the Ruhr on the night of the 14/15th. The targets were Homberg, on the west bank of the Rhine, a few miles to the north-west of Duisburg city centre, and Gelsenkirchen and Sterkrade-Holten further east, but it was a wasted effort as few aircraft reached their respective target areas. Twenty-four hours later a smaller force attacked Homberg again, while a greater number went back to the plant at Sterkrade. 1 Group contributed eight aircraft to the night's proceedings, but these were for an operation to bomb the docks and shipping at Boulogne. 300 and 301 Squadrons each provided four Wellingtons, and they flew "light" from Winthorpe to Waddington, which was the only station serviceable for fully loaded aircraft. F/L Sulinski again took the lead, departing at 18.31, and he delivered his bombs between basins 4 and 5 from 14,000 feet at 20.40. His squadron colleagues followed him in, and bomb bursts were observed, as was a large fire and yellowish glow north of basin 5. Sgt Kazimierczak experienced engine problems on the way home, but landed safely at Fulbeck, and F/O Kaluza's T2608 was hit by a taxying Hampden at Waddington and had to have a wing replaced.

300 and 301 Squadrons each dispatched a freshman crew from the 3 Group airfield at Mildenhall on the 23/24th to join an attack on Boulogne, and they were the only 1 Group aircraft operating on the night. Sgt Dziekonski took off at 19.10 with S/L Cwynar as his second pilot, and dropped a stick of bombs across 6 and 5 basins in a pass from west to east, as the result of which a number of bursts and an explosion were observed. Düsseldorf was the target for eighty aircraft on the night of the 25/26th, for which 1 Group's 103, 150 and 300 Squadrons provided a total of twelve Wellingtons. F/L Sulinski and P/O Jasinski were the 300 Squadron participants, and they took off from Newton at 18.30 and 18.32 respectively. They arrived in the target area two-and-a-half hours later, and bombed through cloud on estimated positions from 16,000 feet, before returning safely. F/L Sulinski's R1178 was approached by an enemy night fighter, but a burst of fire from the rear gunner saw it break away.

The month's penultimate major operation took a force of over a hundred aircraft to Cologne on the night of the 26/27th, for which 300 and 301 Squadrons provided nine Wellingtons between them. W/C Makowski led off the 300 Squadron contribution from Newton at 19.02 in good weather conditions, with

F/O Kaluza and P/O Kula close behind. W/C Makowski spent forty-two minutes over the target, ultimately delivering his two 500lb bombs and three containers of incendiaries from 13,000 feet. It was a similar story for the others, and many fires were reported by returning crews. The Cologne authorities, however, reported only a handful of bombs falling into the city's western fringes and nearby outlying communities. This was the first of a series of attacks on the Rhineland capital spanning the turn of the month. Wilhelmshaven hosted the final operation of the month on the night of the 28th, when a force of more than a hundred aircraft targeted the Tirpitz. 1 Group dispatched nine Wellingtons drawn from 103 and 150 Squadrons, and all returned safely from what was an indeterminate operation.

From an operational viewpoint, it had been an unsatisfactory month for the Polish squadrons because of the unserviceability of the airfield. However there were entertainment and recreational activities including a concert in Lincoln, an all-ranks dance, three performances a week by the station dance band, cinema shows and football and hockey fixtures. The health of the station was described as excellent, and the supply and quality of food was also praised, while trade and test boards offered an opportunity for airmen to qualify for re-mustering. The squadron took part in five operations during the month, and dispatched twelve sorties without loss.

Swinderby, late 1941. Left to Right: F/L Dej (obs.), G/C Makowski, W/C Cwynar and Sgt Dziekonski (pilot). G/C Makowski was Polish Liaison Officer in Bomber Command HQ at this time and W/C Cwynar succeeded him as 300 Squadron Commander. F/L Day had completed his tour of duty by Nov. 1941 and assumed instructor`s post in 18 OTU at Bramcote. Sgt Dziekonski failed to return from Emden on 19th June 1942 in 11th operation of his second tour with 300 Squadron. (B. Klimczak)

March 1941

Cologne opened the March account on the night of the 1/2nd, following on from the attack of a week earlier. A total of 131 aircraft were assigned to two aiming points, and damage was quite considerable for the period, but just a pinprick compared with what was in store for this mighty city in the years to come. 1 Group sat this one out, and waited until the following night to next venture forth in anger. The target was Brest, where the German cruisers Scharnhorst and Gneisenau had put in for provisioning. A force of fifty-four aircraft included five Wellingtons each from 300 and 301 Squadrons, which were again forced to use Newton, as Swinderby remained unserviceable. F/L Sulinski led off the 300 Squadron contingent at 17.47, and the others were all airborne within ten minutes. S/L Cwynar was also involved in this operation, but he chose to act as second pilot to P/O Kula. F/L Sulinski found he was unable to regulate his engines, and flew all the way to the target and back at full speed. He delivered his bombs in a stick from 10,500 feet at 21.41, while passing across the port from north-west to south-east, but probably spent around forty-five minutes in the target area. Three of the others certainly did, and Sgt Kostecki and crew had a lucky escape. He inadvertently switched on his navigation lights, thus attracting the attention of the searchlight and flak batteries. For four hectic minutes he was coned and fired-upon, before eventually escaping. However, on the way home he noticed reflections of lights on the clouds, which caused him to take evasive action in the form of corkscrewing. It was only at this point, that he realized that his lights were showing and causing the reflections. In the meantime, S/L Sulinski had shut down an engine, possibly to reduce speed for landing, and pulled off a perfect touch-down at Newton a full hour ahead of the others.

Another shot at Cologne occupied the night of the 3/4th, a smaller effort than that of the 1st, and this time 1 Group took part with ten aircraft from 103 and 150 Squadrons, and they contributed to slight superficial damage in a number of suburbs. On the 9th of March yet another new Air Ministry directive was received, which changed the emphasis of the Command's operations from oil to maritime matters. Unacceptably high shipping losses to U-Boots in the Atlantic forced the War Cabinet to order an all-out assault on this menace, and its partner in crime, the long-range reconnaissance bomber, the Focke-Wulf Kondor. They were to be hunted down at sea, in their bases, and at the point of their manufacture, and this campaign was to be prosecuted as a priority. Kiel, Hamburg, Vegesack and Bremen all contained shipyards, and the last-mentioned was also home to a Focke-Wulf factory.

The new campaign began at Hamburg and Bremen on the night of the 12/13th, while another force targeted Berlin. 1 Group sent a contingent from Newton and Swinderby to bomb railway installations at Hamburg, while other elements of the eighty-strong force went for the shipyards. Three 300 Squadron Wellingtons took off from Mildenhall in a six-minute slot from 00.30 led by S/L Cwynar. They returned to Swinderby either side of 07.00 and landed safely on the perimeter track. At debriefing they reported attacking their assigned aiming point in excellent visibility with a full moon, and believed it had been a successful operation. Destruction at Hamburg was, indeed, significant, with the Blohm & Voss U-Boot yards sustaining damage to buildings and installations, while the premises of four other ship-building firms were also hit. To complete a good night, a number of high explosive bombs hit the Focke-Wulf aircraft factory in Bremen. At Berlin damage was confined to the southern districts, and no buildings were classed as destroyed.

139 aircraft set off to return to Hamburg on the following night, among them two Wellingtons belonging to 300 Squadron. W/C Makowski took off from Newton at 19.14, followed four minutes later by Sgt Hajdukiewicz, who had S/L Leszczynski beside him as second pilot. W/C Makowski delivered his five

F/O Edward Hajdukiewicz after his commission and DFC award in 1944. He completed two tours of duty with 300 Squadron, the first one in 1940/1941 and the second in 1943. (Z. Dudek)

500lb bombs in a stick from 14,000 feet at 23.03, but was prevented by searchlight glare from observing the result. He landed at Charney Down near Bath at 03.00, after experiencing communications problems and a rough-running port engine. Sgt Hajdukiewicz made two runs across the target, dropping bombs on each, and he observed a total of three bursts before returning safely to Newton. This was another successful operation, which caused further damage at the Blohm & Voss yards and created nineteen large fires. While this operation was in progress, Sgts Szymanowski and Nowakowski joined others in a freshman attack on the oil storage tanks at Rotterdam. Both delivered six 500lb bombs and incendiaries on the aiming point from around 15,000 feet, and observed bursts and evidence of a fire.

The oil directive was not entirely shelved in favour of maritime considerations, and a hundred aircraft set out for Gelsenkirchen on the night of the 14/15th. Although it was a relatively ineffective attack, a number of bomb loads did fall upon the Hydrierwerk Scholven oil plant, and significant damage was inflicted. 300 Squadron was not involved in this operation, and, in fact, would enjoy nine nights off the Order of Battle. Such was the desire of the Polish airmen to avenge their country, however, that they probably didn't appreciate the rest. On the evening of the 18th three 301 Squadron Wellingtons took off from Swinderby for Rotterdam, and, on return, became the first to conduct an entire operation from the station since the 9th of January, a fact which heartened all. Thereafter during March, the accent fell back onto German and French ports but an attempt to hit the U-Boot base at Lorient on the 21/22nd was hampered by poor visibility.

Fourteen Polish crews were scheduled for a raid on Berlin on the night of the 23/24th, using Langham as an advanced base. W/C Makowski led the six 300 Squadron Wellingtons off at 22.04 in weather conditions described as dangerous, with F/L Sulinski and Sgts Dziekonski and Hajdukiewicz following behind at 22.30, 22.33 and 22.52 respectively. After the first four became airborne, the next two collided while approaching the threshold; this incident and the state of the conditions forced the cancellation of the remaining sorties. W/C Makowski dropped a single 500lb bomb on what he believed to be Berlin at 02.00 from 15,500 feet on a south-westerly heading, before noticing a searchlight and flak concentration ahead, which he assumed must be defending the target. This suggested that his first bomb had fallen short, so he continued on only to discover that he had been lured away by a decoy. He eventually delivered the rest of his ordnance of three bombs and two containers of incendiaries at 03.15 from 14,000 feet on buildings thought to be north-east of Hanover. F/L Sulinski reached Berlin at 01.40, and delivered

300 Squadron aircrew who took part in the first Polish raid on Berlin on 23rd /24th March 1941. Left to Right: (back row) - Sgt Talkowski (A.G.), Sgt Kowalski (W.Op.), Sgt Baczak (W.Op.), Sgt Jablonski (A.G.), Sgt Szymanowski (pilot), Sgt Suczynski (A.G.), Sgt Kuflik (pilot), P/O Kozinski (obs.), Sgt Sztul (W.Op.), Sgt Artymiuk (W.Op.), Sgt Swidzinski (W.Op.), (front row) – F/L Jura (A.G.), Sgt Rygiel (A.G.), Sgt Dziekonski (pilot), F/O Miarczynski (obs.), Sgt Nowakowski (pilot), W/C Makowski (pilot) – CO of 300 Squadron, F/L Sulinski (pilot), P/O Dej (obs.), Sgt Zychowski (A.G.), F/O Rogalski (obs.), Sgt Biezunski (W.Op.). (PISM via WM)

his bombs from 15,000 and 18,000 feet, presumably after making two runs, and he also dispensed leaflets (nickels) near Magdeburg before returning to land at Sutton Bridge at 06.15. Sgt Hajdukiewicz overshot Berlin after arriving too early, and dropped his bombs on buildings about fifteen miles to the south-east before landing back at Langham. Sgt Dziekonski bombed from 20,000 feet at 01.55, and observed three bursts about a mile south-west of the target. He also returned safely to land at Waddington. The port of Brest began to take on a particular level of importance from the 29th as the Scharnhorst and Gneisenau were spotted in its waters again, and by the following day they had taken up residence. Their presence over an extended period would be an unwelcome and costly distraction for the Command, which would ultimately end with little to show for the massive effort expended and the high cost in aircrew lives. On the night of the 30/31st more than a hundred aircraft took off to carry out the first of what would be a multitude of attempts over the next eleven months to incapacitate the newly arrived lodgers, and prevent them from going back to sea to threaten Allied surface shipping. 1 Group's effort was provided by fourteen Wellingtons from Newton, but they and the others were unable to score any hits, and the 103 Squadron commanding officer was killed in a crash in Somerset. During the course of the month the squadron managed sixteen sorties on five operations.

April 1941

The new month began with five operations directed at Brest during the first week. The first one, a small effort by 5 Group, resulted in a recall, but larger attacks followed on the 3/4th and 4/5th, neither of which involved 300 Squadron. The latter operation unwittingly produced consequences, one of which was collateral damage to the Continental Hotel, which killed several officers from one of the vessels. The other was a single bomb lodging in the bottom of the dry dock being occupied by the Gneisenau. On the following day the captain opted to remove his ship while the bomb was dealt with, and moored it out in the harbour. While there it was attacked in suicidal fashion by a lone Coastal Command Beaufort torpedo bomber from 22 Squadron, and suffered a direct hit requiring six months of repair work. The Beaufort was shot down with the loss of the entire crew, and the pilot, F/O Kenneth Campbell, was awarded a posthumous Victoria Cross for his gallantry.

The next operation against the port and its guests was mounted on the night of the 6/7th, for which 1 Group contributed twenty Wellingtons from Newton and Swinderby to an overall force of seventy-one aircraft. The Swinderby contingent consisted of four Wellingtons from 300 Squadron and six from 301, and they flew over to Waddington to be fuelled and bombed-up. F/L Sulinski led the 300 Squadron element away at 22.06, to be followed over the next twelve minutes by Sgts Hajdukiewicz, Kostecki and Kazimierczak. S/L Leszczynski was the senior officer on duty, and he was flying as second pilot to Sgt Kostecki. They arrived in the target area to find ten-tenths cloud at 4,000 feet, and were forced to bomb on estimated positions determined by the activity of flak concentrations.

In contrast, good conditions attended a major assault on Kiel by over two hundred aircraft on the following night, when ten Polish crews represented the group. S/L Cwynar was on board R1344 as second pilot to P/O Michalowski, and they led the five-strong 300 Squadron contingent away at 22.04. They arrived in the target area to find that the bright moonlight toned down the intensity of the searchlights, and allowed the crews to identify ground detail. There were already fires burning from earlier arrivals for an operation spread over five hours. The main aiming points were east of the Germania Werft, and all five from 300 Squadron bombed within half a mile of them, although were unable to distinguish individual bomb-bursts because of the fires already burning. They contributed to substantial damage inflicted upon housing and buildings in the eastern docks area, which led to several days' loss of production at two U-Boot construction yards. Sgt Kuflik brought back 1 Group's first successful night target photograph, taken by his observer P/O Kozinski.

A force of 160 aircraft was made ready on the following day for a second attack on Kiel that night. It involved eighteen crews from Newton and Swinderby, including four from 300 Squadron led by F/L Sulinski, who had W/C Makowski alongside him as second pilot. Swinderby was declared serviceable for this operation, and the 300 Squadron element got away in an eight-minute slot from 20.10. They arrived in the target area to find fires burning, and again bombed within eight hundred yards of the assigned aiming points, some observing bomb bursts. The main weight of this night's attack fell upon the town area, rather than the slipways, and the local authorities produced a long list of damaged buildings. Electricity supply failed for a period, and the number of civilian casualties was probably the highest of the war to date, as was the figure of more than eight thousand people bombed out of their homes.

On the following night, the 9/10th, Berlin was the principal target, while two small-scale operations were directed at Vegesack and Emden in line with the latest directive. The first of six further raids on Brest during the remainder of the month took place on the night of the 10/11th, and resulted in four bombs hitting the Gneisenau and killing fifty Germans. 1 Group sat out this operation, but eleven crews were dispatched there from Newton on the night of the 12/13th as part of an overall force of sixty-six aircraft. Only a little over half of them reached the target in poor weather conditions, and the others mostly attacked Lorient as an alternative. Ten Polish crews followed suite on the night of the 14/15th, of which six were provided by 300 Squadron, four of them captained by sergeant pilots. S/L Cwynar was the senior officer on duty, and he and the others took off between 20.15 and 20.30. They arrived over the target to find complete cloud cover, and only S/L Cwynar was able to report observing a bomb burst, while Sgt Ratajczak and crew reported a large, red explosion as they withdrew from the target.

Kiel was the objective again on the night of the 15/16th, for which operation a force of 96 aircraft was made ready. The Swinderby squadrons were not involved in what proved to be an ineffective attack, which was hindered by cloud, but was also indicative of the level of performance generally by the Command. The Polish squadrons were back on the Order of Battle on the following night to represent the group at Bremen, as part of a force of 107 aircraft. F/L Sulinski led the six-strong 300 Squadron element away from Swinderby at 20.21, but on arrival in the target area they encountered mist and cloud that rendered all attempts to see the ground futile. On return at 01.50, R1178 was set upon by a Heinkel 111 as F/L Sulinski was on final approach, but no damage was incurred and he landed safely. The enemy aircraft then proceeded to drop six small-calibre bombs on the north-east corner of the airfield, two of which failed to explode. Two crews were still airborne at this point, and they were forced to orbit the airfield until an alternative runway was made ready, and they also landed safely shortly after 03.00.

Berlin was the destination for 118 aircraft on the night of the 17/18th, for which 300 Squadron briefed four crews led by S/L Cwynar. The crew room was tense as they prepared for the long round trip, particularly as the latest "gen" suggested an increase in anti-aircraft defences and balloons. Because of the shortage of Polish airmen coming into the squadrons, there was a reticence on the part of senior Polish officers to commit large numbers of its men at this stage of the war to long-range and potentially more hazardous operations like those against Berlin. The attitude was, that such operations were not about to bomb Germany out of the war, but would bring home to the German population the reality of war. The war would last a long time yet, and there would be opportunity ahead for the Poles to make their mark. Everyone with 300 Squadron wanted to be chosen for this one, but experience dictated who would go. S/L Cwynar led them away from Swinderby at 20.48, and they reached the target area after midnight to find haze obscuring ground detail. S/L Cwynar observed three bomb-bursts near the Alexander Platz railway station, which started a fire, and Sgt Kostecki also saw three bursts near the target and three fires burning in a western district. L7873 was coned by searchlights, which blinded the crew to ground detail, and was fired upon by flak. The observer, F/O Rogalski, was wounded in the thigh by a splinter, but he carried on with his duties and dropped the bombs onto the target, before Sgt Hajdukiewicz brought the Wellington home to a safe landing. Sgt Kostecki landed at Tern Hill at 04.50, but brushed with two other aircraft in poor visibility, and T2836 was slightly damaged.

The crew of R1061 had boarded their fully loaded Wellington with joy at the prospect of being an unwelcomed visitor in the skies over Germany's capital city, and they climbed away from Swinderby in good weather conditions, glad that this was a moonless night. There was no chatter over the intercom as they droned across the blacked-out English countryside to the south coast, and soon they were over France at 10,000 feet, preparing to climb to 16,000 feet as they passed over the frontier into Germany. It was important to stay below 15,000 feet for as long as possible, as the oxygen supply would last the entire crew of six for just three hours. The Bristol Pegasus engines required a top-up of oil periodically, and after three hours aloft the pressure gauge on the pilot's panel showed a rising temperature on the port power plant as they began to ascend through 12,000 feet. He sent a crew member to the oil tank to hand-pump oil to the engine, but the handle was found to be frozen solid, and further attempts by other members of the crew caused it to break. The only option was to feather the engine, which Sgt Szymanowski did, but he had to level out at 12,000 feet, and battle the tendency of the aircraft to pull to starboard. By this time Berlin was on the horizon, and soon bomb bursts could be seen, and searchlights began sweeping back and forth in front of R1061. There was a stark choice for Sgt Szymanowski to make, sacrifice his crew for the honour of Poland, or live to fight another day. He chose the latter, and the bombs were dropped eight miles south of Potsdam. They descended to 9,000 feet for the long homeward leg, but as the majority of other crews were heading towards England on a direct route across Holland, they met no opposition. Once over the Channel the port engine was restarted, and they arrived home safely after a trip of seven hours and forty-five minutes.

A force of 61 aircraft was prepared for an operation to Cologne on the night of the 20/21st, of which six were provided by 300 Squadron. S/L Cwynar was the senior officer on duty, and he was fourth away from Swinderby at 23.37, four minutes behind F/L Sulinski. It was another disappointing raid, ruined by poor weather conditions, but all located the target area to deliver their bombs before returning home to land either side of 05.00. F/O Michalowski landed R1344 at Upwood, and sustained slight damage in a minor collision. It was back to Brest for five 300 Squadron crews on the night of the 23/24th, as part of an overall force of sixty-seven aircraft. S/L Cwynar took the lead, departing Swinderby at 20.09 in T2623, and he reached the target without incident to deliver his semi-armour-piercing (SAP) bombs. A number of returning crews reported bomb bursts in the area of the torpedo boat station and the dry dock, and one large explosion was also observed. Claims were made of hits on both cruisers, but there was no confirmation.

On the following night, when Kiel was the main target, the squadron sent a single freshman crew, captained by F/O Sedzik, to join others bombing le Havre, but almost complete cloud cover prevented an assessment of results. The third operation of the current series against Kiel took place on the night of the 25/26th, when ten Polish crews represented 1 Group. There were no senior officers among the crew captains of the five participating 300 Squadron Wellingtons, and three of them were sergeant pilots. They took off from Swinderby between 20.17 and 20.50, and all but one reached the target area to deliver their bombs before returning to report observing bursts. Sgt Szymanowski failed to locate Kiel, and delivered his 1,000 pounder, two 500 pounders and 120 X 4lb incendiaries near Lübeck, before returning with engine and radio problems to land at Barkston Heath, a small airfield near Sleaford. This operation was monitored by AVMs Oxland and Saundby and AVM Stanislaw Ujejski of the Polish Air Force. It was on this night also that the Polish element was boosted by the operational debut of five fresher crews from 304 and 305 Squadrons at Syerston. Their target was the oil storage tanks at Rotterdam, which four managed to locate, and all five returned safely.

Another big effort from the Polish squadrons at Swinderby saw them dispatch fourteen Wellingtons as part of an overall force of seventy-one aircraft to attack Mannheim on the night of the 29/30th. 300 Squadron provided six Wellingtons led away by F/L Sulinski, and they reached southern Germany to find clear skies, but intense darkness and ground haze. Some bomb-bursts and fires were observed, and all returned safely home to complete the squadron's operational activity for the month. Newton and Binbrook put up seventeen Wellingtons between them for the group's final outing of the month on the following night, which was yet another attack on Kiel. A new record month for the squadron brought eleven operations and fifty-two sorties without loss.

May 1941

Hamburg was to feature heavily during the first week-and-a-half of the new month, as Peirse continued to prosecute the current directive. The first of five attacks on the city during the period took place on the night of the 2/3rd, when a force of ninety-five aircraft included sixteen Wellingtons from Swinderby, seven of them provided by 300 Squadron and led by S/L Cwynar. The Swinderby contingent had been specially selected by Peirse to lead the attack and create fires to guide the rest of the force in. The 300 Squadron element took off either side of 20.30, and arrived in the target area around midnight to find fair visibility and variable amounts of cloud up to seven-tenths. Some bomb bursts were observed, but searchlight dazzle made it difficult to assess the results, although a number of fires were visible up to thirty miles into the return journey. As the Polish crews headed home they were conscious that Poland's National Day, the 3rd, had dawned. Without doubt, they were proud and emotional at the knowledge that they were striking a blow at the heart of the enemy on behalf of their people, who were suffering unimaginable hardship under Nazi occupation. The Command claimed a successful operation, but, in reality, only modest damage had been achieved. While this operation was in progress on what was an all-Polish 1 Group effort for the night, a single 300 Squadron crew joined eleven others from 304 and 305 Squadrons to carry out freshman sorties at Emden.

Swinderby, September 1941. Wellington X3175 BH-L with its group of 300 Squadron aircrew and ground personnel. Standing (Left to Right): 1st Sgt Szuba (W.Op.), 2nd F/O Mecinski (obs.), 3rd F/L Michalowski (pilot), 4th F/O Morawiak (obs.), 5th Sgt Leszkiewicz (pilot). Sitting (Left to Right): 1st AC2 Wolczek, 2nd LAC Kuch and 3rd AC2 Harasimowski. F/L Michalowski completed his tour of duty, trained as night fighter pilot and became CO of 307 Polish Night Fighter Squadron. He was killed in a training flight on 21st March 1943. Both AC2s Wolczek & Harasimowski later volunteered for flying duties. Wolczek became a bomb aimer and Harasimowski trained as a flight engineer. Both completed full tour of duty with 300 Squadron: Wolczek on Wellingtons in 1943/1944 and Harasimowski on Lancasters in 1944. (PISM via WM)

Swinderby was stood down for the remainder of the day to allow the Polish contingent to observe and celebrate their National Day. Conscious of the importance of the occasion, AVM Oxland, the A-O-C of 1 Group, had visited the station on the previous evening to see the crews off, and this was a gesture appreciated by all. That night Cologne was the target for a force of a hundred aircraft, of which twenty-three Wellingtons of 1 Group were provided by Newton and Binbrook. In the event, cloud covered the target and the operation was a failure. The night of the 4/5th became another all-Polish night for the group, when crews from Syerston and Swinderby attacked le Havre and Brest respectively. The main effort was against the latter, and involved a force of ninety-seven aircraft. W/C Makowski led the 300 Squadron element away at 21.42, to be followed inside ten minutes by five others, four of them with NCO pilots. Their quarry, once again, was the brace of enemy cruisers in residence at the port and, on arrival in the target area after midnight, they found clear conditions and cloudless skies. Some crews returned with reports of observing bomb bursts near the dry dock and straddling the quayside, and there were a number of claims of hits on the Scharnhorst and Gneisenau, although not by members of 300 Squadron.

The following night brought an operation to Mannheim, for which a force of 141 aircraft was made ready. Three crews from 300 Squadron, those of F/Os Cichowski, Sedzik and Michalowski, took off between 22.12 and 22.18, and headed across France without catching a glimpse of the ground. The complete cloud cover persisted over the target, where a house and a barn were destroyed by the twenty-five aircraft whose crews claimed to have reached it, among which were the three from 300 Squadron. Over a hundred aircraft set off to return to Hamburg on the night of the 6/7th, among them ten from Swinderby, of which five represented 300 Squadron. The Polish units were again specially selected to lead the attack. S/L Leszczynski flew as second pilot to Sgt Kazimierczak, and they were one of four to get away on schedule between 21.44 and 21.55. S/L Cwynar was delayed by an hour with intercom problems, but he eventually took off in T2623 at 22.47. The operation was ruined by poor visibility, and although eighty crews claimed to have bombed the target and caused many fires, this was not confirmed by local reports, which suggested only a dozen bomb loads had fallen within the city. On return Sgt Kazimierczak reported seeing a 301 Squadron Wellington come under attack from an enemy night fighter some eighty miles out from the English coast, but it landed safely having shaken off its pursuer.

While a force of eighty aircraft attacked Brest on the night of the 7/8th, the Swinderby squadrons enjoyed a night off. Hamburg hosted its third raid in the space of a week on the following night, when a force of 188 aircraft was dispatched. This was a successful operation, which caused eighty-three fires, of which almost half were classed as large. The death toll of 185 people was the largest to date in a German city. A simultaneous attack on nearby Bremen involved a force of 133 aircraft, of which nine Wellingtons belonged to 300 Squadron. F/L Sulinski was the senior pilot on duty, but he had S/L Leszczynski alongside him as second pilot. They all got away safely between 22.29 and 22.46, and found clear skies over the target, which should have enabled them to identify the important shipyards. The local authorities confirmed widespread bombing of the city, but no damage to the U-Boot yards. 300 Squadron's W5666 and R1061 sustained minor flak damage, and R1642 landed at 04.48 with a hung-up bomb, that fell out and caused slight damage to the tail.

On the night of the 9/10th, 146 aircraft were made ready for an attack on the twin cities of Mannheim and Ludwigshafen, sitting astride the Rhine in southern Germany. The bulk of the 1 Group effort was provided by Polish crews, and five of these were from 300 Squadron, all with officer pilots and led by S/L Cwynar. They got away safely in a ten-minute slot from 22.25, and found good weather conditions in the target area. Bomb bursts were observed and many fires reported, and local authorities confirmed this as a successful raid. This was followed by two further attacks on Hamburg on the succeeding nights, each involving a 1 Group effort. Swinderby was stood down on the 10th, and thus sat out the first operation involving over a hundred aircraft, which caused forty-seven large fires in the city on a night of perfect visibility. Nine 300 Squadron crews were briefed for the same destination on the night of the 11/12th, when F/L Sulinski was the senior pilot on duty, and was last away at 22.23. Weather conditions were again good with bright moonlight, and the attackers took advantage of this to deliver their bombs into the city, causing a further twenty-six large fires and much property damage, although none of an industrial nature.

The busy schedule for the month continued for elements of the Command with another trip to Mannheim and Ludwigshafen on the night of the 12/13th, but there was no operational activity at Swinderby. Crews were detailed for an attack on Kiel, planned for the night of the 14/15th, but this was cancelled, and they sat out an operation to Hanover on the 15/16th, where the post office and telephone exchange were optimistically selected as the aiming points. Cologne was to be raided four more times before the end of the month, and the first of these, on the night of the 16/17th, would prove to be the final operation in May for 300 Squadron. S/L Cwynar was the senior pilot, and he was at the head of the eight-strong 300 Squadron contingent departing Swinderby either side of 23.00. Conditions in the target area were poor, and few of the ninety-three participating aircraft found the city. F/L Sulinski and crew were among a few to report bomb bursts, but the majority saw nothing after bombing on estimated positions. Despite this, the Swinderby ORB hailed the operation as completely successful and a congratulatory message was received from 1 Group HQ. The 1 Group ORB, however, describes the results of the attack as inconclusive, and difficult to assess because of ground haze. Further operations to Cologne were mounted on 17/18th, 23/24th and 27/28th, and only the first-mentioned produced any useful damage.

Swinderby offered aircraft to group on a number of occasions during the remainder of the month, but weather conditions led to most planned operations being scrubbed. The squadron was ordered to stand-by for an operation in the early hours of the 27th, which turned out to be against the battleship Bismarck, but it was cancelled, and news came through later in the day that the pride of the German fleet had been sunk by elements of the Royal Navy. During the course of the month the squadron operated on nine occasions and dispatched a new record of 53 sorties without loss.

June 1941

Düsseldorf, Cologne and Bremen would dominate proceedings during the month, and the first two-mentioned would be attacked on the same night on no fewer than nine occasions during the second half by forces of varying sizes, but not once with better than modest results. What was not known by those taking part, was that their efforts were being scrutinized as never before, and the findings were to form a report to be presented to the highest authorities. 1 Group's contribution to operations continued to grow, but its ambition was thwarted by unfavourable weather conditions at the start of the new month. The Group contributed to operations against Düsseldorf and Duisburg on the night of the 2/3rd, but Swinderby was not invited to participate. 150 aircraft set off for the former, but only two thirds of the force reported bombing the city, and local authorities claimed damage as slight.

Operations were planned and briefings held on succeeding days, but cancellations soon came through, mostly because of poor current or anticipated weather conditions. Minor operations held sway until the night of the 10/11th, when a hundred aircraft were dispatched to Brest for another crack at the Scharnhorst and Gneisenau, which had now been joined by Prinz Eugen. 1 Group was not involved in this attack, which fell accurately across the docks area, but failed to hit the enemy vessels. On the 11th AM Sir Richard Peirse visited the station with the 1 Group A-O-C and other high-ranking officers in tow, and after their departure briefings took place for an operation that night against Düsseldorf. Nine 300 Squadron crews were to be part of a ninety-eight-strong force comprised of Wellingtons and a handful of Stirlings, while eighty other aircraft targeted Duisburg. It was 23.00 when P/O Cichowski lifted R1642 into the air, and fifteen minutes later when Sgt Kostecki brought up the rear in R1617. All but one made it to the target, where ground haze made it difficult to pick out ground detail. Bomb bursts were observed, along with fires, but it proved impossible to assess the outcome. R1347 developed a problem with one engine while outbound, and Sgt Nowakowski opted to bomb Rotterdam as an alternative target. He was last but one home at 04.55, but the arrival of F/O Sedzik and crew was awaited in vain.

W5666 BH-H had taken off at 23.06, and was at 17,000 feet over the target when the starboard engine was hit by flak and had to be shut down. The bombs were dropped and a course set for home, but it was clear that height could not be maintained, and the constant need to open the throttles sent the temperature on the good engine climbing. They were down to 2,000 feet over the North Sea, and could see a beacon in the distance, which they estimated to be twenty-five to thirty miles ahead. The last fix on W5666 actually placed it at position 52.30N and 03.00E, some thirty-five miles out from the English coast. F/O Sedzik risked everything on a short burst of power to get them to the coast for a bale-out, but the engine caught fire and a ditching became inevitable. F/O Sedzik managed to pull off a controlled landing on the sea at 03.20, and he and all but one of the crew managed to escape the sinking Wellington and make it into the dinghy, where second pilot Sgt Maciej was found to have a leg wound caused by scraping against a propeller while swimming. Why the wireless operator, Sgt Chowanski, failed to survive is uncertain, as he was alive during the ditching, and within easy reach of an escape hatch.

At first light an air-sea rescue operation was launched, which included a Hudson and a Blenheim and two crews from Swinderby, but the last-mentioned returned four hours later without having sighted anything. Frustratingly, the men in the dinghy watched both Wellingtons pass overhead, but the low cloud and rain prevented them from being spotted. During the following afternoon German fighters on Texel were sent to attack a convoy and its airborne escort off the Norfolk coast, and one of them also ended up ditching about ten kilometres east of the Sedzik crew. The Polish crew was almost spotted by a Hudson at dawn on Friday the 13th, but lost all hope as it was shot down in front of them by two BF109s.

Later in the morning both dinghies were sighted by German rescue aircraft, and an Arado landed to pick up the injured Sgt Maciej, leaving the others to await a Heinkel float plane to take them into captivity. Although they had been with the squadron for a relatively short time, the loss of this crew was a blow. They had performed outstandingly well, had become popular, and had gained a reputation as an exceptional crew.

Meanwhile, during the course of the 12th, His Royal Highness the Duke of Kent had visited the station and talked with Polish officers, before autographing the operations record book. Sadly, he would lose his life in August 1942, after his Short Sunderland flying boat mysteriously crashed in Scotland, when bound for a secret meeting in Iceland. Four railway targets ringing the Ruhr were selected as the objectives for a combined total of over three hundred aircraft that night. Osnabrück was assigned to 1 Group, which prepared a force of sixty-one Wellingtons, including eleven from 300 Squadron led by W/C Makowski. He took off first at 23.10, and arrived some hours later in the target area to find thick ground haze. Bomb bursts were observed and returning crews claimed a successful operation, which was confirmed to an extent by local reports. A signal from the 1 Group A-O-C was received on the following day, congratulating the crews on their fine performance.

The German raiders at Brest continued to escape damage on the 13/14th, despite the attentions of around a hundred aircraft, including some from 1 Group. It was from this point that Cologne and Düsseldorf became the main focus of attention for the remainder of the month. 300 Squadron returned to the Order of Battle on the night of the 15/16th for an operation against railway installations at the latter, for which eight crews were briefed. F/O Michalowski led them off at 22.46 in X3175, but before reaching the target he was attacked by an enemy night fighter and thrown off course during violent evasive action. Rather than arrive late over Düsseldorf, he opted to deliver his bombs on a target of opportunity on one of the Frisian Islands. Only eleven of the fifty-nine-strong force found the target in poor visibility, and they produced only scattered and ineffective bombing.

While a total of 170 aircraft were divided between the two cities on the 16/17th, thirty-nine Wellingtons were sent to Duisburg, among them ten representing 300 Squadron. W/C Makowski chose to lead from the front, with F/L Sulinski in support and F/O Michalowski also taking part. They were all airborne by 23.27, but Michalowski found that X3175 would not climb above 14,000 feet, and he bombed Deventer aerodrome in north-central Holland before returning home. Only seventeen crews reported bombing the target in conditions of ground haze, and some fires were observed. Cologne, Düsseldorf and Duisburg were back on twenty-four hours later, but the Polish squadrons were not required to operate.

Bremen and Brest were the objectives on the night of the 18/19th, and it was for the former that eight 300 Squadron Wellingtons took off either side of 22.00, as part of an overall force of a hundred aircraft. The 1 Group effort was entirely Polish, and the two stations chose different routes to the target. The Swinderby units selected a north-easterly course up into the North Sea, before turning to attack the target on a south-easterly heading, while the Syerston squadrons opted for a direct approach. It was quite normal for the period for squadrons to determine for themselves the details of an operation with regard to route, time-on-target, bombing altitude and method of attack, and this was one of the procedures to be swept away by the next Commander-in-Chief. F/O Michalowski was on duty again on this night, any problems with X3175 having presumably been fixed, and this time he reached the target area to bomb, although was unable to determine the outcome of his efforts. Nineteen of the twenty-five 1 Group participants bombed as briefed in conditions of low cloud, and six aircraft failed to return. W5665 was shot down

German crew which took the crew of F/O Sedzik from the sea posing in front of their Heinkel He-59 (H. Nauta).

F/O Sedzik being helped off the Heinkel… (H. Nauta)

… followed by Sgt Weinberg. (H. Nauta)

Sgt Kruk-Schuster surrounded by German officers. (H. Nauta)

F/O Sedzik (pilot), Sgt Kruk-Schuster (A.G.), P/O Sojka (obs.) and Sgt Weinberg (A.G.) in the German base at Schellingwoude near Amsterdam. (H. Nauta)

F/O Sedzik, Sgt Weinberg and Sgt Kruk-Schuster as Prisoners of War among German soldiers. (H. Nauta)

into the Waddenzee by a night fighter, killing Sgt Paleniczek and three of his crew, and only the observer and wireless operator survived to be captured and imprisoned.

Sgt Wladyslaw Paleniczek, who was shot down and killed during return from Bremen on his 12th operation. (PISM via WM)

Another of Germany's capital ships, Tirpitz, now, since the recent loss of the Bismarck, the pride of the German fleet, was spotted at berth in Kiel, and a force of a hundred aircraft was sent to seek her out. It proved impossible for the crews to locate the ship, however, and the town was bombed instead. 300 Squadron sat this one out, and remained at home also on the night of the 21/22nd, when the next round of operations against Cologne and Düsseldorf was mounted. The squadron was back on duty for a return to Bremen on the night of the 22/23rd, when seven crews were briefed for an operation involving seventy Wellingtons and Hampdens. Swinderby put up fourteen aircraft, of which half were provided by 300 Squadron. F/O Michalowski led them off at 22.00, but few reached the target in the conditions, and those which did reported isolated bomb bursts. Sgt Kuflik was among those unable to locate Bremen, and dropped his bombs in the Hamburg area, while R1178 developed overheating engines that prevented it from climbing, and P/O Rusiecki bombed a small motor vessel off Heligoland before returning home.

S/L Cwynar led a seven-strong 300 Squadron contingent back to Bremen on the night of the 25/26th, taking off shortly before 22.30 on a night of severe electrical storms. Fifty-six Wellingtons and eight Whitleys were involved, of which fifteen were launched from Swinderby. All but one reached the target despite the conditions, Sgt Kazimierczak having abandoned his sortie early on with a technical issue. F/O Cichowski completed the entire round trip in T2574, but returned with his load after the bomb-bay doors failed to open. It seems that few other aircraft found Bremen, and the outcome of the attack could not be determined. The squadron was not called into action for the fourth attack of the series on Bremen, which took place on the night of the 27/28th. Over a hundred Wellingtons and Whitleys took part on another stormy night that produced icing conditions, and most, it seems, found Hamburg rather than Bremen. The operation was a disaster, which cost a new record loss for a single night of fourteen aircraft. 4 Group Whitleys sustained the bulk of the casualties, as the enemy night fighters enjoyed their best bag to date.

The fifth attack on Bremen was mounted on the night of the 29/30, for which 300 Squadron contributed eight Wellingtons. F/O Michalowski led the squadron contingent away at 21.57 as part of an overall force of 106 aircraft. Ten of the sixteen Swinderby participants reached the target to bomb, but two from 300 Squadron, those captained by Sgt Kuflik and F/O Jasinski, attacked Emden and Bremerhaven respectively, after failing to identify the primary target. Good bombing results were claimed by sixty-nine crews, and seven aircraft failed to return. One of these was R1640, which had been badly shot up by flak at the Dutch coast on the way home, and was successfully ditched in the North Sea some forty miles off Grimsby on the Lincolnshire coast. Sgt Nowakowski and his crew all made it safely into the dinghy, and, meanwhile, two crews took off from Swinderby at first light to carry out a search. Whether or not they were successful in sighting the dinghy is uncertain, but the crew was picked up later, safe and well, by an Air-Sea-Rescue launch. The speed with which this happened was a great boost to morale for Swinderby's Polish residents. The squadron took part in eight operations during the month, and lost three aircraft from a record sixty-eight sorties.

Swinderby, July 1941. A group of Polish airmen posing in front of Wellington T2574 BH-R with symbols denoting 23 sorties on the fuselage. Left to Right: back row – P/O Martusewicz (obs.), F/O Wolanski (pilot), Sgt Swidzinski (W.Op.), front row – Sgt Badelek (A.G.), Sgt Hamerlok (pilot), Sgt Wyporski (A.G.). (PISM via WM)

July 1941

Bremen featured again on the night of the 2/3rd, when returning crews claimed good fires, but Swinderby was not involved. Later on the 3rd Elsham Wolds officially opened for business, and the staff began preparations for the arrival of 103 Squadron a week hence. That night 1 Group put up twenty-nine Wellingtons from Swinderby and Newton for another attack on Bremen, and seven of these were put up by 300 Squadron. P/O Rusiecki was first away at 22.39, but he was back a little over three hours later after suffering intercom failure. S/L Cwynar was second away at 22.41, and he arrived over the target in conditions of cloud and haze to deliver his bombs. No results were observed, but returning crews again claimed an effective operation. R1642 did not arrive back after being shot down by a night fighter over Germany. It was learned later that the second pilot and observer had escaped by parachute, but that F/O Kula and the other three occupants had lost their lives.

Binbrook and Syerston provided twenty-two aircraft for an operation to Lorient on the evening of the 4/5th, while a simultaneous assault went on at Brest. Conditions were fine at both targets, and the Lorient force produced some accurate bombing, but effective smoke screens kept the enemy warships safe. While over sixty aircraft targeted Münster on the 5/6th, the gas works at Bielefeld provided a change of objective for over thirty crews, twenty-four of which were launched from Newton and Swinderby. Six 300 Squadron Wellingtons took part, taking off either side of 23.30, and it appears that they contributed to a successful operation, which resulted in the gas works blowing up. While this operation was in progress a force of freshman crews, including one from 300 Squadron, went to Rotterdam, and left fires burning that were visible up to thirty miles into the return flight.

Nineteen aircraft from Binbrook and Syerston took part in yet another attack on the warships at Brest on the night of the 6/7th, and this was followed twenty-four hours later by an all-Wellington attack on Cologne involving more than a hundred aircraft. Better than half of the participants were provided by 1 Group in response to a call for a maximum effort, and 300 Squadron contributed seven aircraft, which departed Swinderby between 22.39 and 22.51. They helped deliver the most effective attack to date on Cologne, where housing and railway installations sustained the bulk of the damage, and over sixty large fires were started. A simultaneous operation by five freshman crews on Boulogne included a single 300 Squadron Wellington, and this was also described as a successful effort. Thirty-three Wellingtons went back to Bielefeld on the night of the 8/9th to attend to its power station, but only nineteen of the 1 Group element pressed on to bomb as briefed, while twelve others opted for alternative targets. 300 Squadron sent five Wellingtons, but two crews were unable to identify the primary target, and bombed Münster as an alternative.

On the 9th a new Air Ministry directive signalled an end to the maritime distraction, and now called upon Peirse to concentrate his efforts against the German transportation system and the morale of its civilian population. From now on, during the moon periods, the major railway centres ringing and serving the Ruhr were to be attacked, while on moonless nights the Rhine cities of Cologne, Duisburg and Düsseldorf would be more easily identifiable. On dark nights offering less favourable weather conditions, Peirse was to send his forces to the more distant targets in northern, eastern and southern Germany.

103 Squadron operated for the final time from Newton on the night of the 10/11th, when dispatching eleven crews to Cologne as part of a force of 130 Wellingtons and Hampdens. There were also seven 300 Squadron Wellingtons on the Order of Battle, and they took off from Swinderby in a sixteen minute slot from 22.38. R1178 was back within thirty minutes after the intercom failed, but the remainder pressed

on to try to identify two aiming points in the city centre and the Humboldt engineering works on the east bank of the Rhine. Weather conditions were unfavourable, and fewer than half of the crews reported reaching the target, rendering it impossible to repeat the success of three nights earlier. R1617 was on approach to the target when coned in searchlights, and subjected to heavy ant-aircraft fire, and after failing through violent evasive action to break away, Sgt Ceglinski jettisoned the bombs and turned for home. R1184 failed to return after being shot down by a night fighter over Belgium, but Sgt Kuflik and his crew all survived to become PoWs.

On the 11th 103 and 150 Squadrons completed their moves from Newton to Elsham Wolds and Snaith respectively, and for 103 Squadron, its newly-built north Lincolnshire station would be home for the remainder of the war. Seventy-eight Wellingtons and nineteen Whitleys were sent back to Bremen on the night of the 14/15th to attack three aiming points, the shipyards, the goods station and the Altstadt. 300 Squadron contributed six aircraft, taking off shortly before 23.00, but one returned ninety minutes later with engine failure. The remaining crews attacked the city, and most observed bomb bursts and fires. Some returning crews reported that the whole town was ablaze, but there is no confirmation that this was the case.

On the evening of the 15th an impressive ceremony was held at Newark cemetery, where the president of the Polish Republic unveiled a memorial to the Polish fallen. The commander-in-chief of the Polish army, General Sikorsky, also attended, as did many other senior Polish and RAF officers and civilian dignitaries. In front of the memorial monument, all four Polish squadrons were drawn up in review order behind a guard of honour of officers and men from each unit. Wreaths were laid and speeches delivered, and the band played Chopin's Marche Funébre and the national anthem. The 16th was observed as the Polish Air Force Day, and was marked at Swinderby by the blessing and presentation of colours to the Polish Air Force, a ceremony carried out with all the ritual that this solemn and historic occasion demanded. The large number of distinguished guests included Chief-of-the-Air-Staff, Sir Charles Portal, and the C-in-C Bomber Command, Sir Richard Peirse. The Polish units were paraded in front of the saluting base, after which the colours were again blessed by His Eminence Monsignor Jozef Gawlina and presented by General Sikorsky, who then addressed the gathering. Decorations were awarded, before the Polish Commander-in-Chief took the salute during a march-past. That night over a hundred aircraft set off late to attack Hamburg, among them twenty Wellingtons from Binbrook and Snaith. In the event only seven of the 1 Group aircraft were able to identify the target in cloudy conditions, and damage was slight.

On the 17th orders were received for 300 and 301 Squadrons to move to Hemswell, and an advance party was dispatched to begin taking over the facilities. The station was currently in the hands of 5 Group, and the resident squadrons, 61 and 144, flew their Hampdens out on this day to North Luffenham in Rutland. That night the two Polish squadrons dispatched six Wellingtons each as part of a force of seventy five aircraft bound for Cologne. The 300 Squadron element was led away from Swinderby by Sgt Kazimierczak at 22.59, and they were all airborne within ten minutes. They found the target covered by thick ground haze and mist, but judged that they had hit the city centre, and reported many fires and bomb bursts. Local reports suggest that only a small proportion of the bomb loads fell into the city, and damage was insignificant. On the following day the advance party from 50 Squadron arrived at Swinderby, and the station passed officially into the hands of 5 Group. At Hemswell, meanwhile, the Polish squadrons were settling in, and the station became officially part of 1 Group.

Swinderby, 15th July 1941. The ceremony of presentation of colours to the Polish Air Force. According to accepted rules, the colours were to be kept for six months consecutively in each Polish squadron, starting with 300 Squadron. (PISM via WM)

The move provided an appropriate opportunity for W/C Makowski to step down as commanding officer of 300 Squadron, and S/L Cwynar was promoted as his successor. On the following day 304 Squadron departed Syerston for Lindholme, where it was joined on the 20th by 305 Squadron, at which point Syerston was also transferred to 5 Group. On the same day HQ 1 Group moved out of Hucknall and took up residence at Bawtry Hall, located near Doncaster in south Yorkshire. This enabled Hucknall to be closed down next day. 300 Squadron returned to operations on the night of the 21/22nd, when five aircraft joined an overall force of seventy-one Wellingtons and Hampdens bound for Frankfurt for the first major attack on this southern city. F/O Kaluza was the senior pilot on duty, and he took off from Hemswell at 22.57, before setting course for the French coast. Having reached the target all seemed to progress well, and bomb bursts and fires were reported by returning crews. The Frankfurt authorities recorded a few bomb blasts, while nearby Darmstadt reported that fifteen buildings had been hit, and this operation was representative of the ineffective performance of the Command at this stage of the war. Follow-up operations against the city on the ensuing two nights were equally unrewarding.

Mannheim was the main target on the night of the 23/24th, for which fifty-one Wellingtons were made ready. 300 Squadron briefed five crews, of which F/O Kaluza was the senior pilot. They took off between 22.32 and 23.15, and arrived in the target area almost four hours later to deliver their bombs. Claims of a successful attack were again made, with reports of bomb bursts and fires, but local authorities recorded only broken glass and damage to roof tiles. While this operation was in progress S/L Sulinski joined a handful of others to attack the docks at le Havre. He observed no results, while others reported bomb bursts near docks 5 and 6.

The most complex operation for July was to be carried out at Brest in daylight on the 24th, and was a

Hemswell, August 1941. The crew of F/O Tadeusz Jasinski with the group of "erks" posing in the front of Wellington R1211 BH-T with the picture of a bat on the fuselage. Apparently the foundation name "Assam Bomber I" was repainted on this aircraft when Wellington X9639 originally bearing this name was lost on its 3rd operation with 300 Squadron. Standing (Left to Right) –3rd P/O Sobieszczuk (obs.), 4th F/O Jasinski (pilot), 5th Sgt Lapot (W.Op.). 6th P/O Boczkowski (pilot) 7th Sgt Krauss (A.G.). (PISM via WM)

Hemswell, late 1941. The crew of P/O Klecha. Left to Right: Sgt Chanecki (A.G.), P/O Klecha (pilot), Sgt Wize (W.Op.), F/O Zurawski (Obs.), Sgt Tomaszewski (A.G.) (G.Korcz).

concerted effort against the Scharnhorst and Gneisenau under the codename Operation Sunrise. The plan had to be changed at the last minute after it was discovered that Scharnhorst had slipped away and was now at berth at la Pallice, some two hundred miles further south. It was decided to send the 4 Group Halifax element to attend to her, while the rest of the original plan went ahead at Brest. The 1 Group plan, which excluded the Hemswell squadrons, called for its aircraft to attack in eight sections of three aircraft each. Three Fortress 1s of 2 Group's 90 Squadron would go in at 30,000 feet to draw up the enemy fighters, while eighteen 5 Group Hampdens acted as further bait under the umbrella of a Spitfire escort at a lower altitude. This was intended to leave the way clear for the seventy-nine Wellingtons of 1 and 3 Groups to sneak in and attack the objectives unescorted, but fierce flak and fighter opposition brought down ten of them. There were a number of unconfirmed hits on Gneisenau, but Scharnhorst suffered more severely while inflicting heavy casualties on the attacking Halifaxes, and she returned to Brest to take advantage of the superior repair facilities on offer.

The final operation of the month for 300 Squadron took place on the night of the 25/26th, when the target was Hamburg. A force of forty-three Wellingtons was prepared, including four from 300 Squadron, led again by F/O Kaluza, who took off at 23.00. They reached the city to find good weather conditions, and returning crews reported good bombing with fires clearly visible. Local authorities confirmed that four large fires were started, but there were no specific serious incidents. 300 Squadron's X9639, "Assam Bomber I", was shot down by flak over the target, and only the rear gunner in Sgt Sloma's crew survived to fall into enemy hands. R1178 suffered engine failure on the way home, and had to be ditched in the North Sea nine miles off the Norfolk coast. P/O Klecha and his crew took to the dinghy, and were rescued by an Air-Sea-Rescue launch thirty minutes later. R1617 was also in trouble as it approached the English coast with overheating engines, and was eventually force-landed safely by Sgt Kostecki four miles south of Boston. The operational tally for the month stood at a record thirteen operations, generating sixty-one sorties for the loss of four aircraft and three crews.

August 1941

At this stage of the war the Wellington was very much the mainstay of the Command, equipping both 1 and 3 Groups and elements of 4 Group, and almost without exception the operations undertaken thus far in 1941 had featured the type as the most numerous. The weather spanning the turn of the month had been a little unseasonal, with overcast skies and rain, and 300 Squadron had found itself under-employed and not required for operations against Cologne on the 30/31st of July, Hamburg and Berlin on the 2/3rd of August and Mannheim, Karlsruhe and Frankfurt on the 5/6th. It was, in fact, the night of the 6/7th before the squadron was next called into action, when seven crews were briefed for the latest attack in the series against Frankfurt. Southern Germany had become something of a focus for the Command, and on this night simultaneous operations were also mounted against Mannheim and Karlsruhe. F/L Cichowski was the senior pilot on duty, and he led the 300 Squadron contingent away from Hemswell at 22.12 in X9676. R1347 returned within three hours after experiencing severe icing, but the remainder pressed on, and three crews reported bombing in the target area, two of them specifying marshalling yards as their aiming points. Two other crews bombed a town between Frankfurt and Mannheim as they were unable to identify the primary target. X9676 failed to return after crashing into the North Sea, and the bodies of F/L Cichowski and his rear gunner, F/O Jura, were recovered by the Shipwash Lightship, moored off Harwich on the Suffolk coast, on the morning of the 7th.

The squadron sat out operations on the following night, when the Ruhr was the main focus, before attention turned upon northern Germany and the ports of Hamburg and Kiel on the night of the 8/9th. Four 300 Squadron crews were briefed for the all-Wellington attack on railways and shipyards in the former, and they departed Hemswell between 22.27 and 22.41. Sgt Ceglinski turned back over Holland after the intercom in R1327 failed, but the others reached the target area, where only F/O Wolanski reported observing his bombs bursting a mile south of the city, followed by large fires seen through gaps in the cloud. This crew and that of Sgt Wielondek reported being attacked a number of times while over Germany, and the loss of a 301 Squadron Wellington to a night fighter is evidence that they were active. On the way home R1347 hit balloon cables, slicing through two and damaging itself, and Sgt Wielondek was forced to carry out an emergency landing at Hibaldstowe.

The night of the 12/13th typified operations under Peirse at this juncture, when his available forces were divided between Hanover, Berlin, Magdeburg and Essen. Such pinprick attempts to hinder Germany's war effort in poor weather conditions with inadequate navigational tools were rarely productive, and cost the lives of experienced crews. Few aircraft reached their targets, and even fewer were able to identify and hit their briefed aiming points. On this night the 300 Squadron effort was scrubbed just before take-off time. W/C Cwynar had already taken off with a freshman crew to join in a small-scale attack on the docks at le Havre, and, having failed to pick up a recall message, continued on to complete his sortie in six hours. He was also the lone 300 Squadron representative in another small-scale effort at Rotterdam on the night of the 14/15th, but on this occasion he failed to identify the target in very poor weather conditions, and jettisoned his bombs into the sea. The main operation on this night was to Hanover, while Brunswick and Magdeburg were also targeted. A force of 152 aircraft was made ready for Hanover, including six from 300 Squadron. They departed Hemswell in an eighteen minute slot to 21.30, and headed eastwards to north-central Germany with instructions to bomb railway stations. Some success was claimed in conditions of good visibility, with bomb bursts and fires being observed, and all from Hemswell returned safely.

Cologne, Düsseldorf and Duisburg provided the destinations for forces of seventy-two, fifty-two and

Sgt Stanislaw Kuropatwa was killed in a crash on take-off for his 20th sortie. (GK)

fifty-four aircraft respectively on the night of the 16/17th, when railway installations were the briefed aiming points. 300 Squadron put up five Wellingtons for the first-mentioned, while S/L Sulinski joined in a small-scale attack on the oil storage tanks at Rotterdam. Haze and smoke obscured the ground at Cologne, but a large fire was reported, which was probably a decoy as local authorities recorded only light damage and no casualties. T2623 made it only as far as the Dutch coast outbound, before engine failure forced an early return for Sgt Wielondek and crew, who landed at Honington. R1641 was fired upon by an enemy intruder as it prepared to land, but the attack was inconclusive, and Sgt Ceglinski landed safely.

The 18th was the day on which civil servant Mr D M Butt presented his infamous report to the Air Ministry, and its disclosures sent shock waves reverberating around the halls of power. Having studied four thousand photographs taken during a hundred night raids in June and July, he concluded that only a fraction of the bombs delivered had fallen within miles of their intended targets. This swept away at a stroke any notion that the Command was having a material effect on the enemy's war effort, and demonstrated that its claims of success were without foundation. It also provided the detractors with a bountiful supply of ammunition to back up their calls for the dissolution of an independent bomber force, and for the redistribution of its aircraft to the U-Boot campaign and to redress reversals in the Middle East. Peirse had done his best to fulfil the often unrealistic demands of his superiors, but the damning Butt Report was a major blow to morale, and would forever unfairly blight his period of tenure as commander-in-chief.

Cologne and Duisburg were the objectives for forces of sixty and forty aircraft respectively on the night of the 18/19th, when the Cologne force was led astray by a decoy site. Six 300 squadron Wellingtons began to take off at 23.23, and all proceeded without incident until R1641 started rolling at 23.35. The aircraft came to grief at some point as it accelerated down the runway, killing Sgt Ceglinski and second pilot Sgt Kuropatwa, and slightly injuring the other occupants. This tragic incident delayed the take-off of the final two participants, and it was after 00.30 before they were airborne. Sgt Wielondek and crew again had to abandon their sortie because of a fuel shortage, and they bombed the secondary target of Heinsberg, near Aachen. Returning crews claimed good bombing results in clear conditions. While this operation was in progress S/L Sulinski went to Rotterdam.

Bad weather was beginning to frustrate the Command's ability to improve on its poor record during the summer, and typical was an attempt to hit Kiel on the night of the 19/20th, when the effort was thwarted by thick cloud and icing conditions. 300 Squadron sat this one out, but made ready six Wellingtons during the 22nd for an operation that night to Mannheim. A force of fifty-six Wellingtons and forty-one Hampdens was assigned to three aiming points within the city, which was hidden by cloud, and some returning crews claimed to have seen fires. In fact only a handful of bombs found the mark, and just one house was seriously damaged. A small force of freshmen targeted le Havre on this night, and among them was 300 Squadron's S/L Michalowski.

A total of ninety-nine aircraft took off for Cologne on the night of the 26/27th, among them nineteen 1 Group Wellingtons from Binbrook and Hemswell, including four representing 300 Squadron. Aiming points were the city centre and railway yards, and returning crews claimed much damage and raging fires. This is not borne out by local reports, however, which suggest that most of the bombs fell outside of the city limits to the east. Sgt Sobczak and crew experienced navigational problems, and ended up bombing Aachen instead of the primary target. S/L Michalowski returned to le Havre on this night in company with more than twenty other Wellingtons and Whitleys, and some bombs were seen to explode in the docks area. The squadron was not required for operations against Mannheim on the following night, Duisburg on the 28/29th, or Frankfurt and Mannheim again on the 29/30th, when unfavourable weather or ground haze were blamed for poor performances, and none of these attacks caused damage commensurate with the effort expended. The month's activities ended at Cologne on the night of the 31st in another ineffective operation, for which 1 Group provided thirty-two aircraft from Elsham Wolds, Hemswell and Binbrook. Just three 300 Squadron crews took part, one of which, captained by Sgt Leszkiewicz, got lost over France at some point, and had to land at Norwich short of fuel. Also on this night six Wellingtons were sent to Boulogne, and among them was 300 Squadron's commanding officer, W/C Cwynar. The month ended for the squadron with statistics of fifteen operations, forty-eight sorties and one missing aircraft.

Wellington R1641 BH-Z which took part in 14 operations with 300 Squadron from May to Aug. 1941. She was mostly flown by the crew of Sgt Ceglinski. (J. Kubit)

September 1941

September was to be a relatively quiet month for 300 Squadron, and, in fact, Hemswell remained off the order of Battle for the entire first week. During this period operations were mounted against Frankfurt and Berlin on the night of the 2/3rd, Brest on the 3/4th and Hüls on the 6/7th, but only the last-mentioned could claim any degree of effectiveness. The month's largest single effort was directed at Berlin on the night of the 7/8th, for which 197 aircraft were dispatched, among them twenty-seven 1 Group Wellingtons, although none again representing 300 Squadron. By the standards of the period, the 130 or so crews who reported reaching the target area delivered what could be described as an effective attack for the loss of fifteen aircraft. While this operation was in progress, three crews from 300 Squadron were sent to Boulogne in company with thirty-five other Wellingtons and nine Whitleys. They found the port in perfect visibility, and claims were made of excellent bombing results.

The first large-scale attack on Kassel claimed some useful if not excessive damage on the night of the 8/9th, and then it was off to Italy for 1 Group contingents from Elsham Wolds and Snaith to target Turin, where good results were claimed on the night of the 10/11th. The Baltic coast was the destination for elements of 1 Group on the night of the 11/12th, with aircraft from 12 and 142 Squadron assigned to Rostock and others from 150 Squadron to Kiel. 130 aircraft took off for Frankfurt on the night of the 12/13th, with 103 Squadron providing the 1 Group contribution, and more than seventy high explosive bombs found the mark, mostly in residential areas. For whatever reason, Hemswell remained operationally inactive until this night, when S/L Michalowski was the station's only representative in an operation against the docks at Cherbourg. Almost 150 aircraft were committed to an attack on the three warships at Brest on the night of the 13/14th, when 300 Squadron was finally called upon to make a more substantial contribution. Seven crews were briefed to take part, and they began taking off shortly before 23.00. Effective smoke screens hid the targets from view, and bombs were dropped on approximate positions. It was difficult to assess the level of success, some crews reporting clearly observed bomb blasts, while others saw nothing. On return, Z1256 force-landed at Mareham-le-Fen near Coningsby after losing its starboard engine, but the Wellington was only slightly damaged, and F/O Wolanski and crew walked away unscathed. Also on this night, S/L Sulinski and Sgt Nowakowski joined in a small-scale effort at le Havre.

Le Havre was also the destination for 300 Squadron's sole operational sortie on the evening of the 15th, when the main target was Hamburg. F/O Golko was undertaking his first operation with the squadron, and he returned at 23.18 to report observing his bombs bursting in the eastern corner of No 7 dock, and a fire that was visible for seventy miles into the return journey. 305 Squadron's W5526 failed to return from this operation, having crashed in the target area. The squadron's British adviser, W/C Drysdale, was the pilot, and he perished with the rest of the crew. The conditions for the Hamburg raid were good, but despite that, crews found it difficult to pick up individual aiming points. The bombing was spread around the city to fairly good effect, and many fires were left burning as the force retreated. At this point Hemswell began another period of operational inactivity, which stretched until the night of the 29/30th, when Stettin and Hamburg were the main targets. Three 300 Squadron crews took off between 19.14 and 19.24 bound for the latter, with S/L Sulinski taking the lead. They returned safely either side of 02.00 to report observing bomb blasts and a large red fire, but searchlight glare had made it difficult to make an accurate assessment. There were just six operations during the course of the month, which generated seventeen sorties and no losses.

October 1941

Bad weather continued to hamper operations during October, and it would be another relatively low-key month for Hemswell. The first real night of large-scale activity came on the 10/11th, when seventy-eight aircraft were sent to the Krupp works at Essen, while a further sixty-nine targeted Cologne. 1 Group put up twenty-two Wellingtons for the latter, but 300 Squadron stayed at home. In the event, only half of the force found the target area, and the unsatisfactory outcome was compounded by the loss of five aircraft. The night of the 12/13th brought a new record number of 373 sorties, 152 of which were sent to southern Germany to deliver the first large-scale assault of the war on Nuremberg. The operation was a dismal failure in which bombs were sprayed liberally over southern Germany, and few, if any, found the target city at a cost to the Command of eight aircraft. 1 Group put up just ten Wellingtons, but provided forty-seven of ninety aircraft involved in a simultaneous operation to Bremen. Of these ten belonged to 300 Squadron, led by W/C Cwynar, with S/L Michalowski also on duty, and they departed Hemswell between 18.23 and 18.44 for their first outing of the month. They, like the rest of the force here and at a third operation by 5 Group to a chemicals factory at Hüls, encountered cloud cover that led to inconclusive outcomes. Some returning crews reported bomb bursts and fires, while others saw nothing, but at least all returned safely.

Sgt Edward Ekiert took part in 51 operations during his two tours of duty with 300 Squadron between Aug. 1941 and June 1943. (GK)

Düsseldorf and Nuremberg were the principal objectives on the two following nights, but 300 Squadron was not required to take part. It was the same story on the night of the 16/17th, when Duisburg hosted a raid by over eighty aircraft, again without a contribution from Hemswell. The freshman crew of Sgt Ekiert did take off for Dunkerque on this night, but they decided to bomb Calais rather than the primary target because of the poor weather conditions. They delivered their bombs onto the docks area, and on return reported observing a fire for some forty miles into the return journey. The main target on the night of the 20/21st was Bremen, for which 150 aircraft were detailed. 1 Group was not represented, but instead provided thirty-three aircraft from Elsham Wold, Snaith and Lindholme for an attack on the port of Emden. 300 Squadron stayed at home again, but ten crews were called to briefing on the following afternoon, to be told they would be part of another attack on Bremen that night. 136 aircraft were to be involved, of which thirty-four Wellingtons would represent 1 Group, including ten each from 300 and 301 Squadrons. Take-offs at Hemswell began at 18.42, and it took twenty-five minutes to get them all away. S/L Michalowski was the senior pilot on duty, and he arrived in the target area to seek out shipyards as his aiming point. The city was covered by haze, which made identification of ground detail difficult, but he immediately noticed

P/O Zygmunt Radecki took part in 36 operations with 300 Squadron from Aug. 1941 to May 1942. (PISM via WM)

two fires burning. He was also able to pick out the bursts from his bombs, in what was a scattered and relatively ineffective attack, and other returning crews confirmed bomb blasts within the city, although not all saw fires. Also on this night, Sgt Sobczak and crew were sent on a freshman trip to Boulogne, but R1705 experienced an engine failure, and the bombs were jettisoned into the sea as they returned home.

The frequently-visited city of Mannheim hosted another raid on the night of the 22/23rd, with a contribution from 1 Group of nineteen aircraft, of which just eleven managed to battle through the severe conditions of cloud and icing to reach the target area. 300 Squadron stayed at home again, as it did for attacks on Kiel on the 23/24th and Frankfurt on the 24/25th. The night of the 26/27th was devoted to Hamburg, where the important shipyards and two central sites were to act as the aiming points. 300 Squadron made ready nine Wellingtons, and posted the names of S/Ls Sulinski and Michalowski as the senior pilots on duty. They took off either side of 18.00 to join up with more than a hundred other aircraft, and found the city under bright moonlight some three hours later. S/L Michalowski observed a large fire south of the River Elbe as he arrived over the target, and was at 17,000 feet at 21.25 when R1715 was hit by flak. Fortunately, nothing vital was damaged, and he observed his bombs bursting on the aiming point and a fire developing. Other crews reported bomb blasts and fires south of the Aussen-Alster lake, and the consensus was of a successful raid. While this operation was in progress two further crews from 300 Squadron were sent on freshman sorties to Cherbourg, but unfavourable weather conditions prevented both P/O Radecki and Sgt Nowakowski from identifying the target, and they jettisoned their bombs into the sea before returning home. Sgt Nowakowski returned to Cherbourg two nights later in company with Sgt Ekiert, and he again dumped his bombs into the sea from 12,000 feet ten miles off the French coast at 19.30. Sgt Ekiert managed to find what he was looking for, and reported his bombs bursting at the southern end of docks 4 and 5. There were seven operations during the month and thirty-five sorties.

November 1941

The first night of November brought an operation to Kiel supported by elements of 1 Group, including seven Wellingtons of 300 Squadron. The overall force totalled 134 aircraft, which made their way north-east in conditions that would nullify all attempts to deliver an effective attack. Over the target they encountered ten-tenths thick, low cloud with tops at between 10,000 and 19,000 feet, and bombs were released on estimated positions, aided a little by the glow of searchlights beneath the clouds. Some bomb bursts were observed, but generally, crews returned with no clue as to the effectiveness of their efforts. Local authorities reported hearing aircraft above, but no bombs fell within the town, and the operation was another abject failure. Also on this night, Sgt Sobczak and crew went to le Havre, and they returned to report glimpsing the coast line through a gap in the clouds, but being unable to identify the target. The 1 Group ORB, in contrast, states that the two crews involved found le Havre under fairly good weather conditions, and a large red fire was reported after bombing.

The continuing bad weather caused a general grounding of the heavy squadrons over the ensuing days, and an intended operation to Kiel on the night of the 6/7th was scrubbed. In an effort to score a major success during what had been a most frustrating period for Peirse, he planned a large-scale attack on Berlin for the night of the 7/8th, involving more than two hundred aircraft. The weather had not relented, and 5 Group's A-O-C, AVM Slessor, having expressed grave doubts about the conditions on this night, requested that he be allowed to send his force of seventy-five Hampdens and Manchesters to Cologne as an alternative. Peirse agreed, and also sanctioned a third operation to be carried out by fifty-five aircraft against Mannheim, of which forty-six would represent 1 Group. Although a record number of 392 aircraft set out for operations on this night, only 169 of the crews were briefed for Germany's capital city, including twenty-two from 1 Group, of which seventeen were Poles from Hemswell and Lindholme. Six 300 Squadron Wellingtons departed Hemswell either side of 18.15 bound for Germany's capital, but technical problems gradually reduced the number to three. Z1220 suffered engine failure, and bombed Rotterdam before returning home to land at 21.47. Thirteen minutes later Z1264 touched down having also bombed a secondary target because of communications problems. Sgt Leszkiewicz and crew pressed on until 21.06, when they fell foul of the weather conditions, which included severe icing, and dropped their bombs on Wunstorf, west of Hanover, before returning home. The operation developed disastrously, with less than half of the force reaching the target area to inflict a scant amount of damage, and the disappointment was compounded by the loss of twenty-one aircraft.

The Mannheim force, which was supported by four 300 Squadron Wellingtons, failed to find the target with a single bomb, and the cost of this debacle was the failure to return of seven Wellingtons and crews. Among these were two from 300 Squadron, both of which came down over France. Sgt Sobczak and crew were homebound over northern France, when icing conditions and shortage of fuel persuaded them to abandon R1705. The wireless operator and rear gunner were fed through the escape system in southern France and Spain, and eventually arrived back in England, while their colleagues spent the remainder of the war as PoWs. Z1271 was hit by flak in the Calais area, forcing Sgt Nowakowski and his crew to take to their parachutes. They all arrived safely on the ground, and the second pilot, observer and front gunner evaded capture, the first two-mentioned ultimately returning to England after escaping through Vichy France and Spain. The gunner, Sgt Chrzanowski, fell seriously ill, however, and died in Marseille on the 15th of June 1942. [2]

---

[2] *The escape and evasion reports from this and other crews appear at the end of the narrative section.*

F/L Stanislaw Boczkowski. He completed 30 missions from May 1941 to Feb. 1942 before taking up an instructor`s post in 18 OTU at Bramcote. (R. Boczkowski)

F/O Marek Rusiecki. Up till Dec. 1941 he took part in 22 operations with 300 Squadron. In Dec. 1944 he volunteered to fly special missions in 301 Polish (Special Duties) Squadron in Brindisi (Italy). (GK)

The 5 Group element came home unscathed from Cologne after destroying just two houses in the city, but nine other aircraft were missing from the night's minor operations, which included Boulogne, the destination for twelve 1 Group crews. The night's losses amounted to a new record total of thirty-seven, more than twice the previous highest for a single night. Of 1 Group's eighty aircraft, eight returned early and seven failed to return at all. This night of disaster was the final straw for the Air Ministry, and on the 13th Peirse was ordered to restrict further operations while the future of the Command was considered at the highest level. In the meantime Peirse was summoned to a personal meeting with Churchill to explain himself, but his time at the helm of Bomber Command was effectively over, and he would leave his post in January.

In the event, the continuing unfavourable weather would have placed its own restrictions on the Command's operational activity anyway. A force of 103 aircraft took off for Hamburg on the evening of the 9th, among them six Wellingtons from 300 Squadron. They took off either side of 17.45, with their crews briefed to aim for railway stations, but despite the favourable weather conditions of excellent visibility and almost no cloud on this night, searchlight glare made identification of ground detail difficult. Returning crews reported observing bomb blasts and a number of large fires in the city and docks area, and these were confirmed by local authorities.

The weather curtailed operations at this point until the night of the 15/16th, when relatively small-scale operations were mounted against the ports of Emden and Kiel. 300 Squadron was not involved, but sent P/O Boczkowski and crew on a freshman trip to Boulogne. During the course of this they became lost, and eventually force-landed Z1275 on return, happily without injury to the occupants. 300 Squadron remained on the ground for the next nine nights, before two crews were dispatched on the evening of the

Left: Symbols of 24 missions completed and the picture of "Goofy" under the cockpit of Wellington Z1326 BH-B. This aircraft was lost on its 31st mission when Sgt Kubacki had to ditch it while returning from Bremen on 2nd / 3rd July 1942. (PISM via WM). Right: The same picture of Goofy painted on Z1326 BH-B in changed form with RAF battledress tunic and Polish flying badges. (PISM via WM)

25/26th for a small-scale operation against the docks at Cherbourg. The recently appointed station commander at Hemswell, G/C Arthur Wray, took part, flying as second pilot to F/O Rusiecki in Z1282. Wray was born to missionary parents in 1896, and, having been a pilot since 1917, had amassed a great amount of experience of command at squadron and station level. It was typical of the man that he would want to use his experience to help new crews to gain confidence. Both crews on this night reached the target, and returned to report observing bomb bursts across the docks.

On the following night 1 Group was called into action for something other than freshman operations. Twenty-four of the Group's Wellingtons from Elsham Wolds and Hemswell joined a total force of a hundred bound for the port of Emden. There had been an absence on operations of the squadron's senior officers in recent weeks, but on this night S/L Sulinski was on duty, and he lead the seven-strong squadron contingent away at 17.29. They encountered eight to ten-tenths cloud all the way to the target, and those reaching it, which amounted to a little over half of the number setting out, were forced to bomb on e.t.a. Six 300 Squadron crews carried out an attack, two of them reporting bomb bursts and four seeing nothing, and the seventh abandoned their sortie and jettisoned the bombs into the sea. The month ended for the Command with a heavy raid on Hamburg on the last night of the month for which 181 aircraft were detailed. 1 Group contributed thirty-nine Wellingtons, and two-thirds of the force reached and bombed the target, while more than thirty others attacked alternative objectives. A further fifty aircraft were sent to Emden, and among these were three Wellingtons belonging to 300 Squadron. Conditions in the target area were good on this night, with clear visibility, and returning crews claimed good results. Sgt Ekiert had to abandon his sortie because of heavy icing, and he jettisoned his bombs into the sea. During the course of the month the squadron launched thirty-seven sorties for the loss of two aircraft and crews. The squadron operated nine times during the month, and dispatched thirty-seven sorties for the loss of two aircraft.

December 1941

The weather continued to hamper operations for the first half of December, and it was the night of the 7/8th before the first major operation took place. Aachen was the destination for 130 aircraft, including fourteen from 1 Group, but only half reached it in difficult weather conditions. Meanwhile, twenty-two 1 Group aircraft were involved in minor operations directed at French and Belgian ports including Brest, where the German capital ships continued to take shelter. This would be the first of fifteen attacks of varying sizes sent against the port during the month, as the Command sought a conclusion to this annoying distraction. 300 Squadron, meanwhile, contributed four Wellingtons to a freshman attack on Calais, taking off from Hemswell in the minutes leading to 21.00. All four reached the target and returned safely to report bomb bursts across docks 4 to 6. Enemy flak defences were particularly active on this night, and Z1244 was shot up over the target, and sustained damage to the starboard engine and hydraulics system, the latter causing the undercarriage to flop down and create drag. The engine had almost completely failed by the time the Wellington reached home airspace, but F/O Radecki managed to put it down at Mildenhall without crew casualties. When P/O Boczkowski and crew inspected Z1275 after landing, they discovered the fuselage peppered with flak splinters, the port fuel tank punctured and the tail fin damaged.

Sixty aircraft set out for Cologne on the evening of the 11th, among them three Wellingtons representing 300 Squadron. Fewer than half of the force reached the target, but all three from 300 Squadron did so, two reporting a large fire and one reporting bomb bursts. The Cologne authorities reported no attack on this night, and it must be assumed that the fire was a decoy. Sgt Kubacki and crew commendably completed their sortie in Z1326, despite the absence of a functioning intercom and radio. 1 Group participated in an operation against Wilhelmshaven on the night of the 16/17th, when 300 Squadron sent a single freshman crew to Ostend. On the following night, the squadron mounted its largest effort to date, when eleven of its Wellingtons took off either side of 17.30 bound for Brest. They were part of an overall force of 121 aircraft, eighty of which bombed the approximate position of the German warships from between 8,000 and 10,000 feet. W/C Cwynar was the senior 300 Squadron pilot on duty, and he saw no results in the conditions of five to ten-tenths cloud. Some other crews reported bomb bursts and fires, but it was yet another inconclusive operation.

Cologne was the target for over sixty aircraft on the night of the 23/24th, of which thirty-one from the Polish squadrons represented 1 Group. 300 Squadron again put up eleven Wellingtons, led this time by S/L Sulinski, and they departed Hemswell between 17.07 and 17.30. F/L Wolanski was troubled by icing conditions and bombed Calais as an alternative, while F/O Radecki dropped his load near Ostend after losing an engine. The others arrived in the target area to find eight to ten-tenths cloud, and bombed on estimated positions, before returning safely home. Most of the returning crews believed they had bombed the target, but the Cologne authorities recorded no bombs falling. While this operation was in progress a small-scale freshman operation was directed at Ostend, to which 300 Squadron contributed a single Wellington. Forty-one aircraft from the group, including ten belonging to 300 Squadron, contributed to an overall force of 130 bound for Düsseldorf on the night of the 27/28th. Only a handful of crews found the general area, and their bombs caused little damage on the ground. F/O Dreja and crew reported having to make violent course changes to avoid being coned by searchlights, but were uncertain as to their precise location at the time, and P/O Miszewski abandoned his sortie after being attacked four times by a night fighter. The 300 Squadron element bombed a variety of Ruhr locations, including Duisburg, Essen and Remscheid, and all returned safely, although not necessarily to Hemswell.

It had not been a good year for Bomber Command, which had failed to make any significant advance on the previous year's performance. The past twelve months had been characterized by a disappointingly ineffective operational record, and the failure of the new bomber types to match expectations. The Stirling, Halifax and Manchester had all experienced major teething problems following their introduction to squadron service early in the year, and each had undergone annoying periods of grounding while essential modifications were carried out. Following the disastrous night of operations on the 7/8th of November, the Command's future had been left hanging in the balance, and there can have been little confidence of an improvement in prospects as the coming year beckoned. In fact, the Command's salvation was even now waiting in the wings in the shape of the new four-engine Lancaster, which was secretly undergoing proving trials with 5 Group's 44 Squadron. Put into the hands of a new and dynamic commander-in-chief, this "shining sword" was about to carve for itself a place in aviation history.

Sadly, the men of 300 Squadron would have to wait a very long time before they got their hands on a Lancaster, and it brings into question the faith placed by General Sikorski in the fair treatment of Polish airmen by the RAF. It will be recalled that he wrote a letter of appreciation following his visit to Bramcote on the 7th of August 1940, in which he voiced confidence, "that the RAF is giving Polish airmen a really good and fair deal". Over the ensuing months and years, established squadrons would convert to the Lancaster, and new squadrons would be formed on the type. Despite the fact that the rest of 1 Group converted, 300 Squadron, which had been in the front line since almost the start of strategic bombing, would be given the choice of continuing with the outdated Wellington until well into 1944, or agreeing to a transfer to another group and an unpopular aircraft. During the course of the month the squadron operated seven times, launching forty-one sorties without loss.

General Sikorski (left) shown with his fellow Polish General, Marian Kukiel, Clementine and Sir Winston Churchill and the Polish Ambassador, Count Raczynski (Crown Copyright)

January 1942

Hemswell, 2nd Jan. 1942. The first presentation of DFCs to Polish bomber pilots: S/L Sulinski of 300 Squadron (Right) and W/C Piotrowski CO of 301 Squadron (Left) by A-O-C No. 1 Group AVM R D Oxland. (GK)

The New Year began with Bomber Command still under the same cloud, and operational activity somewhat depressed. Sir Richard Peirse would be relieved of his post as C-in-C Bomber Command in mid month, and posted to command Allied Air Forces in south-east Asia. He was succeeded temporarily by the 3 Group A-O-C, AVM "Jack" Baldwin, pending the arrival of a permanent replacement. The weather also played its part in keeping the crews on the ground, and once operational flying became possible, it would be French and German ports that received most of the attention. As already mentioned an average of one raid every other day had been sent against Brest and its lodgers during December alone, and a further eleven would be mounted in January, eight of them during the first eleven days of the New Year. The first event of note for 300 Squadron was the award to S/L Sulinski of the DFC on the 2nd. Eleven 300 Squadron crews reported for briefing at 15.00 on the 5th to be told that they would be joining forces with thirty-seven other crews from the group as part of an overall force of 154 aircraft. Half, including the 300 Squadron element, were assigned to the warships and the remainder to the docks area, and it was actually twelve hours after briefing, during the early hours of the 6th, that they finally took off from Hemswell. S/L Sulinski was the senior pilot, but the station commander, G/C Wray, was the senior officer on duty, flying as second pilot to the freshman crew of P/O Miszewski in Z1250. This Wellington led them away at 03.59, and they were all off the ground in a little over twenty minutes. They arrived in the target area to find unfavourable weather in the form of eight to ten-tenths cloud, and bombed on estimated positions. The reflections of a number of explosions were observed by some from the squadron, and there were reports of fires, but generally, no crew was able to accurately assess results.

The Polish squadrons sat out the small-scale 1 Group attack on Brest on the following night, but 300 Squadron prepared a new record of twelve Wellingtons for a return to the port in the early hours of the 8th. They were part of a thirty-five-strong 1 Group contingent, which represented half of the overall force. F/L Wolanski was the senior pilot on duty as the Hemswell element got away between 03.58 and 04.34, and all reached the target area to find complete cloud cover. Bombing took place from between 8,000 and 12,000 feet, and some returning crews reported seeing the glow of fires beneath the clouds. A much larger force of 150 aircraft was involved at Brest on the following night, when 300 Squadron stayed at home,

F/L Edward Metler. He took part in 38 operations from Oct. 1941 to Aug.1942 and was killed in a training flight in 2 AGS at Dalcross on 12th Apr. 1943. (GK).

Sgt Franciszek Chylewski, Second pilot in the crew of F/O Bak, he was killed on the return from his 2nd operation. (K. Kowalkowski)

and cloud prevented an accurate attack. For the fifth consecutive night, the port was the destination again on the 9/10th, this time for eighty-two aircraft, including eleven from 300 Squadron. They took off between 02.06 and 02.26, and again encountered cloud in the target area. Bombing took place on estimated positions, and returning crews reported a large reddish-orange fire and a big explosion followed by a fire.

It was at this point that attention switched from French ports to northern Germany, and the first of two raids on Hamburg on consecutive nights was mounted on the 14/15th. 300 Squadron was not involved, and, in the event, only half of the ninety-five-strong force reached the target area, where seven large fires resulted. Ninety-six aircraft were made ready for the second operation, eight of them representing 300 Squadron, on what would be an unhappy night for the Polish brigade. Z1250's sortie was scrubbed after an engine problem was discovered on start-up, but the remainder got away safely either side of 18.00. Z1220 was back in the circuit within forty-five minutes, having jettisoned its bomb load after suffering an engine failure, and communications problems on board Z1269 when close to the target forced F/O Metler to turn back also. Z1266 made it all the way to Hamburg, where it was discovered that the face mask of the observer, F/L Zurawski, had frozen, causing him to lose consciousness. There was no time to seek out one of the briefed aiming points, the shipyards and an airframe factory, and the bombs were dropped onto the main city area. Conditions in the target area were relatively good in terms of visibility, and three crews reported bombing close to the Aussen-Alster lake, north-west of the city centre, and observing a number of fires. The weather on return caused problems for a number of crews, with visibility and icing the most testing, and this caused Z1265 to crash at Clipstone, five miles north-east of Mansfield in Nottinghamshire, on return, killing F/O Bak and his entire crew.

The squadron was not required to take part in operations against Bremen and Emden on the succeeding few nights, but briefed nine crews for an attack on Münster on the night of the 22/23rd. This would be the first attack on an inland German target since the turn of the year, and the first of two in a week against this particular town, situated in the flatlands north-west of the Ruhr and within close proximity of the Dutch frontier. P/O Jakusz-Gostomski led them off at 17.35, and the others followed in his wake during the ensuing twenty-two minutes. R1715 was back in the circuit within eighty minutes because of communications problems, while gyro failure on board Z1270 meant that P/O Jakusz-Gostomski was unable to bomb the primary target. Conditions in the target area were described as good, and the others reported fires in the town centre and suburbs. Conditions at home persuaded most crews to land at Horsham-St-Faith on return, where F/O Dreja reported being attacked by a night fighter, and his second pilot, F/O Adrian, was treated for minor wounds.

W/C Romuald Sulinski participated in the maiden operation of 300 Squadron on 14/15th Sept. 1940, taking part in 37 operations up to May 1942. In Jan. 1942 he assumed command of 300 Squadron. Having spent the rest of the war on various staff posts he returned to command 300 Squadron in September 1945. He was killed in a flying accident on 2nd February 1946. (GK)

The main operation on the night of the 26/27th was against Hanover, for which seventy-one aircraft were made available. 300 Squadron briefed six crews, including that of F/L Wolanski as the senior pilot on duty. They took-off from Hemswell between 18.04 and 18.21, but three crews failed to reach the target through technical problems. P/O Pankiewicz delivered his bombs on Nienburg when his wireless operator and observer became ill, P/O Boczkowski attacked Ostend docks after gyro failure, while Sgt Kubacki jettisoned his bombs into the sea having experienced communications failure. Z1269 sustained flak damage to its port wing near Zwolle, but carried on in the hands of Sgt Leszkiewicz and crew, who observed their bomb bursts in the city, but were prevented by haze and a spirited anti-aircraft defence from being able to assess the results. Sgt Wielondek and crew claimed a ME110 as destroyed ten miles north of Rheine, and also observed bomb bursts in the built-up area of the target city. W/C Cwynar relinquished command of 300 Squadron on the 27th, and he was succeeded by W/C Sulinski.

A force of eighty-four Wellingtons and Hampdens took off to return to Münster on the night of the 28/29th in poor weather conditions of thick cloud and icing. None actually found the target area, although some believed they had, and bombs were delivered on a variety of alternative locations. Meanwhile, on this night, 1 Group dispatched twenty freshman crews to attack the docks at Boulogne. Among them were three from 300 Squadron, which took off either side of 19.00, and found more favourable weather conditions than those over Germany. F/L Wolski made a longer-than-expected detour for whatever reason, which would have made him arrive late over the primary target, and he elected to bomb Calais docks instead. Sgts Zalejko and Kostecki found Boulogne, and observed their bombs bursting in the target area before returning safely. This was the squadron's final outing of the month, during which it had dispatched fifty-nine sorties on seven operations for the loss of a single aircraft.

February 1942

The new month would finally bring a resolution to the Brest situation, although not a happy one for the nation and Bomber Command. Before that happened, three further small-scale operations would be mounted again the port in the first week and a half, beginning with one by sixty aircraft on the night of the 6/7th. 300 Squadron contributed nine Wellingtons, led by the newly promoted S/L Wolanski, who had stepped into S/L Sulinski's flight commander shoes following his promotion to command the squadron. The Hemswell gang got away in a sixteen minute slot from 17.14, and arrived in the target area to find complete cloud cover. Almost a third of the 1 Group crews jettisoned their bombs into the sea or brought them home, and this was yet another effort wasted on this target. It was not a good night for 300 Squadron, and began with Z1267 landing twenty minutes after taking-off with an oil system failure. Those reaching the target bombed on estimated positions and had no idea where their bombs landed. Z1282 was attacked and badly damaged by a night fighter on the way home, and a shell splinter caused a photo-flash flare to explode inside the aircraft, blowing the astrodome from its mountings and destroying a section of fuselage fabric. P/O Kracinski was attempting to land at Exeter, in what is believed to have been an emergency landing, but his approach was baulked by another aircraft, and the Wellington crashed just to the west of the airfield killing the second pilot, wireless operator and front gunner. Meanwhile, the crew of R1610 experienced similar difficulties when a photo-flash exploded accidentally inside the aircraft during the return flight. The second pilot panicked and baled out, while the front gunner fell to his death after unaccountably forgetting to attach his parachute. The remaining crew members managed to extinguish the fire, however, and F/O Malec carried out a safe landing at Hemswell.

P/O Franciszek Malec. He failed to return from Essen on 8/9th June 1942 on his 28th operation. (Chelstowski family)

Fifty-five aircraft were detailed to operate against Bremen on the night of the 10/11th, this figure including eight from 300 Squadron. It was actually in the minutes before and after 02.00 on the 11th that they departed Hemswell, and arrived in the target area around two-and-a-half hours later to find conditions ranging from haze and no cloud to up to six-tenths cloud as the operation progressed. There was also snow on the ground, and this made identification of detail difficult. A number of crews returned with reports of a large explosion and fire, but most saw nothing more than bomb bursts. Z1275 suffered an oil system failure, and P/O Boczkowski opted to deliver his bombs on Emden as an alternative target. Z1220 was approaching the target from the north-west, when it came under attack from an unidentified enemy aircraft at 04.50 while at 18,000 feet near the Schillig Roads. The night fighter closed to within sixty yards from the port quarter firing one-second bursts, and the front gunner was slightly wounded, but Sgt Fusinski continued on to bomb through cloud before bringing the Wellington home to a safe landing. Z1269 fell victim to the icing conditions, and turned back when quite close to the target. Later that evening the squadron sent six supposedly freshman crews to join nine others attacking the docks at le Havre. Thirteen aircraft arrived over the target, including all of the 300 Squadron participants, but found it difficult to locate the aiming point in intense darkness. A number of bomb bursts were observed across the docks area, and fires were also reported, which lasted ten minutes.

While the above operation was in progress, the final raid on the German cruisers at Brest was being carried out by a small force of Wellingtons. Weather conditions were described as good, with a cloudless sky and clear visibility at the start of the attack at 19.56, and cloud increasing gradually to two-tenths with tops at 5,000 feet by the end at 20.32. Haze and smoke made precise aiming difficult, but bomb bursts and smoke were observed. Vice Admiral Otto Cilliax, the Brest Group commander, whose flag was on Scharnhorst, put Operation Cerberus into action shortly after the bombers turned for home. Scharnhorst, Gneisenau and Prinz Eugen slipped anchor at 21.14, and headed into the English Channel under an escort of destroyers and E-Boats. It was an audacious bid for freedom, covered by widespread jamming and meticulously planned support by the Kriegsmarine and the Luftwaffe, all of which had been practiced extensively during January. The planning and a little good fortune allowed the fleet to make undetected progress until spotted off le Touquet by two Spitfires piloted by G/C Victor Beamish, the commanding officer of Kenley, and W/C Finlay Boyd, both of whom maintained radio silence and did not report their find until landing at 10.42 on the morning of the 12th. The weather had taken a turn for the worse, which had probably been anticipated, and this would create the most difficult conditions for the Bomber and Coastal Command elements sent to seek out and destroy the enemy under Operation Fuller, a plan devised for precisely this eventuality.

5 Group was already at four hours readiness, and 1 Group was alerted at 11.35. Both groups dispatched their first aircraft at 13.30, 1 Group putting twenty-five into the air, followed later by a further twelve. Among the second batch were four Wellingtons from 300 Squadron, which took to the air either side of 14.00 on what was, in fact, its very first daylight operation. A number of inconclusive attacks were carried out by 1 Group aircraft, and despite the commitment of a record 242 daylight sorties by the Command, the low cloud and squally conditions thwarted all attempts to halt the progress of the enemy flotilla. It passed through the Straits of Dover to make good its escape, and although Scharnhorst struck two air-laid mines, the damage was insufficient to delay her arrival in home port on the following morning. The Channel Dash episode, as it became known, was a major embarrassment to the government and the nation, and cost the Command a further fifteen aircraft and crews to add to all the others lost since the end of March of the previous year. At least, though, this annoying itch had been scratched for the last time, and the Command could now concentrate its resources against more suitable strategic targets.

A number of small-scale operations were mounted on the night of the 13/14th, one of them involving thirty-nine aircraft attempting to hit Cologne's main railway station. 300 Squadron put up five Wellingtons, with W/C Sulinski taking the lead. They took off between 01.37 and 01.50 on the morning of the 14th, and arrived in the target area to find heavy cloud, which obscured the results of their efforts. Later on the 14th, a new Air Ministry directive opened the way to the blatant area bombing of industrial Germany, and an assault on the morale of its civilian population. This had, of course, been going on for more than a year, but now it could be conducted in the open, without the pretence of aiming for industrial and military targets. Waiting in the wings, in fact, at that very moment, on his way across the Atlantic from America in the armed merchantman Alcantara, was a new leader, who would pursue this policy with a will, and have the personality and strength of character to fight his corner against the critics. In the early evening of the 14th four officer pilots took their crews to le Havre to attack the docks, and all returned to report being unable to observe results because of complete cloud cover.

300 Squadron briefed ten crews on the afternoon of the 16th to carry out roving commission sorties over northern Germany. The locations selected were Bremen, Oldenburg, a little to the north-west of Bremen, and Aurich, a small town closer to the coast and west of Wilhelmshaven. It has to be said, that these "nuisance" raids had no effect, and often resulted in the loss of valuable aircraft and crews for no gain. They were airborne either side of 18.30, with W/C Sulinski leading the Bremen element, which included Sgt Wielondek, P/O Pankiewicz and F/O Kusmierz, while P/O Radecki targeted Oldenburg and P/Os Miszewski, Szostak and Jakusz-Gostomski and Sgt Ekiert went for Aurich. It is not clear where P/O Chorazy was headed in Z1213, as engine failure forced him to jettison his bombs a hundred miles east of Mablethorpe at 19.40 and turn for home. Those reaching the target area were generally uncertain of their positions, and bombed through cloud. A number of those attacking Aurich reported observing bomb bursts, but no assessment of the results was possible. At least they all returned safely to land at a number of stations including Drem, Crosby, Hibaldstowe and Squires Gate, Blackpool.

ACM Sir Arthur Harris took up his appointment on the 22nd, and set about the mammoth task of turning Bomber Command into a war-winning weapon. He arrived at the helm with firm ideas already in place on how to win the war by bombing alone, recognizing, that in order to destroy an urban target, it was necessary to concentrate his forces in time and space to overwhelm the defences. This was the birth of the bomber stream, and it brought an end to the former practice, whereby squadrons and even crews determined for themselves the details of their sorties. He also knew that built-up areas are most efficiently destroyed by fire rather than blast, and that by concentrating the effort, fires would have a chance to gain a hold before the emergency services could reach them through rubble-strewn streets. It would not be long before the bomb loads carried in Harris's aircraft reflected this thinking. It was a policy of the bludgeon over the scalpel, but the war to date had demonstrated that precision bombing was a dream still awaiting the scientific means to achieve it.

For the remainder of February Harris continued with the small-scale attacks on German ports, beginning on the night of his appointment, when fifty aircraft were sent to Wilhelmshaven to attack the floating dock being used to repair the recent damage to Scharnhorst or Gneisenau. Ten 300 Squadron Wellingtons took off from Hemswell between 18.14 and 18.30, with F/L Wolski and the newly promoted F/L Jakusz-Gostomski the senior pilots on duty. The senior officer on the operation, however, was S/L Dukszto, who was the observer (navigator) in Sgt Kubacki's crew. They were now well into their first tour of operations, and a few months hence S/L Dukszto would become the squadron's next commanding officer. Complete cloud cover on this occasion thwarted any attempt to bomb accurately, and most delivered their loads on estimated positions. Although bomb bursts were observed, no assessment was possible, and it is likely that few bombs fell within the town.

The Gneisenau was found to be at berth in Kiel, and a force of sixty-one aircraft was made ready to attack the floating dock being used to carry out repairs. Nine 300 Squadron Wellingtons lined up for take-off shortly after 23.00, with F/L Jakusz-Gostomski the senior pilot on duty. On board R1715 with him, and occupying one of the gun turrets, was G/C Lusinski, the Polish station commander at Hemswell. Unfortunately, an air speed indicator problem and icing forced this crew to attack Emden as an alternative

Ingham, summer 1942. The crew of F/O Szostak posing with group of "erks" in front of Wellington (possibly Z1465 BH-S) with individual artwork of a Cracow girl in a dress with coronet on her hair. It was the emblem of pre-war Polish 11th Light Bomber Squadron. Standing left to right: 2nd F/O Wünsche (obs.), 4th Sgt Lubinski (W.Op.), 7th F/O Szostak (pilot) 11th Sgt Platacz (A.G.). Sgt Nowik (A.G.) sitting 1st from left (PISM via WM).

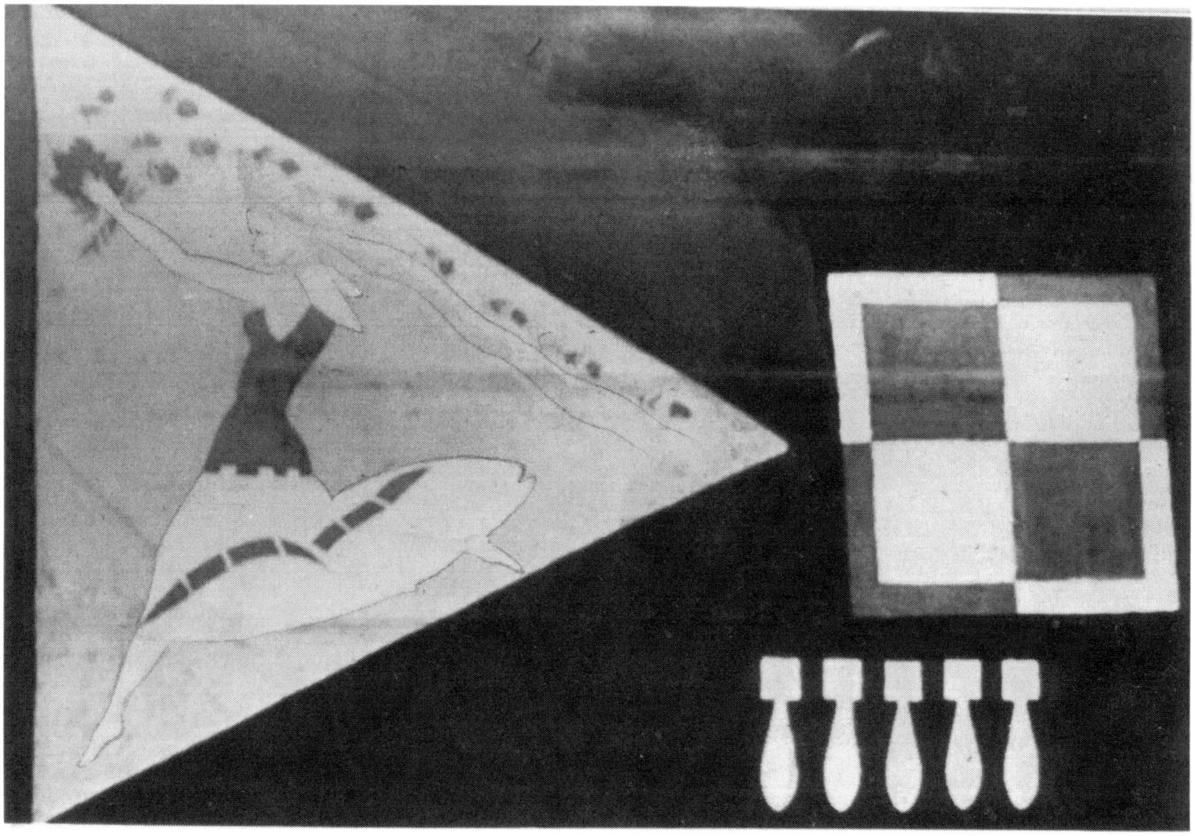

Close up of artwork of a Cracow girl painted on Wellington R1715 BH-S (PISM via WM)

target. Z1183 developed a list to starboard shortly after take-off, which was ultimately traced to a rudder problem. It proved impossible for P/O Chorazy to maintain level flight with a full load, and the bombs were jettisoned twenty miles east of the Humber at 23.40. The remainder arrived in the target area to find generally good conditions and little cloud, according to the 1 Group ORB, but the 300 Squadron record states that cloud prevented an assessment of results. It was probably a case of patchy cloud and ground haze that made it difficult to identify the aiming point, and returning crews reported observing bomb bursts. During the course of the attack two 12 Squadron Mk II Wellingtons delivered 1 Group's first 4,000lb "cookies".

It was at the same target on the following night that the war threw up one of its great ironies. While Wellingtons, Hampdens and Halifaxes were attacking the floating dock, a high explosive bomb struck the bows of the Gneisenau, now supposedly at safe haven after enduring eleven months of almost constant bombardment at Brest. The damage was sufficient to end her sea-going career for good, and her guns were removed for use in coastal defence. She was eventually taken to the port of Gdynia in Poland, where she remained, unarmed and unrepaired until the end of hostilities. 300 Squadron sat out this operation, but was called into action on the following night to attack the same target. Nine Wellingtons prepared for take-off either side of 18.00, and they headed into cloudy skies, which concealed the ground all the way to the target. Bombing took place on estimated positions, and although bomb bursts were reported, none fell within the town. This was the final operation of the month for 300 Squadron, and it brought the total number of sorties for February to seventy-four from ten operations.

F/L Wladyslaw Dukszto standing in front of Wellington Z1250 BH-N in the winter of 1941 at Hemswell. He replaced W/C Sulinski as 300 Squadron Commander in July 1942. Having completed 30 sorties from Aug. 1941 to July 1942, he was appointed CO of 18 OTU at Bramcote and Finningley in July 1943 and remained in this post until the end of the war. (GK)

March 1942

S/L Mieczyslaw Wolanski completed 32 sorties from June 1941 to July 1942. In Dec. 1942 he was posted to 16 (P) SFTS at Newton where he stayed in an instructor's post until the end of hostilities. In June 1945 he returned to 300 Squadron. (GK)

The first unmistakable sign of a new hand on the tiller came early in the new month. In a foretaste of future tactics, a plan was meticulously prepared for an attack on the Renault lorry factory at Billancourt in Paris. The operation was to take place in three waves, led by experienced crews, with extensive use of flares to provide illumination. Bombing would take place from low level, both to aid accuracy and to avoid civilian casualties in adjacent residential districts, and the number of aircraft over the target per hour would represent a 50% increase on the previous best. 235 aircraft were dispatched to Paris in the early evening of the 3rd, of which thirty-five Wellingtons represented 1 Group. This was the largest force yet sent to a single target, and 223 crews bombed as briefed, destroying 40% of the Renault factory buildings. Production of lorries was halted for four weeks, and the operation cost just a single Wellington. The satisfaction at this major success was marred only by the heavy casualties inflicted on French civilians, which amounted to 367 killed, and this was a problem which would never be satisfactorily addressed. It was somewhat paradoxical also, that Harris, as a champion of area bombing, should gain his first victory by way of a precision target.

300 Squadron was not involved in the above operation, and, in fact, had to wait until the early hours of the 9th before next being called into action. Essen was to feature prominently in Harris's future plans, and he mounted three operations against this most important of industrial Ruhr cities on consecutive nights from the 8/9th. The leading aircraft of the three-wave operation were equipped for the first time with the new Gee navigation device, but the ever-present industrial haze would prove to be an insurmountable obstacle to success. It was 01.40 when W/C Sulinski led the nine-strong 300 Squadron contingent off the ground, but Z1320 was back within the hour after suffering a port engine failure. Sgt Kubacki's crew contained S/L Dukszto as observer and G/C Luzinski as a gunner, and they arrived with the others in the target area to find clear skies but thick haze, which made identification of ground detail almost impossible. All returned to report observing many bomb bursts, some within sight of the Krupp works, but it proved impossible to make any assessment of results. Later that evening seven 300 Squadron Wellingtons returned to Essen in two waves separated by three hours. The first four took off between 19.50 and 19.55 with F/L Wolski as the senior pilot, and the second phase departed between 23.02 and 23.11 under the leadership of S/L Wolanski. The skies were clear, but ground haze again led to scattered bombing, and many Ruhr towns reported being hit, while the intended target of Essen suffered the destruction of just two houses.

The third raid in the series against Essen was mounted on the night of the 10/11th, for which 300 Squadron made ready seven Wellingtons to be led by W/C Sulinski. He was first away from Hemswell at 19.27, carrying a single 1,000 pounder, five 500 pounders and one 250lb incendiary, which he delivered in the target area without being able to assess the result. Low cloud made observation difficult, but he did see bursts through gaps, and two small fires. F/O Zelazinski reported many fires south of the target, one of them very large, and the other crews had similar stories to tell of bomb bursts and fires, but no firm impression of the outcome of the attack. At least they all returned safely before 01.00 to spend most of the night in their beds. Six of the squadron's Wellingtons joined up with sixty-two others on the night of the 12/13th to attack the Deutsche Werke U-Boot yards at Kiel, while a smaller force of Wellingtons and Whitleys attacked Emden. There were no senior pilots on duty as the 300 Squadron element took off either side of 19.30, all but one carrying a 1,000 pounder and four 500 pounders. Sgt Wielondek had two 500 pounders in his bomb bay along with thirty-six flares with which to illuminate the aiming point. Unfortunately, he found the glare from the flares impeding his view of his own bomb bursts, and the other crews experienced similar difficulties as a result of being dazzled by searchlights. They all returned safely to report a large fire to the south-west of the dockyards, and local reports confirmed that this was an effective operation, which caused damage to the Germania Werft as well as the intended target, and also hit the town. The Emden raid, in contrast, was disappointing, and bombing photographs showed that no bombs fell within five miles of the target. On the morning after, four 300 Squadron crews took off to carry out a sea-search for a 301 Squadron crew, which, it was believed, had come down in the North Sea, but nothing was seen, and the Wellington and its occupants remained lost without trace.

On the following night over a hundred aircraft took part in the first successful Gee-led raid, which took place at Cologne in the absence of a 300 Squadron participation. Thereafter, adverse weather conditions led to a twelve-night stand-down, which came to an end on the night of the 25/26th, when the campaign against Essen continued at the hands of a new record force of 254 aircraft. 109 of these were from 1 Group, and this represented its largest effort to date. 300 Squadron contributed thirteen Wellingtons led by F/L Jakusz-Gostomski, who had G/C Luzinski on board as a gunner, while S/L Dukszto was flying as observer with Sgt Kubacki. There was also a first operation of his second tour for the returning F/O Jasinski, who had completed twenty-six sorties with the squadron before being posted out in October to join 138 Squadron, one of two highly secret units operating on behalf of the Special Operations Executive (SOE) and Special Intelligence Service (SIS). He carried out a single operation to Poland on the night of the 7/8th of November, which had ended with his Halifax landing in Sweden because of a fuel shortage. A period of internment followed, and he arrived back in England in January 1942, before being posted back to 300 Squadron on the 10th of January.

They began taking off at 20.50, and all but one reached the target to find good visibility, and, according to F/O Jasinski, a smoke screen. F/O Malec had been forced to turn back when Z1268 developed overheating engines, which prevented him from climbing above 14,000 feet. He dropped his bombs on an airfield near the Dutch coast before returning safely to Hemswell. Sgt Zalejko was attracted by a large fire at Oberhausen, situated between Duisburg and Essen, and he delivered his bombs there from 17,000 feet at 23.29. The other squadron participants bombed from 16,000 to 17,000 feet over what they believed was Essen, and returned to report many fires, including a large one visible for twenty minutes after leaving the target. Sadly, despite the commitment of such a large force, the result was the same as before, and, according to local reports, only nine high explosive bombs fell within the city, while a decoy site at Rheinberg attracted many more.

Harris tried again on the following night with a force of 104 Wellingtons and eleven Stirlings, 300 Squadron providing ten of the former, their crews called to briefing at 14.00. There were no senior pilots on duty as they departed Hemswell in a fourteen-minute slot from 19.34. They headed across Holland and reached German airspace some two hours after taking off, where Z1256 was approached by a twin-engine enemy night fighter at 21.43 near Kempen, thirty miles inside Germany and still sixty miles from the target. F/O Dobrzanski jettisoned the bombs from 14,500 feet and took evasive action, while his gunners drove the enemy off before it carried out an attack. The others arrived in the target area to find a hostile flak defence and many night fighters, and searchlight glare added to the dazzling effect of the illuminating flares to make identification and assessment difficult. The 300 Squadron crews carried out their bombing runs from 16,000 to 17,000 feet, and it was then that Z1291 was hit by flak, which killed the rear gunner, Sgt Slabikowski. Nine aircraft returned, each of them damaged to some extent by flak, but Z1269 was not among them, and it was learned later that it had been shot down off the Dutch coast near De Kooy airfield on the Den Helder peninsular, and there were no survivors from the crew of F/O Zelazinski. At debriefing crews reported bomb bursts and many fires, but the truth was, that this was another failed operation, which had deposited a paltry twenty-two high explosive bombs in Essen, at a cost of 10% of the force.

The inability to identify Essen confirmed what Harris already knew, that navigating over a blacked-out, cloud-covered, hostile country at night was a nightmare. However, he believed that if he could provide his crews with pinpoints on the ground, instead of forcing them to rely on dead-reckoning, they would do the rest. Coastlines offered the best reference points, and this was one of the considerations that led Harris to the ancient Baltic port and Hansastadt (free-trade city) of Lübeck. Other inducements were the paucity of its defences, and the half-timbered construction of the buildings in its old centre, where the narrow streets would encourage the spread of fire. In a sign of things to come for Germany, Harris dispatched 234 aircraft on the night of the 28/29th, Palm Sunday, of which fifty-one represented 1 Group, five of them provided by 300 Squadron, led by F/L Jakusz-Gostomski. The two-thirds incendiary bomb loads carried by the force reflected the fire-raising intention of the attack, which was to be conducted on similar lines to those employed against the Renault factory at the start of the month. Aircraft would attack in three waves, led by experienced crews using Gee to assist with navigation for as long as its range lasted. There was a full moon, and crews were instructed to bomb from low level to ensure accuracy. The first four 300 Squadron Wellingtons got away within minutes of 21.30, but F/O Jasinski was not airborne until 22.10. They reached the target to find conditions as forecast, and delivered their bombs from 3,500 to 11,500 feet between 23.25 and 01.05, and all returned safely to report the target to be a mass of flames, with smoke rising to 5,000 feet. F/O Jasinski's rear gunner counted forty-three separate fires, and the success of the operation was confirmed by reconnaissance, which revealed over fourteen hundred buildings destroyed, with a further two thousand seriously damaged. This amounted to 30% of the city's built-up area, and was the first major success for the area bombing policy, which had been achieved for the modest loss of twelve aircraft. There would be no further major attacks on Lübeck for the remainder of the war, because of its importance to the International Red Cross in the shipment of supplies. During the month the squadron was involved in seven operations, and dispatched fifty-seven sorties for the loss of one aircraft.

April 1942

The new month began with minor operations, which did not involve 300 Squadron, and it was the 5th before ten crews were called to briefing. They were told that the first major operation of the month would involve a new record force of 263 aircraft with Cologne as the target. Earlier in the day the crews had attended an Easter church service, followed by a traditional Polish lunch in the Airmen's Institute, attended by all officers and men. 1 Group made ready seventy-nine aircraft for this operation, from all six of its operational stations, and their crews were briefed to aim at the artillery-producing Humboldt Motoren A.G factory complex, which was situated in the Porz district of Deutz, an inner city region occupying the entire right bank of the Rhine. S/L Wolanski was the senior pilot on duty, and he was first away from Hemswell at 23.01, to be followed by the others over a twenty-minute period. They all reached the target area to find good conditions, but the presence of ground haze impeded identification of ground detail. The squadron crews each delivered their eight small bomb containers of incendiaries and single 250 pounder from 15,000 to 19,000 feet between 01.30 and 02.10, and assessed them to have fallen within a mile or so of the aiming point, mostly on the eastern side of the Rhine. Searchlight glare made an assessment difficult, and flak was also a problem. R1725 was hit by flak, but landed safely at West Raynham with diminished fuel reserves. Sadly, this massive effort was not rewarded with success, and left just a scattering of damage across the city. No bombing photos were plotted within five miles of the Humboldt works, and only ninety houses were destroyed or seriously damaged.

During the course of the 6th 157 aircraft were prepared for a return to Essen that night. Eight 300 Squadron crews were briefed to take part, led by W/C Sulinski, and they took off either side of midnight to encounter appalling weather conditions, which included electrical storms and severe icing. This prevented two thirds of the force from reaching the target area, and Sgt Ekiert was one of those forced back by icing on wings and propellers while at 12,000 feet. F/O Chorazy and crew had problems with their oxygen system and bombed Cologne as an alternative before they, too, returned safely home. The others pressed on to bomb the target from 16,000 to 19,000 feet between 02.45 and 03.20, but were prevented by complete cloud cover from assessing the results. Yet another new record was set on the night of the 8/9th, when 272 aircraft took off for Hamburg, of which seventy-eight were provided by 1 Group. W/C Sulinski led the 300 Squadron contingent of eleven Wellingtons, which began taking off at 21.36 on another night of bad weather, characterized by icing conditions and electrical storms. F/O Radecki and crew were plagued by intercom problems as they approached Heligoland outbound, and the front gunner fainted. The all-incendiary load was dropped from 20,000 feet at 00.28 on Marne, on the north bank of the Elbe Estuary, after which the crew returned safely home. The others dropped their loads on e.t.a over ten-tenths cloud from 16,500 to 19,500 feet between 23.50 and 00.44, and returned home with nothing useful to report. The operation was another failure, and despite 188 crews claiming to have bombed in the target area, local authorities reported only about fourteen bomb loads falling into the city.

The first of two further raids directed at Essen took place on the night of the 10/11th, for which 1 Group put up seventy-five aircraft in an overall force of 254. 300 Squadron supported the operation with eleven Wellingtons, led again by W/C Sulinski, and he was first to take off at 22.10, watched by the A-O-C, who was visiting Hemswell. They all reached the target area, where clear conditions had been forecast, but they encountered ten-tenths cloud, and none was able to identify their precise location. They were forced to bomb on estimated positions, which they did from 16,000 to 20,000 feet between 00.03 and 00.30 in the face of a strong flak defence. Fourteen aircraft failed to return, but all from 300 Squadron made it back in one piece.

Wellington Z1398 BH-L photographed at Ingham in summer 1942. She flew with 300 Squadron between April 1942 and Feb. 1943, taking part in no fewer than 50 operations. (PISM via WM)

On the following night S/L Wolanski led ten 300 Squadron Wellingtons away from Hemswell at 21.28, as part of a seventy-strong 1 Group contribution to an overall force of 251 aircraft bound once more for Essen. They adopted a different route on this night, and the mention of nickels being dropped on Bonn suggests a southerly approach to the Ruhr. Certainly, the crews described the outward flight as good, with no interference from the enemy, and conditions were good apart from the usual heavy ground haze. S/L Wolanski identified the target by the River Ruhr, but had nothing specific in his sights as he delivered his seven SBCs and single 250lb incendiary from 18,000 feet at 01.05 on a heading of 270°. Z1256 was shot up by flak during the bombing run, but F/O Adrian was able to bring it home without major incident. The other squadron participants carried out their attacks from 16,000 to 19,000 feet between 00.56 and 01.44 on a variety of headings from 20° to 360°, and all but one returned home. Z1213 was shot down by a night fighter near Uden in south-eastern Holland, almost certainly on the way home, and Sgt Zalejko died alongside four of his crew. The second pilot, Sgt Kuczak, parachuted into the arms of his captors as the sole survivor. This concluded a highly disappointing series of attacks on the home of the giant Krupp armaments-producing concern, during which Harris had mounted eight heavy raids involving 1,555 sorties for the loss of sixty-four aircraft, and although a thousand crews claimed to have bombed in the target area, little damage had been inflicted.

Over two hundred aircraft took off for Dortmund on the night of the 14/15th, ten of them Wellingtons of 300 Squadron, which began departing Hemswell at 22.02 led by W/C Sulinski. Z1250 developed a problem with its starboard engine while outbound, and F/O Miszewski took the opportunity to bomb an aerodrome thirty miles south-east of Cherbourg from 8,000 feet at 00.30 without observing any results. On the way home the engine caught fire and had to be shut down, but a safe landing was made at Tangmere. R1725 made it as far as the Ruhr before flak and searchlights forced Sgt Ekiert to take evasive action, throwing him off course. The bombs were dropped from 13,000 feet at 01.56 on what was believed to be Essen, and it was then that flak hit the starboard engine, causing it to run irregularly. On crossing the English coast it burst into flames, but Sgt Ekiert calmly landed at Horsham-St-Faith on the good engine, and the fire was extinguished. The others pressed on, and those reaching the target area bombed from 17,000 to 20,000 feet between 02.00 and 02.43, although F/O Radecki later believed that he had attacked Hagen in error. Reconnaissance revealed that he was one of many to spray bombs over a forty-mile stretch of the region, and there was only minor damage in Dortmund. The operation was repeated on the following night, when F/L Jakusz-Gostomski led a contingent of six from the squadron, which took off shortly after 23.00. His Z1398 suffered from a misfiring port engine, however, and he brought his bombs home. The others found the target area to be under ten-tenths cloud, and bombed on e.t.a from 17,000 feet between 02.38 and 03.08, with no clue as to results. Z1320 was holed by flak over the target, but F/O Jasinski and crew arrived home safely. It was another failed operation, which delivered the equivalent of just eight bomb loads into the city.

Hamburg was the latest target in this busy month of operational activity, for which a force of 173 aircraft was made ready during the course of the 17th. 300 Squadron briefed ten crews, to be led by S/L Wolanski, and the Hemswell station commander, G/C Arthur Wray, decided to tag along as second pilot to F/O Jasinski. They began taking off at 23.30, and were all safely airborne by 23.58, but R1795 lost the use of both turrets through lack of hydraulic fluid, and F/O Szostak was forced to turn back. He jettisoned part of the bomb load before attempting to land, but hydraulic fluid on the windscreen obscured his view, and he dumped the rest prior to a safe touchdown. Z1267 was shot down into the North Sea by a night fighter while on final approach to Hamburg, and there were no survivors from the crew of F/O Kusmierz, whose presence in the squadron would be greatly missed. Good visibility enable the others to identify the target easily by means of the Elbe and the Binnen-Alster Lake near the city centre, and delivered their bombs from 15,000 to 20,000 feet between 02.59 and 03.50. They returned to report a number of fires, confirmed by local reports, as seventy-five, thirty-three of them classed as large, but there was no significant damage to war industry.

F/O Jan Orsza-Matysek (obs.). He was killed with the rest of the crew of F/O Kusmierz when their Wellington was shot down during the raid on Hamburg on 17/18th April 1942. It was his 23rd operation. (GK)

Gee had proved useful as a navigation device, and in order to assess its potential as a blind bombing aid, an operation was mounted against Cologne on the night of the 22/23rd employing sixty-four Wellingtons and five Stirlings. 1 Group's 150 Squadron was one of those newly equipped with the Gee or TR Wellington, and six of these participated in the operation. The experiment was deemed a failure when only about a quarter of the force found the mark, and the others dropped their bombs up to ten miles away.

Sgt Peczek's crew photographed in Hemswell in late 1941. Left to Right: Sgt Peczek (pilot), F/L Dukszto (obs.), Sgt Kubacki (pilot), Sgt Keryluk (W.Op.) and Sgt Sikorski (A.G.). (GK)

300 Squadron remained at home after Hamburg until the night of the 23/24th, when Harris, in an attempt to repeat the success at Lübeck at the end of March, dispatched the first of four raids on consecutive nights against Rostock, another port further east along the Baltic coast. The presence of a nearby Heinkel aircraft factory was an added attraction, and a contingent of eighteen aircraft from 5 Group was sent to attack it while the main raid was in progress. Four 300 Squadron crews were away from Hemswell by 22.40, with no senior pilots on duty, and they were part of an overall force of 143 aircraft assigned to attack the town. The 300 Squadron crews all reached the target to find clear skies and good conditions other than ground haze. They bombed from 3,500 to 14,000 feet between 02.05 and 02.24, and returned to report a highly successful operation, which left at least seven fires burning that were visible from the Danish coast. In fact, it was a disappointing start to the series, which had missed the aiming point in the Altstadt by two to six miles, and the Heinkel factory had escaped damage altogether.

When the operation was repeated on the following night, just three 300 Squadron crews took part, those of F/O Radecki, P/O Fusinski and Sgt Kubacki, who had S/L Dukszto on board as observer. They took off shortly before 22.30 as part of an overall force of ninety-one assigned to the town, while thirty-four others from 5 Group tried again at the Heinkel works. Conditions were again good, and the Hemswell crews bombed from 6,000 to 12,000 feet between 02.23 and 02.55 in the face of a much heavier flak defence than on the previous night. P/O Fusinski's Z1268 had its hydraulics system damaged by flak, but it came home safely, and the crew reported nine large fires and numerous small ones, the largest appearing to be in the Neptun shipyards. This time the reports were accurate, and reconnaissance showed the town centre to have been heavily bombed, although the Heinkel factory again escaped damage. While this operation was in progress the squadron sent two freshman crews to bomb the docks at Dunkerque, and both returned without incident after fulfilling their briefs.

On the following night S/L Wolanski led off the squadron contingent of four Wellingtons either side of 22.00, as part of a force of 110 aircraft assigned to the town, while the soon-to-be-famous W/C Guy Gibson led a 106 Squadron element to the Heinkel factory. Conditions were again excellent, and bombing was carried out from 7,000 to 15,000 feet between 01.34 and 02.08 in the face of defences that had been further strengthened. Z1397 and Z1465 both sustained flak damage, but returned safely with the others to report another successful outcome. For the second night running two freshman crews were sent to Dunkerque, and one completed their sortie successfully, while the other failed to identify the target. The final raid took place on the night of the 26/27th, for which 300 Squadron dispatched four Wellingtons between 22.05 and 22.41. They were part of an overall force of 106 aircraft divided roughly equally between the town and the Heinkel factory. They all reached the target to find conditions as before, but a pall of smoke hanging over the town threatened to hamper the aiming-point identification. The 300 Squadron element bombed from 14,000 to 17,000 feet between 02.06 and 02.55, and returned safely to report another accurate attack. Over the course of the four operations 1 Group launched 165 sorties, and these contributed to the destruction of over seventeen hundred buildings. This left an estimated 60% of the main town area in ruins for the modest overall loss of eight aircraft.

Sgt Jan Fusinski was shot down on his 28th operation, evaded capture and returned to the UK. After his commission he trained as night fighter pilot and was posted to 307 Polish Night Fighter Squadron, but failed to return from night patrol over Germany on 27/28th May 1943. (PISM via WM)

Cologne hosted one of its more effective raids on the night of the 27/28th at the hands of a predominantly Wellington force of ninety-seven aircraft, of which six represented 300 Squadron. There were no senior pilots on duty as they departed Hemswell in a fourteen-minute slot to 21.52, and made their way across France in favourable weather conditions to the target area. Z1276 was approaching the Franco-Belgian frontier outbound when it was attacked by a night fighter near Givet, and shot down. The crew of P/O Fusinski all took to their parachutes, and landed safely on the ground, where they received help from the locals to put them in touch with the French underground. The observer, F/O Wawerski, was captured in Paris, and the front gunner, Sgt Sierpina, opted to remain in neutral Switzerland for the remainder of hostilities, but the others all eventually made it back to England. *(See escape and evasion reports at the end of the narrative section).* Four of the others from the squadron reached the target area after approaching from the south, and delivered their bombs from 16,000 to 18,000 feet between 01.00 and 01.12. The fifth, Z1397, was running low on fuel as it crossed into Germany, and rather than swing north to Cologne, F/O Chorazy elected to carry on eastwards to bomb the town of Andernach before turning for home. Z1264 was attacked six times by a night fighter on the return flight, and the observer and rear gunner sustained wounds. The rear turret and communications system were knocked out, but F/O Mendela skilfully evaded the enemy, and made a safe landing at Coltishall in Norfolk. While this operation was in progress, S/L Wolanski and Sgt Dziekonski went to Dunkerque, where they encountered unusually heavy flak. Z1215 was on its bombing run when caught by an exploding flak shell, which sent it spinning temporarily out of control, but Sgt Dziekonski managed to recover the situation, and bombed the target from 15,000 feet at 00.01. S/L Wolanski dropped his bombs from 12,000 feet, and watched them explode across docks 7 and 8 and railway lines. One of the bursts was described as very brilliant, and three minutes later an enormous explosion occurred in the docks area.

300 Squadron was not involved at Kiel on the following night, when all three shipyards were hit, but six of its crews were briefed on the 29th for an attack that night on the Gnome & Rhone aero-engine factory

Hemswell, spring 1942. Wellington Z1250 BH-N in the foreground during preparation for a night operation. R1715 BH-S is in the middle and possibly Z1279 BH-Z is on the right. (PISM via WM).

at Gennevilliers, in the loop of the River Seine in northern Paris. 1 Group put up twenty-nine Wellingtons in an overall force of eighty-eight aircraft, and the 300 Squadron element was led by W/C Sulinski. They took off shortly after 21.00, and arrived over the French capital, mostly to find excellent visibility, and easily-identifiable ground detail to assist with orientation. Sgt Kubacki circled Paris from 23.56 to 00.45, but failed to identify the aiming point because of the similarity of the 180° bends in the river in the north and the centre. The others pressed home their attacks at altitudes varying from 3,500 to 6,000 feet, and a number of hits were observed on the main target, and also on the power station, the Thompson-Houston works and the Goodrich Tyre factory. All returned safely to Hemswell, where reports were filed of a successful operation. In fact, the Gnome & Rhone factory had not been hit, but damage to others in the Port de Paris was confirmed. The squadron took part in a record seventeen operations during the month, which generated a new record of 109 sorties for the loss of three aircraft.

May 1942

Sgt Alojzy Dreja completed his operational tour with 300 Squadron between Oct. 1941 and June 1942. (PISM via WM)

May opened with a raid on Hamburg on the night of the 3/4th, for which a force of eighty-one aircraft was made ready, including nine from 300 Squadron. They were all airborne by 23.02, led by F/L Wolski, and headed towards a partially cloud-covered north-western Germany. Z1268 refused to climb above 15,000 feet, and this meant that F/O Malec was unable to pick up wireless fixes. There was also doubt about being able to reach the target in time, and it was decided to bomb the airfield at Jever in the Friesland region of Holland as an alternative. It was identified in good visibility by the flare path, along which an aircraft was seen to be taking off, and was attacked from 15,000 feet, although the bombs were believed to have fallen short. F/O Dreja encountered ten-tenths cloud while about twenty miles north of Hamburg, and decided to bomb Tönning on the Schleswig-Holstein peninsular as an alternative. However, searchlights and flak at Meldorf further south drove him off, and persuaded him to jettison his bomb load and return home. Z1270 was attacked by a JU88, which F/O Radecki evaded after also jettisoning his bombs. Z1183 was shot down into the sea by a night fighter, and only the second pilot, Sgt Lis, managed to bale out to land in the sea, where he was rescued by a German patrol boat and taken into captivity. The bodies of the observer and a gunner eventually came ashore for burial, but F/L Wolski and the others were never found, and the loss of this experienced crew would be keenly felt. The others were among a modest fifty-four aircraft known to have attacked the target on estimated positions, after finding it to be completely cloud-covered. Despite this, over a hundred fires were started, and besides other damage, eleven blocks of flats were destroyed by the blast from a 4,000 pounder. While this operation was in progress, Sgt Dziekonski was on his way to bomb the docks at St Nazaire, but an encounter with a night fighter at 2,000 feet forty miles off Bridport saw him jettison his bombs and turn for home. Meanwhile, the freshman crew of Sgt Peczek carried out a leafleting sortie over Paris, in company with three crews from 304 Squadron, which was operating with Bomber Command for the final time before being transferred to Coastal Command on the 7th.

On the following night the first of three raids on consecutive nights was mounted against Stuttgart, where the Bosch AG factory at Fuerbach was the main target for the twenty-four participating 1 Group Wellingtons in an overall force of 121 aircraft. 300 Squadron stayed at home on this night, when complete cloud cover led to a scattered and ineffective attack. The effort was further compromised by a decoy fire site fifteen miles north of the city, cleverly "defended" by over thirty searchlights, which inevitably attracted many bomb loads. 300 Squadron briefed seven crews for the second Stuttgart operation, which involved just seventy-seven aircraft. The Hemswell crews began to depart at 21.59, with no senior pilots on duty. Z1220 suffered instrument and fuel pressure problems on the way out, and there was also some concern about the undercarriage. It was the last-mentioned issue that persuaded Sgt Ekiert to jettison the bomb load rather than face the dangers of an undercarriage collapse on landing. F/O Tomaszewski arrived in the Stuttgart area on ETA to find thick haze, which prevented him from identifying ground detail. He was able to see an aerodrome, however, and attacked this from 15,000 feet at 01.15, without being able to determine any results. The remaining five 300 Squadron crews also reached the target area, but cloud thwarted all attempts to identify the aiming-point, and not one of the 1 Group crews found it. They bombed on estimated positions from 14,500 to 16,000 feet between 01.05 and 01.34, before returning safely. Under cover of this operation the squadron contributed three Wellingtons to a small-scale effort at Nantes, on the River Loire, inland from St Nazaire. One must assume that the docks were the target, and two of the squadron representatives bombed in clear conditions from 16,000 feet, while the third was beset with engine problems and jettisoned its load.

The third Stuttgart operation was mounted on the night of the 6/7th, and involved an overall force of ninety-seven aircraft. Ground haze again thwarted the crews, and no bombs fell in the city. The decoy site was in operation again, and it backfired to some extent by attracting crews to the town of Heilbronn, five miles away and twenty miles from Stuttgart. Many bomb loads fell into the town, and 150 buildings sustained damage. 300 Squadron was not involved, but sent the crews of P/O Kaluzny and Sgt Peczek back to Nantes along with seventeen others. Both suffered engine problems, and neither completed their sortie.

On the night of the 8/9th, almost two hundred aircraft, set out for the Baltic port of Warnemünde. Thirty-four aircraft from 1 Group were assigned to the town and its port facilities, while twelve others targeted the nearby Heinkel works. A further element was sent in to supress searchlight activity, and three of these were from 1 Group. W/C Sulinski led the seven 300 Squadron participants away at 21.39, and they were all safely airborne by 22.10. Z1382 lost an engine while outbound, and Sgt Ekiert dumped his bombs in the sea before turning for home. W/C Sulinski arrived to find clear skies and good visibility, and was able to identify the target from the coastline and a river. He ran in on the target from north to south at 11,000 feet at 01.20, and saw his bombs burst in the eastern half of the town. The others from the squadron attacked from 14,000 to 16,000 feet between 01.14 and 01.30, and bursts were seen, along with a number of fires. All in all the night was a disaster, with inconclusive results and heavy losses amounting to nineteen aircraft, four of which were 44 Squadron Lancasters.

On the 13th the squadron was visited by F/Os Taras and Radwanski, who had failed to return in Z1271 on the night of the 7/8th of December 1941. They told their stories of evasion from the Germans and escape from internment in France and return to England. Three days later the General Inspector of the Polish Air Force, AVM Stanislav Ujejski, visited the station, and bestowed awards upon members of 300 and 301 Squadrons. Minor operations occupied most of the next ten nights, and it was during this period, on the 18th, that 300 Squadron moved south from Hemswell to Ingham, situated about eight miles north of Lincoln. The first major operation thereafter saw 197 aircraft take off for Mannheim on the night of the 19/20th, and among them were seven from 300 Squadron. There were no senior pilots on duty as they got away safely by 22.30, and, for once, all reached the target to deliver between them fifty-five small bomb containers (SBCs) of incendiaries from 16,000 to 18,000 feet between 00.57 and 01.25. Thick haze made it impossible to assess the results, but fires were observed as the crews turned away from the target, and a large forest fire was seen to be developing to the north. While this operation was in progress two freshman crews were sent to join an attack on the docks at St Nazaire, and both completed their sorties before returning safely.

Apart from the isolated notable successes already mentioned, the Command had failed to impress thus far under Harris, and voices in high places, particularly at the Admiralty, were still calling for bomber aircraft to be diverted to other theatres. When Harris took up the reins of command, he demanded a massive increase in the number of bombers made available to him, with which, he asserted, he would win the war. While there was not the slightest chance of getting as many as he wanted, he needed to ensure that those earmarked for him were not spirited away to what he considered to be less deserving causes. He required a major victory, and, perhaps, a dose of symbolism, to silence the critics, and out of this was born the Thousand Plan, Operation Millennium. This called for the commitment of a thousand aircraft in one night to erase from the map an important German city, for which Hamburg had been pencilled in. Harris did not have a thousand frontline aircraft at his disposal, and he needed the support of other Commands, principally Coastal and Flying Training, to make up the numbers. This was forthcoming in letters to him on the 22nd and 23rd respectively, but following an intervention from the Admiralty, Coastal Command underwent a change of heart, withdrew its contribution, and sent a handful of navigators instead.

Undaunted as always, Harris, or more likely his able Deputy, AM Sir Robert Saundby, set about scraping together every airframe capable of controlled flight, or something close to it, and pulled in the screened crews from their instructional duties. Come the night, not only would the magic figure of one thousand be achieved, it would be comfortably surpassed. There was little operational activity after Mannheim, and the arrival on bomber stations from Yorkshire to East Anglia of aircraft from the training units during the final week of the month gave rise to much speculation. F/Os Miszewski and Dreja took off on the evening of the 22nd to lay mines off St Nazaire, but they were recalled a few hours into the outward flight because of anticipated bad weather at home. The weather also remained the only question with regard to Operation Millennium, and as the days ticked by inexorably towards the end of May, it was showing no signs of cooperating. Harris was aware of the genuine danger, that such a large fleet of aircraft might draw attention to itself and, thereby, compromise security, and the point was fast being reached when the operation would either have to be launched, or be abandoned for the time being. The Polish crews found this period of inactivity particularly frustrating, such was their desire to get at the enemy, and every cancelled operation sent them deeper into despondency. On the night of the 29/30th Harris released some pressure by allowing seventy-seven aircraft to carry out another raid on the Gnome & Rhone aero-engine factory at Gennevilliers in Paris, to follow up the attack there a month earlier. 300 Squadron was not included on the Order of Battle for this operation, which as before, failed to find the mark.

It was in a tense atmosphere of uncertainty and frustration that "morning prayers" began at Harris's High Wycombe HQ on the 30th, with all eyes turned upon the bespectacled chief meteorological adviser, Magnus Spence. After deliberating for some time, he was able to give a qualified assurance of clear weather over the Rhineland after midnight, while north-western Germany and Hamburg would be concealed under buckets of cloud. Thus did the fickle finger of fate swing away from Germany's Second City, and point unerringly at Cologne as the host for the first one thousand bomber raid in history. One of the concerns for the planners had been the risk of collisions over the target, as the unprecedented concentration of at least ten aircraft per minute funnelled towards the aiming point during the intended ninety-minute duration of the raid. At briefings crews were informed that the experts had predicted that just two aircraft would collide over the target. It is reported, that at least one "wag" on every station asked whether the statisticians knew which two aircraft would be involved! Whether or not they did, their prediction of one collision would prove to be accurate, although it would occur at home, not in the target area. Fifteen 300 Squadron crews listened with relish as the details of the operation were laid out before them, while out on the dispersals the ground crews and armourers toiled to ensure that this record effort would go off without a hitch. Planning for the operation had been meticulous, and involved the first large-scale use of the bomber stream, in which all aircraft would adopt a common route and speed to and from the target, and adhere to a height and time slot to ensure an orderly procession across the aiming point. These innovations would become a feature of all major operations henceforth.

1 Group's contribution to the overall force of 1,047 assorted aircraft was 156 Wellingtons, and some of these would be in the leading wave of Gee-equipped aircraft flown by experienced crews. 12 Squadron would make the greatest contribution of the night when putting up a magnificent twenty-eight Wellingtons from Binbrook, and the Polish element of 300, 301 and 305 Squadrons would contribute a combined total of forty-two Wellingtons from Ingham, Hemswell and Lindholme respectively. The second wave was to contain the other twin-engine aircraft including those from the training units, while the genuine heavies brought up the rear. Among the contingent from the various training units were a further twenty-five Polish crews from 18 O.T.U at Bramcote, and these brought the total number of polish crews taking part to sixty-seven. They began to take off for Germany at around 22.30 hours, and some of the older training hacks took somewhat reluctantly to the air, and were, perhaps, lifted more by the enthusiasm of their crews than by the power of their engines. A few of these, unable to climb to a respectable height, would fall easy prey to the defences, or just drop from the sky through mechanical failure. There were no pilots above flying officer rank among the 300 Squadron contingent, but the Polish station commander from Hemswell, G/C Luzinski, and S/L Dukszto were on board F/S Kubacki's Z1326 as rear gunner and observer respectively.

They took off either side of 23.30, and all fifteen reached the target to find conditions precisely as predicted by Magnus Spence, clear skies, good visibility and moonlight. By the time the Polish crews arrived the city was already a mass of flames, with smoke rising to 10,000 feet. As the ORB commented, "Lübeck was nothing to this spectacle". The Ingham crews were each carrying nine SBCs of 4lb incendiaries, which they delivered onto the target from 15,000 to 19,500 feet between 01.28 and 02.00. Z1326 was hit by flak, which damaged an engine and holed the fuel tanks, but it returned safely with twenty holes for the riggers to patch, and F/S Kubacki described it as a "very nice trip". Z1279 lost its port engine on the way home, and crash-landed at Barkstone Heath airfield near Sleaford with no casualties among the crew of F/O Dreja. In all, 1,400 tons of bombs had reigned down on the target, and the operation was an outstanding success by any standards, resulting in the destruction of over 3,300 buildings, with a further two thousand seriously damaged. A new record of forty-one aircraft failed to return, but in conditions favourable to both attackers and defenders alike, and in the context of the size of the force and the scale of the success, this was an acceptable loss of 3.9%. During the course of the month the squadron was involved in eleven operations, launching fifty-six sorties for the loss of a single aircraft.

June 1942

Hemswell, spring 1942. Group of 300 Squadron aircrew sitting on a trolley with bombs. Left to Right: Sgt Chanecki (W.Op.), S/L Wolanski (pilot), Sgt Kostecki (pilot), F/O Jezewski (obs.), F/O Martusewicz (obs.), P/O Cieplinski (A.G.), Sgt Sosinski A.G) (L. Gredys).

Wishing to capitalize on his success, Harris determined to use the Thousand force again as soon as possible, and selected Essen as the target for the night of the 1/2nd of June. Only 956 aircraft were available to answer the call to arms, and 12 Squadron again put up the largest effort in 1 Group with twenty-three Wellingtons in an overall total of 137. 300 Squadron briefed fourteen crews, and they took off between 23.12 and 00.14 led by S/L Wolanski. F/O Chorazy and crew were recalled for an unspecified reason after midnight, when they were fifteen miles east of Leiden, north-east of the Hague, but the others pressed on to reach the target, where ground haze and a thin layer of low cloud presented the usual difficulties of identification. S/L Wolanski described the visibility as good, but not as good as at Cologne, and he believed his nine SBCs of incendiaries hit the northern part of the Krupp works. F/S Kubacki struggled to maintain height, even with superchargers, but he arrived over the target at 15,000 feet, identifying it by means of flak and searchlight concentrations. The others bombed from 17,000 to 18,000 feet between 01.15 and 02.04, and all returned safely to report what they believed was a successful attack, which had left many fires burning. In fact, and in stark contrast to the raid on Cologne, this operation followed the same pattern as past attempts on Essen, and bombs were distributed all over the Ruhr, with the main concentration west of Essen at Oberhausen, Duisburg and Mülheim. Only eleven houses were destroyed in Essen at a cost of thirty-one aircraft.

F/O Franciszek Jakusz-Gostomski. He successfully completed all 36 operations in which he took part with 300 Squadron from July 1941 to June 1942. In Aug. 1943 he joined 138 (Special Duties) Squadron at Tempsford and started flying special missions in Polish "C" Flight. Failed to return from a supply dropping operation to Poland on 14/15th Sept. 1943. (PISM via WM)

A follow-up raid by under two hundred aircraft twenty-four hours later did not involve 300 Squadron, and failed to bring any improvement in performance. Harris switched his force to Bremen on the night of the 3/4th, for which 300 Squadron contributed ten Wellingtons to an overall force of 170. They took off either side of 23.00 with F/L Jakusz-Gostomski the senior pilot on duty. F/O Miszewski turned back with engine failure, but the others pressed on to find the target in fairly good visibility, which enabled F/O Jasinski to identify it by means of bends in the River Weser. He released his SBCs from 18,000 feet at 01.18 before the first flares had gone down, and it was three minutes later before they illuminated the target. He believed his incendiaries had fallen on the southern edge of the old town on the south-west bank of the river, and noted fires beginning to break out after other aircraft had bombed. The others bombed from 17,000 to 18,500 feet between 01.30 and 02.00, and all but one returned safely to report a successful operation. Z1291 lost its port engine shortly after crossing the Dutch coast at Alkmaar, and eventually had to be ditched some thirty-six miles out from Great Yarmouth at 03.35. F/O Mendela and his crew spent five-and-a-half hours in their dinghy before being picked up by a rescue boat. This raid produced the best result yet at this target, with damage inflicted on the docks and residential districts, but Harris's attention was still on Essen, and he would not give up yet.

Eight 300 Squadron crews attended briefing on the 5th to be told that Essen would be their destination that night as part of a force of 180 aircraft. S/L Wolanski took the lead, and was first away from Ingham at 23.00. Visibility was poor as he arrived in the target area, with heavy ground haze concealing detail. The light from flares enabled him to identify the river as he approached at 18,000 feet, and he dropped his nine SBCs at 01.27 on an almost north to south heading. By this time Sgt Fojud had turned back with communications difficulties when fifteen miles west of Egmond, and F/O Malec had jettisoned part of his load twenty miles out over the North Sea because R1725 was climbing sluggishly. They all ultimately found what they believed was the target, and bombed from 17,000 to 18,500 feet between 01.35 and 01.52 before returning safely home. The ORB hailed this as another very successful operation, but, in truth, it was another scattered and ineffective attack, which cause no significant damage.

Before Harris tried again at Essen, he would send over two hundred aircraft to Emden, the port situated on the north bank of the Ems Estuary opposite northern Holland. However, the first business at Ingham on the morning of the 6th was to dispatch F/L Jakusz-Gostomski and crew at 10.56 to search the North

Sea for a missing 301 Squadron crew, and, although a parachute was identified, no other trace was found. Eight 300 Squadron crews were briefed for the Emden operation that night, for which S/L Wolanski would again take the lead, and he was first off the ground at 23.16 to be followed over the ensuing twenty minutes by the others. Conditions in the target area were good, and the coast line assisted in orientation, but some found ground haze a problem. The 300 Squadron crews bombed from 16,500 to 18,000 feet between 01.27 and 02.00, and the consensus was of a successful outcome based on numerous fires, including one large one. Reconnaissance confirmed the effectiveness of the operation, which destroyed around three hundred houses and seriously damage a further two hundred. Harris would attempt to capitalize on this success with three further raids later in the month, but each would fall well short of this one.

170 aircraft set out for Essen on the night of the 8/9th, among them eight representing 300 Squadron led by the newly-promoted F/L Jasinski. He was airborne at 23.06, followed by his squadron colleagues over the next fifteen minutes. Z1489 was eight miles south of Amsterdam when attacked by a JU88 at 17,000 feet, and Sgt Szychowiak opted to jettison his SBCs of incendiaries and head for home. R1725 disappeared into the sea at some point, presumably after also encountering a night fighter, and the crew of F/O Malec was never found. The others all definitely reached the target area, but none was able to positively identify Essen. F/L Jasinski bombed from 18,000 feet at 01.18, believing Essen to be beneath him, but after landing he felt that Bottrop was more likely the recipient, which meant that his true position had been some distance to the north-west. The others also bombed on estimated positions from 16,000 to 18,000 feet between 01.10 and 01.29 before heading for home. Z1382 was thirty-five miles west of Essen when it was attacked by a BF110, which caused a fire in the port wing and engine, damaged the rear turret, seriously wounded the rear gunner and slightly wounded the wireless operator. The engine was shut down and the fire extinguished, but damage to the hydraulics system meant that the bomb doors could not be closed and the undercarriage was inoperable. The second pilot, Sgt Offierski, panicked and baled out over enemy territory, where he was captured. Sgt Fojud calmly flew the crippled Wellington home on one engine with the bomb doors creating drag, and force-landed at Martlesham Heath, between the Suffolk coast and Ipswich, without further crew casualties. The crew claimed their assailant as probably destroyed after it was seen to dive away. The operation was later revealed to be another widely-scattered failure, at a cost of nineteen aircraft. Thus far during the month 1,600 sorties had been launched against Essen for the loss of eighty-four aircraft, and there was little to show for it.

Sgt Leopold Peczek. He completed 37 sorties with 300 Sqn from Oct. 1941 to Aug. 1942. After spending three months as instructor in 18 OTU at Bramcote he volunteered to join 138 (Special Duties) Squadron at Tempsford and took part in another 19 special operations from Dec. 1942 to April 1943. The CO of 138 Squadron assessed Peczek as 'a pilot of exceptional skill' in his logbook. (GK)

On the following night the squadron contributed six Wellingtons to mining duties in the Nectarines garden, off the Frisians. They were led away by F/L Jasinski at 23.02, and mostly selected the island of Schiermonikoog as a pinpoint from which to make their runs. Each delivered their vegetable into the briefed location from around 700 feet shortly after 01.00, and returned safely to report a quiet and successful trip. After a period of minor operations, 106 aircraft were detailed for a return to Essen on the night of the 16/17th, but only sixteen crews reported bombing as briefed, and many of the others found alternative targets, mostly Bonn. 300 Squadron remained at home on this night, and it was the 19th before the crews were next called to briefing. The target was to be Emden, and this would be the first of three further attacks on the port in the space of four nights. Eight 300 Squadron Wellingtons took off either side of midnight in the absence of a senior officer, and joined up with the rest of the 190-strong force over the North Sea. Weather conditions were unfavourable, and most crews were unable to identify the target under ten-tenths cloud, and were forced to bomb on e.t.a. F/S Peczek was the only one to make a positive identification, having recognized the coastline of Dollart Bay, into which the River Ems fed. He released his nine SBCs from 17,400 feet at 02.18, but was unable to observe any results, and returned safely to comment, "Weather so poor the trip was just a waste of petrol". Five other squadron crews bombed on e.t.a from 16,000 to 17,000 feet between 01.55 and 02.15, and returned home with no clue as to the effect of their efforts. Two others failed to return on what was a bad night for the squadron. Z1215 crashed into the sea at some stage during the operation, and only two bodies washed ashore a month later for burial, those of the pilot, Sgt Dziekonski, and the observer, F/O Lech. Sgt Dziekonski was a very experienced pilot, who, at the time of his death, was mid way through his second tour with the squadron. Z1256 was hit by flak over the target, and made it out into the estuary before crashing about seven miles north of the target, killing F/O Tomaszewski and his crew. Hardly any bombs fell on Emden, and, in fact, Osnabrück, some eighty miles away, received more attention after part of the flare force began an attack there.

A force of 185 aircraft set out to return to Emden on the following night, of which six Wellingtons represented 300 Squadron. F/O Miszewski led them away from Ingham at 23.19, and they headed out over the North Sea towards the Waddensee and the Frisian islands of Borkum and Juist off the mouth of Dollart Bay and north of the target. Z1398 was five miles south of Juist when it was attacked by a night fighter, which Sgt Szychowiak successfully evaded after jettisoning his bomb load. The others all identified the target area by coastline detail, and carried out their attacks from 13,500 to 16,000 feet between 01.25 and 01.36, before returning safely home. It was learned later that only a proportion of the force had found the target, and around a hundred houses had sustained damage. After a night's rest seven 300 Squadron crews joined 227 others for a return to Emden on a night of better weather conditions and good visibility. F/O Miszewski was first off again, at 23.20, and the remainder got away safely by 23.31, only for F/S Hulas to abandon his sortie and return to Ingham at 00.15 after his front gunner reported sick. The others pressed on to find the target easily identifiable, and attacks took place from 14,200 to 18,000 feet between 01.25 and 01.36. Returning crews described Emden as "well alight", and the general impression was of a successful operation. Local reports detailed fifty houses destroyed and a hundred damaged, and it is believed that decoy fire sites drew off many bomb loads.

Mining operations were a constant feature of activity, particularly for freshman crews, although it was four experienced 300 Squadron crews who took to the air from 23.00 on the 23rd to plant their vegetables in the Nectarines garden off the Frisians. F/O Miszewski again took the lead, and he made a fix on the Simonszand sand bank east of Schiermonikoog, before delivering his mines into the briefed locations. The others were also successful at other nearby map references, and all returned safely from an uneventful trip.

Sgt Henryk Kaluzny. After completion of his tour of duty from Oct. 1941 to July 1942, he trained as a night fighter pilot and was posted to 307 Polish Night Fighter Squadron. (PISM via WM)

The final outing for the Thousand force was to be directed at Bremen on the night of the 25/26th, when 960 aircraft and crews answered the call for a maximum effort, among them 111 Wellingtons from 1 Group. Ordered by Churchill to participate, Coastal Command contributed 102 aircraft, in what was classed as a separate operation, but the numbers converging on the target would exceeded those going to Cologne at the end of May. 300 Squadron detailed thirteen crews, led by S/L Wolanski, and they got away in a twenty-five minute slot from 23.20. They reached the target area to encounter complete cloud cover, and most crews established their location by the glow of fires started by the first wave crews, who had used Gee to guide them. The squadron crews delivered their nine SBCs each from 16,500 to 18,000 feet between 01.45 and 02.06, and a few caught glimpses of fires through gaps in the cloud as they withdrew. Z1415 was on its way home at 12,000 feet near Dokkum in northern Holland, when it was attacked by a BF110, which probably came from the Luftwaffe night fighter station at Leeuwarden, the famed Wespennest (wasps nest), situated just a few miles to the south-west. The Wellington's rear turret and hydraulics system were knocked out, but P/O Kaluzny was able to escape, and landed safely at Ingham with the bomb doors hanging open. While not achieving the hoped-for success, the results at Bremen far surpassed the Essen debacle, and 572 houses were destroyed, while over six thousand others sustained varying degrees of damage, and a number of shipyards and other war industry factories were hit. The Command registered a new record loss of forty-eight aircraft, but only two were from 1 Group. Among them was the Wellington of 301 Squadron's commanding officer, W/C Krzystyniak, which was hit by flak over the target, forcing him and his crew to parachute into the arms of their captors.

The month ended with two smaller-scale follow-up raids on Bremen on the 27/28th and 29/30th, both of which resulted in some useful industrial damage. 300 Squadron took no part in these operations, but sent three crews on a sea search for a missing crew on the morning of the 28th, without result. The squadron participated in eleven operations during the month and dispatched ninety-two sorties for the loss of three aircraft.

July 1942

It fell to Bremen also to open the July account on the night of the 2/3rd, for which a force of 325 aircraft was made ready. 1 Group contributed ninety-one aircraft, fourteen of them Wellingtons provided by 300 Squadron, and led by F/L Jasinski. He took off first at 23.03, and headed for the coast at Mablethorpe, followed by the others over the ensuing thirty minutes. Z1409 returned at 00.41 with the crew of Sgt Rokosz, after his port engine began to lose power ten miles east of Mablethorpe, and Sgt Ekiert landed R1795 at 01.57, after surviving an encounter with two night fighters at 15,000 feet over the North Sea at 00.20. Z1490 landed fourteen minutes later with the crew of Sgt Szychowiak, after the lack of an oxygen feed to the front turret left its occupant incapacitated. To their credit, all three crews brought their incendiary loads home. The others reached the target area to find no cloud and good visibility, and delivered their incendiary loads from 15,000 to 18,000 feet between 01.43 and 02.00. P/O Kubacki identified the target by the River Weser and the docks, and he believed his load fell into the town just north of a railway bridge over the river. Z1326 was then hit by flak, which holed a petrol tank, and it failed by twenty-five miles to reach the coast at Mablethorpe. P/O Kubacki pulled off a controlled ditching, after which the trusty Wellington remained afloat for twenty minutes. The crew spent two hours in their dinghy until being rescued by a British patrol boat, HMS Corsair. Damage at the target was again quite widespread, reported at about a thousand houses damaged, and a number of ships were hit in the port, one of them sinking.

By the middle of 1942 plans were afoot to convert the whole of 1 Group to the Halifax, and 103 Squadron was selected as the first to receive the type. A little later 460 Squadron would also begin training on Halifaxes, but would not achieve operational status before a change in policy decreed that the Group would operate Lancasters instead. There was only one further major operation during the first half of the month, but first, five 300 Squadron crews were sent on a sea search on the morning of the 4th to try to find a missing crew, and they returned later with nothing to report. Nine crews took off either side of 22.30 on the 5th to conduct mining operations off St Nazaire, and apart from Sgt Szychowiak and crew, who were thwarted by a navigational error, all successfully fulfilled their briefs. Ten crews took off from Ingham either side of midnight on the 7/8th to carry out a similar operation around the Frisians, and this time all completed their assigned tasks from between 500 and 700 feet before returning safely.

285 aircraft were made ready for a raid on Wilhelmshaven on the night of the 8/9th, of which fifty-eight Wellingtons represented 1 Group. Ten 300 Squadron crews attended the briefing during the afternoon, and it was approaching midnight when F/L Jasinski took off to lead them away from Ingham. Z1332 lost an engine while outbound, and had to turn back, P/O Kaluzny opting to retain his bombs and bring them home rather than dump them in the sea. Z1250 had the target in sight ten miles ahead, and the crew of Sgt Rokosz could make out bomb bursts, when they were attacked by an enemy night fighter, and had to jettison the bomb load north-west of the target in order to escape. The others delivered their two 1,000 pounder and three 500 pounders from 15,500 to 18,000 feet between 01.53 and 02.20 in poor visibility, having mostly identified the target from coastal features and ground detail illuminated by flares. Z1489 was leaving the target area when the starboard engine cut out momentarily, before restarting, and it did this a number of times before failing altogether. The crew of Sgt Szychowiak had noted intense heavy flak during the bombing run, and realised that they must have been hit. An empty fuel tank confirmed this, but 230 gallons remained in the port tank, and that was sufficient to carry them a good distance towards the English coast. Ultimately a ditching became inevitable, and at 04.10 Sgt Szychowiak put the

Wellington down in a heavy swell, which forced the nose under water and propelled the front gunner, Sgt Rawski, towards the forward escape hatch. The pilot made a desperate attempt to get to him, but the Wellington was sinking too fast, and he and the other members of the crew had to get out. It was all over within thirty seconds, and the gunner went down with the aircraft. An air-sea rescue launch picked them up at 11.30 and delivered them to Grimsby. The pilot had a slight head wound, but otherwise the survivors were none the worse for their harrowing experience. Some damage was inflicted on Wilhelmshaven, but generally the bombing missed the target.

Sgt Leon Szychowiak failed to return from his 26th sortie on 4/5th Sept. 1942. (PISM via WM)

On the 9th W/C Sulinski was succeeded as commander of 300 Squadron by W/C Dukszto, who unlike his predecessors was a navigator rather than a pilot. Late that morning four crews took off for a sea search, but found nothing. On the night of the 13/14th, Harris began a five raid series against Duisburg, which would take place over a three-and-a-half week period, and would prove to be equally as frustrating as the campaign against its neighbour, Essen. A force of 194 aircraft was prepared on this night, among them seventy-five from 1 Group, including eight provided by 300 Squadron. They were led away by F/L Jasinski at 23.46, and take-offs were safely completed by shortly after midnight. Conditions outbound were not good, and F/S Hulas was caught in ten-tenths rain-bearing cloud and beset with icing, which prevented him from climbing above 11,000 feet. He jettisoned his bomb load at 01.16 and turned back. The others encountered nine-tenths cloud in the target area, with tops at 16,000 feet, and bombing took place on e.t.a from 15,000 to 19,000 feet between 02.03 and 02.22. Returning crews reported the glow of fires beneath the cloud, but no meaningful assessment was possible. In fact, only eleven houses had been destroyed, along with sixty others damaged, and it was a poor return for the effort expended.

On the following night fifty-two aircraft were sent to a variety of garden areas to lay mines, and four from 300 Squadron were assigned to the Nectarines region off the Frisians. They took off either side of 23.30, and found good visibility beneath the cloud base, which enabled them to find pin-points and deliver their stores from 700 to 800 feet, before returning without incident. Daylight cloud-cover operations on the 16th, 17th and 19th involved aircraft from 1 Group's 150 Squadron carrying out nuisance raids on Essen. These, as previously mentioned, were highly dangerous operations of questionable value, and frequently resulted in the pointless loss of valuable and experienced crews. Only four sorties were completed as briefed during this series, and no results were observed. The second operation to Duisburg was mounted on the night of the 21/22nd, when 291 aircraft were made ready, of which sixty-six were from 1 Group. Thirteen 300 Squadron crews attended briefing, and they began to depart Ingham at 23.30. S/L Wolanski was the senior pilot on duty on a night of reasonable weather conditions, but not all from Ingham would reach the target. First, Z1465 developed a port engine problem, persuading P/O Siadek to bring his bombs home, and then Z1409 refused to climb above 11,000 feet because of excessive oil temperature, and Sgt Rokosz also brought his bombs back. F/S Peczek was another to experience engine problems, and he bombed an aerodrome south of Haarlem near the Dutch coast, and observed five bursts across the airfield.

Ingham, summer of 1942. Wellington Z1387 BH-Q which was lost on her 37th operation on 14/15th Jan. 1943 with the crew of Sgt Gosiewski. (PISM via WM)

The others pressed on and found the target identifiable by ground detail, such as a lake and an aerodrome west of the River Rhine, the Rhine itself, its large inland docks area and a canal. They delivered their two 1,000 and three 500 pounders from 14,000 to 18,000 feet between 01.45 and 02.06, and all returned to report a successful operation. In all, 253 crews reported bombing within the city, and local authorities confirmed that ninety-four residential buildings had been destroyed, and 256 seriously damaged, and this definitely represented an improvement at this target, but was still a poor return for the effort expended. The problem had been the inaccurate dropping of flares by the lead Gee-equipped aircraft, and this was responsible for a proportion of the bombing falling into open country west of the Rhine.

It was a similar story on the night of the 23/24th, when a force of 215 aircraft set out for Duisburg, while 300 Squadron stayed at home. The flares were again scattered, but some bombs did find the target to hit housing. Two nights later 300 Squadron was back on the Order of Battle for the next swipe at Duisburg, for which 313 aircraft were detailed. Thirteen Wellingtons lined up for take-off at Ingham led by F/Ls Jasinski and Kropinski, but F/S Hulas was first away at 23.58, and F/O Metler brought up the rear twenty-eight minutes later. They headed for the target in poor weather conditions, and most crews were forced to bomb on e.t.a., as they failed to pick out any ground detail. A number of crews were able to positively identify Duisburg by a distinctive bend in the River Rhine, and others took flak and searchlight concentrations as proof that they were in the right area. They delivered their bombs from 17,000 to 19,000 feet between 02.09 and 02.40 in the face of a heavy flak barrage, and Z1490 picked up a few splinters. Z1387 came home with damage to its aerial and rudder, and this was attributed to a night fighter, although no sighting of one was reported. While returning over the North Sea Z1244 was definitely engaged by a night fighter, and the rear gunner, Sgt Janek, was killed instantly. The Wellington was badly damaged,

Ingham, summer 1942. Left: Wellington Z1320 BH-K with the symbols of 41 bombing operations and the artwork of a constellation of stars which were supposedly left over from the aircraft's previous service with 458 Squadron RAAF. 4th from left F/L Szymanski (obs.) flew 29 operations in this Wellington. 3rd from right – S/L Wolanski, "A" Flight commander. Right: 'Erks' decorating the nose of the aircraft (PISM via WM).

but F/O Metler pulled off a one wheel landing at Ingham, and there were no further injuries to report. There was again damage to residential property, although not as much as on the two previous raids, and the operation was chalked up as another major disappointment.

Harris switched his attention to Hamburg on the night of the 26/27th, for which a force of 403 aircraft answered the call for a maximum effort. 1 Group contributed eighty-three Wellingtons, of which fifteen were provided by 300 Squadron, led by the station commander, G/C Arthur Wray, who was a month short of his forty-sixth birthday. He was first to take off at 22.26, to be followed by the others over the ensuing forty-seven minutes. Z1279 was attacked outbound by a BF109, which was evaded after the bomb load had been jettisoned, and P/O Miszewski made a safe return. P/O Jan Miszewski was the older brother of the previously-mentioned F/O Andrzej Miszewski, and this was a rare, though not unique case of two brothers operating with the same squadron at the same time. Happily, both would complete their tours. Z1490 developed an oxygen system failure to the front turret, and F/O Dziubinski decided to attack a last-resort target, for which the island of Heligoland presented itself. The bombs were dropped from 18,000 feet at 00.42, and bursts were observed, but not on the island, which they missed. The last of the early returners was Z1320, which was attacked by a night fighter, forcing F/L Jasinski to dump his two 1,000 pounders, two 500 pounders and single 250 pound delayed action bomb, and thereby evade the enemy and any consequent damage. The others pressed on to find Hamburg under clear skies with excellent visibility. G/C Wray easily picked out the River Elbe and the docks, and bombed from 19,000 feet at 01.20 on an almost north-south heading. He believed his bombs had hit between the old town and a railway junction to the north-west, but he was too busy evading flak and a searchlight cone to worry too much about that. Some of the shrapnel from flak bursts found the mark, and there were holes to patch in Z1465 when he got home. The others bombed from 13,500 to 19,000 feet between 01.07 and 01.35, and all but one returned to report a successful outcome. R1795 came back with its bomb doors hanging open, and one wheel loose, both as a result of flak over the target. Z1270 failed to return with the freshman crew of Sgt Bakalarski, after being badly damaged by a night fighter while on the way home at 19,000 feet over the North Sea. The pilot turned towards Sweden to seek sanctuary there, but the Wellington was mortally wounded, and a forced landing was carried out on the island of Sylt. The rear gunner, P/O Boguszewski, failed to survive, and the other crew members were captured. Sgt Bakalarski escaped from Jaworzno PoW camp in Poland, and, with the help of underground organisations, undertook a perilous journey which took him through Berlin to France, and then across the Pyrenees into Spain and back to England. The attack on Hamburg was, perhaps, the most effective thus far of the war after Cologne, and resulted in the destruction of over eight hundred houses, while more than five hundred large fires had to be dealt with. The success was paid for with the loss of twenty-nine aircraft, over 7% of the force, and this was very high for the period.

Sgt Koscien and crew were sent on a sea search on the afternoon of the 27th, and returned in the evening to report no sightings. The penultimate operation of the month was directed at Saarbrücken on the night of the 29/30th. This was the first large-scale operation to this city, situated in south-western Germany, close to the border with France. A force of 291 aircraft was made ready, ten of the crews attending briefing at Ingham, with F/Ls Jasinski and Kropinski the senior pilots on duty. The former led them away at 23.16, and all were safely airborne by 23.33. Z1490 was intercepted by a night fighter two hours into the outward journey, but escaped damage, and Sgt Szychowiak brought the all-incendiary bomb load home. It was anticipated that the selection of this target would be unanticipated by the enemy, and that it would be lightly defended. Crews were encouraged to attack from lower than of late, and some complied in conditions of varying amounts of cloud with large gaps, while others preferred the safety of height. F/L Jasinski arrived early over the target, and identified it by means of the reflection of the moon in the river as he made a dummy run to kill time. He eventually bombed from 11,800 feet at 01.45, and observed his bombs burst before returning well-satisfied with his night's work. The others from the squadron bombed from 7,000 to 18,500 feet between 01.50 and 02.09, and also came home with stories of a job well done. Of the 248 crews claiming to have attacked the primary target, 75% did so from below 10,000 feet, and almost four hundred buildings were destroyed in central and north-western districts.

Düsseldorf provided the objective for a record non-1,000 force on the night of the 31st, when a sizeable contribution from the training units enabled an overall figure of 630 aircraft to take part. 1 Group provided eighty-four aircraft, including seven Halifaxes of 103 Squadron on its return to operations following conversion, and 300 Squadron's contribution amounted to fourteen Wellingtons, led by S/L Wolanski. They took off either side of midnight, and set off over the North Sea to gain operational altitude and form up into a stream. Z1465 was at 11,000 feet over the sea and closing on the target when it was intercepted by a night fighter at 01.47. P/O Siadek jettisoned his load and returned home. Conditions in the target area were ideal, with clear skies and good visibility, and S/L Wolanski identified the city by the docks and ground detail on both banks of the River Rhine. He delivered his all-incendiary load from 17,000 feet at 02.06, and watched it burst between the old town and the main railway line. Z1245 was held in a searchlight cone, and by the time he had evaded it, F/O Polnik knew he was a mile-and-a-half west of the aiming point as he let his bombs go from 15,000 feet at 02.27. The others from the squadron bombed from 17,000 to 19,000 feet between 02.10 and 02.28 before returning safely home to report another successful operation. In all, 484 crews claimed to have bombed in the target area, where some of the bombing spilled across the Rhine into Neuss. 453 buildings were destroyed in the two locations, and a further three thousand sustained more than slight damage, while over nine hundred fires were started. Eleven operations during the month generated a record 120 sorties and one missing aircraft.

August 1942

There was a gentle introduction to operations for the new month, and 300 Squadron stayed at home until the night of the 4/5th, when a dozen of its crews were briefed for mining duties off St Nazaire and Brest. The six assigned to the former took off first as they had a little further to travel, and they were all safely airborne by 23.21. The second section of six completed their take-offs by 00.01, and all reached their respective target areas to find five-tenths cloud and fairly good visibility. Four of the St Nazaire crews pinpointed on Belle Ile on le Palais island west of St Nazaire, and carried out timed runs of between eight and fourteen minutes at a steady indicated air speed of 130 to 160 mph, and the other two oriented on the Quiberon peninsular, north of le Palais. Each planted two parachute mines into the correct locations, five seconds apart, from between 600 and 850 feet, and returned safely. The Brest contingent pinpointed on the island of Ushant, west of the mainland, and also carried out timed runs to deliver their vegetables into the briefed locations.

The final raid of the Duisburg series was mounted on the night of the 6/7th by a force of 216 aircraft, of which forty-two were provided by 1 Group. Ten 300 Squadron crews attended briefing, and they departed Ingham either side of 00.30 led by F/L Jasinski. For the first time in his fifty-seven sorties to date, he was forced to return early after the supercharger failed in his starboard engine. The others carried on to the target in unfavourable weather conditions, and all bombed on e.t.a from 15,500 to 18,000 feet between 02.37 and 02.57, before returning to report a most unsatisfactory operation. Reconnaissance revealed that most of the bombs had fallen into open country short of the target on its western side, and it was another major disappointment. Over the five-raid series 1,229 sorties had been dispatched for the loss of forty-three aircraft, in return for the destruction of a little over two hundred houses and a number of industrial buildings.

The next operation was directed at Osnabrück, a town in the flat Münsterland region, north-east of the Ruhr and within fifty miles of the Dutch frontier. Eight 300 Squadron crews were briefed on the afternoon of the on the 9th, and told that they would be part of a 1 Group contribution of forty-six aircraft to an overall force of 192. The 300 Squadron effort was reduced to six before take-off, which happened shortly after midnight with the now acting S/L Jasinski the senior pilot on duty. Z1465 was outbound when its port engine failed suddenly, and P/O Miszewski was left with no option but to turn back. He landed at Hemswell at 03.25, to his credit, with his two 1,000, two 500 and single 250 pound bombs still on board. The others reached the target to find good visibility, and they identified the approximate aiming point by means of ground detail, including the river and a railway junction. They bombed from 14,500 to 19,000 feet between 02.34 and 02.43, and all returned home to report a highly successful operation, which left a number of large fires burning and a pall of smoke rising. Z1332 had its reserve oil tank punctured by fire from a night fighter, and Z1421 was hit by machine-gun fire, but there was no serious damage and no crew casualties. Reconnaissance revealed that the attack had left over two hundred houses destroyed, and a further four thousand buildings damaged to some extent. There was also damage to a number of industrial buildings and the inland docks, where ten barges were hit.

The first of two raids on Mainz took place on the night of the 11/12th, for which 1 Group contributed thirty-three aircraft to an overall force of 154. 300 Squadron detailed seven Wellingtons, which took off either side of 22.30 with F/O Metler the senior pilot on duty. Z1389 experienced an electrical system failure while outbound, and P/O Wlodarczyk brought his bombs home. The others reached the ancient and historic city of Mainz, situated on the Rhine to the south-west of Frankfurt, and identified it through

Left: Hemswell, summer 1942. 300 Squadron Wellington with the picture of an elephant throwing the bomb. The crew posing in front of the aircraft belongs to 301 Squadron. In the middle – W/C Adam Dabrowa CO of 301 Squadron. Right: The board with examples of pictures painted on various Wellingtons flown in Polish squadrons stationed at Hemswell. (PISM via WM)

gaps in the cloud by the confluence of the Main and Rhine rivers. F/O Metler was at 18,000 feet over the target from 01.08 until 01.25, and saw no fires within the city, but a large one to the north on the northern bank of the river. The others bombed from 12,000 to 16,000 feet between 01.09 and 01.25, and P/O Miszewski described a line of fire about three miles in length. Reconnaissance revealed much damage in central districts, where the castle and its museum were burnt out.

A force of 138 aircraft set out on the following night to return to Mainz, and this time thirty-seven 1 Group aircraft were among them, including seven again representing 300 Squadron. S/L Jasinski was the senior pilot on duty, and he was first away from Ingham at 21.59. Z1407 lost the use of its communications system, and Sgt Chmielewski brought his bombs home. The others pressed on to find plenty of cloud in the target area, and some crews were able to pinpoint their position by islands in the river. S/L Jasinski released some flares, and established his position on the basis of the ground detail illuminated by them, before dropping his all-incendiary load from 10,000 feet at 00.53. Not all obtained a clear view of the ground, and a number of crews bombed on e.t.a without seeing any results, or even fires started by other bomb loads. Bombing took place from 8,000 to 14,000 feet between 00.42 and 01.05, and all from Ingham returned safely uncertain as to the effectiveness of the operation. In fact, central districts had again been heavily damaged, along with some industrial areas, and it was estimated that 135 acres of the town had been destroyed.

A new era began on the 15th, with the formation of the Pathfinder Force under the then G/C Don Bennett, an Australian with unparalleled experience as an airman and navigator. Harris had been opposed in principle to the formation of an elite target finding and marking force, a view shared by all but his 4 Group commander, AVM Roddy Carr. Among Harris's supporters was AVM Baldwin of 3 Group, under whose control the new outfit would nominally fall, and upon whose stations it would lodge for the time being. The four founder heavy squadrons, which each represented a Group from which they would draw fresh recruits, were 7, 35, 83 and 156 Squadrons, and they moved into their new stations on this day to begin preparations for their operational debut. Once overruled by higher authority, Harris, in typical fashion, gave the Pathfinders his unstinting support, and his choice of Bennett, a relatively junior officer as its leader, although controversial, would prove to be inspired. A matter of great significance for the future success of the Command was the posting to the Pathfinders at the same time of 109 Squadron, which would spend the remainder of the year marrying the Oboe blind-bombing device to its Mosquitos, and ironing out the technical problems. This magnificent pioneering work under W/C Hal Bufton would bear fruit in the coming year, and enable the Command to hit effectively at the hitherto elusive Ruhr towns and cities.

On the night of the new force's formation 1 Group contributed forty-two aircraft to an overall force of 131 to attack Düsseldorf. 300 Squadron prepared seven Wellingtons, which took off either side of midnight, and headed into good conditions, which allowed identification of ground detail. P/O Sawicki and crew were approaching the western rim of the Ruhr at 17,000 feet, when Z1407 was attacked by a night fighter. It was decided to jettison the bombs to aid an escape, and this was done in the Krefeld area to the north-west of the target at 02.15. The others found the target visually, identifying it by means of bends in the River Rhine, the docks and the main railway station. Bombing took place from 14,000 to 16,000 feet between 02.15 and 02.23, and returning crews reported watching their all-incendiary loads bursting to the east and south of the planned aiming point. Z1409 came home with flak damage after being held in searchlights and shot up over the target, but there were no injuries among the crew of P/O Prykiel. Local authorities described a light raid, with the most serious damage in Neuss, Düsseldorf's neighbour on the west bank of the Rhine to its south-west.

Harris had intended to "blood" the Pathfinder Force on the night of the 17/18th, when Osnabrück was selected as the target, but the commanding officers declared their units to be unready, and a standard operation was mounted instead by a force of 139 aircraft. 300 Squadron contributed seven Wellingtons, which took off either side of 22.00. Z1421 was soon back in the circuit, after the pilot's escape hatch opened and could not be closed. The others found the target to be easily identified by ground detail, and they bombed from 12,000 to 15,000 feet between 00.28 and 00.40, all but one returning to report a successful attack. Z1409 was shot down by a night fighter and crashed near Emlichheim, just inside Germany's border with Holland, after the crew had baled out. All were captured, but the pilot, Sgt Konderak, succumbed to his wounds on the 22nd. Local reports confirmed the effectiveness of the operation, citing the destruction of seventy-seven residential buildings and four belonging to the military, with more than a hundred others seriously damaged.

It was on the following night, that of the 18/19th, that the fledgling Pathfinder Force led its first raid on Germany, for which the port of Flensburg was selected. A force of a little over a hundred aircraft included eighteen from 1 Group, but none from 300 Squadron. The target's location in Schleswig-Holstein, on the narrow neck of land where Germany and Denmark meet, should have made it relatively simple to find, but in the event, no bombs fell within miles, while a number of Danish towns reported being hit. It was an inauspicious beginning to what would, ultimately, become an illustrious career for the Pathfinders. 300 Squadron briefed six crews on the 20th for mining duties off Brest that night. They took off either side of 20.30, and all successfully delivered their mines into the required locations from 600 to 700 feet around midnight before returning safely.

The second Pathfinder-led operation was directed at Frankfurt on the night of the 24/25th, when 1 Group put up fifty aircraft in an overall force of 226. 300 Squadron contributed five Wellingtons, which took off either side of 21.00 led by F/L Kropinski. Z1320 developed a starboard engine problem, and F/S Twardawa decided to drop his bombs on an alternative target before turning back. He found a gun and searchlight concentration on the enemy coast between Dunkerque and Ostend, which he attacked from 16,000 feet at 22.25, and watched his two 1,000 pounders, two 500 pounders and single 250 pounder burst across the beach and set off a number of violet-coloured explosions radiating in all directions. Those reaching the target found excellent visibility above the cloud with bright moonlight, but six to ten-tenths low cloud made it difficult to see the ground in detail. F/S Hulas caught glimpses of the Rhine between Bingen and Mainz, to the south-west of the target, and maintained a course from there until seeing flares some ten minutes short of the aiming point. He delivered his bombs from 14,000 feet at 00.05, and believed that they fell into the city centre. F/L Kropinski and F/O Polnik had already bombed from 16,000 feet shortly before midnight, the former confident that his bombs had fallen into the west of the town area close to the railway station, while the latter let his go on e.t.a without observing any results. Z1488 failed to return from this operation, and it was learned later that it had been shot up by a night fighter, and had been force-landed near Dijon in eastern France. Sgt Koscien and his crew were unhurt, but were rounded up and became PoWs.

The third Pathfinder-led operation was directed at Kassel, a city to the east of the Ruhr in central Germany. A force of 306 aircraft was made ready, of which ninety-three were provided by 1 Group. 300 Squadron briefed seven crews on the afternoon of the 27th, and they took off either side of 20.30 with F/L Kropinski the senior pilot on duty. There were no early returns, and they arrived to find the target sufficiently illuminated by Pathfinder flares for ground detail to stand out. Crews identified the city by its shape, its waterways and railway junctions, and this was the first time that the Pathfinders had successfully fulfilled their brief. Sgt Wojno was the first from the squadron to deliver his all-incendiary load, which he did from 6,000 feet at 23.28, by which time fires had already gained a hold. F/L Kropinski bombed a minute later from 9,000 feet, and the others followed up from 5,000 to 11,500 feet over the ensuing fifteen minutes. All returned safely, two of them with non-serious flak damage, and the general opinion was of a successful operation. This was confirmed by local reports, which catalogued 144 buildings destroyed and more than three hundred seriously damaged, but the defences had claimed thirty-one bombers, a loss rate of 10%, off which fourteen were from 1 Group.

On the following night, while a force of 159 aircraft was engaged over Nuremberg, 113 others targeted Saarbrücken, and among these were nine from 300 Squadron. They were all safely airborne by 20.00, led by F/L Kropinski, and arrived at the target under the light from an almost full moon, which allowed crews to identify the river and its docks. Bombs were delivered from 8,000 to 12,000 feet between 22.38 and 23.13, but returning crews expressed doubts about the effectiveness of their efforts. Their pessimism turned out to be justified, as only fifteen houses were destroyed by the widely scattered bombing. The squadron operated twelve times during the month, mounting eighty-four sorties for the loss of two aircraft.

September 1942

The intended target for the night of the 1/2nd was Saarbrücken, for which a force of 231 aircraft was made ready, seven of them Wellingtons belonging to 300 Squadron. They began taking off at 23.08, and there were no early returns. They arrived in the target area to find what was believed to be the target well marked by the Pathfinder element, and they confirmed identification by a bend in the River Saar. Each of the Polish crews was carrying an all-incendiary load, and these were delivered from 11,000 to 16,500 feet between 02.03 and 02.15 into the already blazing town. Returning crews reported numerous fires, which could be seen up to sixty miles away on the return trip. F/O Polnik was of the opinion that the target had been so completely destroyed, that it would not need to be attacked again. He was correct in that, but for the wrong reason. Not all of the 205 crews claiming to have bombed the target were convinced that the Pathfinders had marked the intended location, and, in fact, it became clear afterwards, that they had posted a "black", by marking the non-industrial town of Saarlouis, some thirteen miles to the north-west. They had been confused by a similar bend in the river, and the unfortunate town and nearby communities were heavily damaged on a night when the main force crews were uncharacteristically accurate with their bombs.

This could have been an ill-omen for the month, but from this point on, the Command embarked on an unprecedented series of effective operations, which would take it through the first two weeks of the month. Karlsruhe was the destination for two hundred aircraft on the night of the 2/3rd, of which forty-six were from 1 Group. 300 Squadron contributed six Wellingtons, which were led away from Ingham at 22.16 by F/O Polnik. There were no early returns, and they arrived in southern Germany to find good conditions, which enabled them to pick out ground detail, like the Rhine and the docks. There was praise for the efforts of the Pathfinders, which illuminated the target well, and the squadron crews delivered their all-incendiary loads in and around the centre of the town from 13,000 to 17,000 feet between 01.44 and 02.06. On return, crews claimed to have seen many fires burning, and reported that they erupted even more quickly than on the previous night. The Bomber Command report stated that up to two hundred fires had been observed, and reconnaissance confirmed the level of destruction to residential and industrial buildings.

Two nights later, a few hours before a force of 251 aircraft set out for Bremen, a single 300 Squadron Wellington took off to mine the waters off the Frisians. F/O Szostak took a pin-point off the eastern end of the island of Terschelling, and then made a five-minute run to the drop zone to deliver his mines accurately. There were seven Wellingtons representing 300 Squadron in the main operation, during which the Pathfinders would introduce the new three-phase system of illuminators, visual markers and backers up. They got away safely from Ingham in the minutes leading to midnight, and once again there were no early returns. They arrived at the target to find it well marked, and ground detail clearly visible. The all-incendiary bomb loads were delivered from 15,000 to 17,500 feet between 02.02 and 02.08, and many fires were reported, particularly in areas north of the river. Searchlight glare was a slight problem, but flak was not troublesome until Z1407 caught a packet, and had its fuselage fabric catch fire. P/O Machej was an experienced pilot, and dived the Wellington to extinguish the flames. By the time they landed the fabric had been stripped from the trailing edge of the main-plane right back to the leading edge of the tail-plane. There was a degree of surprise on the ground that such a badly-damaged aircraft had managed to get back, but this was down to the geodetic design and construction of the type. Sadly, this did not help Sgt Szychowiak and his crew, who disappeared without trace in Z1320, and it must be assumed that they were lost in the North Sea. Returning crews were confident that a successful operation had taken place, and this was confirmed by local reports of 480 buildings destroyed, including some large industrial concerns, and fourteen hundred others seriously damaged.

F/O Szostak returned to the Frisians on the night of the 6/7th, taking off at 20.15 and heading for Boschplaat Island, which was actually the eastern half of Terschelling. He pin-pointed on the northern tip before carrying out a short timed run to the release point, where he delivered his parachute mines into the briefed location. He was safely back on the ground at Ingham at 00.05, forty-five minutes before three other crews took off as part of a two-hundred-strong force bound for Duisburg. The recent good record of no early returns was spoiled on this night, when Z1475 came back with a failed supercharger on its starboard engine, and was followed thirteen minutes later by Z1465, also with an engine failure. Before turning back, however, P/O Nowak dropped his bombs from 16,000 feet onto an airfield near Haamstede on the island of Schouwen in the Scheldt Estuary. F/O Waszkiewicz pressed on to deliver his all-incendiary load from 15,000 feet at 03.03, and believed they fell one to two miles south-west of the town. He returned to report many fires in the town area and to the west of the river, and smoke rising to 14,000 feet. He also claimed that the glow of fires was visible from the English coast. This last point is unlikely, as the operation was not an outstanding success, and destroyed only 114 buildings, while seriously damaging a further three hundred. In the context of operations generally, this was a modest return, although, perhaps, it represented something of a victory at this particular target.

The night of the 7/8th was devoted to mining operations, for which four 300 Squadron crews were assigned to the Nectarines garden off the Frisians. They took off shortly before 20.30, and, as on the previous night, they used Boschplaat as a pinpoint for their timed runs to the drop zone. Each planted two vegetables into the correct location before returning safely home after a round-trip of a little over five hours. The Command's run of successes was temporarily halted at Frankfurt on the night of the 8/9th, although this, quite understandably, was not apparent at the time to the author of the squadron ORB. Seven 300 Squadron Wellingtons were made ready, and they were to join up with 242 others for the long trip to southern Germany. They were led off by F/O Waszkiewicz at 20.36, and arrived in the target area to find good conditions, and the urban spread below illuminated by Pathfinder flares. The target was identified by a bend in the river, the docks and the main railway station, as well as a moat encircling the old town, and the concentration of searchlights seemed to confirm that the crews were over a major city. The 300 Squadron crews were each carrying an all-incendiary load, which they delivered from 13,000 to 18,000 feet between 23.32 and 23.55, and returned home, mostly with reports of many fires in and around the old town. Sgt Kazmierczak confirmed this, but also claimed that flares were dropped thirty miles to the north-east and ten miles to the south. An hour into the return flight his gunners observed two large explosions in Frankfurt. The consensus was of a successful operation, which was duly entered into the ORB, but it emerged later that the Pathfinders had been unable to identify Frankfurt, and only a handful of bomb loads had found the mark. The majority fell on Rüsselsheim, fifteen miles to the south-west, which happened to be the location of the Opel tank works and a Michelin tyre factory, which, reconnaissance suggested, had sustained some damage.

There would be a return to winning ways with the next operation, which was against Düsseldorf on the night of the 10/11th. It involved 479 aircraft, including sixty-two provided by 1 Group and a large contribution from the training groups. 300 Squadron supported the operation with six Wellingtons, which took off either side of 20.30 with F/L Wojcik the senior pilot on duty. Z1398 was soon back in the circuit with the crew of P/O Wlodarczyk, after the pilot's escape hatch became unlatched and would not lock

Above: The crew of Wellington Z1407 BH-Z for Zosia in front of their flak-damaged aircraft. Left to Right: Sgt Tomiec (A.G.), P/O Brzezinski (A.G.), P/O Machej (pilot), Sgt Muszynski (W.Op.), F/L Bilinski (obs.). Below: The same crew posing for the press photograph inside the partially burnt out fuselage of Z1407. (J. Cynk)

shut even after twenty minutes of trying. The Pathfinders were to employ "pink pansies" in converted 4,000lb bomb casings as target indicators for the first time, and they were put to good use after the aiming point, for once, was correctly identified. The 300 Squadron crews picked out the characteristic south-east bend in the River Rhine, and fires had already gained a hold by the time they released their all-incendiary loads over the old town and nearby marshalling yards. They bombed from 16,800 to 18,000 feet between 22.48 and 23.05, and the only problem was caused by flares bursting at too high an altitude and creating glare. All but one from Ingham returned safely to claim a successful operation, which was confirmed by reconnaissance and local reports, that revealed the destruction of over nine hundred houses and eight public buildings in the city and nearby Neuss. Many industrial premises also sustained damage, but it was not a one-sided affair, as it turned into a good night also for the defenders. Thirty-three aircraft failed to return, 7% of the force, and among them was Z1258, which was shot down by a night fighter eight miles south-south-west of Rotterdam, with fatal consequences for F/O Waszkiewicz and his crew. Sixteen of the missing aircraft were from the training units, which had also suffered disproportionately heavy losses during the three 1,000-bomber raids earlier in the year.

The night of the 13/14th brought Bremen's second heavy raid of the month, this one at the hands of an initial force of 446 aircraft, of which fifty-seven were provided by 1 Group, and just three of these were 300 Squadron Wellingtons. There was also another sizeable contribution from the training units, demonstrating, perhaps, that lessons had not been learned with regard to their unsustainable losses to date. The Ingham trio took off shortly after midnight, and arrived over the target to find clear skies but very thick ground haze. Large fires were already burning, and these negated to some extent the haze, and the three-fingered docks layout was proof that they were at the correct location. P/O Sawicki was the first from the squadron to arrive, and he could tell from the concentration of searchlights and flak that he was where he was supposed to be. He bombed from 17,000 feet at 02.39, and observed many fires in and around the old town area. Sgt Kazmierczak followed the southern-most finger of the docks, dropping his incendiaries into the old town from 14,600 feet at 02.49, and F/S Twardawa followed up at 23.05 from 18,000 feet. All returned safely to claim a highly successful outcome, and this was confirmed by reconnaissance and local reports. Over eight hundred houses were destroyed, and among the industrial buildings hit were the Focke-Wulf aircraft factory and the Lloyd dynamo works, both of which lost vital production for a number of days. The level of destruction surpassed that achieved by the thousand force back in June. Sixteen of the twenty-one missing aircraft were from the training units.

The run of successes continued at Wilhelmshaven on the night of the 14/15th, when 202 aircraft were dispatched, of which six were provided by 300 Squadron. They got away from Ingham shortly before 20.00, and on arrival in the target area, they were able to pick out ground detail by the light from Pathfinder flares. The square Bauhafen was easily identified, as was the entire harbour area generally, but P/O Nowak noted that plenty of incendiaries were falling into open country north-west of the town. The squadron crews bombed from 14,500 to 17,000 feet between 22.22 and 22.28, and returned home safely to describe many very large fires, particularly in an area to the south of the naval dockyards and in some residential districts. Local reports confirmed that the town had registered its most destructive raid of the war to date, with housing and city-centre type buildings the hardest-hit. On the following night F/L Kropinski was the senior pilot among four crews taking off to mine the waters off the Frisians. They were all safely airborne by 19.45, and headed into poor weather conditions, which included electrical storms. Despite this they all arrived off the eastern end of Langeoog, and delivered their mines into the correct locations from between 600 and 800 feet.

Essen had been left relatively unmolested for some time, when it faced its latest test on the night of the 16/17th at the hands of a bomber force numbering at the outset 369 aircraft. The training units were called upon once more, as was 1 Group, which provided thirty-two aircraft, including three Wellingtons from 300 Squadron captained by P/O Machej, and Sgts Kazmierczak and Przedpelski. They took off either side of 20.30 on a night of doubtful weather conditions, and they arrived in the target area to encounter cloud, which prevented them from making a positive identification. They bombed on e.t.a from 17,000 feet between 22.26 and 22.50, and P/O Machej caught sight of two very large fires through a gap in the clouds, which he believed to be in the northern part of the city. Post raid analysis suggested that this was probably the most effective raid of the war to date, and local reports cited over a hundred large and medium fires. Residential districts suffered the most, but fifteen high explosive bombs hit the Krupp works, as did a crashing bomber loaded with incendiaries. This was one of thirty-nine aircraft failing to return, the heaviest loss from a non-1,000 raid thus far, although the Command suffered the heavy loss of thirty-nine aircraft for its troubles.

The night of the 18/19th was devoted to wide-ranging mining operations, for which 300 Squadron assigned five crews to the Elbe Estuary. They took off either side of 20.00, and encountered unfavourable weather conditions outbound and in the target area. Four of them pin-pointed on St Peter Point (Heligoland), and delivered their mines into the correct location from 700 to 800 feet, before returning safely. P/O Miszewski was unable to find a pin-point, and reached the Schleswig-Holstein coast before giving up. 1 Group's final operation of the month against a German target came on the night of the 19/20th, when thirty-five aircraft joined elements from other groups to attack Saarbrücken. Just three 300 Squadron Wellingtons were involved, and they took off either side of 19.45, and experienced difficulty in identifying the target in hazy conditions. F/S Kazimierczak followed the River Saar, which was clearly visible, until he reached what he believed to be the target. He bombed from 11,000 at 23.08, four minutes later than Sgt Kazmierczak and from a thousand feet higher. These were following in the wake of P/O Sawicki, who had already sneaked in at 5,000 feet at 23.00. His closer view of the ground persuaded him that the attack had produced some useful damage, while his colleagues were less optimistic. Most of the bombs had, in fact, been scattered to the west of the target, and only thirteen houses were destroyed.

It can be no coincidence that the highly effective series of operations during the first two weeks of the month came at a time when the Pathfinders were emerging from their shaky start, and the crews were coming to terms with the complexities of their demanding role. It would not be an overnight transformation, and failures would continue to outnumber successes for some time to come. The encouraging signs were there, however, and it boded ill for Germany's industrial heartland in the coming year. Thereafter, there was a steady diet of mining operations to see the month out, beginning for 300 Squadron on the night of the 24/25th, when eight crews were briefed for the Nectarines garden off the Frisians. They took off shortly after 20.00, with F/Ls Wojcik and Kropinski the senior pilots on duty. Weather conditions in the target area were excellent, and four crews pin-pointed on the eastern end of Terschelling, while the others used the eastern tip of Ameland from which to make their individual timed runs to ensure a chain of mines across this important enemy shipping lane. It was similar fare on the following night for five crews from Ingham, who were all safely airborne by 20.31 bound for the same target area. This time four crews pin-pointed on the eastern end of Norderney, and one on the western tip of Baltrun, and all successfully laid the mines in the briefed positions from 500 to 700 feet either side of 23.00. During the course of the month the squadron equalled its record of seventeen operations, totaling seventy-nine sorties for the loss of two aircraft. The number of sorties was reduced by a shortage of operational crews, caused by the posting out of those who had completed their tours. The number available for operations fluctuated throughout the month between five and ten. The situation would improve early in the coming year with the disbandment of one Polish squadron.

300 Squadron ground personnel decorating bombs with 'good wishes' to the Germans. (W. Zmyslony)

October 1942

The new month's operations began at Krefeld on the night of the 2/3rd, when eight 300 Squadron Wellingtons were among fifty-eight 1 Group aircraft in an overall force of 188. They took off in the early evening for the town of Krefeld, perched right on the western rim of the Ruhr, south-west of Duisburg and north-west of Düsseldorf. The Ingham contingent got away either side of 19.00, with F/Ls Kropinski and Kucharski the senior pilots on duty, and they all reached the target area to encounter thick haze. This had already caused problems for the Pathfinder element, which arrived late on target, and the marking was not concentrated. P/O Wlodarczyk pinpointed on the Rhine, and identified the target by the light of flares and fires in built-up areas, while Sgt Chmielewski recognised the railway yards and town layout. F/L Kropinski map-read his way there, and F/L Kucharski found it easily distinguishable in the light of flares. Others, in contrast, were not able to positively identify Krefeld, and bombed on e.t.a. The 300 Squadron element delivered their all-incendiary loads from 11,500 to 15,000 feet between 20.46 and 21.04, and returned home less than satisfied with the results of their labours, one commenting that flares were spread over a wide area, with some illuminating fields. The lack of effectiveness of this operation was confirmed by local reports, which mentioned that only a number of streets were hit in the north of the town.

After two nights off, eight 300 Squadron crews attended briefing on the afternoon of the 5th to be told they would be attacking Aachen that night. They were to be part of a force of 257 aircraft targeting the town, situated in Germany's Eiffel region, south-west of the Ruhr and right on the border with Belgium. F/L Wojcik was the senior pilot on duty as they departed Ingham either side of 18.45 on a night of poor weather conditions. Z1244 reached Cambridge before turning back with a failed engine, but the others pushed on through thunderstorms and icing to reach the target area, where they found sparse Pathfinder marking. F/O Polnik seemed to have no problem in identifying his whereabouts, possibly because he was down at 7,000 feet, and he dropped his incendiary load at 21.38 onto the eastern half of the town, immediately west of the marshalling yards. Sgt Chmielewski was also below 8,000 feet when he picked out the marshalling yards and a large factory, and watched his load fall across the former. He and his crew observed large fires at the eastern end of the town, and picked up some flak damage before they headed for home. P/O Sawicki was at 8,700 feet over an industrial area to the north-east, and reported widespread fires for five miles towards the west, but not all were able to positively identify the target, particularly if they were higher up. The others from the squadron delivered their attacks from 13,000 to 15,000 feet between 21.35 and 22.13, and returned safely to provide a variety of statements as to the effectiveness of the operation. In fact, it had failed to produce any significant damage, and many bombs had fallen on the Dutch town of Lutterade some seventeen miles to the north-west.

Twenty-four hours later, Osnabrück was targeted by a force of 237 aircraft, of which just six represented 300 Squadron. They took off shortly after 19.00, and all made it to the target area after pinpointing on the Dümmer See, a large lake to the north-east, which had been illuminated by the Pathfinders. The ground was largely obscured by cloud, and not all crews could make a positive identification, but a timed run from the lake all but guaranteed that their incendiary loads would find their way into built-up areas. The squadron crews went in at 11,000 to 15,000 feet between 21.25 and 21.33, and F/O Polnik was certain that he hit the marshalling yards on the eastern side of the town. His report was the most specific, while the others observed many fires or the glow from them, but no detail. In fact, it had been a very effective and concentrated raid, which had caused substantial damage in central and southern districts. 149 houses

G/C Arthur Mostyn Wray, CO of RAF Station Hemswell. He was very popular among Polish aircrew and flew no fewer than six operations with 300 Squadron crews in 1941/1942. (P. Tulinski)

were destroyed and more than five hundred seriously damaged, and a number of industrial premises were also reduced to rubble.

The following week was occupied by minor operations, which included mining, and 300 Squadron sent four crews to the waters between Den Helder and Texel on the night of the 8/9th. They took off over a thirty-minute period to 20.57, and found their allocated drop zones with ease two hours later. Each delivered two parachute mines from 700 feet and returned without incident. Two nights later F/Ss Kazimierczak and Leszkiewicz took off shortly before midnight, and successfully delivered their mines into the sea lanes off Brest. There was a larger effort on the night of the 11/12th, involving eighty aircraft assigned to a variety of gardens. 300 Squadron dispatched nine Wellingtons to Nectarines, off the Frisians, and they were all safely airborne by 19.17 led by F/Ls Kropinski and Wojcik, althought S/L Wesolowski was the senior officer, and he was flying as observer with the crew of Sgt Chmielewski. All but one delivered their mines into the briefed location from 600 to 850 feet between 21.02 and 21.13, and only Sgt Przedpelski was defeated by ten-tenths cloud, and he brought his stores home. On the following night the squadron sent seven crews to the waters off the island of Heligoland. There was an early departure time, beginning at 17.12, and all reached the target area to make timed runs from Hjels Lake, Brandso Island or Norderney. All but one successfully carried out their brief, but P/O Prykiel was defeated by fog, and brought his mines home. Z1244 was badly shot up by flak, and was heavily damaged on landing at 00.40, happily without casualties among the crew of Sgt Wojno.

There was a return to bombing operations on the night of the 13/14th, when the port of Kiel was selected as the destination for 288 aircraft, of which four belonged to 300 Squadron. F/L Wojcik was the senior pilot on duty as they began taking off at 18.35, and three of them arrived in the target area in clear skies and good visibility, which enabled them to establish their position based on the shape of the urban layout below and the harbour. They released their all-incendiary loads from 16,000 to 17,000 feet between 21.30 and 21.35, and watched them burst on or near the aiming point, west of the harbour. On return they spoke of many fires and a very successful operation, which, to an extent, was correct. A decoy fire site drew off 50% of the effort, but the remainder caused widespread damage, although probably nothing of major significance. Z1250 failed to return with the crew of F/L Wojcik DFC, and no trace was ever found of the aircraft or crew, suggesting that it was lost in the sea.

The night of the 15/16th was devoted to a large-scale attack on Cologne, involving 289 aircraft, of which just five represented 300 Squadron. They began taking off shortly after 18.30 on a night of unfavourable weather conditions, and P/O Wlodarczyk turned back early on because of severe icing. The winds were not as forecast, and this caused major problems for the Pathfinders, which failed to establish their position and provide adequate marking to attract the main force element away from a large decoy fire site. Three of the 300 Squadron crews identified a bend in the River Rhine, and a large fire, which was almost certainly the decoy, and they dropped their all-incendiary loads from 14,000 to 15,000 feet between 20.51 and 20.56. Only Sgt Chmielewski and crew described a built-up area beneath them in the centre of the town, and perhaps their incendiaries were among the 210 of more than 68,000 that actually fell within the city boundaries. Z1475 failed to return with the crew of Sgt Szymen, and they were posted missing without trace.

Wellington Z1250 BH-N photographed at Hemswell in April/May 1942. She flew with 300 Squadron from Dec. 1941 to Oct. 1942 but failed to return from her 49th operation. (R. Bolczyk)

It was at this juncture that a campaign began in support of Operation Torch, the Allied landings in North Africa, which would ultimately lead to Montgomery's victory over Rommel at El Alamein. Bomber Command's role was to carry out an assault on the major cities in Italy, and fifteen such operations would be mounted between the 22/23rd of October and the 11/12th of December. Milan was the target for seventy-one aircraft from 1 and 3 Groups and a Pathfinder element on the night of the 24/25th, of which five belonged to 300 Squadron. They would be following hard on the heels of a highly successful daylight raid by 5 Group Lancasters during the afternoon. This was to be the squadron's first foray into Italy, and it created much interest at Ingham. Characteristically, G/C Wray put himself on the Order of Battle for this one, choosing to fly with Sgt Leszkiewicz and crew in Z1421. They flew down to Tangmere to top up their tanks before taking off in a fifteen minute slot from 19.12, each carrying a single 1,000 pounder and incendiaries. All made it safely across the Alps to northern Italy, but unfavourable weather had dispersed the stream by then, and some aircraft wandered over the Swiss frontier. Only W/O Kazimierczak seemed certain that he had bombed the primary target, which he did from 10,000 feet at 22.53. Three others bombed on what they suspected was the target from 8,500 to 15,000 feet between 22.50 and 22.56, while F/L Polnik believed he had attacked Montara, some twenty-five miles south-west of Milan. It proved to be an unsatisfactory operation, in which only a little over half of the force bombed, and it is unlikely that they added significantly to the damage caused by 5 Group. W/C Dukszto completed his tour as commanding officer of 300 Squadron on the 31st, and he was succeeded by the newly promoted W/C Kropinski. The squadron operated eleven times during the month, dispatching fifty-eight sorties for the loss of two aircraft.

November 1942

The new month began as the old one had ended, with a week of minor operations. 300 Squadron called seven crews to briefing on the afternoon of the 3rd, when they were told they would be conducting mining sorties off the French coast that night. Six were assigned to the sea lanes off Lorient, while P/O Machej went alone to St Nazaire. He had a little further to travel and took off first at 17.07, to be followed away by the others over the ensuing seventeen minutes. He arrived in the target area to be met by poor visibility caused by sea mist and ten-tenths cloud, which had its base at 800 feet. Despite searching, he failed to locate his pinpoint, and, at 21.00, he reluctantly abandoned his sortie and turned for home with his mines. Three of the Lorient contingent described the visibility in their target area as good, while two disagreed, but all delivered their mines into the briefed locations from 500 to 700 feet between 20.24 and 21.41. Z1421 failed to return home with the crew of P/O Sawicki, and was the latest from the squadron to be lost without trace, presumably in the sea.

Four nights later the drop zone was the Little Belt (Carrots), the western-most of the three Denmark Straits, which lay between Denmark's eastern coast and the island of Funen. Five 300 Squadron Wellingtons took off between 01.33 and 01.48, but, on reaching the west coast of Denmark at the islands of Mandø and Fanø, four of them were forced by low, sleet-bearing cloud and mist to abandon their sorties and return home with their mines. Only Sgt Furmaniak made it across the Schleswig-Holstein peninsular to find good visibility and pinpoint on Aerø Island, from where he and his crew map-read their way to the allocated drop zone, and delivered their two mines accurately from 700 feet at 04.32. Six of the squadron's Wellingtons returned to the Little Belt on the following night, the 8/9th, when F/L Polnik was the senior pilot on duty. Sgt Chmielewski was first to take off at 18.54, and the others followed during the ensuing sixteen minutes. This time they all made it across the peninsular to Denmark's eastern coast, and pinpointed on various landmarks, including Vejle Fjord, to the north-west of Funen Island, and the headland of Funen opposite Fredericia. They delivered their two mines each from 400 to 700 feet between 21.47 and 22.44, and five returned safely home. Z1343 lost an engine and ditched in Vejle Fjord at 22.30, and only Sgt Chmielewski and front gunner Sgt Dadej managed to get clear of the Wellington before it sank, and were the only survivors. Local people heard the crash, and rescued them, but they were soon picked up by the Germans and taken into captivity.

The first bombing operation of the month against a German target came on the night of the 9/10th, when Hamburg was the destination for 213 aircraft, of which forty-five of the Wellingtons were provided by 1 Group, including five from 300 Squadron. W/C Kropinski put himself on the Order of Battle, which already contained the name of S/L Kucharski, in contravention of the group's strict rule that the squadron and flight commanders should not operate on the same occasion, in case they were both lost. As a consequence, S/L Kucharski's participation was scrubbed, as was that of F/S Leszkiewicz, who reported sick at the last minute, leaving just four to take off, headed by the commanding officer at 17.31. It was to be a night to forget for the Polish contingent, after P/O Wlodarczyk was forced to turn back at 18.36, when Z1332 suffered a port engine failure at just 1,390 feet. At 19.08 F/L Polnik found himself in a similar position, after Z1286 developed a starboard engine malfunction at 4,000 feet. The remaining two crews encountered heavy cloud and icing conditions in the target area, along with winds not as forecast. The result was that most crews were unable to positively identify Hamburg, and dropped their bombs on estimated positions. Sgt Wojno and crew were at 17,000 feet over what they believed was Hamburg, but in the absence of any Pathfinder flares it was decided to abandon the sortie at 20.38 and bring the incendiaries home. W/C Kropinski had already bombed, five minutes earlier, from 16,000 feet, with absolutely no clue as to his precise position in relation to the target.

Thereafter, from the night of the 13/14th, Genoa and Turin became the main focus of attention as the Italian campaign continued. Six 300 Squadron crews were called to briefing on the afternoon of the 13th, to be told they were on gardening duties that night off Lorient. They took off shortly after 16.30, but less that two hours later Z1332 suffered a hydraulics failure that paralyzed the rear turret, and P/O Wlodarczyk was forced to turn back. Sgt Wojno reached the target area, but was unable to find a pinpoint in conditions of low cloud and fog, and turned back with his mines at 19.13. Visibility was poor as F/L Polnik sought out the Pont-Aven Estuary, north-west of Lorient, for his pinpoint, and delivered his two mines from 500 feet at 19.11. He was on his way home and crossing Douarnenez Bay when he realised that he had mistaken Quimper for Lorient, and the coast south of Pont-L'Abbe for the southern coast of Ile de Croix, and, that consequently, he had dropped his mines in the wrong location. To make matters worse, flak had cut the hydraulic pipes in Z1286's port wing, preventing the flaps from lowering for landing, and F/L Polnik ultimately pulled off a wheels up touchdown at Ingham. The other three crews completed their sorties as briefed, delivering their mines from 700 to 800 feet either side of 19.30.

On the night of the 16/17th the squadron sent six crews to lay mines off the Frisians, and this time there were no early returns after they took off shortly before 17.00. They met with a variety of conditions depending on the location of each individual drop zone. Sgt Sowa found the visibility to be moderate under five-tenths cloud with a base at 2,500 feet. He pinpointed on the centre of Langeoog Island, before running on a heading of 042° for two-and-a-half minutes to deliver his mines from 800 feet at 19.50. P/O Prykiel found the cloud base down at around 700 feet as he pinpointed on the eastern tip of Langeoog, and ran on a heading of 353° also for two-and-a-half minutes to drop his mines from 800 feet at 19.59. A few miles to the west the cloud base was at 2,000 feet as F/S Leszkiewicz picked up the eastern tip of Norderney and began a five minute run on a heading of 024° to plant his vegetables from 700 feet at 20.02. F/L Polnik had the same brief as F/S Leszkiewicz, but he described the visibility as poor at first, as he encountered rain falling out of the 1,500 foot cloud base. Conditions improved as he made a four-minute run to deliver his mines short of those dropped by his colleague two minutes earlier. P/O Machej and Sgt Wojno were also able to fulfil their briefs, and all returned safely either side of midnight to report successful sorties.

The following night brought a return to the French coast for five gardeners from 300 Squadron, of which F/L Polnik was the senior pilot on duty. They were all safely airborne before 17.00, bound for the waters off St Nazaire, and there were again no early returns. Conditions in the target area were excellent, with cloudless skies and bright moonlight, and the mines were released from 500 to 700 feet between 19.55 and 20.04. Z1286 met with considerable opposition in the form of flak, and had its aerial shot away and ailerons damaged, but F/L Polnik brought it home without further incident, and commented that he preferred going to Hamburg! He was no doubt happy, then, when he found his name on the Order of Battle for Turin on the night of the 20/21st, as the senior pilot of six from the squadron to take part in an overall force of 232 aircraft, of which thirty-five represented 1 Group. The Ingham crews flew down to Tangmere on the Sussex coast to top up their tanks, before departing for the French coast either side of 18.30. The 300 Squadron crews were each carrying a single 1,000 pounder and incendiaries, and they arrived in the target area to find good visibility but ground haze. They were able to identify the city by its outline and

F/O Kazimierz Konopasek. In April 1942 he started flying in 305 Squadron only to be posted to 300 in November 1942. He flew 8 operations with 300 Squadron from Nov. 1942 – March 1943 and took up the post of "A" Flight Commander. In April 1943 he assumed command of 305 Squadron and flew Mitchells & Mosquitoes. (PISM via WM)

F/O Jan Gerstel (navigator) completed 26 operations with 300 Squadron between July and Nov. 1942 only to be shot down and taken prisoner on his 27th sortie, a daylight operation to Essen. (PISM via WM)

the river junction to the north, and they delivered their loads from 9,000 to 12,000 feet between 22.00 and 22.34, before returning safely to report a highly successful outcome. All believed their bombs had fallen close to the aiming point, and within the city's central districts, and their confidence was confirmed by the large number of fires and the dense smoke rising to 10,000 feet.

Four 300 Squadron Wellingtons taxied for take off as the clock ticked towards 19.00 on the 22nd, their crews briefed to attack Stuttgart as part of an overall force of 222 aircraft. Z1401 was well into its journey across France when engine problems forced F/O Konopasek to turn back, and they landed at Tangmere at 00.17 with their bombs still on board. The others reached the target, which they could pick out as they approached, and identified by a bend in the River Neckar. The main problem was vertical visibility, which was impaired by thick ground haze, and this had produced difficult conditions for the Pathfinder element. The Polish crews bombed from 12,000 to 13,000 feet shortly after 22.00, but were not able to observe the burst of their bombs. It was revealed later that most of the bombing had fallen into southern and south-western districts and outlying communities, destroying fewer than a hundred houses.

The senior officers at Command and group level sometimes lost their common sense, and sanctioned operations of minimal value that exposed crews to extreme danger. Daylight intruder operations, known as "moling", involved the use of cloud cover to enable single aircraft to sneak in and bomb a specific target, or one of opportunity under a roving commission order. They were purely of nuisance value, and to risk the lives of an entire crew to annoy the enemy can not be justified. The majority of such sorties were abandoned because of a lack of cloud cover, and many others resulted in the brave crew being shot out of the sky. Thus far 300 Squadron had been spared this madness, but three crews were selected to carry out Operation Bullhead over Essen on the afternoon of the 25th. P/O Wlodarczyk, W/O Kazimierczak and Sgt Kazmierczak were airborne by noon, and headed for the Dutch coast, where the cloud became too thin for two of them to continue, and they turned back.

The cloud tops were relatively low as Z1495 approached the Dutch coast, but over land it could be seen to rise steeply to reveal blue sky ahead in the east. Navigator, F/O Gerstel, left his cubicle and stood beside the pilot, map in hand, ready to identify pinpoints on the ground to confirm his navigation as they crossed the coast. The bomb-aimer was in the front turret ready to open fire if ordered, and the wireless operator was in the astrodome, the tension palpable as the green fields of Holland drew near. Gerstel had a bad feeling about daylight forays into enemy territory, but orders were orders, although the captain could abandon the sortie if he felt the risk too great. Had Sgt Kazmierczak been more experienced, he might well have turned back, but he decided to press on, barely cresting the waves until climbing sharply to flash across the expanse of sand, before dropping back to tree-top height. Suddenly the air was full of coloured tracer, and the crew members could feel the Wellington shudder under repeated hits. The fuselage was filled with the smell of cordite, and then the starboard engine erupted in flames, which the pilot tried to quell with the extinguisher. It failed to operate, and, as if in sympathy, the port engine also caught fire. A military barracks could be seen under camouflage netting directly below, and the Wellington's gunners fired at running uniformed men, who fired back. The pilot was hit in the leg, but he remained fully in control, and began to jettison the bombs safe. He gestured for Gerstel to drag the bomb-aimer out of the front turret, by which time the rear turret had fallen silent and the whole aircraft was ablaze. The Wellington sank towards the ground with trees and buildings all around, and when the crash came, the wreckage burst into flames. Gerstel temporarily lost consciousness, and as he came to there was blue sky above and he was being dragged by the collar of his tunic from the inferno by a German soldier who was shouting "Bomben". There were no bombs still on board, but the petrol tanks and ammunition were a danger and the fire was intense. The soldier dragged him to a hut, where the other crew members were sitting on beds, the wireless operator, Sgt Skonieczny, having sustained severe burns to his face and hands, to which he would succumb in a German prison hospital two months later. The crash had occurred right next to the camp's sick quarters, and the staff did all they could to tend to the wounded men. Gerstel deduced from the German conversations that the rear gunner had been burned to death, but Gerstel was certain he had died in the air. The survivors all sustained injury, and while in hospital in Amsterdam, Gerstel worked out what had happened. On impact, he, the pilot and the bomb-aimer had been flung through the windscreen clear of the aircraft, but the wireless operator, dazed and injured, had walked the whole length of a burning wing, before falling off the end and being found by German soldiers wandering around in a state of confusion. Gerstel praised the Germans for risking their own safety to rescue him and his colleagues, and for their humanitarian treatment. They were put into a ward full of wounded German soldiers, and kept together so they could talk. Sgt Kazmierczak was the most severely injured of those who would survive, and underwent many operations and blood transfusions until his eventual transfer to Dulag III.

The squadron operated for the final time during the month on the evening of the 27th, when sending five crews to lay mines off the Dutch coast near Den Helder. They took off between 17.00 and 18.00, and found their pinpoints on either Zwanen Water or Callantsoog, on the coast south of Den Helder, and carried out timed runs towards Cromer, before delivering their mines into the allocated positions. The squadron undertook twelve operations during the month, and dispatched fifty-seven sorties for the loss of three aircraft.

December 1942

The first large-scale operation of the new month involved a force of 272 aircraft, whose crews were briefed on the afternoon of the 6th to attack Mannheim. 300 Squadron prepared six Wellingtons for this operation, and another for a freshman crew to take on a mining sortie off Terschelling in the Dutch Frisians. The bombing brigade took off first, either side of 17.00, but Z1407 immediately developed an exhaust problem, while climbing for height over base, and W/O Kazimierczak was forced to abandon his sortie. A similar problem afflicted Z1286 as it approached the English coast at Clacton-on-Sea. A hole appeared in the starboard exhaust pipe, from which a long tongue of flame passed beneath the wing, threatening to set it on fire, and F/L Polnik had no choice but to turn back. Z1401 was hit by flak at the French coast, and crashed near Boulogne, killing Sgt Furmaniak and his crew, and whether this occurred outbound or inbound is uncertain. The others arrived in the target area to be confronted by complete cloud cover, and none was able to positively identify his position. Sgt Sowa had picked up a visual pinpoint at Trier, some one hundred miles west-north-west of Mannheim, and made a timed run to deliver his all-incendiary load onto what he believed to be the target, encouraged by the glow of fires beneath the clouds. F/S Wojno saw the same glow, and also some coloured marker flares, and he bombed on a north-westerly heading from 15,000 feet at 02.11. P/O Prykiel bombed twelve minutes later from the same altitude before starting the long journey home across France, and by the time he reached the English coast his fuel state was critical. He carried out a forced-landing at Manston, which resulted in a slight injury to the wireless operator. The operation was a failure, largely because the Pathfinders withheld their flares, and only around five hundred incendiaries found their way into the city. On a more positive note, Sgt Kuzminski and crew successfully delivered their two mines off Terschelling from 700 feet at 18.54, and returned safely.

The Italian campaign was approaching its conclusion when the second of three operations in the space of four nights took place against Turin on the 9/10th. This was the largest effort, involving 227 aircraft, of which five Wellingtons represented 300 Squadron. They took off either side of 18.00 led by F/L Polnik, and there were no early returns. On arrival in the target area they found the ground partially obscured by haze and smoke from the previous night's very destructive attack, and the Pathfinders struggled to provide consistent marking. F/L Polnik was the first of the squadron participants to arrive, and he found the centre of the city to be obscured, but the outskirts clearly visible. He dropped his all-incendiary load onto a concentration of fires from 10,000 feet at 21.24, and their glow was still visible sixty miles into the return trip. P/O Wlodarczyk noted ten to fifteen searchlights to the west and north-west of the city, and intense but inaccurate light and heavy flak. He dropped his all-incendiary load from 15,000 feet at 22.15, and was coned by searchlights and subjected to a heavy flak barrage from an unknown location during the return flight. Sgt Przedpelski bombed at 22.16 from 11,000 feet on a due-north heading, and by the time he wheeled away from the target, smoke was drifting up to 8,000 feet.

While the final operation of the Italian campaign took place rather ineffectively at Turin on the night of the 11/12th, 300 Squadron committed five Wellingtons to mining duties off the French coast. They took off either side of 16.45, and found their respective drop zones easily by pinpointing off the Ile de Groix or Pont-Aven, respectively south-west and north-west of Lorient. They planted their vegetable into the required locations from 600 to 700 feet either side of 20.00, and returned without incident. A further three crews departed Ingham shortly after 17.00 on the 12th to mine the waters off Borkum, the Frisian island facing the Ems Estuary. Sgt Sowa took a run of six-and-a-half minutes north-west from the Boschplaat end of Terschelling whilst W/O Kazimierczak carried out a similar run from Rottumerplaat, further to the east, F/S Leszkiewicz pinpointed on Simonszand, off the eastern tip of Schiermonikoog, and all delivered their stores into the allocated locations. Extensive mining operations on the night of the 14/15th involved five crews from 300 Squadron, but the participation of two of them was scrubbed before take-off. The others headed for the Dutch coast near Callantsoog, a dozen miles or so south of Den Helder, with the intention of pinpointing on Zwanen Water or Petten. Sgt Skowron was at 350 feet on approach to Petten and just a few miles out, when he was persuaded by the conditions to abandon his sortie, and, at 17.55, he turned for home. Three minutes later P/O Wlodarczyk released his mines into the correct position, and Sgt Sowa followed suit at 18.05.

Sgt Czeslaw Przedpelski took part in 31 operations with 300 Squadron from Aug. 1942 to May 1943. (W. Ratuszynski)

The lunacy of single daylight sorties continued on the 17th, when six Wellingtons and four Mosquitos were sent out to attack railways and other targets. Sgt Przedpelski and crew were invited to bomb the small German town of Leer, situated just across the northern-most border with Holland on the east bank of the River Ems, where the railway station was probably the specific aiming point. They took off at 13.08, and decided to remain below the cloud to avoid the icing conditions predicted to be at 2,000 feet. The ten-tenths cloud began to break up to six-tenths as they flew eastwards, and the cloud base dropped to 50 feet with visibility at five hundred yards. The likelihood of picking up a firm pinpoint in those conditions at that altitude was considered small, and the sortie was abandoned at 14.40. The final operation of the year for 300 Squadron involved five crews mining off Lorient on the night of the 19/20th. They took off after 01.00 with F/L Polnik the senior pilot on duty, and arrived in the target area to find good conditions and fair visibility. They released their mines into the allocated positions from between 600 and 700 feet between 04.13 and 05.17, and all returned safely.

When Duisburg provided the target for over two hundred aircraft on the following night, six 109 Squadron Mosquitos carried out the first Oboe raid, for which a power station at Lutterade in Holland was the target. The operation was to serve as a calibration exercise to assess the electronic device's margin of error, but this was thwarted, when photographic reconnaissance revealed a mass of craters left by misdirected bombs from the October attack on Aachen, and it proved impossible to plot those delivered by Oboe. The Oboe trials would continue into the New Year, and would ultimately prove to be vital in the success of the Command's spring offensive. Nine operations during the month had generated the year's fewest sorties at thirty, for the loss of a single aircraft.

January 1943

New Year's Day brought with it the formation of 6 Group RCAF, which was financed by Canada but existed under the control of Bomber Command. Its founder squadrons had mostly served with 4 Group on Wellingtons, and the stations occupied by them were duly transferred to new ownership. It would be some time before the new group fully converted to a mixture of Halifaxes and Lancasters, and, in the meantime, they would help maintain the number of Wellingtons available to Harris until well into the second half of the year. The first two weeks of January were dominated by the continuing Oboe trials program, involving the Mosquitos of 109 Squadron and Lancasters from 1 and 5 Groups. Essen would feature on seven occasions during this period, and Duisburg once, but the group's first operational activity involved twelve Wellingtons of 199, 301 and 305 Squadrons laying mines off the French coast on the night of the 2/3rd. The first of the small-scale operations against Essen took place on the following night, when only nineteen Lancasters were employed. 1 Group was not involved, but instead sent seventeen Lancasters and fourteen Wellingtons on mining sorties. 300 Squadron dispatched three crews to the sea lanes off St Nazaire, P/O Nowak and Sgts Sowa and Przedpelski taking off between 16.11 and 16.20, and delivering their mines into the required location from around 700 feet either side of 20.00.

Sgt Stanislaw Gosiewski (pilot) who was shot down on his 4th operation). (PISM via WM)

On the following night twenty-nine 1 Group Lancasters formed the main force at Essen, and forty-two buildings were destroyed for the loss of two aircraft. The Pathfinders were granted group status on the 8th as 8 Group, and the titles are interchangeable for the purposes of this work. 1 and 5 Groups each provided twenty-five Lancasters for Essen on the night of the 9/10th, when over 120 buildings were either destroyed or seriously damaged. Essen was again the target for 1 and 5 Groups on the nights of the 11/12th and 12/13th, for which 1 Group put up thirty-three and twenty-one Lancasters respectively. The latter operation required a late take-off, after 03.00, and under cover of this activity, thirty-two gardeners set off for the Biscay coast to lay mines. 300 Squadron was undertaking only its second operation of the year when sending F/L Polnik, P/O Wlodarczyk and Sgt Sowa to the waters off Lorient, and all were safely airborne by 03.06. They each found their respective drop zones without difficulty, before releasing their mines from 650 to 700 feet between 06.31 and 06.46. The series of Oboe attacks on Essen concluded on the night of the 13/14th at the hands of over sixty Lancasters of 1 and 5 Groups, but the trials would continue on, as there were many wrinkles in the system to iron out.

A new Air Ministry directive was issued on the 14th, which authorized the area bombing of those French ports providing bases and support facilities for U-Boots. A list of four such targets was drawn up

Sgt Gosiewski with his crew during their training course in 18 OTU at Bramcote in late 1942. Left to Right: 1st Sgt Kozakiewicz (A.G.), 2nd Sgt Gosiewski (pilot), 3rd P/O Zukotynski (nav.), 4th Sgt Imiolek (B.A.). Sgt Burda (W.Op.) is sitting in the front. Sgt Kozakiewicz failed to return from his first operation with the crew of Sgt Furmaniak on 6th Dec. 1942. The rest of the crew except Sgt Gosiewski were also killed on their maiden operation with 300 Squadron. (PISM)

accordingly, headed by Lorient, which, that night, would receive the first of its eight raids over the ensuing month. First, however, a handful of Halifaxes and Wellingtons were sent on a daylight, cloud-cover foray to Leer, and the 300 Squadron crews of W/O Kazimierczak and Sgt Sowa were the lucky ones selected to put their necks on the block as a means of irritating the Germans! They took off either side of noon, and reached the enemy coast before deciding that there was insufficient cloud to continue. Main force Lancasters were not involved in the assault on Lorient at this stage, and the 1 Group effort for that night amounted to fifteen Wellingtons, of which four were provided by 300 Squadron. Z1387 was last away from Ingham at 22.34 with the crew of Sgt Gosiewski on board for their maiden operation, and those on the ground, watching it fade into the darkness, were unaware that the Wellington and its crew would never be seen again. Sgt Cholewa saw the first evidence of flak when thirty or more miles out over the Channel, and surmised that it came from a flak ship. It may also have been responsible for the port engine failure, which curtailed his sortie at that juncture. The remaining two crews arrived in the target area to find the port already well-alight, and W/O Szafran came down to 9,500 feet in order to identify it for himself. He delivered his bombs into existing fires, and reported inaccurate light and heavy flak from the town, and

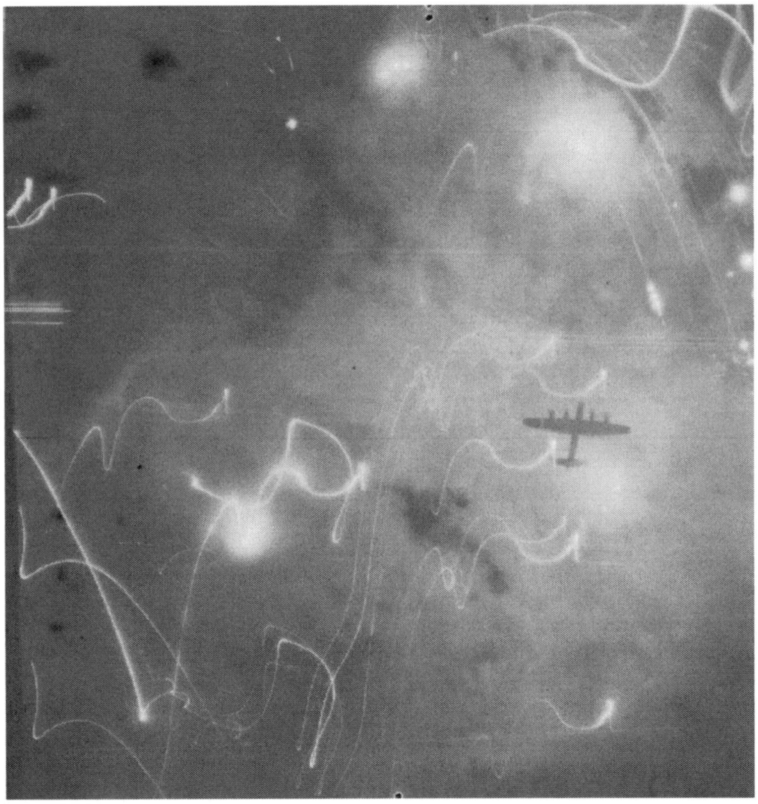

Cloud-covered targets were often marked using parachute flares which provided a virtual aiming point for the bomb aimers. These show as the bright circles in this photo. Note the lower-flying Lancaster; being hit by bombs from above was a constant danger over crowded target areas (Crown Copyright).

heavy flak over to the east. Sgt Skowron carried out his attack from 13,000 feet at 01.23, and echoed the comments about flak, adding that some of it reached 22,000 feet.

The second attack on Lorient took place on the night of the 15/16th, and destroyed at least eight hundred buildings. 300 Squadron carried out a supporting role by sending four Wellingtons to lay mines in the approaches to the port (Artichokes). They took off shortly before 18.00, and pinpointed on Glenan Isle off Pont-Aven, before delivering their mines into the briefed locations from 700 feet between 21.36 and 21.46. There would be no further operational activity for 300 Squadron for ten nights, during which period the Command carried out a number of major raids. The Lancasters were out in strength on the 16/17th for the first of two operations to Berlin on consecutive nights. The force of two hundred aircraft included forty-seven from 1 Group, but twelve of these returned early for a variety of reasons. Germany's Capital lay beyond the range of Gee and Oboe, and the H2S navigation and blind-bombing device was not yet quite ready for its operational debut, and this was reflected in the scattered nature of the attack. Despite good visibility and the first use by the Pathfinders of genuine target indicators, the only building of note to be hit was the ten thousand-seat Deutschlandhalle, the largest covered arena in Europe, and this was completely wrecked. A bonus was the loss of just one aircraft, but this was redressed somewhat on the following night, when a slightly smaller force returned to Berlin, and lost twenty-two of its number in return for another disappointing raid.

The next stage of the Oboe development programme brought a raid by eighty Lancasters from 1 and 5 Groups on Düsseldorf on the night of the 23/24th. 1 Group dispatched twenty-eight, but losses and the usual crop of early returns reduced those reaching the target to nineteen. The attack was delivered through complete cloud cover on estimated positions, as few if any crews caught a glimpse of the "Wanganui" flares (skymarkers), and the operation was inconclusive. Also on this night came the third raid on Lorient, which was carried out successfully by a force of more than a hundred aircraft. The fourth raid was mounted on the night of the 26/27th, and it brought the return to operations of 300 Squadron, which dispatched three crews shortly before 20.00, led by F/L Konopasek. They found some low cloud over the target, but F/L Konopasek was able to pick out the town and the harbour by the light of flares, and dropped his all-incendiary load from 12,000 feet at 20.33. Sgt Przedpelski bombed a minute later from 9,000 feet, and believed that his load fell into the town, west of the docks. Finally, Sgt Sowa attacked at 20.36 from

12,000 feet, and his bombs also fell to the west of the aiming point, which was the military dockyard. This was the first operation conducted by the squadron on Wellington IIIs.

On the following night, Düsseldorf was selected as the objective for the first ground marking by Oboe Mosquitos, a method far more reliable than the parachute flares employed thus far. A force of 160 aircraft set off, of which twenty-six Lancasters were provided by 1 Group. Despite the presence of thin cloud, the bombing was concentrated, and over four hundred houses were destroyed, while many public and industrial premises sustained serious damage. While this operation was in progress four 300 Squadron Wellingtons joined fifty other aircraft to carry out mining sorties off the Frisians. The Ingham contingent was safely airborne by 18.00, each carrying two 1,500lb parachute mines. They found five to ten-tenths cloud with a base at 2,000 feet, but good visibility below, and Sgt Marciniszyn took a pinpoint off Simonszand, a sandbank between Schiermonikoog to the west and Rottumerplaat to the east, before delivering his mines into the allocated positions from 700 feet on a north-westerly heading at 19.36. W/O Szafran followed a minute behind on the same heading to add more links to the deadly chain, and Sgt Zielinski completed the job on a slightly more northerly heading at 20.40. Meanwhile, further to west, F/S Leszkiewicz had picked up the western tip of Boschplaat on the island of Terschelling, and delivered his mines from 500 feet at 20.38.

A 1, 4 and 6 Group Wellington and Halifax assault on Lorient took place on the night of the 29/30th, for which 1 Group put up twenty-eight aircraft and lost one. The month's operations concluded at Hamburg on the night of the 30/31st, when Stirlings and Halifaxes of 7 and 35 Squadrons respectively, carried H2S into battle for the first time. Although it would become a useful device as the war progressed, it required great skill on the part of the operator to interpret the light and dark blotches on the cathode-ray tube, and its maiden operation was not an outstanding success. Twenty-five 1 Group Lancasters took off, but more than a quarter of them returned early or failed to bomb the primary target in unfavourable weather conditions. Dozens of large fires were started, but there was no significant industrial damage, and the destruction of a railway bridge, which brought the city's network to a standstill, was an unanticipated bonus. Five 300 Squadron Wellingtons took off on this night to participate in mining operations off St Nazaire, but four abandoned their sorties because of the conditions, and only F/L Polnik pressed on to the target area. He found ten-tenths cloud with a base at 2,000 feet, and also intense darkness and showers, which reduced visibility to ¾ of a mile. He carried out a ten-minute run from the island of Hoedic on a south-easterly heading, and delivered his mines into the briefed locations from 500 feet at 21.12. It was too dark to observe whether or not the parachutes opened, but now fuel became the issue, and by the time he reached the English coast his reserves were low. He managed to reach Finmere in Buckinghamshire before he felt it prudent to land, and he did so safely with just fifty gallons left in his tanks. 300 Squadron moved back to Hemswell on the 31st, to make way for 199 Squadron to take up residence at Ingham, but the competition between the two stations to be home to the Poles was not yet over. During the course of the month the squadron operated on eight occasions, launching twenty-eight sorties for the loss of one aircraft.

February 1943

Sgt Jan Kropacz (pilot) and Sgt Feliks Lazowski (B.A.) photographed during their training course in 18 OTU at Bramcote. Both were posted to 300 Squadron as one crew on 11th June 1942. Sgt Kropacz was killed on his maiden operation as second pilot in the crew F/O Tomaszewski on 19/20th June 1942. Sgt Lazowski failed to return from his 12th sortie in the freshmen`s crew of Sgt Zielinski on their first operation. (Lazowski family)

The new month began with a raid on Cologne on the night of the 2/3rd, to which 1 Group contributed twenty-six Lancasters to an overall force of 161 aircraft. The Pathfinders used a combination of Oboe and H2S to mark the target on this night, as attempts continued to find a reliable system. The attack again failed to achieve any degree of concentration, and no significant damage was inflicted. On the following night icing conditions over the North Sea made life difficult for the 260 crews bound for Hamburg, and twenty-one of the thirty-five 1 Group Lancasters and Wellingtons turned back early. 300 Squadron supported the operation with two crews, those of W/O Szafran and Sgt Zielinski, who took off at 18.11 and 18.23 respectively. The former made it through the weather to reach the target area, where he found ten-tenths cloud at 10,000 feet, but good visibility. He established his position by means of fires and red and green Pathfinder star markers. He delivered his all-incendiary load from 16,000 feet at 21.09, and returned safely to report many large fires and what seemed to be a successful operation. His assessment was partially confirmed by local reports, which detailed over forty large fires, but damage was still not commensurate with the effort expended. Night fighters were out in force on this night, and sixteen aircraft failed to return. Among them was 300 Squadron's BK511, which was lost without trace with the crew of Sgt Zielinski, and was presumably shot down into the sea.

While this operation was in progress three crews from the squadron joined others to lay mines off Lorient. They had taken off either side of 17.30, and two of them are known to have reached the target area to find between three and six-tenths cloud at around 1,000 feet. They pinpointed on the islands off the coast and made timed runs of four and thirteen minutes on a heading slightly south of east, before delivering their mines into the briefed locations from 500 to 700 feet at 20.53 and 20.59. BK303 failed to return with the crew of Sgt Sowa, and presumably suffered a similar fate to the above-mentioned BK511. The night of the 4/5th brought a change of scenery for 156 crews, who crossed the Alps to bomb Turin, and returned to confirm an accurate and destructive attack. 1 Group provided twenty-one Lancasters for this operation, and a single Lancaster and twenty-five Wellingtons for a simultaneous attack on Lorient. F/S Leszkiewicz was 300 Squadron's sole representative for the latter, taking off at 18.07, and finding the target by pinpointing on Groix Island and the estuary in visibility estimated at five miles. He ran in at 11,500 feet on a south-easterly course, identifying his aiming point by the light of flares, and delivered his all-incendiary load at 20.22. He saw their bursts south of the town, half a mile west of the aiming point, and then remained in the target area for thirty minutes watching the raid develop, and noting some bombs falling outside of the target.

Mining operations occupied the night of the 6/7th, when the sea lanes off St Nazaire provided the drop zone for a single 300 Squadron Wellington. P/O Hajdukiewicz and crew took off at 17.50, and found the target area under intense darkness with poor visibility. They pinpointed on Callabasse Rocks, and ran for five minutes on a heading of 142°, before delivering the two mines from 700 feet at 20.59. The campaign against Lorient continued on the night of the 7/8th, when Lancasters were employed against it in numbers for the first time. 1 Group provided 25% of the eighty of the type, along with twenty-six Wellingtons that made up an overall force of over three hundred aircraft for the two-wave assault. 300 Squadron sent just two Wellingtons, with the crews of Sgt Przedpelski and W/O Kazimierczak, who took off at 19.15 and 19.18 respectively. They found the target in good visibility with little or no cloud, and identified it by the estuary of the River Scorff, and by the fires already burning in the town. Sgt Przedpelski delivered his all-incendiary load from 9,500 feet at 21.39, but its burst was lost among the many fires raging across the entire town. W/O Kazimierczak followed up from 10,000 feet four minutes later, and returned safely to confirm the accuracy and concentration of the raid.

Complete cloud cover forced the use of skymarking at Wilhelmshaven on the 11/12th, but despite this, the bombing was concentrated, and at least one bomb load hit a naval ammunition depot, which blew up, and laid waste to 120 acres of the town and dockyard. 300 Squadron was enjoying six nights away from the operational scene, and missed this one, but briefed six crews for the penultimate attack on Lorient to be mounted on the night of the 13/14th. This was the largest force of the series thus far, and involved over four hundred aircraft, of which Lancasters were the most populous type. 1 Group's contribution amounted to forty-four Lancasters and forty-two Wellingtons. W/C Kropinski added his name to the Order of Battle on this night, and was the third to take off from Hemswell at 17.39. There were no early returns, and all from the squadron arrived in the target area to find clear skies, no haze and excellent visibility. W/C Kropinski located the aiming point by map-reading, flares and fires, and delivered his all-incendiary load from 11,000 feet at 20.31 on a heading of 035°. Not everything went perfectly for him, however, as his automatic pilot, fine pitch control and camera failed, and the photo-flash hung up. The others bombed from 10,000 to 12,000 feet between 20.23 and 20.44, and, in so doing, helped to deliver over a thousand tons of bombs accurately onto the target.

Another disappointing raid was directed at Cologne on the night of the 14/15th, when the Pathfinder marking was based on H2S skymarking. 300 Squadron contributed four Wellingtons, which departed Hemswell between 18.16 and 18.27, and all reached the target despite Sgt Hajdukiewicz losing his intercom and W/T shortly after take-off. There was ten-tenths cloud over the target, with tops between 6,000 and 12,000 feet, and the location of the city was established by means of warning and release-point flares. The Polish crews delivered their single 4,000 pounder each from 15,000 to 16,200 feet between 20.16 and 20.32, and all returned safely, Sgt Hajdukiewicz's X3548 displaying flak damage to its port wing. Only around fifty bomb loads fell into the city, despite the fact that more than four times that number of crews claimed to have attacked, and it demonstrated that the problems of target marking were not yet solved. While this operation was in progress, the Lancaster brigade was elsewhere, pounding Milan to good effect, and starting fires that could be seen from a hundred miles away.

The eighth and final raid of the series on Lorient took place on the night of the 16/17th at the hands of a force of 363 aircraft, which included forty-one Lancasters and eighteen Wellingtons from 1 Group. What they left behind them as they retreated was a town reduced to a deserted ruin by an accumulative total of four thousand tons of bombs. What had not been destroyed, however, were the U-Boot bunkers at Keroman, which were home to the 2nd and 10th U-Boot flotillas. While this operation was in progress, three crews from 300 Squadron were laying mines further south off St Nazaire. They had taken off either side of 18.00, and arrived in the target area to find little cloud and bright moonlight. They each made a timed run from the Calebasse Rocks on a south-easterly heading, and delivered their mines from 600 to 700 feet between 20.27 and 21.02. Sgt Ponc's Z1661 was hit by two light flak shells, one in the dinghy casing and the other in the starboard fuel jettison pipe, and with dwindling fuel reserves, landed at Brize Norton in Oxfordshire after seven-and-a-half hours aloft. F/O Romaniszyn and crew reported seeing the glow of fires from Lorient over to starboard on the way home, but were too low to gain a firmer impression.

W/O Jan Cholewa. Between Jan. and Aug. 1943 he took part in 30 operations with 300 Squadron. Later he volunteered for 1586 Special Duties Flight at Brindisi (Italy) where he completed another two tours of duty between April 1944 and Feb. 1945 having recorded an impressive total number of 110 bombing and special operations flown in his Log-book. (W. Zmyslony)

The first of three disappointing raids on Wilhelmshaven took place on the night of the 18/19th, and involved 1 Group Lancasters but no Wellingtons. The second one, on the following night, was supported by thirty-two Wellingtons from the group and no Lancasters, and 300 Squadron contributed six aircraft in an overall force of 338. They began taking off at 18.00, but BK443 was soon back with overheating engines. Sgt Cholewa made a heavy landing, which damaged the tail wheel. The others reached the target, where they found a thin layer of eight to ten-tenths cloud, and almost daylight conditions above. The target was identified by the coastline to the north, and Pathfinder warning and release-point flares, which were clearly visible ahead. The squadron crews delivered their all-incendiary loads from 13,000 to 18,000 feet between 20.02 and 20.24, and returned safely to report large and concentrated fires, and what they believed was a successful operation. In fact, most of the bombs had fallen to the north of the town, and it was discovered later that the Pathfinders had been using out-of-date maps. Later on the 20th two crews were sent on a sea-search for missing crews, but found nothing. At 14.40 that afternoon W/O Szafran and crew took BK305 for an air-test, and ten minutes later it was seen to dive out of cloud over Scampton, and crash onto farmland three miles north-north-east of Lincoln, killing all on board. The squadron ORB notes that "bad luck has dogged W/O Szafran since he came to the squadron".

The night of the 21/22nd was devoted to Bremen, for which a force of 143 aircraft was made ready, included forty-two Lancasters from 1 Group. Those reaching the target bombed through cloud, and no assessment of the results could be made. On the 24th Air Commodore Edgar Rice was installed as the new A-O-C. 1 Group, and his two year tenure would prove to be controversial. He had joined the RFC in 1915, and had commanded a number of squadrons by the end of the Great War. When the Second World War began he was the station Commander at Hemswell. 6 and 8 Groups concluded the series of attacks on Wilhelmshaven on the night of the 24/25th, and produced little damage in return for their efforts.

Nuremberg was the next destination on the 25/26th, where poor weather conditions hampered the marking, and although three hundred buildings were damaged within the city, most of the bombing from the three hundred-strong force fell around the northern suburbs and onto outlying communities. 1 Group put up forty-five Lancasters, and all returned safely. Gardeners were also out in numbers on this night, and three from 300 Squadron returned to the St Nazaire region. They took off either side of 20.00, and reached the target area to find intense darkness and foggy conditions, which reduced visibility to a thousand yards. Sgt Skowron pinpointed the Calebasse Rocks, and made a timed run of five minutes on a roughly south-easterly heading, before delivering his two mines from 700 feet at 23.39. F/O Romaniszyn carried out a similar delivery from 400 feet six minutes later, while Sgt Ponc pinpointed on the Ile du Pilier, and made a two-minute run due north.

A force of over four hundred aircraft again failed to make its mark at Cologne on the night of the 26/27th, when much of the bombing missed the target altogether. 1 Group dispatched forty-three Lancasters and twenty-eight Wellingtons, of which 300 Squadron provided three of the latter. Sgt Skowron took off at 19.00 in BK236, and landed back fifty-six minutes later with a malfunctioning oxygen system. Skies over the target were clear, but ground haze hampered vertical visibility, and the target was identified by red and green Pathfinder markers. F/O Nowak hung around the target for twenty-four minutes until he saw the first markers, and then delivered his all-incendiary load from 18,000 feet at 21.24. He estimated that 25% of the bomb loads fell up to ten miles west of the target, but many large fires could be seen in the city, and he described it as an enjoyable and successful trip. F/O Romaniszyn attacked from 15,000 feet at 21.25, and he returned to describe two lines of fires two miles long running west to east and north to south across the city, and fires visible up to eighty miles into the homeward flight. The truth was that only about a quarter of the bomb loads had hit the city, causing significant housing damage, but the rest had fallen to the south-west. Two other 300 Squadron Wellingtons had taken off on this night to mine the waters off the Frisians, but Sgt Ponc had to turn back while still over base after BK443's port engine failed. Sgt Kuzminski and crew carried on to reach the target area in poor visibility, caused by intense darkness and fog, but made a run of eight-and-a-half minutes from Simonszand in a north-westerly direction, before dropping the two mines in the briefed location from 500 feet at 20.48.

Sgts Skowron and Ponc were involved in a sea-search for missing crews on the 27th, but returned having seen nothing. That evening Sgt Kuzminski and S/L Konopasek took off for the Frisians to lay mines, but the latter was soon back on the ground at Coltishall after experiencing engine failure. Sgt Kuzminski reached the target area to find patchy fog, but successfully delivered his mines from 800 feet at 20.19. Having dealt with Lorient, the Command's attention was now turned upon St Nazaire on the last night of the month, when 437 aircraft were made ready, including four Wellingtons from 300 Squadron. The Hemswell contingent took off either side of 18.30, two of them carrying a 4,000lb cookie, and two an all-incendiary load. The town was already well-alight by the time they arrived over the target, and three of them dropped their bombs from 13,000 to 15,000 feet between 21.17 and 21.35. F/O Romaniszyn thought his cookie hit the marshalling yards, and F/O Nowak confirmed two columns of smoke rising up from the centre and south-western corner of the yards. Sgt Ponc reported arriving late over the town, which was burning from end to end, and he delivered his cookie from 14,000 feet at 22.40. Sgt Skowron landed at Abingdon in Oxfordshire with diminishing fuel reserves. The attack destroyed an estimated 60% of the town's built-up area, and it would not be targeted again for three weeks. Fourteen operations were undertaken by the squadron during the months, and the forty-three sorties resulted in the loss of two aircraft.

Ingham, July-Aug. 1943. The crew of F/Sgt Skowron posing in front of Wellington LN299 BH-G. Left to Right: Sgt Brozek (A.G.), F/O Segno (nav.), P/O Szczerbaniewicz (B.A), F/S Skowron (pilot) and Sgt Trzcinski (A.G.). They carried out their tour of duty between Dec. 1942 and Aug. 1943. (Skowron family via R. Gretzyngier)

March 1943

The profile of the Polish element in Bomber Command was about to change. Of the original four squadrons formed at Bramcote in 1940, only three remained, 304 Squadron having been transferred to Coastal Command in May 1942. The shortage of Polish personnel would lead to the disbandment of 301 Squadron at the end of March, and the dissemination of its air and ground personnel between 300 and 138 Squadrons. The latter was one of the two highly-secret Special Operations Executive (SOE) squadrons at Tempsford, which delivered agents, arms and supplies to resistance organisations in occupied Europe, and also spies and assassination squads for the Secret Intelligence Service (SIS). 138 Squadron would have a Polish C Flight bearing the 301 legend, and thus keep the proud number alive. A change of role for 305 Squadron was also in the planning stages, and it would eventually convert to Mosquitos and join the 2nd Tactical Air Force in September. On the 2nd of March AVM Ujejski KCB of the Polish Inspectorate General, wrote to Air Commodore Beaumont at the Air Ministry to discuss the matter of the conversion of 300 Squadron from Wellingtons to Lancasters. Beaumont's response, dated the 5th, presented Ujejski with two options, either of which was acceptable to the Air Ministry. Beaumont made it clear that there was absolutely no prospect of the squadron receiving Lancasters in 1943, and there was no guarantee, either, that they would be available even in 1944. There had also been a suggestion in earlier discussions that Liberators might be made available, but Beaumont quashed that notion by confirming that there was no allotment, whatsoever, of Liberators in Bomber Command. Therefore, the squadron could be brought up to full operational strength with some of the air and ground crews from 301 Squadron, and continue to operate Wellington IIIs, or convert to Halifaxes, beginning, perhaps as early as the 1st of April, and transfer to 4 Group.

For Ujejski, the long-term viability of a Polish presence in Bomber Command was the priority, and in order to achieve that goal he would have to husband the limited Polish human resources. The training of new Polish air and ground personnel, many from the Middle-East, was ongoing, but it was a trickle rather than a steady flow, and the prospect of entering the new phase of heavy bomber operations with the unpopular Halifax was not appealing. The type's poor record to date threatened to wipe out the available Polish manpower in a short time, and this, ultimately, forced Ujejski's hand. Beaumont ended his letter with the comment that he was being pressed for an answer, and required the matter to be resolved by the 8th. Ujejski's reply in a letter dated the 8th of March read; "With regard to 300 Squadron. In view of the statement in your letter, to the effect that conversion into Lancasters will not be possible in 1943, and also that Liberators are out of the question, I wish to ask you to leave this squadron on Wellington III aircraft, on condition that it would be supplemented to its full establishment strength both in aircrew and ground personnel." The decision was made, and 300 Squadron would remain a Wellington unit for the foreseeable future. This was a sound move on Ujejski's part, because it meant a limited involvement in the forthcoming campaigns, which would prove to be very expensive in manpower terms, and would ensure the enduring presence of passionate Poles in Bomber Command for the remainder of the war.

March would bring the start of the year's first major offensive, against the industrial Ruhr, but first, Berlin was attacked on the night of the 1/2nd by a mixed four-engine force of under three hundred aircraft, for which 1 Group dispatched forty-two Lancasters. The problems of interpreting H2S returns were demonstrated by the lack of accuracy and concentration in the marking, and this led to widely scattered bombing, and the main weight of the attack falling into the south-western districts. Despite the failings, the total of 875 buildings destroyed represented the best result yet at the Capital. Two 300 Squadron Wellingtons had taken off in the early evening to lay mines off St Nazaire, but BK516 developed a variety of technical problems, and Sgt Cholewa was forced to abandon his sortie. Using la Calebasse Rocks as his pinpoint, Sgt Przedpelski delivered his two mines from 700 feet at 21.38. Later on the 2nd Sgt Ponc carried out a sea-search for missing crews, but returned with nothing to report.

Hamburg came next on the night of the 3/4th, when a force of four hundred aircraft included forty-three Lancasters and thirty-one Wellingtons from 1 Group. 300 Squadron dispatched four Wellingtons, but engine failure over the North Sea midway between Hemswell and the target, forced Sgt Ponc to turn back at 20.08. The others pressed on, and found clear skies over the target, but ground haze and smoke from the fires already burning. F/O Nowak was carrying an all-incendiary load, which he released on Pathfinder red and green markers from 18,000 feet at 21.32. Sgt Przedpelski and F/O Romaniszyn each had a cookie on board, and they went down from 14,500 and 16,000 feet at 21.36 and 21.49 respectively. Similar difficulties to those at Berlin were encountered on this night with regard to H2S, but a hundred fires were, never the less, started in the city. However, it was the small town of Wedel, some thirteen miles downstream of the Elbe, which received the bulk of the main force effort, and heavy damage was inflicted.

Two nights after Hamburg, Harris embarked on what would become a five month long offensive against Germany's industrial heartland. Within two weeks of his appointment as C-in-C a year earlier, he had made his intentions clear with regard to the likes of Essen and Duisburg, but had failed repeatedly to deliver a telling blow at either. Düsseldorf, alone of the Ruhr cities, had experienced a number of effective operations, but now the means were to hand to negate the ever-present blanket of haze, which had so often frustrated the best endeavours of the crews. The Ruhr campaign would be the first for which the Command was genuinely well equipped and prepared, and with Oboe demonstrating a reasonable degree of reliability, the time was right to strike. Essen, with its giant Krupp armaments complex, was the obvious choice to open proceedings, and on the night of the 5/6th, 442 aircraft took off either side of 19.00 hours and headed towards the east to deliver the three wave attack.

300 Squadron Wellingtons at dispersal. (PISM via WM)

1 Group contributed forty-one Lancasters and thirty-eight Wellingtons, five of the latter representing 300 Squadron. They took off from Hemswell between 19.27 and 19.54, and three of them were among the unusually high number of early returns, which, ultimately reduced the size of the force actually attacking the target to 362. Sgt Cholewa and crew were at 7,000 feet east of Skegness and north of the Norfolk coast at 20.04, when the rear turret became unserviceable, and they brought their bombs home. Sgt Skowron abandoned his sortie at 20.30, when at the midpoint between the English and Dutch coasts. BK236 developed a number of engine problems, which reduced it to flying at just ninety mph indicated air speed (i.a.s.). Despite the handicap, the crew undertook a slow return home with the bombs still on board. F/L Konopasek had Sgt Ponc alongside him as second pilot, and they were at 14,000 feet when rising temperatures in the starboard engine and a failed IFF (identification friend or foe) system persuaded them to turn back at 21.02 from almost the same position as Sgt Skowron. F/O Nowak reached the target, which he found under four-tenths cloud and in good visibility. He saw the Pathfinder markers, and delivered his all-incendiary load onto them from 18,500 feet at 21.17, before returning home to report intense fires.

The plan had worked to perfection, and after accurate marking of the city centre, first by the Oboe Mosquitos, and then by the heavy backers-up, the main force delivered a concentrated assault. Over three thousand houses and apartment blocks were destroyed, while fifty-three buildings within the Krupp works were hit, and this was by far the most successful raid of the war on this target. Among fourteen missing aircraft was the 300 Squadron Wellington BK150, containing F/O Romaniszyn and his crew, which included as navigator on this night S/L Jankowski, the first commanding officer of 305 Squadron back in 1940. The Wellington was hit by flak outbound, probably while passing through the searchlight belt between Mönchengladbach and the Ruhr, and F/O Romaniszyn ordered his crew to bale out. Once alone in the aircraft, he turned back towards the Dutch border to make a forced landing, which he accomplished, but sustained injuries in the process. He was captured and taken to a hospital in Holland, and joined four others of his crew as PoWs. S/L Jankowski failed to survive, and the circumstances of his death are uncertain. According to Romaniszyn's post-war testimony, the navigator opted to remain on board. The reason for this decision is not known, and one can speculate that, perhaps, he had been wounded by the flak, and was unable to abandon the aircraft, or even that his parachute had been rendered unusable. It is also possible, that F/O Romaniszyn's decision to attempt a forced landing was prompted by such a scenario.

F/O Kazimierz Romaniszyn (pilot) was shot down and taken prisoner on his 8th operation with 300 Squadron. (PISM via WM)

Before launching round two of the campaign, Harris turned his attention to southern Germany, and raided Nuremberg, Munich and Stuttgart over the succeeding week. The first mentioned operation took place on the night of the 8/9th, at the hands of a force of over three hundred aircraft. The force experienced the usual problems with marking beyond the range of Oboe, and visual identification proved difficult in the face of ground haze. As a consequence the markers delivered by H2S were not concentrated, and much of the bombing fell short. Even so, six hundred buildings were destroyed, and a number of important war industry factories were damaged. It was a similar story at Munich on the following night, when 1 Group provided forty-seven Lancasters to an overall force of 260 aircraft. On this occasion it was the wind that

Left: Hemswell, 6th March 1943. Polish airmen shortly after receiving the Virtuti Militari decoration. 1st from left – S/O Yvonne Gerstel WAAF receiving VM on behalf of her husband F/O Jan Gerstel who was shot down and taken PoW on 25th November 1942. 2nd from left – W/C Adam Kropinski CO of 300 Squadron. The other officers are from 301 Squadron. Note that Mrs Gerstel is keeping the official diploma and case with the VM in her hand while other officers are proudly sporting their medals on uniforms. Right: Close up of S/O Yvonne Gerstel and W/C Adam Kropinski, who took command of 300 Squadron on 31st Oct. 1942 and completed his tour of duty between June 1942 and Feb. 1943. (PISM via WM)

influenced the outcome of the raid, and a more modest 291 buildings suffered destruction, mostly in western districts. The Stuttgart raid on the night of the 11/12th was disappointing in comparison, despite accurate marking, and it is possible that the first recorded use of dummy target indicators caused most of the bombs to fall into open country. 1 Group put up forty-one Lancasters, and all returned safely.

The second operation of the Ruhr offensive took place on the night of the 12/13th, and was also directed at Essen. A force of 450 aircraft took off, among them forty-five Lancasters and thirty-nine Wellingtons from 1 Group, four of the latter provided by 300 Squadron. Sgt Ponc was last away from Hemswell at 20.05 in Z1661, but intercom failure forced him to turn back thirteen minutes later while at 4,000 feet, a dozen or so miles short of the exit point at Skegness. The others carried on to reach the target in clear skies with moonlight, but thick haze obscuring ground detail. Red and green target indicators guided the crews to the aiming point, and the 300 Squadron participants delivered their all-incendiary loads from 12,000 to 17,000 feet between 21.28 and 21.40. They returned safely to report many and concentrated fires, the glow from which could be seen from the Dutch coast. The Krupp works was in the centre of the bombing area on this night, and sustained 30% more damage than a week earlier, and a further five hundred houses were destroyed. Twenty-three aircraft failed to return, five of them from 1 Group.

A period of minor operations followed, during which much of the Command's effort would be directed towards mining. On the night after Essen, 300 Squadron dispatched five Wellingtons shortly before 19.00 to lay mines in the St Nazaire area. Thick fog over the Devon coast persuaded Sgt Ponc to abandon his sortie after reaching Start Point, and he turned back at 21.00. The others reached what was now familiar territory off the Brittany coast, and pinpointed on the Calebasse Rocks, before making timed runs to their individual drop zones. Three delivered their vegetables into the correct location from 700 feet between 21.36 and 22.05, and returned safely to report a successful operation. The return of BK516 was awaited in vain, and no trace of it or the crew of Sgt Kuzminski was ever found.

The next assault on St Nazaire was carried out on the night of the 22/23rd, when 283 crews bombed as briefed for the loss of a single Lancaster. The Ruhr campaign continued at Duisburg four nights later, when 455 aircraft were dispatched, among them fifty-two Lancasters and forty-three Wellingtons from 1 Group. 300 Squadron contributed four of the Wellingtons, which took off shortly before 20.00, and all reached the target, where they found that matters were not proceeding according to plan. Five of the Oboe Mosquitos returned early with technical problems, while a sixth was lost, and this was partly responsible for the disappointing outcome, which reflected previous attempts at this target. Sgt Skowron found the target area hidden beneath ten-tenths cloud, and identified Duisburg by means of red, green and white Pathfinder flares. He aimed for the centre of these from 17,000 feet at 21.46, and returned home to report four main clusters of widely dispersed markers, suggesting a scattered attack, but large explosions and the reflection of fires in the clouds visible from a hundred miles away. The others from the squadron attacked from 15,000 to 17,000 feet between 21.51 and 21.55, and returned safely with similar stories.

Berlin was the target for a force of 396 aircraft on the night of the 27/28th, but it failed to produce the hoped-for outcome after inaccurate Pathfinder marking led to no bombs falling within five miles of the city-centre aiming point. The following night was devoted to the next assault on St Nazaire, for which 323 aircraft were made ready. 300 Squadron dispatched five Wellingtons between 19.07 and 19.26, and they arrived in the target area to find a thin veil of cloud, which others identified as haze, but, otherwise, good visibility. The docks and the town were picked out visually, and red and green target indicators marked out the aiming point. BK267 was hit by flak north of the town at the start of the bombing run, and lost all of the hydraulic fluid to the rear turret, as well as gaining many holes in the starboard side of the fuselage. Sgt Przedpelski carried on, and he and the other squadron participants released their all-incendiary loads from 8,000 to 14,500 feet between 22.02 and 22.19. They all arrived safely home, and at debriefing F/O Nowak described a large explosion, which lasted for seven seconds.

A second Berlin operation in three nights took place in unfavourable weather conditions at the hands of three hundred aircraft on the night of the 29/30th. Most of the bombing fell into open country, and the failure was compounded by the loss of twenty-one aircraft. A simultaneous operation against Bochum involved thirty-eight aircraft from 1 Group, and it proved to be the final operation for 301 Squadron, which, because of a lack of available Polish airmen, was about to be disbanded. 300 Squadron contributed five crews, which departed Hemswell either side of 20.00. Sgt Ponc's regular aircraft, Z1661 again proved troublesome, and refused to climb above 13,500 feet, even after part of the all-incendiary load had been jettisoned. He was just beyond mid-point between the English and Dutch coasts at 20.58 when he decided to turn back. The others kept going, and reached the target area to find no cloud, but the usual industrial haze providing only moderate visibility. They followed the red and green route marker flares, and bombed on the red target indicator flares and green stars from 14,000 to 16,000 feet between 21.50 and 22.01. Returning crews suspected a scattered attack, but it proved to be not even that successful, as problems with late and sparse marking led to only a few bombs falling within the town. Eight operations were mounted during the month, which generated thirty-four sorties and two missing aircraft.

April 1943

April would prove to be the least rewarding month of the Ruhr period, but this was largely because of the number of operations directed against targets in other regions of Germany, and, consequently, beyond the range of Oboe. Meanwhile, at Hemswell, 300 Squadron described itself as being in the throes of reconstitution, as it was about to welcome not only fresh blood from 301 squadron, but also the return of experienced battle-hardened crews who were to embark on a second tour. The prospect of increasing its striking power and bringing greater resources against the enemy served to energise the squadron anew, and the coming month would prove to be a busy one. The first night of operational activity of the month involved forces of fifty-five and forty-seven aircraft respectively, carrying out the final attacks on St Nazaire and Lorient on the night of the 2/3rd. 300 Squadron provided Sgt Przedpelski for the former, and he took off at 19.40 to reach the target some two-and-a-half hours later in good visibility, but with a smoke screen operating below and a hostile flak and searchlight defence. He delivered his bombs on a north-south heading from 10,500 feet at 22.25, and then took violent evasive action, which prevented him from observing their bursts. He and his crew were in Z1661, which had enjoyed a chequered career to date, and picked up some fresh flak damage on this night, although nothing serious. There was a hot reception also for the crews over Lorient, but the two 300 Squadron crews carried out their attacks from 9,000 and 16,000 feet shortly after 23.00, and returned to report a successful operation. It was on this night that that the experienced crew of P/O Tomicki took to the air in the squadron's first Wellington Mk X, HE148. It would not be long before all of the squadron's Mk IIIs were replaced with the more powerful and reliable Mk X.

The bombing campaign against Germany began in encouraging fashion with the third attack of the series on Essen on the following night, and this left over six hundred buildings in ruins, and five hundred more displaying signs of serious damage. 1 Group dispatched seventy-two Lancasters in an overall force of almost 350 aircraft, while the Wellington brigade remained at home. A new record non-1,000 force of 577 aircraft sent against Kiel on the night of the 4/5th included a contingent from 1 Group of sixty-seven Lancasters and twenty-seven Wellingtons, of which four of the latter represented 300 Squadron. They took off in a ten-minute slot from 20.35, and X3548 was over the North Sea, east of Mablethorpe, when the starboard engine failed, and P/O Brochocki was forced to turn back. The Wellington crashed on landing, but there were no crew casualties. The others pressed on to find heavy cloud over the target, and W/O Kazimierczak hung around for fifteen minutes waiting for markers to appear. Once the green target indicators went down, he bombed from 16,000 feet at 23.30 on a north-south heading, and returned with an unenthusiastic impression of the outcome. There was also a claim that the gunners had shot down an enemy night fighter, after it attacked three times over the target. P/O Hajdukiewicz and F/O Nowak had bombed fifteen minutes earlier from 16,000 and 17,000 feet respectively, and they were more positive about the effectiveness of the attack, based on the glow of many fires beneath the cloud. In the event the massive effort was not rewarded with success, for which strong winds and decoy fires may have been to blame. Only a few bombs fell within the built-up area of the town, and twelve aircraft were lost to this failure. The end came for 301 Squadron when it was disbanded on the 7th, and its personnel were posted to other units as already outlined.

Almost four hundred aircraft set off for Duisburg on the evening of the 8/9th, among them thirty-eight Lancasters and twenty-nine Wellingtons from 1 Group, of which eight of the latter represented 300 Squadron. They began taking off at 21.25, the crews of F/S Leszkiewicz and F/L Kunowski in aircraft borrowed from 199 Squadron. Weather conditions were unfavourable throughout, and F/S Leszkiewicz and Sgt Cholewa both abandoned their sorties and jettisoned their bombs because of severe icing. On arrival over the target the others encountered thick cloud, which led to inaccurate marking, and all from 300 Squadron bombed on e.t.a from up to 18,000 feet. Sgt Skowron actually stooged around for ten minutes waiting for markers to appear, but he was to be disappointed. He was unable to determine the fall of his bombs, but observed many photo-flash bombs going off and the reflected glow of new fires apparently starting up. Nineteen aircraft failed to return, and among them was the previously-mentioned HE148, one of the new MkX Wellingtons recently delivered to the squadron, and the first to be lost. It crashed into the sea about fifteen miles west of Ijmuiden at 23.07, after being shot down by a Kriegsmarine flak ship as it approached the coast outbound. There were no survivors from the crew captained by P/O Tomicki, who had fought courageously during the Polish campaign in September 1939, and had gained his commission in the field as a result. Before being posted to 300 Squadron, he had completed a tour of operations with 305 Squadron. There is a possibility, suggested by the timing of the crash, that this crew may have been returning home early with some kind of problem, as the only bombing times specified in the ORB are 23.16 and 23.28, nine and twenty-one minutes after the time of the crash, and some 140 miles further east. On return a number of crews landed away from Hemswell because of deteriorating weather conditions and dwindling fuel reserves.

104 Lancasters and five Mosquitos returned to Duisburg twenty-four hours later, but the city's apparently charmed life continued, and a modest fifty houses were destroyed. A force of 502 aircraft made ready for Frankfurt on the 10th included forty-six Lancasters and twenty-eight Wellingtons from 1 Group, six of the latter provided by 300 Squadron. They were all safely airborne from Hemswell by 23.50 and heading for the exit point over the south coast. They reached the target area to find complete cloud cover, and established their positions by means of Pathfinder route and release point flares. One crew reported that the latter were dropped from too close to the cloud tops and quickly disappeared from sight. They delivered their all-incendiary loads from 13,000 to 17,000 feet between 02.34 and 02.46, and had no real clue as to their effect. F/L Kunowski complained that the Pathfinder target indicators were not released until 02.53, by which time many crews were on their way home. The reflection of fires in the clouds seemed to cover a wide area, and suggested to some a scattered attack, while others reported a successful operation. Sgt Cholewa's HE373 was damaged by flak, and he landed at West Malling with dwindling fuel reserves. It was established later that the operation had failed, and that only a few bombs had fallen within the city south of the River Main.

Matters improved somewhat on the night of the 13/14th, when an all Lancaster main force successfully bombed the docks area in the Italian town of La Spezia. The following night was devoted to attacking Stuttgart, for which a force of 462 aircraft was made ready. Unusually for the period, Lancasters were not the most numerous type committed to the fray, Wellingtons and Halifaxes taking that honour with 146 and 135 respectively. Eleven 300 Squadron Wellingtons took off between 21.28 and 21.48, and made their way south-east to rendezvous with the rest of the force. X3459 developed a fuel system problem, forcing P/O Krzehlik to turn back at 22.05 when at 6,000 feet over Boston, and Sgt Cholewa abandoned his sortie at 23.05 after his oxygen system failed when over the sea north of Dieppe. Sgt Ponc and crew were only about thirty miles north-west of the target when they were attacked by a night fighter, and they jettisoned the bomb load in order to escape. The Pathfinders had dropped yellow route markers north of Saarbrücken, some hundred miles north-west of the target, and crews were able to navigate from there in bright moonlight. Stuttgart itself was easily identifiable by the River Neckar, and also by the green and yellow markers cascading over it. The 300 Squadron crews delivered their all-incendiary loads from 15,000 to 19,000 feet between 01.00 and about 01.20, and returned home to report many fires across the city and a successful operation. The Pathfinders claimed to have marked the centre, but the attack developed to the north-east along the line of approach, and was rescued from failure by the almost inevitable creep-back, a feature of most heavy raids. It could work in favour of, or against, the Command, and on this occasion it fell across the industrial suburb of Bad Canstatt and into nearby residential districts, where almost four hundred buildings were destroyed.

Three 300 Squadron crews went mining on the night of the 15/16th, joining twenty others at various locations off the French coast. The Beeches garden off St Nazaire provided the target area for the Polish element, which took off from Hemswell shortly after 20.30, and found perfect weather conditions on their arrival over the drop zone. They made timed runs from la Calebasse Rocks, and delivered their two mines each from around 1,000 feet, before returning safely. When Germany took Czechoslovakia under its wing, it acquired for itself the huge Skoda armaments works at Pilsen, and this was the target for the Lancaster and Halifax squadrons on the night of the 16/17th. 327 aircraft took off for the former, where the plan was to identify the target visually in bright moonlight, and for the Pathfinder markers to provide a route-marker reference for the start of the bombing run. This was a plan doomed to fail, and it did so spectacularly when most main force crews became confused and bombed on the route markers seven miles short of the Skoda works. Many loads fell onto an asylum, and the intended target escaped damage. The failure was compounded by the loss of thirty-six aircraft, split evenly between the two types.

While this operation was in progress, a simultaneous predominantly Wellington and Stirling raid on Mannheim was intended to provide a diversion to split the night fighter defences. 300 Squadron provided thirteen Wellingtons, which took off either side of 21.30, but W/O Kazimierczak had to turn back early after being unable to draw fuel from his overload tank. Sgt Ponc was also unable to carry on when his navigator reported sick. The others reached the target to find it easily identifiable by the River Rhine and its junction with the Neckar, and the Pathfinders exploited the favourable conditions to mark it accurately. The squadron crews delivered their all-incendiary loads from 11,000 to 15,000 feet between 01.00 and 01.25, some of them after waiting up to seven minutes for the target indicators to be released. All crews returned home to report a successful operation, describing many large fires and concentrated bombing. F/O Stadtmüller returned with damage courtesy of a light flak battery seven miles east of Dieppe, and complained that the return journey should have been at high altitude, rather than the low level ordered at briefing. The operation achieved some success, destroying 130 buildings and damaging to some extent three thousand others, while forty-one industrial firms lost production. Eighteen aircraft failed to return, and these added to those lost from Pilsen, brought the total to fifty-six, the heaviest loss to date in a single night.

The following night brought further mining operations off the French coast, for which 300 Squadron dispatched seven crews, five for Beeches off St Nazaire, and two for Artichokes off Lorient. They were all safely airborne before 21.00, but P/O Myszkowski was taken ill during the outward flight to St Nazaire, and was forced to turn back. Weather conditions were excellent as Sgt Zielinski and W/O Kazimierczak pinpointed on Pont-Aven, and made seven and five-minute timed runs respectively, to deliver their mines into the correct locations from 1,000 feet at around 23.45. The others found pinpoints on la Calebasse Rocks and Hoedic Island, and dropped their mines as briefed from 1,000 feet between 23.59 and 00.45. The heavy losses from Pilsen were no doubt still fresh in the mind for the next two long-range operations, the first of which was a return to the naval base at La Spezia on the night of the 18/19th, and the other to the Baltic port of Stettin on the 20/21st. 170 Lancasters took part in the former, and there were no losses from among the sixty-two sent by 1 Group. The latter involved a force of over three hundred aircraft, of which seventy Lancasters were provided by 1 Group. They helped to lay waste to a hundred acres in the centre of the town at a cost of twenty-one aircraft overall, eight of them from 1 Group.

300 Squadron was not required for the above-mentioned operations, and was next in action on the night of the 22/23rd, for a return to the Lorient and St Nazaire shipping lanes. Six crews were briefed for each garden, and they were all safely airborne by 20.53. Sgt Garczynski was bound for Lorient, but lost his Gee early on, and then experienced hydraulics problems, before encountering poor visibility, which persuaded him that he would be unable to plant his vegetables accurately. He turned back when over the Channel west of Guernsey, and landed without being able to deploy flaps. P/O Krzehlik abandoned his sortie to Lorient because of poor visibility, and P/O Myszkowski did likewise at St Nazaire. He reached the target area on dead reckoning, and searched for fifteen minutes without finding his pinpoint. The others delivered their stores either side of midnight, despite also encountering unfavourable weather conditions, and a number of crews reported being shot at. HE291 failed to return from St Nazaire with the crew of F/L Przysiecki, after being brought down over the sea by flak. There were no survivors, but the bodies of all but the rear gunner were recovered for burial.

The next major operation was against Duisburg on the night of the 26/27th, for which a force of 561 aircraft was made ready. 1 Group dispatched sixty-two Lancasters and thirty-one Wellingtons, eleven of the latter provided by 300 Squadron. There was a late take-off, with the many-times-previously-mentioned Z1661 last away at 01.02 with the crew of Sgt Garczynski. HE147 developed a problem with its port engine while circling over base, and P/O Hajdukiewicz landed back with his bombs as soon as the others had cleared the circuit. HE267 was unable to maintain height and had a defective rear turret, as a result of which Sgt Kalfas turned back at 02.06 shortly after crossing the Dutch/German frontier. The others pressed on to approach Duisburg from the north, and found clear skies and smoke from the already burgeoning fires. The aiming point was identified by the Pathfinder target indicators, and the squadron crews delivered their all-incendiary loads from 14,000 to 18,000 feet between 02.27 and 02.41 in the face of a heavy and accurate flak defence. They returned full of praise for the Pathfinders, and Sgt Ponc reported that the target appeared to be one large fire, which could be seen from the Dutch coast. One pilot was so convinced that the operation had been an outstanding success, that he made the comment, "Duisburg existed yesterday". Daylight reconnaissance revealed that, although it was the most effective raid yet on this city, destroying three hundred buildings, it still fell short of what might have been expected from such a large force. The conclusion was that the main force had bombed too early, creating a creep-back to the north-east along the line of approach.

The largest mining effort to date took place on the night of the 27/28th in French and Dutch coastal waters, for which 300 Squadron contributed nine Wellingtons to an overall force of 160 aircraft. Eight crews were briefed for St Nazaire and one for Lorient, and the former element got away in a twenty-minute slot to 21.20, to be followed at 21.52 by F/S Ekiert, who was back for a second tour. F/O Stadtmüller abandoned his sortie at 23.38 because of poor visibility while crossing the Brest peninsular, having been unable to pick out a navigation point on the Normandy coast in low cloud, haze and intense darkness. F/L Kuzian was south-west of Jersey when he came to the same conclusion at 23.35. Sgt Ponc had not long crossed the Normandy coast when he also gave up, after being unable to pick up a Gee fix. The others pushed on to their respective drop zones, where they found improved conditions and increased visibility. They picked

Ingham, summer of 1943. Wellington HF598 BH-W being loaded with sea mines during preparations for another minelaying mission. (PISM via WM)

up the familiar pinpoints, and delivered their mines from 1,000 to 1,500 feet after midnight, and returned safely to complete the squadron's operational activity for the month. An even larger force of 207 aircraft was committed to the mining of northern waters on the following night, and although the number of mines laid was a new record, at twenty-two aircraft, so was the scale of losses from this type of operation. The month ended with a tilt at Essen on the last night, which produced more modest returns than the previous raids on this target during the campaign. The squadron carried out fifteen operations during the month, and launched eighty-eight sorties for the loss of two aircraft.

May 1943

May would bring a return to winning ways, with a number of records and spectacular successes. 300 Squadron was back to full strength with an influx of experienced crews from 301 and 305 Squadrons and a full complement of Wellington Xs. The new month began for 300 Squadron with a mining operation off Brest (Jellyfish), for which six crews were briefed. They were all safely off the ground by 21.20, and found the target area in conditions of good to fair visibility. They pinpointed on Pointe du Toulinguet, south-west of the port, and carried out short timed runs to deliver their two 1,500lb mines each from 1,000 to 2,700 feet between 23.49 and 00.15. There was a change at the top of 300 Squadron on the 4th, as W/C Kucharski took over from W/C Kropinski.

W/C Marian Kucharski succeeded W/ C Kropinski as CO of 300 Squadron in May 1943. He flew his first tour of duty in 304 Squadron. From Sept. 1942 to Nov. 1943 he completed 18 operations of his second tour. In Feb. 1944 he assumed command of the Polish 45 Transport Group in Canada. (PISM via WM)

That night a new record non-1,000 force of 596 aircraft carried out the first genuinely heavy raid of the war on Dortmund. 1 Group provided seventy-six Lancasters and thirty-four Wellingtons, and eleven of the latter represented 300 Squadron. They took off in a fifteen minute slot to 22.51, and all reached the target area to find clear skies, good visibility, many already-established fires and well-placed Pathfinder red and green target indicators. The 300 Squadron crews were at 14,000 to 18,000 feet as they began their bomb runs from the north, and had the TIs in their sights as they delivered their all-incendiary loads between 01.18 and 01.30. On return in poor visibility, HE420 collided with another Wellington at 1,300 feet over Ingham, and lost the rudder and top of its tail fin, but W/O Kazimierczak pulled off an excellent landing without further mishap. At debriefing he described the concentration of fires appearing to cover the entire city, and mentioned a huge explosion occurring when he was thirty miles into the return trip, which lit up the sky sufficiently for him to see other aircraft. From the Dutch coast he could see a pall of smoke rising and moving westwards, and there was no doubt in his mind and of the others, that this had been an outstandingly destructive attack. In fact, only about half of the force had managed to bomb within three miles of the aiming point after some of the backers-up dropped their markers short, and a decoy fire site had also attracted some attention. Never-the-less, it was a very successful operation, which destroyed over twelve hundred buildings, and inflicted useful damage on industrial premises and dock facilities. The defenders fought back to claim thirty-one aircraft, and high casualty figures would prove to be a feature of the campaign.

The main force and Pathfinder crews were rested over the succeeding week, and it was on the night of the 12/13th that they were next called to arms, for yet another crack at the elusive city of Duisburg. 572 aircraft took off, among them sixty-one Lancasters and thirty-two Wellingtons of 1 Group. 300 Squadron provided thirteen of the Wellingtons, and it was fifteen minutes after midnight before the first one lifted off from Hemswell, to be followed into the air by the others before 00.30, each carrying an all-incendiary bomb load. HE381 developed an overheating port engine, and was between Boston and Skegness, about to cross The Wash at 01.00, when F/O Myszkowski decided to turn back. HZ374 was almost at the Dutch coast when its port engine began to fail at 01.35 at 18,000 feet, and P/O Korczak-Krzeczowski also took the only possible decision to jettison his load and return home. The others reached the target to find cloudless skies and near perfect visibility, which, despite the expected haze and smoke, allowed the crews to identify ground detail. The Pathfinder marking was accurate and concentrated, and the crews had red and green TIs in their bomb sights as they delivered their loads from 14,000 to 18,000 feet between 02.12 and 02.27. Returning crews were unanimous in their conviction that Duisburg had suffered a massive blow, describing a sea of flames, explosions and black smoke rising high into the air, and the glow of fires visible from the Dutch coast. This time Germany's largest inland port had, indeed, succumbed to an outstandingly accurate and concentrated assault, which destroyed almost sixteen hundred buildings, and sank or damaged sixty thousand tons of shipping. Again this was not a one-sided affair, and the enemy defences claimed thirty-four bombers, a new record for the campaign thus far. 300 Squadron's HE295 failed to return, and was lost without trace with the crew of Sgt Werner.

On the following night over four hundred aircraft targeted Bochum, situated west of Dortmund and south-east of Gelsenkirchen, for which 1 Group managed put up a new record of eighty-three Lancasters along with thirty-four Wellingtons. 300 Squadron made ready a dozen Wellingtons, which took off either side of midnight, and within minutes one was on its way back. HE381 had reached 4,500 feet when all electrical power to the instruments failed at 00.30, and for the second operation running, F/O Myszkowski was forced to turn back. Sgt Ponc and crew were closing in on the target at 17,000 feet at 02.12, when they were attacked by a BF109, which they managed to evade after jettisoning their incendiary load live. The others from the squadron reached the target, which they found under clear skies in bright moonlight, with just the usual haze and smoke impairing vertical visibility. There were some Pathfinder markers to aim at, but F/S Kleinschmidt claimed to have arrived at the target at 02.09, and circled for more than ten minutes waiting for the first TI to appear, which didn't happen until after he had bombed at 02.35. The other squadron crews carried out their attacks from 15,000 to 17,000 feet between 02.14 and 02.35, and on return described smoke rising to around 5,000 feet as they were leaving the target area. F/S Ekiert reported a very large explosion at 02.27 followed by a column of black smoke, and added that the glow of fires was still visible seventy miles into the homeward trip. Post raid analysis suggested that the operation began well, but after fifteen minutes German decoy markers succeeded in drawing off much of the later bombing. Even so, almost four hundred buildings were destroyed, and a further seven hundred seriously damaged for the loss of twenty-four aircraft. 5 Group and a Pathfinder element, meanwhile, were engaged over Czechoslovakia, attempting in vain to rectify the recent failure at the Skoda works at Pilsen.

Another nine day break allowed the squadrons to rest and replenish, during which, on the night of the 16/17th, 617 Squadron earned its place in bomber folklore, with its epic attack on the Möhne, Eder and Sorpe Dams east of the Ruhr. 300 Squadron returned to operations on the night of the 21/22nd, when eight crews began taking off at 22.16 for a mining operation in the Nectarines garden off the Frisians. They found varying amounts of cloud and some haze at sea level, but visibility was reasonable, and all crews were able to make pinpoints before embarking on a timed run and delivering two 1,500lb parachute mines each from 1,000 to 2,000 feet either side of midnight.

When the rest of the Command returned to action on the night of the 23/24th, it was for a record breaking operation to Dortmund by the largest non-1,000 force to date. The 826 aircraft included another new record for 1 Group of 122 Lancasters and fifty-eight Wellingtons, of which 300 Squadron contributed a very creditable sixteen. It was some time since a senior officer had been on the Order of Battle, but on this night W/C Kucharski led the squadron contingent away at 23.04 in HE464. There were no early returns as they headed eastwards to the Ruhr in favourable weather conditions, which persisted all the way to the target. When still eighty miles short, a heavy pall of smoke could already be observed from the burning city, but this did not seem to present a visibility problem to those on their bombing run. W/C Kucharski bombed from 14,500 feet at 01.09, by which time the northern half of the city was well alight, but the attack had not yet reached the southern districts. He praised the work of the Pathfinders, and reported the glow of fires visible from 140 miles into the return journey. The other squadron crews bombed from 11,000 to 16,500 between 01.10 and 01.55, and all but one returned without major incident to report a highly successful operation. The success was confirmed by reconnaissance, which revealed massive damage in central, northern and eastern districts, where some two thousand buildings had been destroyed, and serious damage had been inflicted upon the city's industry. The defenders fought back, however, and claimed their biggest haul for the campaign yet of thirty-eight aircraft, of which nine were from 1 Group. 300 Squadron's HZ374 was shot down by flak roughly five miles north-north-west of Düsseldorf before bombing, and there were no survivors from the crew of F/O Piatkowski.

Another very large force of 759 aircraft was prepared for an operation to Düsseldorf on the night of the 25/26th, for which 1 Group detailed 116 Lancasters and forty-seven Wellingtons. 300 Squadron had fourteen Wellingtons ready for take-off from Hemswell as the clock ticked towards midnight, and the senior pilot on duty was the station commander, G/C Henry Cozens. There were no early returns, and the squadron crews arrived in the target area in the early stages of the operation to find varying amounts of cloud, and no concentration of marking and bombing. G/C Cozens assessed that fires were scattered over fifteen square miles, and crews, who had been at Dortmund two nights earlier, could tell that this was not going according to plan. They carried out their attacks from 11,000 to 16,500 feet between 01.41 and 02.03, and apart from one aircraft sustaining a little flak damage to the rear turret, they all returned safely to report modest results. Sgt Garczynski and crew made it all the way to the target and back, only to discover that their incendiaries had hung up and were still on board. Reconnaissance confirmed that the operation had not been successful, largely because the Pathfinders had been unable to establish their position, and enemy decoy markers and fire sites were also in use. Twenty-seven aircraft were missing, and this was a high price to pay for little return.

The next round of the Ruhr offensive was directed at Essen, and came on the night of the 27/28th, when a force of over five hundred aircraft included 104 Lancasters and twenty-nine Wellingtons from 1 Group. Ten 300 Squadron crews underwent briefing, eight of them with NCO pilots, and they lined up for take-off shortly after 23.00. By this time two crews had already departed for mining duties off the Frisians, and they would return safely after successfully delivering their stores into the allocated positions. HE289 took off for Essen at 23.04, and an hour later, when it was at 17,000 feet just beyond the midpoint between Great Yarmouth and the Dutch coast, the intercom failed. A repair was attempted, but at 00.20 Sgt Jawoszek abandoned the sortie and turned for home. HE749 was deep into Holland and heading in a south-easterly direction towards the German frontier when it was attacked three times in eleven minutes by a BF110. The bomb load was jettisoned from 16,500 feet at 00.47, and Sgt Garczynski was able to evade further attention. The others arrived in the target area to find up to ten-tenths cloud with tops above 10,000 feet, and this caused the Pathfinders to employ skymarkers. P/O Hajdukiewicz attacked from 18,000 feet at 01.04, after following Pathfinder route markers to the target from the north. Two minutes earlier he had witnessed two large explosions, which seemed larger than those typically created by a 4,000 pounder. As he left the target he noticed a red ground marker some sixteen miles to the north-west, which was darker than usual and burned in a suspicious manner. This was probably a decoy, and reconnaissance would later reveal, that, as much of the bombing had fallen short, it may well have been very effective. F/S Lech and crew had completed their attack when the port engine failed, and they came home on the other one. The remaining 300 Squadron crews delivered their ordnance from 16,000 to 19,000 feet between 01.02 and 01.05, and returned safely to report large explosions and fires visible for forty minutes into the homeward leg. Almost five hundred buildings were destroyed, mostly in central and northern districts, but ten other towns were also hit in an echo of pre-Oboe times. Twenty-three aircraft failed to return.

The final bombing operation of the month took place on the night of the 29/30th, and was directed at Barmen, one of the twin towns known jointly as Wuppertal, situated on the southern rim of the Ruhr region, roughly twenty miles east of Düsseldorf. The force of seven hundred aircraft included ninety-six Lancasters and thirty-one Wellingtons from 1 Group. 300 Squadron contributed ten aircraft, which began to take-off at 23.00, and all reached the target to find clear skies, but haze and smoke obscuring ground detail. The Pathfinders had provided plentiful and accurate markers, and the Hemswell crews homed in on these from 14,000 to 18,500 feet between 00.55 and 01.15, before returning home to describe the target as "blitzed". F/O Myszkowski and crew went off track outbound, and found themselves coned by about twenty searchlights and targeted by heavy flak. They took violent and effective evasive action, and bombed Düsseldorf from 14,000 feet as an alternative. This operation was one of those relatively rare occasions when all facets of the plan came together in perfect harmony, and it spelled catastrophe for the unfortunate inhabitants of the doomed town. Concentration of marking and bombing had always been the key to success, and it was achieved completely on this night, gutting by fire the centre of the town, and destroying in all four thousand houses and over two hundred industrial premises. Unusually, the number of buildings classed as completely destroyed was double the number seriously damaged, and the level of devastation was reflected in the estimate, that 80% of the town's built-up area had been reduced to ruins. The death toll, at 3,400 people, was also many times higher than in any previous raid on an urban target, but Bomber Command's losses were high as well, amounting to thirty-three aircraft.

While the bulk of the Command remained at home on the following night, six 300 Squadron Wellingtons joined other aircraft to lay mines off the Biscay coast. It was familiar territory for the Hemswell brigade, which got away safely before 22.00, and found the target area off St Nazaire under clear skies with good visibility. They located la Calebasse Rocks without difficulty, and carried out their timed runs to complete a successful operation. The squadron was involved in eleven operations during the month, and dispatched 108 sorties for the loss of two aircraft.

June 1943

The moon period at the start of June kept the heavy brigade on the ground for the first ten nights, but mining continued, and five 300 Squadron Wellingtons took off shortly before 23.00 on the 3rd to sow two vegetables each in the waters off Lorient. They made timed runs from Pont-Aven, and delivered their mines from 1,500 feet between 01.33 and 01.42, before returning safely home. When the main force returned to the fray on the night of the 11/12th, Düsseldorf was selected as the objective for a force of 783 aircraft, including a new record for 1 Group of 128 Lancasters along with fifty Wellingtons. Sixteen crews were briefed at Hemswell during the afternoon, and twelve of them had NCO pilots. They took off either side of 23.30, but F/L Winiarek was forced to turn back at 00.43 after HE289 developed an unspecified technical problem. The others pushed on to the target, following yellow Pathfinder route markers, until the red and green skymarkers began to descend towards the cloud tops and identify the aiming point. They delivered their all-incendiary loads from 17,000 to 19,500 feet between 01.35 and 01.58, and returned home to report a massive concentration of fires, a very large explosion at 01.51, a pall of black smoke drifting up to 15,000 feet, and the reflection of the inferno still visible from the Dutch coast on the way home. Reconnaissance confirmed the success of the operation, which might have been even more destructive but for an errant Oboe marker fourteen miles north-east of the city, which persuaded a proportion of the force to bomb open country. The main weight of the attack fell squarely onto central and southern districts, where the fires covered an area of forty square kilometres. More than forty war industry factories suffered a complete stoppage of production, while almost thirteen hundred people were killed, and 140,000 others were rendered homeless. The Command had to contend with the loss of thirty-eight heavy bombers, however, another new record for the campaign, and "Happy Valley's" evil reputation was now set for all time.

The main operation on the night of the 12/13th was against Bochum, for which a force of five hundred aircraft took off. Wellingtons were not involved in this highly successful raid, but thirty-four of the type were sent mining. Two 300 Squadron crews were assigned to the Nectarines region off the Frisians, F/L Winiarek and F/S Ekiert taking off at 22.50 and delivering their two mines each into the allocated positions from 1,200 and 2,000 feet between 00.29 and 00.35 respectively. Two nights later, a relatively modest main force of 197 Lancasters, almost half of them from 1 Group, took off for Oberhausen, and those arriving over the target accurately bombed the Oboe markers, and destroyed 267 buildings. The seventeen failures to return represented an 8.4% loss rate, which demonstrated, that although Lancasters fared best in a mixed force, when operating alone they were equally vulnerable to night fighters. In a further effort to fine-tune target marking techniques, sixteen H2S equipped Pathfinder heavy aircraft led a raid on Cologne on the night of the 16/17th, for which 1 and 5 Groups provided the main force of two hundred Lancasters. This would be the first of four attacks on the city over a three week period. A high level of equipment failure on this night led to late and sparse skymarking, and the resultant bombing was scattered, although moderately effective. Four hundred houses were destroyed, many public buildings and railway stations were hit, and sixteen industrial premises sustained damage.

300 Squadron had spent more than a week away from the operational scene by the time that air-tests were in progress on the morning of the 21st. HF591 took off at 10.17 with the crew of F/L Pokorniewski, as one of two engaged in height tests. At 10.50 it was seen to break cloud in a steep dive and crash four miles east-south-east of Lincoln, killing all on board. Sixteen crews were called to briefing later that afternoon, and were told that that night's operation would be against the Ruhr town of Krefeld, situated on the

300 Squadron Wellingtons at Hemswell in mid-June 1943. Note the picture of a dwarf painted on unidentified aircraft in the foreground. (PISM via WM).

western edge of the region, north-west of Düsseldorf. It would be the first in a hectic round of four major operations in the space of five nights for the Command, and it would also be the final operation for 300 Squadron from Hemswell. A force of seven hundred aircraft was made ready, of which 110 Lancasters and thirty-seven Wellingtons were provided by 1 Group. This time there were senior officers lining up for take-off at Hemswell in the twenty minutes before midnight, not least among them G/C Cozens, the station commander. W/C Kucharski was also taking part, and they all got away safely, each carrying an all-incendiary bomb load.

Conditions in the target area were ideal, and the Pathfinder marking near perfect, all of which provided the main force crews with an opportunity to exploit the situation to the maximum. The 300 Squadron crews aimed at ground markers from 16,000 to 18,000 feet between 01.39 and 01.48, and fourteen returned safely to report highly concentrated bombing, masses of large fires and few if any examples of loads falling outside of the target. They also described smoke rising high into the air, and the glow of fires visible well into the return journey. A number, including G/C Cozens, poured scorn on the "pathetic" decoy markers fired up from the ground by the enemy, which were clearly distinguishable from the genuine article. Post-raid analysis revealed that most of the 2,300 tons of bombs had fallen within three miles of the aiming point. The whole centre of the town was engulfed in flames, and over 5,500 houses were reduced to ruins, a new record for the war, while more than a thousand people lost their lives. The bomber losses were also a new record for the campaign, however, and the seventy-two thousand people made homeless by the raid would have been cheered to know, that over three hundred of their assailants in forty-four aircraft would not be returning home either. There were two empty dispersals at Hemswell, those belonging to HE327 and HE985, which had contained the crews of Sgt Bronicki and F/S Bialobrowka respectively. Both disappeared into the sea, and only one body from the former was eventually washed ashore at Castricum on the Dutch coast for burial.

Sgt Jozef Zawistowski (W.Op.) who flew 26 sorties with 300 Squadron between June and November 1943. On his first operation on 21/22nd June 1943 to Krefeld his Wellington was badly shot up by flak. He bandaged the severely wounded navigator and took over navigation assisting his pilot on successful return home. For his navigational knowledge and exceptional bravery in the face of the enemy on his maiden operation he was awarded the Virtuti Militari Cross. (A. Sinclair).

Later on the 22nd 300 Squadron departed Hemswell to return to Ingham, where it would remain for more than eight months. On the following night a force of 557 aircraft was made ready for a raid on Mülheim, a town on the east bank of the Rhine, north-east of Cologne. Another highly accurate and concentrated attack ensured that it suffered the destruction of over eleven hundred houses, while dozens of public buildings sustained damage, and many industrial premises suffered loss of production. The Command's losses remained high at thirty-five, but just three came from 1 Group's contribution of 102 Lancasters. On the following afternoon the funerals took place at Newark cemetery of the 300 Squadron crew killed on the 21st. Afterwards nine crews were briefed for mining operations that night off Lorient and St Nazaire, and they all got away safely either side of 22.00. The Lorient contingent pinpointed on Pointe de Trevignon to the north or Etel to the south, while the St Nazaire crews timed their runs from la Calebasse Rocks, and all completed their sorties as briefed, with just one sustaining slight flak damage. One crew commented on the number of times the letter V was flashed to them as they crossed France.

After a night's rest following Mülheim, 630 aircraft took off for Wuppertal, to attack the Elberfeld half, having destroyed its twin Barmen a month earlier. 1 Group dispatched ninety-five Lancasters and thirty-three Wellingtons, eleven of the latter provided by 300 Squadron. W/C Kucharski was the senior pilot on duty as they began taking off shortly after 23.00, and S/L Kuzian was also on the Order of Battle. The route to the target took them between Cologne and Düsseldorf, where they were subjected to heavy flak, and a number of the squadron's aircraft, including the commanding officer's HE464, sustained damage. The target was well-marked by the Pathfinders with red and green TIs, and the squadron participants delivered their loads from 13,000 to 19,000 feet between 01.10 and 01.31, before nine of them returned home. At debriefing they spoke of many large and medium fires, explosions and smoke, and a glow reflected in the sky visible from the Dutch coast. It would be established later, that they had participated in a raid even more devastating than the one on Barmen a month earlier. It had resulted in the destruction of three thousand houses and 171 industrial premises, with a further 2,500 buildings suffering serious damage. Over 90% of the town's built-up area was laid waste on this one night, and eighteen hundred people were killed. Another thirty-four Bomber Command crews paid the price for this success, five of them from 1 Group, and among these were two belonging to 300 Squadron. HF606 was shot down by flak and crashed at Kevelaer, close to the Dutch border north-west of Duisburg, and there were no survivors from the crew of Sgt Jawoszek. HZ376 was also brought down by flak near Krefeld, but the pilot, F/O Turecki, and his rear gunner, Sgt Kosiarski, escaped with their lives to become PoWs.

An attempt by a force of 450 aircraft to hit the important oil town of Gelsenkirchen foundered on the night of the 25/26th, when a proportion of the Oboe aircraft experienced equipment failure. In an echo of the past, bombs were sprayed all over the Ruhr, and the disappointment was compounded by the loss of thirty aircraft. 1 Group had put up eighty-eight Lancasters and ten Wellingtons, and seven of these were among the missing. 300 Squadron did not participated in the main operation, but sent four crews mining in the Nectarines garden off the Frisians. All delivered their mines as briefed from 1,000 to 1,500 feet between 00.50 and 00.56 after pinpointing on or near Schiermonikoog, and returned without incident.

Either side of midnight on the 28/29th over six hundred aircraft departed their stations for the first of three raids on Cologne in the space of ten nights spanning the turn of the month. 1 Group sent eighty-nine Lancasters and twenty-seven Wellingtons, nine of the latter provided by 300 Squadron. S/L Kuzian was the senior pilot on duty as they all got away safely, but two abandoned their sortie at Knokke on the Belgian coast just south of the Scheldt Estuary. HF590 developed an overheating engine, and F/O Myszkowski turned back at 00.59, to be followed one minute later by HF598 with a malfunctioning starboard engine. It seems that Sgt Cholewa had lost height during evasive action, and had been unable to regain it when the engine faltered. He hung on to his incendiaries until almost at the mid-point of the sea crossing, but ultimately decided to dump them. F/L Winiarek and crew were at 19,000 feet over Germany when attacked by night fighters, and they also jettisoned their incendiaries at 01.43 some twelve miles south-west of Bonn, before making it safely back home. Those reaching the target found the skies heavy with cloud, making it necessary for the Pathfinders to employ predominantly the less reliable skymarking method. Only half of the Oboe Mosquito crews were able to mark as briefed, and did so some seven minutes late. Despite these setbacks, the operation developed into the most awesomely-destructive assault yet visited upon a German city. The crews followed green route markers to the target, and aimed at red release-point flares with green stars. The 300 Squadron crews bombed from 16,200 to 19,000 feet between 01.56 and 02.00, before returning home unable to give an assessment of the outcome. In fact, 6,400 buildings had been totally destroyed, including forty-three industrial premises, and 4,377 people lost their lives, while a further 230,000 were rendered homeless. In return, a slightly more modest twenty-five aircraft were shot down, and among those missing from 1 Group was a 300 Squadron Wellington. HZ438 was on its way home when intercepted and shot down by a night fighter over Belgium at 02.22, and there were no survivors from the crew of the experienced F/S Kleinschmidt, who was close to the end of his first tour.

On the following night four of the squadron's crews took off shortly before 22.30 to mine the waters off St Nazaire. Working off the usual pinpoint for this region, la Calebasse Rocks, they each delivered two mines from 3,000 to 5,000 feet between 01.08 and 01.26, and returned without incident to land at Harwell in Oxfordshire. During the course of the month the squadron operated ten times, generating seventy-six sorties and a new record loss of five aircraft.

July 1943

Ingham, late 1943. Wellington LN297 BH-P with a crew, probably of W/O Ludwik Lech. This aircraft took part in 28 operations from July – Dec. 1943. (PISM via WM)

The month began for 300 Squadron with a celebration of the anniversary of its formation, and the 1st was devoted entirely to this momentous occasion. A presentation of awards to flying personnel was followed by a communal lunch held in No 3 hangar, and then by an exhibition of the work of the squadron's mechanics. At 16.00 there was a performance by actors of the Lwowska Fala Theatre in the airmen's institute, and finally at 18.00 a garden fete was held on the playing field.

It fell to Cologne to open the operational account for July on the night of the 3/4th, for which a force of 653 aircraft was made ready. I Group was represented by one hundred Lancasters and twenty-nine Wellingtons, 300 Squadron providing a dozen of the latter. They were all safely airborne from Ingham by 23.20 led by S/L Kuzian, but F/L Stadtmüller was forced to turn back at 00.10, after HE869 developed an oxygen system problem when at 16,000 feet. They tried for twenty minutes to repair a leak in the distributor with insulating tape, but were unsuccessful, and the entire oxygen supply was gone within forty-five minutes of being turned on. The others pressed on in favourable weather conditions to find the target under clear skies and in good visibility, which enabled the crews to identify ground detail. The aiming point, on the industrialized eastern bank of the Rhine, was well marked by the Pathfinders with red and green target indicators, and the crews had these in their sights as they delivered their all-incendiary bomb loads from 13,000 to 18,000 feet between 01.20 and 01.28. Fires were seen to be taking hold in many parts of the city on both sides of the river, and F/L Spychala described a line running from north to south through the city centre close to the river. He also witnessed a very large explosion at 01.20 in a north-western district, which was followed by an intense and substantial fire. His estimation, that the glow from the burning city was visible half way to the coast on the return journey, was echoed by other crews. F/S Lech had difficulty opening his bomb doors, and he was past the aiming point before he could let his load go some two miles south-east of the city. It was on this night that the Luftwaffe introduced its new Wilde Sau (Wild Boar) night fighter tactic, in which single engine day fighters were employed over the target city to pick off bombers silhouetted against the fires below. The operation was another outstanding success for the Command, which destroyed a further 2,200 houses and twenty industrial premises for the loss of thirty aircraft, six of them from 1 Group.

The Cologne series was concluded on the night of the 8/9th, when an all-Lancaster heavy force from 1, 5 and 8 Groups destroyed almost 2,400 more houses and apartment blocks, along with nineteen industrial premises. When the Cologne city authorities were able to assess the cost of the three raids, they catalogued eleven thousand buildings destroyed, 5,500 people killed, and a further 350,000 made homeless. Also on this night, five 300 Squadron crews, all with officer pilots, joined forty others for mining duties at various locations. For the Polish crews it was familiar territory off St Nazaire, and all successfully delivered their mines from 1,500 to 2,000 feet between 03.02 and 03.10 before returning home without incident.

Another failure at Gelsenkirchen on the night of the 9/10th effectively brought an end to the Ruhr campaign, although two further operations to the region would be mounted at the end of the month. Harris could look back over the past five months with genuine satisfaction at the performance of his squadrons, and point to Oboe as the crucial factor. Most of the operations attended by Oboe Mosquitos had been a major success, while those beyond the device's range had continued to be something of a lottery. Losses had been grievously high, and "Happy Valley's" reputation had been justifiably earned, but much of Germany's industrial heartland now lay in ruins, and the aircraft factories at home had more than kept pace with the rate of attrition. The training units were continuing to feed fresh crews into the fray to fill the gaps, and a gradual expansion was taking place to further strengthen Harris's hand. With confidence high, Harris now sought to rock the very foundations of Nazi morale, by erasing from the map one of Germany's most important cities in a short, sharp series of raids until the job was done.

In the meantime, 1, 5 and 8 Groups carried out a highly destructive attack on Turin on the night of the 12/13th, in which almost eight hundred people were killed, but the Command also lost one of its favourite sons. W/C Nettleton, the commanding officer of 44 Squadron, who had earned a Victoria Cross for his part in the epic daylight raid on the M.A.N. diesel engine factory at Augsburg in April 1942, was shot down into the English Channel on the way home, and died with his crew. On the following night a force of 374 aircraft departed their stations for the town of Aachen, situated in the Eiffel region of Germany close to the Dutch and Belgian frontiers. 300 Squadron contributed fifteen Wellingtons, which were all safely airborne by 00.23, and not one was forced to return early. They arrived in the target area to find a layer of seven to nine-tenths thin cloud at 10,000 to 12,000 feet, and identified the aiming point by means of the Pathfinder target indicators. It is believed that most of the Ingham contingent were carrying all-incendiary loads, but F/L Stadtmüller had a 4,000 pounder on board, which he delivered from 18,000 feet at 01.58. His squadron colleagues carried out their attacks from 16,000 to 19,000 feet between 01.52 and 02.05, but none could gain a clear picture of what was happening on the ground. Explosions and fires were seen beneath the clouds, and the reflected glow was visible from up to eighty miles away, but returning crews suggested a scattered raid. It was, in fact, a devastating blow, which, according to local reports, destroyed more than 2,900 individual buildings, containing almost seventeen thousand dwelling units, and severely damaged many more of a cultural, administrative and public nature.

Minor operations occupied the following week and a half, and 300 Squadron's next outing came on the night of the 18/19th, when five crews were sent to mine the sea lanes off St Nazaire. They took off either side of 22.00, and found their pinpoint on la Calebasse Rocks with ease in good visibility. They made their timed runs and dropped their mines into the briefed locations from 1,200 to 2,000 feet between 00.52 and 01.00, before returning without incident. Having been spared by the weather from hosting the first one thousand bomber raid in May 1942, Hamburg became Harris's choice for Operation Gomorrah, to be mounted during the final week of July. As Germany's Second City, its political status was undeniable, and as a centre of U-Boot construction and other important war industries, it had always been at the top of the Command's list of priority targets. There were other considerations of an operational nature, however, which also made it an attractive proposition, chief among which was its location. Close to a coastline, it could be approached from the sea, without the need to traverse large tracts of hostile territory, and would be fairly easy to pinpoint. It was also close enough to the bomber stations to allow a large force to approach and withdraw in the few hours of total darkness afforded by mid summer. Finally, beyond the range of Oboe, it boasted the wide River Elbe to provide a strong H2S signature for the navigators high above. Operation Gomorrah would also benefit from the first use of Window, the tinfoil-backed strips of paper, which, when dispensed into the slipstream, produced radar-reflecting clouds. The effect was to swamp the enemy night fighter, searchlight and gun-laying radar with false returns, making it impossible to pick out a genuine hostile aircraft. The device had actually been available for a year, but its use had been vetoed in case the enemy copied it. Germany had, in fact, already developed a similar system under the code name Düppel, which it too had withheld for the same reason.

Briefings for the opening round of what might be termed the Battle of Hamburg, took place on the 24th, and that evening 791 aircraft took off, 158 of them from 1 Group, of which thirty-five were Wellingtons. 300 Squadron dispatched nine aircraft from Ingham for the main operation, while three others went mining in the Eglantine garden between Heligoland and the Elbe Estuary. They got away safely by 00.24, with S/L Kuzian the senior pilot among the Hamburg element. An early indication of the effectiveness of Window was the relatively low number of combats before the target was reached. A number of aircraft were shot down during this stage of the operation, but they were well off track, and may have been returning early with technical difficulties. Whatever, they were well outside of the protection of the Window screen.

The efficacy of Window became clearly apparent in the target area, where the usually efficient co-ordination between the searchlight and flak batteries was absent, and anti-aircraft defence was at best random. The Pathfinder marking was slightly misplaced and scattered, but close enough to the aiming point to make little difference to the outcome, had the main force crews produced concentrated bombing. The 300 Squadron crews reported no cloud, but hazy conditions, and a considerable amount of smoke beginning to rise skyward from the already-burgeoning fires. They bombed from 17,000 to 19,500 feet between 01.21 and 01.33, and all returned safely to report concentrated fires, thick, black smoke up to 16,000 feet and the glow of fires visible from seventy miles away. Reconnaissance revealed that an extensive creep-back had developed, which cut a six-mile-long swathe of destruction from the city centre along the line of approach, out across the north-western districts and into open country, where a substantial number of bomb loads were wasted. Fifteen hundred people on the ground lost their lives, but in terms of the heavy damage inflicted, it was an encouraging start to the campaign. A bonus was the loss of just twelve aircraft, which suggested that, for the time being at least, Window had handed the advantage to the bombers. Meanwhile, the gardeners in northern waters had pinpointed on St Peter Head, and carried out timed runs of eight minutes to the drop zone, where each delivered two mines from 1,300 to 1,500 feet between 01.07 and 01.17.

On the following night Harris planned another attack on Hamburg, but a combination of lingering smoke over the target and the proximity of a cold front persuaded him to switch his force to Essen, where he could take advantage of the body blow dealt to the enemy's defensive system by Window. 705 aircraft took off, including 148 from 1 Group, of which seventeen were Wellingtons provided by 300 Squadron. W/C Kucharski was the senior pilot on duty as they all got away safely in the minutes leading to 23.00, but F/S Cholewa had to abandon his sortie at 23.57 midway between the English and Dutch coasts. They had reached 17,000 feet, when HF598 dropped to 15,000, and refused to climb again, even after some of the incendiary load had been jettisoned. The others reached the target to find thin, patchy cloud, but good visibility, and they delivered their all-incendiary loads from 16,500 to 19,500 feet between 00.51 and 01.01. All but one returned to report a highly successful operation, with many large fires and smoke rising to 12,000 feet. HZ486 was the missing 300 Squadron Wellington, one of twenty-six failures to return, and it was established later that it had been hit by flak and crashed west-south-west of Hagen, and, therefore, south-east of Essen. The crash location strongly suggests that Sgt Garczynski and crew had carried out their attack, and were victims of the Essen flak, which was always intense. They continued on the same heading as the bombing run while they dealt with the consequences of their situation, and three of the crew managed to take to their parachutes, leaving the bomb-aimer and wireless operator to perish in the crash. It seems that the pilot struck his head on leaving the stricken Wellington, and died soon after reaching the ground, while the navigator and rear gunner were soon in enemy hands. The operation was a triumph, which destroyed over 2,800 houses and fifty industrial premises, while the Krupp works suffered its worst night of the war. On the following morning Dr Gustav Krupp apparently suffered a stroke, which he survived, but from which he never recovered.

A night's rest preceded the second round of Operation Gomorrah, for which 787 aircraft were made ready during the course of the 27th, including a contribution of 159 from 1 Group, of which sixteen Wellingtons represented 300 Squadron. They began taking off shortly after 22.30, with S/L Kuzian the senior pilot on duty. HE805 refused to climb above 14,500 feet, and Sgt Kalfas decided to bomb a last resort target of St Peter Head, before returning home with a very disappointed crew. What followed the arrival of the rest of the force over Hamburg was both unprecedented and unforeseeable, and was the result of a conspiracy of factors. A spell of unusually hot and dry weather during July had left tinderbox conditions within parts of the city, and when the Pathfinders dropped their markers, they did so with unaccustomed concentration two miles to the east of the planned city centre aiming point, and into the densely populated working class residential districts of Hamm, Hammerbrook and Borgfeld. 729 main force crews followed up with uncharacteristic accuracy and scarcely any creep-back, and delivered most of their 2,300 tons of bombs into this relatively compact area. The 300 Squadron crews were over the target at 16,500 to 19,500 between 01.17 and 01.41, and returned to describe a good concentration of fires visible from a hundred miles away. F/L Spychala had trouble with the bomb doors on HE807, and made three runs across the target before being able to release his all-incendiary load. The crews could not have known the extent of

Nose art of a fire-breathing dragon painted on the fuselage of unidentified 300 Squadron Wellington. (PISM via WM)

the disaster unfolding below as the individual fires took hold, and joined together to form one giant conflagration, which sucked in oxygen from surrounding areas at hurricane velocity to feed its voracious appetite. Such was the ferocity of this meteorological phenomenon, that trees were uprooted and flung bodily into the flames, along with debris and people. The temperature at the seat of the inferno reached a thousand degrees Celcius, and it was only once all of the combustible material had been consumed, that the fire began to subside. An estimated forty thousand people perished on this one night alone, and on the following morning the first of an eventual 1.2 million inhabitants began to file out of the tortured city. Of the seventeen missing aircraft just three were from 1 Group.

305 Squadron changed leaders for the final time as a Bomber Command unit on the 28th, when W/C Czolowski was succeeded by W/C Konopasek, who had operated seven times with 300 Squadron before his posting to 305 Squadron at the beginning of April. The assault on Hamburg continued on the night of the 29/30th at the hands of another force of nearly eight hundred aircraft, to which 1 Group contributed 150 Lancasters and Wellingtons, including fourteen of the latter provided by 300 Squadron. They took off either side of 22.30, with no less than five pilots of flight lieutenant rank on the Order of Battle. There were no early returns, and they reached the target to find fires already burning fiercely, and too much smoke to be able to pick out ground detail. The Pathfinders made their approach from the north, and again dropped their markers to the east of the city centre, and a little south of the districts afflicted by the firestorm. The main force reverted to type on this night, and allowed a four mile creep-back to develop, which spread across the devastation from the previous raid, before hitting other residential districts beyond, and creating a large area of fire. The 300 Squadron crews bombed on the yellow and green target indicators from 17,000 to 20,000 feet between 01.08 and 01.14, and returned home safely to report another

Buildings blaze in the Hamburg inferno during Operation Gomorrah. The raid demonstrated to the German people and their leaders the awesome, and awful, potential of Bomber Command at full strength.

highly effective attack. F/L Stadtmüller delivered his 4,000 pounder onto what he believed was the docks area, and he described a pillar of black smoke rising to 6,000 feet from the same one-thousand-yard-square area. F/S Skowron reported the smoke to be at 17,000 feet, and Sgt Rech and crew could see the reflection some 180 miles away as they flew home at 15,000 feet. Their impressions were confirmed after another 2,300 tons of bombs continued the city's torment, but as the Luftwaffe began to recover from the effects of Window, so the bomber losses began to escalate. Twenty-eight were missing on this night, but only three of them came from 1 Group.

Before the final assault on Hamburg took place, a relatively modest heavy force of under three hundred four-engine aircraft destroyed over 80% of Remscheid's built-up area on the night of the 30/31st, to finally bring down the curtain on the Ruhr campaign. 1 Group was called upon to provide thirty aircraft, and all returned safely. There were nine operations for 300 Squadron during the month, with ninety-six sorties and one missing aircraft.

August 1943

The fourth and final act of Operation Gomorrah opened the new month's account on the night of the 2/3rd, and brought an unsatisfactory conclusion to what had been an awesome display of Bomber Command's potential. 1 Group provided 153 aircraft towards the 740 that were to complete the destruction of Germany's second city, and of these, fifteen Wellingtons represented 300 Squadron. A late take-off had them all safely airborne by 23.51, but it was not long before the first one was on its way back. HE807 lost its starboard engine when at 800 feet, and found itself on approach to the town of Worksop, some twenty miles to the west of Ingham in the neighbouring county of Nottinghamshire. By this time it had sunk to 300 feet, and despite dumping the incendiary load, F/L Spychala was unable to climb on one engine, and sought out the first apparently flat field he could find. This was at Clumber Park, two miles south-east of the town, where a successful forced landing was carried out at 00.05. The Wellington caught fire, but all of the crew had scrambled clear with bruises and grazes before the wreckage was consumed by the flames.

The other crews pressed on in increasingly unpleasant weather, and encountered severe icing conditions and electrical storms over the North Sea. Many were persuaded to jettison their loads and turn back at this stage, and a number of 300 Squadron crews were among them. F/L Stadtmüller was carrying a 4,000 pounder, which he let go from 18,000 feet at 02.12 over Germany, when still some miles to the south-west of Hamburg. He described the conditions as the worst he had experienced. Sgt Kalfas found ten-tenths cloud with tops at 23,000 feet as he crossed the German coast, and, on seeing no evidence of Pathfinder activity, dumped his all-incendiary load in the Bremerhaven area, some sixty or so miles short of the target. Those from the squadron who pressed on to the target delivered their loads from 14,000 to 19,500 feet between 02.23 and 02.35, and contributed to a widely scattered attack. After bombing, F/L Winiarek passed over the eastern extremity of the city, and, through a break in the clouds, caught sight of a dummy fire site about nine miles north-east of the aiming point. He also got a good view of Hamburg, and confirmed that there were very few fires to be seen anywhere within the city boundaries. HF605 had apparently been damaged by a night fighter and flak by the time the crew began searching for the target on ETA. Suddenly the aircraft became encased in ice, and the crew members had just enough time to don their parachutes before the Wellington broke into three sections. Rear gunner, Sgt Jaremko, opened the doors of his turret and fell out backwards to land safely, and the bomb-aimer and wireless operator also survived after simply falling out as the aircraft broke up. They all became PoWs, but the pilot and navigator, F/O Smyk and P/O Skalisz respectively, lost

Sgt Jan Kalfas completed his tour of 30 operations with 300 Squadron between April and November 1943. Later he flew 11 special missions with 301 Special Duties Squadron at Brindisi (Italy) during 1944/1945. (PISM via WM)

their lives. Gunner, Sgt Pilat, had already spent two years as a Russian PoW, and now faced the prospect of almost two more in German hands. The operation was a complete failure, and inflicted no significant new damage, but, in truth, the damage had already been done. Thirty aircraft failed to return, eight of them from 1 Group, the two Polish squadrons losing two Wellingtons between them. This proved to be the final operation in Bomber Command for 305 Squadron, which would join the 2nd Tactical Air Force in the following month.

Italy was by now teetering on the brink of capitulation, and the second week of August was devoted largely to nudging it over the edge. The campaign began on the night of the 7/8th, with attacks on Genoa, Turin and Milan by 1, 5 and 8 Groups, G/C Searby of 83 Squadron using the Turin raid as a trial run for the Master Bomber role he would be assuming for a very important operation ten nights hence. Before the next trip across the Alps, over four hundred aircraft destroyed thirteen hundred buildings in Mannheim on the night of the 9/10th, despite the presence of cloud, which made identification of the Pathfinder markers very difficult. This was followed by an attack on Nuremberg twenty-four hours later by a force of six hundred aircraft, which included 114 Lancasters from 1 Group. Again cloud intervened to prevent an accurate assessment of the outcome, but the glow of fires visible from up to 150 miles away suggested an effective attack, and there were no losses from the Group. While this operation was in progress, the only two remaining Wellington units in the group, 166 and 300 Squadrons, sent six and twelve aircraft respectively on mining sorties. S/L Kuzian was the senior pilot on duty as they departed Ingham shortly after 21.30, and headed for the Nectarines garden off the Frisians. They found varying amounts of cloud up to ten-tenths, and fair to moderate visibility beneath the cloud base, which was somewhere between 1,500 and 3,500 feet. The drop zones were in open sea, well to the north of Terschelling and Ameland, and this meant obtaining a Gee fix as the starting point for the timed runs. All twelve from the squadron completed their assigned tasks from 1,000 to 2,200 feet between 23.26 and 23.36, and returned safely.

111 Lancasters from 1 Group joined an attack on Milan on the 12/13th, while a simultaneous assault on Turin was delivered by a predominantly Stirling force. The attack at Milan proceeded in perfect weather conditions following accurate Pathfinder marking, and the defences were described in the 1 Group ORB as "well up to their standard of hopelessness". Meanwhile, eight 300 Squadron crews carried out mining off St Nazaire in excellent weather conditions characterized by clear skies and bright moonlight. F/L Winiarek had led them away at 20.49, and, as usual, la Calebasse Rocks provided the pinpoint for the timed runs. Each crew delivered two mines into the required locations from 1,200 to 2,000 feet between 23.53 and 00.21, before returning home without incident. 1, 5 and 8 Groups returned to Milan on the night of the 14/15th, when twenty-eight of the forty-four 1 Group participants were assigned to attack the Breda Pirelli works just outside the city. In the event it proved difficult to identify, and most crews opted to join in the main raid. The group put up sixty-seven Lancasters for a return to Milan on the night of the 15/16th, and the ensuing attack was described as even more destructive than the previous efforts, with smoke rising to ten thousand feet. This concluded the main force Lancaster interest in Italy.

While this operation was in progress, extensive mining operations were taking place off the French coast and the Frisians, for which 300 Squadron contributed thirteen Wellingtons. Nine were assigned to Nectarines, the northern Frisians islands, and four to Trefoil, between Den Helder and the southern tip of Texel, and they took off either side of 21.00 led by W/C Kucharski. He was bound for Trefoil, along with F/Ls Stadtmüller, Winiarek and Wojtulewicz, and they found the target area under cloudless skies and bright moonlight. They delivered their mines from 1,300 to 1,500 feet between 22.18 and 22.23, and returned without incident to report a successful operation. The Nectarines contingent were operating in the same area as on the night of the 10/11th, over open sea north of Terschelling, and F/O Ochedzan was forced to abandon his sortie after his Gee equipment failed. Seven of the others delivered their mines as briefed from 1,000 to 1,500 feet between 22.35 and 22.49, and also returned safely. An SOS message was received from HE768 at 23.20 stating that an engine was on fire. F/S Rech and his crew were just four minutes short of their drop zone at the time, and decided to carry on to deliver their mines as briefed. At 23.50 the Wellington was shot down into the sea off Borkum by a night fighter, killing three of the crew, but the pilot and bomb-aimer, F/S Poddany, survived to spend eight days in their dinghy before being rescued by Germans and taken into captivity. The final raid by the Command on Italy was delivered by elements of 3 and 8 Groups on the night of the 16/17th, after which, all attention turned to a target of great significance for the security of Britain and the free world.

Since the start of hostilities, intelligence had been filtering through to London concerning German research into rocket weapons. As the war progressed and the Enigma codes were broken, it became possible to identify Peenemünde, on the island of Usedom off the Baltic coast, as the centre of such activity. Through the interception and decoding of signals traffic, it was possible for the brilliant scientist, Dr R V Jones, to monitor the V-1 trials taking place over the Baltic, and thereby to assess the weapon's range capability, data he would use in 1944 to feed disinformation to the enemy. Reconnaissance flights over northern Germany frequently passed, as if by accident, over the research and development establishment, to enable a picture of its activities to be built up, and by the summer of 1943, enough evidence was to hand to cause alarm. Curiously, Churchill's chief scientific adviser, Professor Lindemann, or Lord Cherwell as he became, steadfastly refused to give credence to rocket weapons, and even when confronted with a photograph of a V-2 on a trailer at Peenemünde, taken by a PRU Mosquito in June, he remained unmoved. It required the combined urgings of Dr Jones and Duncan Sandys to impress upon Churchill the need to act, and it was at last decided to attack the site at the first suitable opportunity. This arose on the night of the 17/18th, for which a complex and detailed plan was prepared under the code name Operation Hydra. The operation was largely successful, and delayed the development of the V-2 by a number of weeks, and forced the production of secret weapons underground, while the rocket's flight testing was moved eastwards into Poland.

300 Squadron had not been involved in operational activity since the night of the 15/16th, and the time was fast approaching when the venerable old Wellington would be retired from bombing operations, although it would continue on in a mining role in the hands of 300 Squadron until well into the coming year. Harris had long believed that Berlin, as the seat and symbol of Nazi authority, held the key to ultimate victory, and that its destruction would bring an early end to the war. There has long been a question over the true starting date of the Battle of Berlin. Between the 23/24th of August 1943 and the 24/25th of March 1944, a total of nineteen major operations and one diversionary operation would take place. There is no question that the main battle began on the 18/19th of November, but the question remains, did Harris intend the three operations in late August/early September to be the start of the campaign? There seemed to be no question at Elsham Wolds, where the 103 Squadron ORB states for the 23/24th; "Berlin. Twenty-four aircraft were detailed to attack this target, which begins the so-called Battle of Berlin". Before opening this first phase of his assault on Germany's Capital, however, he dispatched over four hundred aircraft to Leverkusen in the Ruhr on the night of the 22/23rd, wherein lay an important I G Farben chemicals plant. The operation degenerated into something resembling the raids on Ruhr targets in 1942, and bombs were sprayed over twelve other towns in the region.

Sgt Kazimierz Artymiuk started his operational career in 305 Squadron where he completed 21 operations before being posted to 300 Squadron. Then he added another 11 operations to his tally from Aug. to Oct. 1943. In late 1944 he volunteered to fly special missions in 301 Special Duties Squadron at Brindisi (Italy). (PISM via WM)

On the following night 727 aircraft were prepared for the first raid on Berlin since the end of March, and this number included 107 Lancasters from 1 Group. A contingent of Pathfinder Mosquitos was also on hand to lay route markers at predetermined points. The difficulties associated with identifying an aiming point by H2S in an urban sprawl the size of Berlin were made manifest on this night. Instead of the city centre, the Pathfinders marked the southern outskirts, and much of the bombing fell onto outlying communities, something which would become a feature of the entire campaign. Never the less, over 2,600 buildings were destroyed or seriously damaged, and this was the best result yet at the Capital. On the debit side, a new record of fifty-six aircraft failed to return in the face of a spirited defence. 300 Squadron returned to the fray on the night of the 24/25th, when sending fourteen Wellingtons to lay mines in the Nectarines region. G/C Cozens and W/C Kucharski were the senior pilots on duty, the latter leading them away at 20.06. HE869 developed port-engine problems immediately after take-off, and had covered ten miles towards the Lincolnshire coast, when it became necessary to jettison the mines and find somewhere to land. They dumped them three miles east of Faldingworth at 20.37, and Sgt Kalfas made an emergency landing on the airfield, which, unknown to him, had recently opened as a decoy airfield to protect Lindholme, and would, in the coming year, become home to 300 Squadron. The others all arrived in the garden area, off Schiermonikoog, and found slightly misty conditions up to around 800 feet, but visibility of two to three miles, and delivered their stores into the allocated positions from 1,200 to 2,000 feet between 22.05 and 22.08, before returning safely. HF590 picked up a little flak damage to the top of its starboard wing, and F/L Wojtulewicz complained that the Mablethorpe flak battery had fired at him on the way out and on the way back, but was too inaccurate to pose a danger.

On the following night the Squadron dispatched a dozen Wellingtons to the Jellyfish garden area off Brest. S/L Kuzian was the senior pilot on duty as they became airborne by 19.29, and all reached the approximate target area where their fortunes differed. Sgt Nowocin and F/S Artymiuk found heavy rain and low cloud reducing visibility to nil, and preventing them from locating their final pinpoint. They were well out over the Atlantic, however, some distance from the Pointe-Saint-Mathieu reference point being used by the others. F/L Stadtmüller was experiencing similar difficulties, having travelled too far south and into a bay that resembled the approaches to Brest. They all turned back, while the remainder found their pinpoints in clear weather with some cloud but good visibility, and delivered their mines into the briefed locations from 1,000 to 1,500 feet between 22.18 and 22.43.

The main operation on the night of the 27/28th was against Nuremberg, for which a force of 674 aircraft was made ready. Although the initial marking was accurate, many of the Pathfinder backers-up experienced problems with their H2S sets, and this allowed a creep-back to develop. Despite the attentions of a Master Bomber, it proved impossible to rescue the attack, and much of the bombing was wasted in open country, a disappointment compounded by the loss of thirty-three aircraft. Nine 300 Squadron Wellingtons went mining off St Nazaire on this night, departing Ingham in a very smart seven-minute slot from 19.41. JA116 developed a hydraulics leak at 19.47, when near Abingdon in Oxfordshire, which caused the undercarriage and flaps to deploy. F/L Osmialowski followed protocol by continuing on out to sea to jettison the mines in deep water before returning to land at Wittering in Cambridgeshire. The others all reached the target area to find good visibility, and deliver their mines into the briefed locations from 1,000 to 3,000 feet between 22.50 and 23.01.

For just the second time in the month the squadron prepared to take part in a bombing operation, and briefed fifteen crews on the afternoon of the 30th for an attack that night on the twin towns of Mönchengladbach and Rheydt, situated close to the Dutch border about eighteen miles west of Düsseldorf. A force of 660 aircraft took off, 134 of them provided by 1 Group, and it was 00.31 when G/C Cozens began the procedure at Ingham, with W/C Kucharski in his wake. Sgt Markiewicz was at 11,000 feet on approach to Sheringham on the Norfolk coast at 01.25, when his navigator reported being too ill to continue. Sgt Weyna was also at 11,000 feet fifteen miles south-east of Sheringham at 01.31, when his navigator reported a problem with his oxygen mask tube, forcing them to turn back. The saga of the oxygen mask tubes had actually begun twenty minutes before take-off, when the rear gunner found his missing, and on locating the spare mask, found that deficient too. The captain, who in this crew was the navigator, F/O Koncewicz, gave his to the rear gunner, intending to improvise for his own needs, and they took off. Whatever F/O Koncewicz's plan, it proved to be impracticable, and when the Gee and Monica equipment failed as well, they called it a day.

The others arrived safely in the target area, where they found a thin layer of eight to ten-tenths cloud with tops estimated at between 4,500 and 8,000 feet. Otherwise, visibility was good, and the pathfinder marking, which seemed to begin at 01.56, was accurate and concentrated on the centre, first of Mönchengladbach, and then Rheydt. The 300 Squadron crews had been briefed to attack the former, and they were predominantly carrying all-incendiary loads, but F/O Ochedzan had a 4,000 pounder in his bomb bay. The 300 Squadron crews bombed from 16,000 to 20,000 feet between 02.07 and 02.45, mostly on red target indicators, and many reported being able to pick out the explosions of multiple cookies, while being prevented by the cloud from making a meaningful assessment of the raid. It had, in fact, been highly successful, and had destroyed more than 2,300 buildings in the two towns, including 171 of an industrial nature. Twenty-five aircraft failed to return, and among them was 300 Squadron's JA116, which was shot down by a night fighter at the Dutch coast and crashed west-north-west of Rotterdam, killing F/L Osmialowski and his crew.

The last night of the month brought the second raid of the series on Berlin, and involved a force of over six hundred aircraft, of which 102 Lancasters were provided by 1 Group. Again the marking was inaccurate as the H2S sets proved to be temperamental, and many crews undershot the city, some by up to thirty miles. Less than a hundred houses were destroyed, while Berlin's industry escaped altogether, and the defenders hacked down forty-seven bombers, including 16% of the Stirlings. The squadron carried out nine operations during the month, sending out ninety-seven sorties and losing three aircraft.

September 1943

Operations for the new month began for 300 Squadron with involvement in a small-scale attack on an ammunition dump in the Foret de Mormal in north-eastern France, close to the border with Belgium. Thirty Wellingtons provided the main force element, with Pathfinder Mosquitos and Lancasters carrying out the marking. Twelve crews were briefed at Ingham, and S/L Kuzian was the senior pilot on duty as they began to depart at 20.00. Weather conditions in the target area were good, with varying amounts of cloud at fairly low level obscuring the ground, but the target was identified by red and green Pathfinder markers confirmed by a Gee fix. The Wellingtons were each carrying nine 500lb bombs, which were delivered from 17,500 to 19,000 feet between 22.01 and 22.16, and one returning crew reported a white explosion at 22.02, while another described four large, dull explosions which lit up the clouds for a number of seconds. S/L Kuzian abandoned his sortie at 22.17 and returned with his bombs still on board, after a navigational error and unserviceable Gee equipment prevented him from locating the target.

The final raid on Berlin before the autumn recess was delivered by three hundred Lancasters on the night of the 3/4th. The marking and bombing again fell short, but some loads were deposited in the industrial Siemensstadt district, where a number of war industry factories suffered a serious loss of production. Wide-ranging mining operations occupied the following night, and 300 Squadron provided eight crews for Artichokes, the sea lanes off Lorient. Sgt Klatkiewicz led them away from Ingham at 19.16, and they reached the target area in good order under clear skies with good visibility. They pinpointed on Pont-Aven, confirmed by a Gee fix, and carried out their timed runs from 1,200 to 2,500 feet between 22.22 and 22.35. Sgt Klatkiewicz ran into intense light flak fired simultaneously from the Ile de Groix and the mainland, and dropped his mines about a thousand yards short. 305 Squadron was posted from Bomber Command on the 5th, and became part of the 2nd Tactical Air Force, with which it would fly Mosquitos. This left just 300 Squadron and the C Flight in 138 Squadron to represent Poland in Bomber Command.

The Command's persistently heavy losses continued at the twin cities of Mannheim and Ludwigshafen on the night of the 5/6th, when thirty-four aircraft failed to return from a highly successful operation. The location of the cities astride the Rhine made them ideal for a dual attack, in which the creep-back tendency could be incorporated into the plan. An approach from the west with the aiming point on the eastern side of Mannheim on the eastern bank, guaranteed the spread of the bombing across the city and onto the western bank of the river, where lay Ludwigshafen. Mannheim reported a catastrophe, while the Ludwigshafen authorities recorded almost two thousand fires, and over a thousand buildings destroyed. While this operation was in progress eight 300 Squadron Wellingtons carried out mining sorties, four each in the Rosemary and Trefoil gardens, respectively off Heligoland and the southern end of Texel. Those bound for Rosemary took off first, beginning with F/L Winiarek at 20.17, and S/L Kuzian led the Trefoil element away shortly after 21.00. F/L Winiarek was well to the north of Schiermonikoog when he abandoned his sortie at 21.54, after believing that his Gee had been jammed when at a position sixty miles further east. He had continued on in the hope of picking up a fresh fix, but on failing to do so, brought his mines home. The others reached their respective target areas, where visibility was moderate under four to six-tenths cloud with a base at 2,000 to 3,000 feet. Mines were planted from 1,000 to 1,500 feet as briefed between 22.17 and 22.25, and all returned safely.

On the following night, four hundred aircraft were sent to Munich, eighty-six of them representing 1 Group. Most of the crews bombed on estimated position after a timed run from the Ammersee, and results were inconclusive. Operation Starkey was an attempt to mislead the enemy into believing that an invasion was imminent, and had begun in mid August with highly visible troop movements, and the assembling of landing craft and gliders. Harris was not amused at being ordered to participate in what he considered to be play-acting, but in the event, bad weather prevented the planned Bomber Command involvement during the final week of the month. It was not until the night of the 8/9th of September, that the opportunity arose to for him to carry out his orders to bomb heavy gun emplacements at either end of the small resort town of Le Portel near Boulogne. Perhaps in a gesture of his attitude towards the whole Starkey affair, he committed only his two Oboe Mosquito squadrons and two heavy Pathfinder units, along with the Stirlings of 3 Group, and Wellingtons from 300 Squadron and the training units. Phase I was aimed at the northern site, code-named Religion, and phase II at the southern site, Andante. 300 Squadron briefed fourteen crews, and they were led away by W/C Kucharski at 21.25, only for HE813 to develop terminal engine problems immediately after take-off, and force Sgt Markiewicz to abandon the sortie at 21.33. Two attempts to land with the bombs on board were rendered unsuccessful, because one engine was over-revving and out of control, and caused an overshoot on both occasions. With the likelihood of an emergency landing looming, the nine 500lb bombs and the photo-flash were jettisoned safe three miles east of Ingham at 21.59, but one bomb and the photo-flash detonated. In preparation for the landing, the wireless operator fired off a red warning cartridge, which somehow set fire to fabric and sound-proofing material in the cabin. Sgt Markiewicz eventually put the Wellington on the runway under the most difficult circumstances, immediately cutting both engines to avoid running off the end, and, when it came to a halt, ground crews used chemical extinguishers to put out the fire before it consumed everything. Meanwhile the other crews were well on their way to the French coast, and they found the target under clear skies in bright moonlight. W/C Kucharski and F/L Spychala were the only two with a cookie on board, and these were dropped into the centre of red and green target indicators from around 18,500 feet at 22.46 and 22.50 respectively. The others bombed from 17,000 to 19,000 feet between 22.24 and 22.55, and all returned safely to report what appeared to be a successful operation. F/O Myszkowski and crew had to be thawed out on return, after completing the entire trip with the pilot's escape hatch open. Reconnaissance revealed that neither coastal battery had been put out of action, but the town of le Portel had sustained heavy damage and civilian casualties.

The main force Lancaster squadrons remained off the order of battle for two weeks after Munich, and, in the meantime, one of the most fascinating aspects of the bomber war was taking another step forward. The field of electronics was championed by Harris as the tool by which Bomber Command could at last overcome the difficulties of accurate bombing by night, and thwart the enemy's attempts to make it an uneconomical undertaking. Every gain, however, was temporary, as the enemy always seemed to find a countermeasure. Now that the effectiveness of Window was waning, it was decided to equip 101 Squadron with frequency-jamming apparatus, code named "Jostle". The device provided an opportunity to jam three frequencies simultaneously, with the aim of interfering with ground-to-air night fighter communications. An extra crew member was required to operate Jostle, which was renamed Airborne Cigar or ABC in 101 Squadron usage. He was not required to be a German speaker, capable of broadcasting spurious instructions to enemy pilots, but needed only sufficient knowledge of the language to be able to recognise genuine German transmissions, which he would drown out with engine noise. Once the ABC Flight became operational, a minimum of eight of its aircraft would accompany every major Bomber Command operation for the remainder of the war, spread through the stream not more than ten miles apart, whether or not the rest of 1 Group was on the battle order.

Sgt Kajetan Ignatowski (pilot) who flew 22 operations in 305 Squadron before being posted to 300 Squadron where he added another 8 sorties to his logbook in August and September 1943. (M. Ignatowski)

300 Squadron had enjoyed ten nights without operations when fourteen crews were called to briefings on the afternoon of the 18th, to be told that they would be on gardening duties that night, eight for Beeches (St Nazaire) and six for Nectarines (Frisians). 166 Squadron was also taking part on what would be its final Wellington operation before being stood down to begin conversion to the Lancaster, and this would leave 300 Squadron as the sole Wellington unit in 1 Group, and one of only two in the Command. First away with furthest to fly were the St Nazaire crews, who were all safely airborne by 18.49, led by W/C Kucharski, while the second element departed an hour later with no senior pilots among them. Both target areas were partially cloud-covered, but pinpoints were located at le Croisic and la Calebasse Rocks at St Nazaire, and by Gee fix off Terschelling in the Frisians, and all of the mines were dropped into the correct locations from 1,400 to 3,000 feet between 21.17 and 21.45. Two nights later twelve crews were divided equally between St Nazaire and Lorient, and all but Sgt Kalfas completed their sorties as briefed. He found the cloud base off St Nazaire down to 300 feet, and, despite searching for some time for his pinpoint on la Calebasse, he was unable to locate it. He abandoned his sortie at 02.11, and brought his mines home. Twenty-fours hours later the target area was Jellyfish, the sea lanes off Brest, for which seven crews began departing Ingham at 21.14. Weather conditions off the French coast were good, and provided excellent visibility for the timed runs from Pointe Saint-Mathieu. The mines were delivered into the briefed locations from 1,000 to 2,500 feet between 23.36 and 23.54, and all returned safely from an uneventful trip.

The night of the 22/23rd brought the first of a month-long four-raid series against Hanover, a city in northern Germany about 150 miles west of Berlin. This first operation would prove to be the largest of the series, and involved over seven hundred aircraft, including 101 Lancasters and twelve Wellingtons from 1 Group, all of the latter now provided by 300 Squadron. Eight of the 101 Squadron Lancasters were of the ABC variety, and were operating over Germany for the first time. W/C Kucharski was the senior pilot on duty, and was among the first to take off, shortly after 19.00. They got away safely, and headed for Northern Holland to cross into enemy territory near the night fighter airfield at Leeuwarden, where some of the Luftwaffe's most skilled night fighter crews were stationed. Even before this point was reached, however, Sgt Kleczanski experienced control column problems while at 17,000 feet at the mid-point of the North Sea crossing. The starboard wing dropped, making control difficult, and at 20.15 it was decided to jettison the all-incendiary load and turn back. LN393 had just crossed the enemy coast a few miles north-west of Leeuwarden at 16,000 feet, when it was attacked three times by an enemy night fighter at 20.57. Good visibility favoured the enemy, but a layer of cloud with tops at around 12,000 feet provided a means of escape, and Sgt Klatkiewicz and crew made it safely home after jettisoning their load safe. A minute later, a little further to the north-east and 3,000 feet higher, LN299 was attacked by three single engine fighters, which F/O Myszkowski managed to evade after dumping his incendiaries live two miles north-east of Dokkum.

P/O Kazimierz Toziczka completed 28 sorties with 300 Squadron from July to Dec. 1943. He was comissioned in October 1944. (J. Stevens)

The others from the squadron continued on to the target, which they found under two-tenths cloud in excellent visibility. The target was identified by green Pathfinder markers, and bombing was carried out from 17,000 to 20,000 feet between 21.31 and 21.40. One of the Wellingtons was carrying a 4,000 pounder, two others had nine 500 pounders on board, while the remaining loads were all-incendiary, and these were apparently delivered to good effect into the heart of the city. Returning crews reported huge explosions, large fires and smoke up to 12,000 feet, and the entire city ablaze. W/C Kucharski described the attack as equalling that on Hamburg, and he claimed to be able to see the glow of the inferno from the Dutch coast, some two hundred miles away. According to the account in the indispensable Bomber Command War Diaries tome by Martin Middlebrook and Chris Everitt, the crews' efforts were effectively wasted, when stronger than forecast winds pushed the marking and bombing some two to five miles south-south-east of the city centre. In the absence of a local report, they speculate that little significant damage was inflicted. Having studied many reports from participating crews, I conclude that this was, indeed, a highly destructive operation, and that a substantial amount of the disproportionately massive damage credited to the attack on the 8/9th of October, was actually inflicted during this and the second raid of the series.

Mannheim received its second heavy assault of the month on the night of the 23/24th, when well over nine hundred buildings were destroyed, and some of the later bombing spilled across the Rhine into Ludwigshafen, and the small towns of Oppau and Frankenthal. 300 Squadron stayed at home on this night, and on the following afternoon briefed thirteen crews for mining duties, six in the Nectarines and seven in the Trefoil gardens, which were off the Frisians and south of Texel respectively. They were all safely airborne by 19.18, and made their way without incident to their allocated drop zones, which were some distance out from land, off Vlieland to the north, and the Dutch coast between Zandvoort and Castricum to the south, and required a Gee fix to establish position. The mines were successfully delivered into the assigned locations from 1,000 to 2,000 feet between 20.25 and 20.34, and all crews returned safely.

Ingham, November 1943. Wellington HF450 BH-V with the crew of F/L Wojtulewicz and a group of ground personnel. Left to Right in the back row: F/S Jarzab (B.A.), F/L Wojtulewicz (pilot), F/L Dymek (nav.), F/O Wilczynski (W.Op.) and F/L Krol (A.G). They completed their tour of duty from March - October 1943. After his commission P/O Jarzab returned to 300 Squadron in October 1944 and commenced his second tour of duty on Lancasters in early 1945. (PISM via WM)

The second Hanover raid took place on the night of the 27/28th, for which 1 Group put up 108 Lancasters and fifteen Wellingtons from 300 Squadron in an overall force of 678 aircraft. They took off either side of 20.00 with S/L Kuzian the senior pilot on duty, and all but one made it safely through thick rain cloud to emerge into clear skies at 18,000 feet. HF490 was still over Ingham when Sgt Kleczanski decided to abandon the sortie after repeated unsuccessful attempts to close the pilot's escape hatch. LN390 was 500 feet above the cloud tops a few miles out from Southwold at 20.40, when the navigator reported sick, and Sgt Markiewicz turned back to bring his bombs home. HF480 was at 12,000 feet south of Bramsche, and following the course of the Mittelland Canal eastwards, when F/L Wojtulewicz reluctantly decided to turn for home. This was his twenty-fourth operation, and he had never had to abort before. Even after losing his W/T immediately after take-off, he had refused to be beaten, and was well on his way to the target when the first enemy night fighter was encountered at 21.45. This and a combat ten minutes later forced him to dive into the cloud to escape, and it would also delay his arrival at the target just eighty miles ahead. He concluded that he would be too late on target, and, anyway, dare not climb to a safe bombing height because of the strong presence of enemy night fighters. He dropped his bombs in the area of Egmond on the Dutch coast at 22.50, and landed safely, if frustratingly, at two minutes after midnight.

The others arrived over the city to find much better weather conditions and good visibility, and aimed their all-incendiary loads on green Pathfinder target indicators from 17,000 to 20,000 feet between 22.09 and 22.20. Returning crews claimed concentrated fires and smoke rising to 10,000 feet, and again reported being able to see the glow of fires from the Dutch coast. Post raid assessment suggested a successful attack, and the bombing was, indeed, concentrated, however, Middlebrook and Everitt suggest that wrongly forecast winds had caused it to be concentrated outside of the city and onto outlying communities and open country. This is not supported by the reports of scores of participating crews, and while eyewitness accounts have been proved to be wildly misleading on numerous occasions, I do not believe that this is one. Decoy fires and the destruction of small communities simply do not create a glow visible from two hundred miles away. This was the final operation of the month for 300 Squadron, and it remained at home while over three hundred aircraft were unleashed on the Ruhr town of Bochum on the night of the 29/30th. During the course of the month the squadron undertook fourteen operations, and lost a single aircraft from 115 sorties.

Hanover was devastated by a succession of raids, this historic city paying the price for its part in the Nazi was effort.

October 1943

The new month began in hectic fashion for the Lancaster squadrons, which were called on to operate six times in the first eight nights, beginning with an attack by 240 aircraft of 1, 5 and 8 Groups on Hagen in the Ruhr on the night of the 1/2nd. The eighty-five 1 Group participants to reach and bomb the primary target helped to devastate the town's industry. On the following night, the same groups went to Munich with 290 aircraft and destroyed over three hundred buildings. While this operation was in progress 300 Squadron dispatched sixteen crews to the Brittany coast to mine the waters off Lorient and St Nazaire. Seven crews were assigned to the former and nine to the latter, and they took off either side of 21.00 with S/L Kowalczyk the senior pilot on duty. He was a former fighter pilot and commander of the famous 303 Squadron in 1940/41, but now, because of his advancing years, he had chosen to switch to bombers and had undertaken the appropriate training. Sgt Toziczka was at 1,000 feet west of Guernsey when his Gee equipment failed at 22.56, and without it he had no chance of locating his drop zone. The others continued on to find good conditions with minimal cloud and excellent visibility. The Beeches contingent pinpointed on Gee fixes a little out to sea from the mouth of the Loire Estuary, while the Artichokes gang positioned themselves north-west of Belle Isle and west of the Quiberon peninsular. They planted their mines as briefed from 1,000 to 3,000 feet between 23.51 and 00.13, and all returned without incident.

On the 3rd, for the third night running, a major operation was mounted, and this time the Halifaxes and Stirlings joined in to make up a force of 540 aircraft. The target was Kassel, a city situated east of the Ruhr, about ninety miles from Dortmund. It succumbed to a partially successful operation that resulted in the devastation of one of the city's eastern districts, and damage to the Henschel and Fieseler aircraft factories. Frankfurt was the objective on the following night, where all previous efforts had achieved only modest results. To operate on four successive nights was a new record for the group, but the ground crews worked hard to prepare for what turned out to be two operations. Twenty-seven Lancasters from the group joined forces with 370 others to hit the primary target, while fifty-four acted as the main force for a "spoof" raid on Ludwigshafen. The Frankfurt operation was the most effective yet on the city, and the eastern half and the inland docks area was left a sea of flames. After a two night rest 340 Lancasters of 1, 3, 5, 6 and 8 Groups went to Stuttgart on the 7/8th, when 101 Squadron employed its ABC communications-jamming Lancasters in numbers for the first time. In all the squadron put up nineteen Lancasters in a 1 Group effort of 107, and they enjoyed moderate success at a cloud-covered target. It cannot be determined whether the two tiny 8 Group diversions at Munich and Friedrichshafen were responsible for the low loss figure, or the presence of the ABC Lancasters, but just four aircraft failed to return from Stuttgart, and for the third operation in a row 1 Group had no losses to report.

It was on this night that 300 Squadron returned to the operational scene to carry out mining sorties off the French coast. Sixteen crews were briefed, five for Jellyfish (Brest), five for Beeches (St Nazaire) and six for Artichokes (Lorient). They were all safely airborne by 23.29, with S/Ls Kowalczyk and Morawski the senior pilots on duty, but it was not long before the first early return occurred. F/S Zoltanski had crossed the Devon coast at 2,000 feet without picking up a pinpoint from which to set course for the French coast and, thereafter, his drop zone off St Nazaire. He spent twenty minutes trying to identify his position and pick up a navigation beacon, but abandoned the attempt at 23.59 and turned back on a reciprocal course, only then to locate the beacon at Exeter. By this time it was too late to continue with the operation, and he brought his mines home. Having touched down safely, the Wellington slewed suddenly to port a hundred yards down the runway, causing the starboard wheel to break away and tipping the aircraft onto its starboard wing. HF590 broke its back and was declared a write-off, but no injuries to crew members were reported. F/S Ziejka was bound for the Artichokes garden at 800 feet, when he abandoned his sortie in conditions of low cloud and fog as he approached the northern stretch of the Brest Peninsular at 01.30. F/S Artymiuk was much closer to the target area when similar conditions prompted him to turn back at 01.50. He had been unable to pinpoint on Ile de Batz, an island just off the northern coast, and had flown across the peninsular in solid cloud, from which he had been unable to escape despite alternating altitude between 600 and 2,000 feet. The other pressed on, and all of the Jellyfish contingent successfully completed their assigned tasks from 1,300 to 1,500 feet between 02.04 and 02.10. The weather conditions off Lorient were good, with no cloud, and the crews assigned to its sea lanes had no difficulty in pinpointing by Gee fix and delivering their vegetables into the required locations. Those arriving in the waters off St Nazaire also found clear skies, with mist at sea level, and they were able to make timed runs off Gee fixes in the mouth of the Loire Estuary to plant their vegetables as briefed. HF490 failed to return with the crew of S/L Morawski, and no trace of the Wellington or its occupants was ever found.

The Polish commander-in-chief and a party of dignitaries flew in to Ingham on the afternoon of the 8th, to be met by the 1 Group A-O-C, AVM Rice, the RAF and Polish Air Force station commanders, G/C Cozens and G/C Kropinski respectively, and the squadron commander W/C Kucharski. They proceeded immediately to the intelligence/operations section, where they attended the briefing for that night's operation, which was the third of the series of attacks on Hanover. They learned that 1 Group was to contribute ninety-six Lancasters and twelve 300 Squadron Wellingtons to an overall force of five hundred aircraft. What they did not know, was that these Wellingtons and fourteen others from 432 Squadron RCAF, would be carrying out their final bombing operations in Bomber Command service. From this point on the type would conduct only mining operations until they were eventually replaced by Lancasters. After the briefing the Polish C-in-C presented the Cross of Valour to a number of airmen, before undertaking an inspection of the station, and delivering a short speech to officers in the concert hall, to update them on Polish Air Force matters. Later still he spent half an hour in the sergeants' mess, before visiting Hemswell briefly, and returning to Ingham to watch the crews take-off for Germany.

F/L Winiarek led the take-off procedure at 23.11, to be followed over the ensuing twelve minutes by the others, including the senior pilot on duty, S/L Kuzian. JA117 was at 16,500 feet over the North Sea closing on Texel, when the port engine overheated. It could only be cooled by losing height, and with Holland and half of Germany to traverse, this was out of the question for Sgt Klatkiewicz and his crew, and they brought their bombs home. LN242 had crossed into northern Holland when it was attacked at 15,000 feet by two single engine enemy fighters, and this was a problem exacerbated by the fact that three of the four guns in the rear turret had become jammed. The situation demanded that the bombs be jettisoned live, and this was done at 00.52 before a safe return was made. Sgt Toziczka and crew rued the loss of the rear turret, and would otherwise have attempted to fight their way to the target. The others did manage to reach their destination, and found clear skies and excellent conditions, along with plenty of red and green Pathfinder markers to aim at. F/L Stadtmüller was in LN552 with a freshman crew, and they were hit by flak at 18,500 feet during the bombing run, which damaged the rear turret, blew off the emergency door and wounded the rear gunner and bomb-aimer. They were also attacked by an FW190 at the same time, but shrugged it off and came home to report concentrated fires and an orange explosion at 01.36. For his actions in evading destruction at the hands of the enemy and for bringing his crippled aircraft home, F/L Stadtmüller received the immediate award of the DFC. The other 300 Squadron crews bombed from 17,000 to 19,000 feet between 01.33 and 01.39, and all returned safely to be greeted by the Polish C-in-C, who had flown back to Ingham from Hemswell in time to see them land. The operation was an outstanding success, credited with destroying almost four thousand buildings and damaging to some extent thirty thousand others. As mentioned earlier, I believe that a substantial proportion of this destruction was achieved during the two previous raids.

Most of the main force crews were allowed a welcome break from operations thereafter, but extensive mining operations off the Frisians and the Biscay coast involved a dozen 300 Squadron crews on the night of the 17/18th, six each briefed for the waters off Lorient and St Nazaire. They took off either side of 18.00, and all reached their respective target areas without incident, to find mostly clear skies and excellent visibility. They pinpointed by means of Gee fixes, and delivered their two mines each into the designated locations from 1,000 to 2,000 feet between 21.02 and 21.25, and returned home to report a quiet trip. The night of the 18/19th brought the fourth and final attack on Hanover by an all-Lancaster force of 360 aircraft, of which 108 were provided by 1 Group. This was almost certainly the least effective raid of the series, after the Pathfinders failed to achieve concentration in conditions of complete cloud cover, and this resulted in the main weight of the bombing falling into open country north and north-west of the city.

The first major operation against Leipzig took place on the night of the 20/21st, when appalling weather conditions conspired to render the attack ineffective. 1 Group put up 104 Lancasters, five of which failed to return. In contrast to this dismal failure, a second attack during the month on Kassel on the night of the 22/23rd produced outstanding results. 569 Lancasters and Halifaxes took off, of which 105 represented 1 Group. The marking and most of the bombing were stunningly accurate, and achieved the kind of concentration that inevitably led to massive destruction. It also led to a firestorm, and although not as extensive as that experienced in Hamburg in July, it contributed to the destruction of 4,349 apartment blocks, containing 26,782 dwellings, and serious damage to a further 6,700 blocks. More than 3,500 fires were dealt with and at least six thousand people lost their lives, but the defenders fought back to claim the high figure of forty-three bombers, among which were seven from 1 Group. There were no other major operations to occupy the main force crews during the month, but 300 Squadron briefed eleven crews for a spot of gardening on the night of the 24/25th. The target areas were off the Frisians for six crews, and the Dutch coast south of Texel for five, and they took off safely either side of 18.00 with W/C Kucharski the senior pilot on duty. The weather conditions were not ideal, and were described by most as poor, but, employing Gee fixes, all successfully planted their vegetables in the correct positions from 1,000 to 2,000 feet between 19.24 and 20.05.

Four days later a signal was received from HQ Bomber Command, which read: “On the night of the 24/25th of Oct., a number of crews returning from operations sighted several ships of various categories, and gave accurate reports on return, which were of considerable value to C-in-C Nore. As a direct consequence HM ships intercepted an attack by a force of 25 enemy E-Boats on an east coast convoy, sank 4, damaged 7 and took 19 prisoners. The accuracy of the reports and the speed of transmission to C-in-C Nore has been commended. It should be pointed out to all crews that such reports can be of considerable value to naval authorities, as has been explicitly shown by this incident.” The 300 Squadron ORB adds further, “The information which led to this successful naval engagement was secured from reports provided by the following captains and crews, all of 300 Squadron, W/C Kucharski, F/L Winiarek, F/L Pluta, F/O Kowalczyk, F/S Zablocki, F/S Szmaciarz and F/S Kleczanski.” There had been ten operations involving 300 Squadron during the month, with sixty-seven sorties and one missing aircraft.

F/L Roman Stadtmüller flew 8 sorties in 301 Squadron and was transferred to 300 Squadron in April 1943 where he took part in another 26 operations by Nov. 1943. (PISM via WM)

November 1943

In a minute to Churchill on the 3rd of November, Harris stated that he could "wreck Berlin from end to end", if the Americans were to join in, and, although he estimated it would cost between them four to five hundred aircraft, it would, he asserted, cost Germany the war. Harris was holding firm to the belief that a victory could be achieved by bombing alone, and he was the first commander in history with the means to put this theory to the test. Having personally witnessed the carnage of the trenches in the Great War, he wished to avoid a protracted and bloody land campaign this time round. The Americans, of course, were committed to victory by land invasion, where the film cameras could be present to record the heroic actions, and there was never the slightest chance of enlisting their support. Harris would go to Berlin alone, as he had done in late August/early September, and would resume the campaign in mid-month.

For the crews of 1 Group there was only one major operation to negotiate during the first half of November, and this was to Düsseldorf on the night of the 3/4th. 140 Lancasters of 1 Group joined 440 other Lancasters and Halifaxes heading towards the Ruhr city in conditions of heavy cloud. As if by royal command the cloud disappeared when the force was twenty-five miles from its destination, and the residents braced themselves for what was destined to be a torrid time. The Pathfinder marking was both punctual and accurate, and the main weight of the attack was delivered onto central and southern districts, where substantial damage was inflicted on housing and industry. 300 Squadron's future, while it remained a Wellington unit, was restricted to mining operations, and sixteen crews were briefed on the 4th for activity off the Biscay ports that night. Five crews each were assigned to Brest and St Nazaire, and six for Lorient, and they all got away safely either side of 17.15 with W/C Kucharski heading the Brest contingent, with S/L Kuzian in support, and S/L Kowalczyk leading the St Nazaire element. There were no senior pilots briefed for Lorient. All completed their sorties successfully in conditions of moonlight and excellent visibility, and although a number of crews reported limited light flak, only S/L Kowalczyk brought back evidence in the form of slight aileron damage.

There would be little further activity for the heavy brigade for the next two weeks, but 300 Squadron was up again on the night of the 6/7th for mining operations off the Biscay ports and the Dutch coast. Four crews each were assigned to Brest, Lorient, St Nazaire and south of Texel, and it was the south-west-bound crews who departed first, beginning at 21.17, with S/L Kowalczyk the senior pilot on duty. They all completed their sorties successfully, and were already on their way home when the eastbound quartet departed at 00.44 for the Dutch coast between Castricum and Den Helder. The senior officer among these crews was S/L Chrzanowski, who was flying as wireless operator with F/O Myszkowski. They also successfully completed their assigned tasks and returned safely. Fifteen crews were divided equally between Brest, Lorient and St Nazaire on the following night, and they took off either side of 22.45 with S/Ls Kuzian and Kowalczyk the senior pilots on duty. F/S Drobny and crew took off in LN508 at 22.36 bound for St Nazaire, but soon developed engine problems, which caused the port and then the starboard power plants to fail. They had reached the county of Warwickshire by this time, and the mines were jettisoned safe about six or seven miles east-south-east of Rugby. The nearest airfield was the relief landing ground at RAF Southam, a few miles further to the south-west, east of Royal Leamington Spa, and a forced landing was made there at 23.30. The Wellington was written-off, but the crew members sustained only minor injuries. A search for the missing vegetables was organised by the county police, and one assumes they were located.

The group was alerted on the 10th to provide aircraft for an attack on the distant Baltic port of Königsberg. At midday the target and bomb load were changed, and the ground crews worked frantically to prepare 102 Lancasters to join more than two hundred others from 5 and 8 Groups for an attack on the railway tunnel at Modane in southern France, which linked Turin and Grenoble through the Alps. The Pathfinder marking was slightly off, but over two hundred aircraft brought back aiming point photographs showing serious damage. 300 Squadron remained at home on this night, but dispatched sixteen crews twenty-four hours later to mine the waters off Brest, Lorient and St Nazaire. They took off either side of 17.00, with G/C Cozens and S/L Kuzian leading the six-strong Brest element, while S/L Kowalczyk headed the five bound for Lorient and F/L Pluta the St Nazaire contingent. Weather conditions were excellent, with bright moonlight, and Sgt Klatkiewicz described the visibility as too good, inferring that it was helpful to the defenders. Certainly, there was a spirited light flak defence at Lorient, and F/O Skwarczynski, who was in LN299 heading for St Nazaire, reported seeing an aircraft held in searchlights and engaged by flak, before falling in flames at 20.08. The highly-experienced F/L Winiarek and crew failed to return in LN393, and it must be assumed that the above report referred to their demise, as they were assigned to Lorient and no other aircraft were lost. However, according to Bill Chorley in his superb Bomber Command Losses for 1943, LN393 was shot down by a flak ship off Brest, and the timings suggest that F/L Winiarek and crew were about twenty-five minutes into their return journey when the end came, and this would put them in the Brest area. The pilot managed to ditch the burning aircraft near the enemy coast, and he and two of his crew were able to scramble into the dinghy, only to be taken into captivity two hours later. Sadly, F/L Korecki and F/S Winiarczyk lost their lives.

W/C Kazimierz Kuzian. CO of 300 Squadron from 18th Nov. 1943. He completed his tour of duty from Apr. 1943 to Jan. 1944 and later assumed the post of Chief Flying Instructor in 16 (P)SFTS at Newton. (PISM via WM)

W/C Kucharski concluded his six month tour of duty as commanding officer of 300 Squadron, and he was succeeded on the 18th by W/C Kuzian. That night sixteen crews departed Ingham for four gardens, Den Helder (Limpets) for three crews, Brest for five crews and four crews each for Lorient and St Nazaire. S/L Kowalczyk was the senior pilot on duty as they got away safely either side of 17.30. Visibility off the French and Dutch coasts was described as moderate to good, with some mist, and all successfully completed their assigned tasks. As Harris's recent hint to Churchill concerning an American involvement in the Berlin campaign had generated no positive response, he made preparations to resume the campaign alone. While the Wellingtons of 300 Squadron were conducting the above-mentioned mining operations, the Lancaster squadrons were heading for the Capital, at the same time as a predominantly Halifax and Stirling effort made for Mannheim and Ludwigshafen to act as a diversion. Complete cloud cover over Berlin necessitated blind marking and bombing, and in the absence of any concentration, a modest 169 houses were destroyed, along with four industrial premises, while a further five hundred buildings were seriously damaged. One useful victim of the operation was the Daimler-Benz car factory, which suffered

P/O Zygmunt Pluta (obs.) in the middle with Sgt Alfred Kleniewski (W.Op.) on the left and Sgt Roman Wysocki (A.G.) on the right. All three had completed their tours of duty with 300 Squadron by 1941/1942. P/O Pluta finished pilot training and returned to 300 Squadron for the second tour in Oct. 1943. Later he joined 1586 (Polish) Special Duty Flight at Brindisi (Italy) for the third tour in June 1944 and failed to return with entire crew from the supply-dropping flight to Warsaw on 16/17th Aug. 1944. Sgts Kleniewski and Wysocki were posted to 138 SD Squadron in October 1942 and were killed when their Halifax crashed in Malta on 16/17th Dec. 1942 during transit flight to UK (Wysocki family)

a 90% loss of production for a period. The diversionary raid was moderately effective, and may well have contributed to the relatively low loss from Berlin of nine aircraft.

On the following night, thirteen 300 Squadron crews took off for the three Biscay ports and the Dutch coast, and all delivered their mines into the briefed locations, mostly without incident. The senior officer on duty was S/L Chrzanowski, who was with F/L Kurowski, and had succeeded the newly promoted W/C Kuzian as a flight commander. The Brest contingent encountered sleet and visibility of one to two miles, and this may have cloaked a flak ship, which escaped F/L Spychala's notice until it fired at him as he was delivering his mines. He took violent evasive action, and returned safely, landing, as did all but the Trefoil crews, at Davidstow Moor, near Camelford in Cornwall. The Lancaster squadrons sat out a disappointing raid on the Ruhr city of Leverkusen on this night, which scattered bombs over a wide area after a poor performance by the Pathfinders in testing weather conditions.

The Lancaster brigade returned to the fray on the night of the 22/23rd, for a maximum effort assault on Berlin. 764 aircraft set out either side of 17.00 hours for the long slog eastwards on a relatively direct route, in weather conditions that were generally unfavourable for night fighters. Complete cloud cover over the target prevented the crews from making an immediate assessment of their work, but beneath the clouds, Berlin was undergoing its worst night of the war. From the city centre westwards, three thousand houses and apartment blocks were reduced to ruins, along with twenty-one industrial premises, and a number of fire areas developed with firestorm characteristics. Around two thousand people lost their lives, while 175,000 others were rendered homeless. This outstanding success was gained at a cost of twenty-six aircraft, and not a single one of the 169 contributed by 1 Group failed to return. Five of the fifty participating Stirlings were among the casualties, however, and after a succession of disproportionately high losses, Harris decided to withdraw them from future operations over Germany. While this operation was in progress, fourteen 300 Squadron Wellingtons headed for the Dutch coast, eight to mine the waters off the Frisians and six off the Dutch mainland further south. W/C Kuzian led the Trefoil element, and S/L Kowalczyk those bound for Nectarines, and all completed their assigned tasks in variable weather conditions without major incident. F/L Kurowski burst a tyre on take-off, but landed safely, and one crew had a mine hang up.

On the following night an all Lancaster main force set off to return to Berlin with 111 of their number provided by 1 Group. Perhaps the strain of back-to-back Berlin operations had something to do with the twenty-three early returns experienced by the group, but those pressing on continued the good work of the previous night, guided by the glow of fires still burning beneath the clouds. Another two thousand houses were destroyed, along with eight industrial premises, and around fifteen hundred people were killed. The main defence in the target area was provided by single engine day fighters operating in the Wilde Sau role, and these probably accounted for many of the twenty shot-down Lancasters, six of which were from 1 Group. Halifaxes provided the main force for an ineffective attack on Frankfurt on the night of the 25/26th, when 300 Squadron sent five Wellingtons each to mine the sea lanes off Brest, Lorient and St Nazaire. G/C Cozens led the St Nazaire contingent, S/L Kowalczyk the Brest element, and F/L Pluta those bound for Lorient, and all completed their sorties as briefed without incident.

The fourth raid on Berlin since the resumption took place on the night of the 26/27th, and involved an all-Lancaster heavy force numbering over four hundred aircraft, including 153 from 1 Group. It was a busy night for 101 Squadron, which provided seventeen aircraft for the main operation and six ABC Lancasters for a diversionary attack on Stuttgart by a Halifax main force. Approaching Berlin from the south in clear conditions, the Pathfinders overshot the aiming point by many miles, and marked an area in the north-west of the city, where a number of industrial suburbs were situated. More by luck than judgement, therefore, thirty-eight war industry factories were destroyed, but there was less damage to housing. Sadly, the zoo was hit, and although some animals had been evacuated, most of those remaining were killed. Twenty-eight aircraft failed to return home, and many more crashed in England, 1 Group losing eleven from Berlin and one from Stuttgart. This series of three raids on Berlin in five nights had inflicted terrible damage, with fatalities in the city amounting to 4,330, but its modern layout, with wide thoroughfares and open spaces, created natural firebreaks, and from now on the law of diminishing returns would apply and further successes would have to be ground out at a high cost in Bomber Command lives.

While this operation was in progress fourteen 300 Squadron Wellingtons headed for the various points off the enemy coast to lay mines. Ten went north to the Nectarines garden off the Frisians, three to Limpets, off Den Helder, and one to Trefoil, further south off the Dutch mainland. S/L Chrzanowski was the senior officer on duty, flying in the crew piloted by F/S Weyna and bound for Nectarines, and all completed their assigned tasks, except for F/L Krzepisz, who lost his Gee some twenty miles out from Mablethorpe while at 2,000 feet, and brought his mines home. Two nights later S/L Kowalczyk led a mining operation by five crews to the waters off Brest, and four successfully delivered their two mines each into the briefed locations. F/S Gluba abandoned his sortie after his rate of climb indicator became unserviceable. A further fifteen crews were briefed on the 30th for mining operations off the Biscay ports that night, five for Brest, seven for Lorient and three for St Nazaire. S/L Kowalczyk again led the Brest contingent, and all completed their assigned tasks without incident. One crew returned early from Lorient with a vibrating engine and unserviceable W/T receiver, and one likewise failed to reach St Nazaire with a malfunctioning artificial horizon. Because of the many small-scale mining operations during the month, the squadron smashed all previous records by taking part in thirty-three, for which a record of 155 sorties was dispatched for the loss of a single aircraft.

December 1943

It fell to the "Big City" to open Bomber Command's December account on the night of the 2/3rd, when over four hundred Lancasters represented the main force. 1 Group put up 144, two of them from 460 Squadron RAAF containing war correspondents. These very courageous people placed their lives at risk in the pursuit of their journalistic art, and no one could have known that they had chosen to fly on the squadron's blackest night of the war thus far, and that the aircraft to which they had been assigned would be among those failing to return. The direct route to the target helped the Luftwaffe night fighter controller to identify the destination of the bomber stream in good time, and he was able to assemble a proportion of his aircraft in the target area. Wrongly forecast winds scattered the stream, and presented the Pathfinders with great difficulty in establishing their position. This led to a scattering of bombs from east to west, and across southern districts, where some useful industrial damage occurred, but many bomb loads were wasted in open country. Night fighters continued to be active on the return flight, and a massive forty aircraft were lost, eighteen of them from 1 Group. Five of these were from Binbrook, and all fell within the Berlin defence zone. The war correspondent from the Sydney Sun, Norman Stockton, and a Norwegian war correspondent, Capt. Grieg, were among the fatalities.

On the following night over five hundred aircraft were detailed for a raid on Leipzig, and the famous American broadcaster, Ed Murrow, hitched a lift in a 619 Squadron Lancaster of 5 Group. 1 Group provided ninety-six Lancasters for what turned out to be a highly successful and destructive operation, despite the presence of complete cloud cover. The operation demonstrated that skymarking under favourable conditions could be as effective as visual marking. It helped that the Luftwaffe controller had wrongly identified Berlin as the target, and had sent the night fighters there. As a result the operation proceeded without undue interference from the defences, and much residential and industrial property was destroyed. Twenty-four aircraft failed to return, at least half of them as the result of flying into the Frankfurt defence zone on the way home. 300 Squadron's first operation of the new month involved sixteen Wellingtons mining off the Frisians, and yet another war correspondent got in on the action. Listed as Sgt Walter C Peters, USA, he flew in the crew of F/S Niezrecki and made it back safely. The squadron participants had got away after 21.00 on a night of difficult weather conditions, which would severely impact the success of the operation. On board with F/L Kurowski was G/C Macpherson, who was the successor to G/C Cozens as station commander at Hemswell, the latter having been posted to 1 Group HQ. Otherwise, the senior officer on duty was S/L Chrzanowski, who was again flying in the crew of F/S Weyna. Ten crews managed to locate suitable pinpoints despite heavy cloud, some of which had its base at sea level, but six other crews were defeated by the conditions or the failure of their Gee equipment, and brought their mines home.

On the 15th notification was received that the squadron was to convert to Lancasters, and three crews, together with specialist officers and ground crews, proceeded to Blyton to begin training. Eight crews were to remain operational on Wellingtons to complete their tours as A Flight, while the remaining crews became B Flight, re-designated the Conversion Flight, to be fed through the conversion system over the ensuing weeks. After the lengthy stand-down the main force and Pathfinder Lancaster crews were briefed on the 16th for the next trip to Berlin. 483 Lancasters took off in the late afternoon of what would become known as "Black Thursday", and this number included a new record of 161 aircraft from 1 Group. Berlin was cloud covered, but most of the bombs found the mark in central and eastern districts, although there was no recognizable point of concentration. Housing, railway installations and public buildings were the chief victims of the attack, but the defences claimed twenty-five aircraft, of which seven were from 1 Group. The real problems arose when the tired crews arrived back over England to encounter a blanket of fog concealing their airfields, principally in the 1, 6 and 8 Group regions. Most had insufficient fuel reserves to even contemplate the long flight to a diversionary station, and as they stumbled around in the murk in search of somewhere to land, accidents were inevitable. Twenty-nine Lancasters either crashed or were abandoned by their crews, and around 150 airmen lost their lives in these most tragic of circumstances. Losses to enemy action were part and parcel of the job, but to have to battle the weather on return to base at the end of an exhausting seven or eight hour slog was asking too much. While this operation was in progress eight 300 Squadron Wellingtons went mining off Brest and Lorient, and all completed their assigned tasks before returning safely.

F/O Jan Ochedzan, who completed 24 operations from June to December 1943. (PISM via WM)

HF598 took off for an air-test at 11.00 on the 19th, and crashed eleven minutes later on the other side of the A15, seven miles north-north-east of Lincoln. Both occupants, pilot, F/O Ochedzan, and bomb-aimer, Sgt Bluj, were killed, and the wreckage was burnt-out. On the 20/21st, Frankfurt was the objective for over six hundred Lancasters and Halifaxes, while a small 1 and 8 Group raid on Mannheim acted as a diversion. 1 Group contributed 103 Lancasters to the main operation and twenty-eight to the diversion. The crews had been briefed to expect clear skies and ground marking, but in the event, marking had to take place through gaps in the cloud, and the confusion was exacerbated by a decoy fire site some miles away. Some of the creep-back fell across residential districts, and 466 houses were destroyed, while many cultural and historic buildings sustained severe damage. It was a costly night for the attackers, and it was the Halifax brigade that sustained the bulk of the casualties among the forty-one missing aircraft. 1 Group came off lightly with just three missing aircraft. There was a late-afternoon take-off for five 300 Squadron crews on the 22nd, either side of 16.30, and they made their way to the waters off Lorient to lay mines. Conditions were good, particularly with regard to visibility, and all were successful, although two crews reported being troubled by intense flak in the target area. Over 350 Lancasters made up the main force for Berlin on the night of the 23/24th, of which 128 represented 1 Group. The bombers failed to make a major impression on the Capital, after many Pathfinder crews experienced technical failures with H2S. Under three hundred buildings were destroyed, but at least the losses were substantially down on recent operations, and a more modest sixteen were absent from their dispersals on the following morning.

The bombing campaign resulted in the Germans having to devote massive resources of weapons and manpower to the defence of their homeland. These would otherwise have been freed up to support their forces in occupied territories. A flak battery is shown here in Berlin.

The fifth wartime Christmas came and went in relative peace, the Polish personnel observing a traditional Polish catholic observance and festive dinner on Christmas Eve. On Christmas Day an RAF tradition was observed, the officers serving the other ranks with their Christmas lunch. It was not until the 29th that the main force crews were ushered once more into the briefing rooms, to learn that they must endure yet another trip to the Capital. This was a maximum effort operation, involving over seven hundred aircraft, and would be the first of three against Berlin in the space of five nights spanning the turn of the year. 1 Group provided 136 Lancasters for this operation, and like the rest of the force the crews found the city again concealed beneath a layer of cloud, forcing them to bomb on skymarkers. As they retreated westwards at the end of the attack, they remained uncertain as to the effects of their efforts. Reconnaissance later showed the main weight of the attack to have fallen into southern and south-eastern districts, where around four hundred buildings were destroyed. Twenty aircraft were brought down by the defences, and among these were five from 1 Group. 300 squadron completed its operational year with seven mining sorties on the night of the 30/31st. Three crews were briefed for the sea lanes off Lorient, and four for St Nazaire, and all successfully carried out their orders before returning safely home.

The frequent operations to Berlin were by now having an effect on the resolve of all crews, and this would be reflected in the rate of early returns. It was not the most opportune time for new crews to be beginning their first tour of operations, and in the minds of most of them, there can have been little prospect of surviving to complete thirty sorties. It had, of course, been a tough year for all squadrons, but, on balance, a highly successful one, which had seen the enemy's industrial heartland devastated, and many cities in other regions bearing the scars of battle. Both sides must have known that the future promised nothing other than more of the same. The slackening pace of the month was reflected in the squadron's tally of just six operations, thirty-six sorties and one aircraft lost from a training flight.

January 1944

The beleaguered citizens of Berlin and the hard-pressed crews of Bomber Command doubtless shared a common hope as the New Year dawned, that Germany's Capital would cease to be the main focus of Harris's attention. For their part, the Berliners were a hardy breed, and just like their counterparts in London during the blitz of 1940, they would bear their trials with fortitude and humour, and develop a strong sense of community. They were proud of their status as Berliners first and Germans second, and during this, their "winter of discontent", they taunted their tormentors by parading banners through the shattered streets, proclaiming, "you may break our walls, but not our hearts". The radio played endlessly the melodic strains of the most popular song of the period, Nach jedem Dezember kommt immer ein Mai, After every December comes always a May, the lyrics catching the mood of the time, and hinting at a change of fortunes with the onset of spring. Harris, however, remained single-minded in his purpose, and both camps would have a long wait before their hopes were realized.

As the last few minutes of New Year's Day passed, the first of 421 Lancasters took off for the rendezvous over the North Sea, among them 117 from 1 Group. Cloud began to build up as they left the English coast behind, and by the time the bombers reached the Continent it was ten-tenths with tops at ten 10,000 to 12,000 feet. The force proceeded almost due east to pass south of Hamburg, and on reaching the "Big City" the crews found it impossible to pick out the Pathfinder ground markers. As a result they delivered most of their bombs into wooded and open country, and managed to destroy only twenty-one houses and one industrial building. It was a poor return for the loss of twenty-eight Lancasters, and the death toll among RAF airmen was greater than that suffered on the ground.

The crews were late to bed on the morning of the 2nd, but that didn't prevent many of them from being on the Order of Battle for that night, for the third trip to Berlin in five nights. Such back-to-back long range flights were exhausting, and many men must have been incredulous at the prospect of another seven or eight-hour round trip. This was reflected in the very high number of sixty early returns, which amounted to almost 16% of the 383 aircraft dispatched. Twenty-eight of 1 Group's contingent of 116 Lancasters returned early, but fifteen of these resulted from a misunderstood signal, which used the group's collective call sign for Lancasters, but was intended for the eight 300 Squadron Wellingtons on a simultaneous mining operation. It was once the Bomber stream had reached the target area that the night fighters caught up, and they contributed to the loss of twenty-seven Lancasters, in return for another very disappointing operation. A modest eighty-two houses were destroyed in the scattered attack, and again, there were more fatalities among the bomber crews than on the ground.

The above-mentioned mining operation by 300 Squadron had begun with take-off from Ingham shortly after 19.30, and the now very familiar outward flight across the Channel to the waters off Brest and Lorient. W/C Kuzian headed the five assigned to the former, and F/L Pluta was the senior pilot among those bound for Lorient. There was moonlight above the ten-tenths cloud, but weather conditions were not particularly favourable, and visibility at Brest was described variously as good, by W/C Kuzian and F/S Nowocin, the latter assessing it as four miles, while F/S Uram reported bad light and visibility of half a mile. He also commented on the intensity of the searchlight activity, but all confirmed that Gee had worked perfectly throughout. Each crew planted their mines as briefed between 22.30 and 22.42, before returning to land at Exeter, having picked up the divert signal from group that had confused some of the Lancaster element on their way to Berlin. Further south, the Lorient crews found clear skies, and good visibility at sea level, and experienced no difficulty in delivering their mines into the briefed locations between 22.41 and 22.50. W/O Blachowicz and crew were on their way home at 750 feet at 23.14, when LN242 was hit by light flak from a seven-ship convoy. The hydraulics system sustained damage, which caused the bomb bay doors to drop, while rendering the flaps, undercarriage and rear turret unserviceable. Some of the ammunition in the rear turret also exploded. Not wishing to compromise the serviceability of Exeter for the other crews by force-landing there, W/O Blachowicz pressed on to Barford St John, just south of Banbury, and pulled off a belly-landing, from which the Wellington recovered and was eventually returned to the air.

Small-scale operations occupied the night of the 4/5th, and 300 Squadron contributed six Wellingtons to another mining effort off the Biscay ports. Taking off after midnight, three crews each went to Lorient and St Nazaire, and found their respective target areas lying under clear skies with moonlight and generally good visibility. All successfully delivered their mines as briefed between 03.01 and 03.12, and returned home safely to report a good and quiet trip. In a change from Berlin, over three hundred Lancasters provided the main force for a raid on Stettin on the night of the 5/6th, in the first major operation to the Baltic port since the previous April. 1 Group contributed 113 aircraft, whose crews encountered ten-tenths cloud most of the way to the target area, but found it clear over the city, with just a little haze. As always seemed to happen at this target, the marking and bombing were accurate, and much damage was inflicted on housing and industry, while eight ships were sunk in the harbour. 300 Squadron stayed at home on this night, but briefed six crews for mining duties off Lorient on the following night. They departed in the late afternoon, and found cloudless skies and bright moonlight in the target area, which afforded excellent visibility and almost daylight conditions. The mines were delivered into the required locations between 19.20 and 19.32, and all returned safely, although not entirely unscathed. LN544 was hit by light flak, which perforated the fuselage and tail, but, fortunately, despite causing damage to cable control rods, the escape hatch and dipole aerial, did not affect the handling of the aircraft for the pilot, F/S Klatkiewicz.

On the 12th, 300 Squadron officially became the proud owner of three Lancasters, which were resident at Blyton and being used for conversion training. These aircraft were training hacks, not fit for operational duties, and it would be April before the first war-ready examples of the type reached the squadron. A period of rest extended through to mid month, and when briefings took place on main force and Pathfinder stations on the 14th, there must have been a degree of relief when the target was revealed to be Brunswick, an historic city some forty miles to the east of Hanover, and well short of Berlin. Almost five hundred aircraft, all but two of them Lancasters, took off either side of 17.00, among them 151 from 1 Group. The city was cloud covered and the marking scattered, and this virtually virgin target escaped with only light superficial damage, after most of the bombs fell onto outlying communities to the south. The bombers did not escape lightly, however, having been under attack from night fighters from the moment they crossed the enemy coast near Bremen, and thirty-eight Lancasters were shot down. Losses had been high since the turn of the year, and the Pathfinders in particular were taking a beating. 156 Squadron alone had lost fourteen aircraft and crews during these first two weeks of the year, a figure equivalent to almost a full two-flight squadron, and it was putting a terrible strain on the force. It was now struggling to find adequate resources to fill the gaps, and the original intention to recruit only experienced tried and tested crews would no longer sustain 8 Group. The opportunity to become Pathfinders became opened up to the leading crews leaving training units, the prospect of a straight-through tour of fifty operations balanced out in part by the one step up in rank enjoyed by all of its aircrew. Many sideways postings took place between the squadrons to maintain a leavening of experience, but the situation was becoming critical.

300 Squadron had also returned to the fray on this night after a period on the ground, during which the crews had attended daily lectures. Eight crews had been assigned to the waters off Brest for a further mining effort, and they were led by G/C Macpherson, the recently-appointed station commander at Hemswell. Gee had again played an important part in locating pinpoints, and all crews completed their tasks successfully despite unfavourable weather conditions. F/L Krzepisz was bringing LN707 home after a quiet trip, but undershot the runway at Ingham and landed on the Lincoln Road, effectively writing off the Wellington, but, happily, without doing the same to the crew. There were no operations at all over the succeeding five nights, and during this period, on the 18th, W/C Kuzian concluded his two month period of tenure as 300 Squadron's commanding officer, and was posted to 16 (Polish) SFTS at Newton, to be succeeded by W/C Kowalczyk.

W/C Adam Kowalczyk. CO of 300 Squadron from 18th Jan. 1944 who flew 19 operations between Oct. 1943 and Feb. 1944. (W. Zmyslony)

A maximum effort was called on the 20th, for which Berlin was to be the destination. 769 aircraft and crews answered the call, of which 144 represented 1 Group. Almost 10% of the force returned early, and the captains would have to face interrogation from their commanding officers, to ascertain that they had a cast-iron reason to abort their sorties. The others pressed on, passing into enemy territory a little south of Denmark, and shortly thereafter the night fighters made contact, and remained with the bomber stream all the way to the target and part of the way home. Berlin was cloud-covered, and it was impossible for the crews to make an immediate assessment of the outcome of the raid. It was later learned that the main weight of bombs had fallen into the hitherto less severely afflicted eastern districts, where a moderate amount of damage was achieved, and this was paid for by the loss of thirty-five aircraft, two-thirds of them Halifaxes. While this operation was in progress, eight 300 Squadron crews carried out mining sorties off Brest and Lorient. The four crews assigned to the former enjoyed moderate to good visibility, while those further south experienced less favourable conditions, with rain and intense darkness, but all delivered their stores as briefed between 19.54 and 20.07 before returning safely.

On the following night, 132 Lancasters from 1 Group joined more than five hundred other aircraft setting out for the first major raid of the war on Magdeburg. On this occasion, some night fighters infiltrated the bomber stream even before it crossed the German coast. The two combatant forces remained in contact all the way into eastern Germany, where stronger than forecast winds drove some main force crews to the target ahead of the Pathfinders. Some of these bombed before Zero Hour, and the resultant fires attracted bomb loads, while decoy fires lured away others, and the Pathfinders were unable to bring the attack back on track. The early bombing fell into the south-eastern quadrant of the city before a degree of concentration was achieved. In return for this disappointing outcome, a record fifty-seven aircraft were lost, but only three of them were from 1 Group. Meanwhile, eight 300 Squadron crews were mining the waters off St Nazaire, led for the first time as commanding officer by W/C Kowalczyk. They all dropped their mines into the briefed locations in favourable weather conditions and moderate visibility between 19.56 and 20.03, and returned home without incident. A small mining effort on the night of the 23/24th saw six 300 Squadron crews take off for the waters off Brest. F/L Kowalczyk (not to be confused with the W/C) led them away at 21.26 in JA451, but a radio malfunction forced him to turn back at 21.54 when at 2,000 feet eight miles east of Leicester. The others continued, and all completed their assigned tasks in good conditions between 00.09 and 00.27, before returning without incident.

A few days of rest would allow the Command to lick its wounds, but the end of the month was to bring a major effort against the Capital in the form of three operations in an unprecedented four nights. This would test the resolve of the crews to the absolute limit, and would prove to be the last concerted attempt to bring Berlin to its knees. The series began on the night of the 27/28th, and involved an all Lancaster heavy force numbering 515 aircraft, of which 149 were from 1 Group. 7% of the force returned early, which was about average, while the others pressed on to deliver a scattered attack through complete cloud cover, with more bombs falling into the south of the city than the north. A number of important war industry factories sustained serious damage and loss of production, and twenty thousand people were bombed out of their homes, but there was a large wastage of bombs onto dozens of outlying communities. Thirty-three Lancasters were brought down, and, on a bad night for 1 Group, it posted missing twelve, more than a third of the overall loss figure. While this operation was in progress, six 300 Squadron crews were engaged in mining sorties off the Dutch coast, two in the area of Den Helder, and four further south. Weather conditions were reasonable, and all delivered their mines either side of 21.00, but F/L Kowalczyk's were dropped in error a few miles to the north of the intended drop zone, which should have been off Zandvoort.

The Halifax squadrons joined in at Berlin on the following night to create a force of 670 aircraft, of which 125 belonged to 1 Group. Berlin lay under ten-tenths cloud with tops at 10,000 feet, but the Pathfinders seemed to achieve a degree of concentration, and the consensus was of an effective assault. Western and southern districts bore the main weight of the attack, and 180,000 people were bombed out of their homes. A high number of public and administrative buildings were also hit on this night, as were seventy-seven communities outside of Berlin. The defenders also enjoyed a successful night, hacking down forty-six bombers, although only four from 1 Group. After a night's break, a predominantly Lancaster heavy force of over five hundred aircraft returned to Berlin, and caused heavy damage in central and south-western districts in particular, where fires raged out of control. A thousand people died under the bombs, and thirty-three aircraft were shot down, all but one of them Lancasters. 129 aircraft took part from 1 Group, of which thirty were assigned to Pathfinder support duties, and nine failed to return home.

This concluded the current round of operations against Germany's Capital, and there is no question that it had been sorely afflicted as a result of these three latest assaults, but it was still a functioning city, the seat of government, and nowhere were there signs of collapse. During the course of the month the squadron carried out twelve operations, and dispatched fifty-six sorties without loss.

February 1944

Ingham, February 1944. The crew of Wellington LN697 BH-U in preparation for a minelaying operation. Left to Right: F/S Uram (pilot). Sgt Grzeslowski (A.B.), Sgt Krzyszkowski (nav.), F/S Kulagin (W.Op.) and Sgt Klak (A.G.). (PISM via WM)

Had bad weather not kept most of the Command on the ground for the first two weeks of February, Harris would have followed up the recent successes at Berlin with another attack early in the month. As it was, 300 Squadron kept the war mobile by carrying out mining operations on four nights during the period beginning on the 3rd, when seven crews were assigned to Brest and Lorient. W/C Kowalczyk led the four-strong element to Lorient, and F/O Ingling the others, and both sections found favourable weather conditions with variable amounts of cloud, but moonlight and good visibility. Mines were delivered into the briefed locations between 01.59 and 02.11, and all returned safely from a quiet trip. The squadron sent six crews back to Lorient on the following night, when the recently promoted Air Commodore Cozens left his 1 Group desk to lead the effort. They arrived in the target area to find favourable weather conditions and good visibility, but this time they were met by heavy flak, both from Ile de Groix and from four ships nearby. HE813 sustained some damage, which would require F/L Labiszewski to land at Stanton Harcourt in Gloucestershire with a suspected fuel shortage. Despite the opposition, all of the mines were dropped into the briefed locations either side of 21.00, and there were no casualties to report.

After a few nights away from operations, briefings took place at Ingham on the 10th for mining operations that night off Brest and Lorient. Seven crews were involved, W/C Kowalczyk leading a section of three bound for Lorient, while F/L Kowalczyk was the senior pilot amongst four with the waters off Brest as their destination. They got away safely at around 22.30, and enjoyed favourable weather conditions on the way out, and good visibility in the target area. One of the Brest contingent reported inaccurate tracer from three ships, and four heavy machine guns firing from the coast, but it was not troublesome, and all mines were delivered as briefed at both locations between 00.53 and 01.07, and all returned safely in deteriorating weather. On the following night four crews returned to Brest, while three others headed for a drop zone off St Nazaire. F/L Kowalczyk was the senior pilot on duty for the early take-off either side of 17.45, but LN507 hadn't even left the circuit before engine problems persuaded W/O Blachowicz to abandon his sortie at 18.00. The others pressed on in good weather conditions and visibility, and found their target areas without difficulty. Three ships, reported to be stationary off Brest, poured accurate machine-gun fire into the air, but it did not hamper the success of the operation, and all crews at both locations carried out their assigned tasks between 20.21 and 20.35, before returning safely.

It was not until the night of the 15/16th that Harris could mount another heavy raid on the Capital, and this was a record breaking effort in a number of ways, and would be the penultimate raid of the war on Berlin by RAF heavy bombers. The 891 aircraft represented the largest non-1,000 force to date, and those reaching the target would deliver an unprecedented 2,640 tons of bombs. It was also the first time that over five hundred Lancasters and three hundred Halifaxes had operated as part of the same force. It was a record night also for 1 Group, which dispatched 161 Lancasters, of which 139 are known to have bombed the primary target. Despite the long lay-off, during which the crews had rested and recuperated, seventy-five aircraft turned back early, more than 8% of the force, and twelve of these were from 1 Group. The remainder pressed on and the bomber stream was left largely unmolested by night fighters during the outward flight, which took place in cloud. Berlin itself lay under a blanket of ten-tenths cloud with tops at eight thousand feet, into which the Pathfinder markers quickly disappeared. The bombing was most heavily concentrated in central and south-western districts, and over eleven hundred fires sprang up, half of them classed as large. Around a thousand houses were destroyed, along with over five hundred temporary wooden barracks, and many important war industry factories sustained damage. Forty-three aircraft failed to return home, and nine of these belonged to 1 Group. 300 Squadron dispatched six crews on this night for mining duties off Lorient. They took off either side of 17.30, but LN600 suffered an electrical system failure while at 2,300 feet with the airfield still in sight, and F/O Brochocki was forced to turn back. The others reached the target area to find visibility ranging from poor to good, but all were unanimous regarding the intensity of the darkness. They delivered their mines as briefed between 20.43 and 20.54, and returned home without incident.

A slimming down of the Halifax contribution reduced the size of the force taking off for Leipzig on the night of the 19/20th to 823 aircraft, but 1 Group put up another record of 170 Lancasters. They departed their stations either side of midnight for the long trek into eastern Germany, and headed in broken cloud towards the greatest disaster to afflict the Command thus far. A proportion of the night fighter force met the bomber stream as it crossed the Dutch coast, and the two camps remained in contact all the way to the target. The meteorologists had been experiencing difficulty in predicting the winds over Germany, and this had hampered a number of recent operations. So it was on this night, when an unanticipated strong tail-wind led to some crews reaching the target area ahead of the Pathfinders, where they were forced to orbit and await the opening of the attack. Around twenty of these fell victim to the local flak batteries, while four others were involved in collisions. The attack was delivered through cloud, and many returning crews described seeing the glow of fires and heavy columns of smoke rising towards them. Never the less, the cloud prevented an assessment of the results, but the performance of the enemy defences was all too clear to see. When all returning aircraft had been accounted for, there was an unbelievable shortfall of seventy-eight, the heaviest loss to date by a clear twenty-one. The Halifaxes suffered a 13% casualty rate, and from this point on, the less efficient Merlin powered Mk II and V variants were excluded from operations over Germany, as had been the Stirlings in November.

Despite the prohibitive losses, almost six hundred aircraft set out on the following night for Stuttgart, among them 130 Lancasters from 1 Group. Cloud in the target area varied from three to ten-tenths, and inaccurately forecast winds led to some aircraft arriving early. The Pathfinders opened proceedings on time, and the impression was of concentrated marking and bombing in the built-up area until the later stages, when it spread to the north. Photo-reconnaissance confirmed extensive damage in central districts and in the northern quadrant, and this was achieved for the modest loss of nine aircraft, none of which was from 1 Group. 300 Squadron dispatched six crews on this night for mining operations off Brest, and they were led away by W/C Kowalczyk at 18.06. He was followed a minute later by his F/L namesake, whose sortie was curtailed by the failure of his a.s.i., probably through icing, when he was ten miles north of Oxford at 19.51. The weather conditions outbound were not ideal, but the remaining crews all reached the target area, where they found visibility much improved under clear skies. They also found many machine guns firing at them from ships dispersed off the port, but this did not hamper the work in hand, and four crews delivered their mines as briefed between 20.36 and 20.48. JA117 did not return home with the crew of F/S Kabacinski, and no trace has ever been found of man or machine. This would prove to be the very last Wellington to be lost on operations with Bomber Command. On the following night four crews returned to Brest, once more encountering adverse weather during the outward flight over the Channel and France. This time there was no machine-gun fire to greet them, and they all completed their assigned tasks in good visibility between 20.39 and 20.57, before returning home safely.

A new tactic was employed for the next two operations to Germany in an attempt to address the problem of unacceptably high losses. This involved splitting the force into two waves, with a two hour gap in between, to catch the enemy night fighter force on the ground refuelling and rearming as the second phase force passed through. 392 aircraft represented the first wave for Schweinfurt on the night of the 24/25th, taking off after 18.00 hours, and 342 others followed after 20.00 hours. 1 Group provided seventy Lancasters for the first wave and eighty-six for the second, and each found similar conditions of cloud over France and clear skies in the target area. The impression was of a successful initial assault, which set fires burning that were visible by the approaching second phase crews from 150 miles away. Heavy smoke tended to obscure the ground for the second phase attack, and there was some undershooting and a gradual spreading of the bombing towards the north. Photo-reconnaissance suggested that the operation was not as effective as at first believed, but the second phase lost 50% fewer aircraft than the first, in an overall casualty figure of thirty three, which suggested some merit to the policy of splitting the force. 300 Squadron was also active on this night with five crews mining off Lorient led by F/L Kowalczyk. There were clear skies in the target area, but intense darkness, and there was some light flak directed at them ineffectively from the coast. They delivered their mines as briefed between 21.38 and 21.55, and returned without incident.

On the following night, Augsburg became the victim of another of those rare occasions beyond the range of Oboe, when an operation proceeded almost entirely according to plan. 590 aircraft took part in the two-phase attack, 1 Group contributing 102 Lancasters to the first and thirty-nine to the second. The operation

Despite often being written off as a failure for Bomber Command, the Battle of Berlin resulted in considerable destruction to the city's war industries and iinfrastructure, and brought the war back to the Nazi regime's doorstep, a source of grim satisfaction to the Poles who suffered so grievously as a nation at the hands of the Germans.

was characterised by highly accurate and concentrated marking and bombing, which left the old centre of this beautiful and historic city ravaged by fire, destroying forever centuries of irreplaceable culture. Almost three thousand houses were wrecked, as were many public buildings, and millions of pounds worth of art treasures were also lost. For its part, the bomber force returned home without twenty-one of its number, which again suggested that there was some merit in splitting the force, and this would become a regular feature of operations from the coming autumn. 300 Squadron operated for the final time in the month on this night, when sending five crews to mine the waters off St Nazaire. It was also to be the final operation from Ingham, as preparations were in hand for the imminent move to Faldingworth, a few miles away on the other side of the A15 north of Lincoln. Perhaps to mark the occasion, G/C Macpherson and W/C Kowalczyk shared Wellington LN553, and took off at 17.58, followed by the others over the ensuing twelve minutes. It turned out to be a quiet trip under clear skies in the target area, but there was also intense darkness and limited visibility. Never the less, all crews fulfilled their briefs between 20.53 and 20.56, and returned safely home. The 29th was devoted to clearing snow from the vital points of the airfield, and preparing for the move scheduled for the next day. Fifty-three sorties from twelve operations during the month resulted in the loss of one aircraft.

March 1944

It was the opening of Sandtoft at the start of March that enabled 1667 HCU to leave Faldingworth and make room for 300 Squadron to move over from Ingham. The transports carrying the squadron equipment departed Ingham at 10.00 on the 1st, leaving just the aircraft and air and ground crews behind. The living quarters at Faldingworth were found to be less comfortable than at Ingham, but in other respects the facilities were superior. The month's operations began for the main force on the night of the 1/2nd with a return to Stuttgart by over five hundred aircraft, the majority of which were Lancasters. Eighty of these were provided by 1 Group, and they set out in clear conditions, which persisted until the force was south of Paris, where ten-tenths cloud developed with tops as high as 15,000 feet. At the target the Pathfinder markers disappeared quickly into the cloud, forcing the crews to bomb on release-point flares. Some H2S-equipped crews became aware that the marking was concentrated too much in the south and south-western districts, but it did spread towards the north in the later stages of the attack. The cloud prevented an immediate assessment of results, but it was a successful operation, which caused fresh damage in central, western and northern districts.

There followed a two-week lull in major operations, during which period 300 Squadron went to war for the final time as a Wellington unit. F/L Kowalczyk, W/O Blachowicz and F/S Danieluk took off from Ingham shortly after 18.00 on the 3rd to mine the waters around Lorient, and arrived in the target area to find excellent visibility and almost daylight conditions. They delivered their mines into the briefed locations between 20.42 and 20.53, and all returned safely, with the intention of landing at Wickenby. F/S Danieluk and crew, who were on just their third operation, landed at Kelstern in error, but this was put down to inexperience. Also, during this period, the first salvoes were fired in the pre-invasion campaign against the French and Belgian railway systems, when Halifaxes were the predominant type in attacks on railway yards at Trappes and le Mans on the nights of the 6/7th and 7/8th respectively. These raids would continue throughout the month, and would be stepped up when the rest of the main force joined in at the conclusion of the winter offensive. Conversion training was rarely completed without at least one serious accident, and for 300 Squadron this happened on the night of the 7/8th, when P/O Ingling and crew were engaged in a night bombing exercise. They were in Halifax HR657, which belonged to 1662 Heavy Conversion Unit, and around midnight they collided with Halifax EB184 of 1667 HCU over the bombing range. Both aircraft came down near Haxey, eleven miles south-west of Scunthorpe in north-west Lincolnshire, and there were no survivors from either crew.

The first crew to complete conversion training, that of F/S Nalepa, arrived back on the squadron from 1 Lancaster Finishing School (1LFS) on the 9th. The Command returned to operations after the long lay-off on the night of the 15/16th, and did so in unprecedented strength. The main effort involved 823 aircraft taking off for the third raid in three weeks on Stuttgart, while 140 Halifaxes, Stirlings and Mosquitos went to Amiens to target the railway yards, and a small 5 Group raid was directed at an aero-engine factory at Woippy in France. 1 Group dispatched a record number of 190 Lancasters to southern Germany, and they took off in conditions of thin broken cloud, which had thickened to seven to ten-tenths by the time they reached the target area. The enemy night fighters arrived at the same time and remained in contact with the bombers until they were well on their way home. The cloud prevented an assessment of results, but it would become clear that it had not been as effective an attack as that at the start of the month. Thirty-seven aircraft were brought down, eight of them from 1 Group. The first air-test of a 300 Squadron Lancaster from Faldingworth took place on the 17th, and, during the remainder of the month, crews filtered back following the completion of their conversion, and limited exercises took place in the form of cross-countries, fighter affiliation and bombing practice.

The first of two heavy and successful operations against Frankfurt took place on the night of the 18/19th, when more than eight hundred aircraft took part. The 194 Lancasters from 1 Group represented a new record, and they contributed to the destruction of, or serious damage to, over six thousand buildings. Of the twenty-two missing aircraft just two were from 1 Group, and this enabled it to put up another 194 Lancasters for the second assault on this southern city on the night of the 22/23rd. The outcome was even more catastrophic for the residents, who came out of their shelters to find half of the city without electricity, gas and water, a situation that would persist for an extended period. Fires could be seen from up to two hundred miles by returning crews, all but four of those from 1 Group making it back home.

On the night of the 24/25th, Harris mounted what would be the final raid of the war by RAF heavy bombers on Berlin, and the sixteenth since the resumption of the campaign in November. 1 Group put up 184 Lancasters in an overall force of 811 aircraft, of which fifty-three returned early. Having set course at cruising altitude, the crews encountered an unusually strong wind from the north, which broke up the cohesion of the bomber stream and pushed the aircraft continually south of the intended track. This inevitably led to the Pathfinders' skymarkers being driven to the south-west of the city, as a result of which two areas of concentration developed. The release-point flares were identified as being five to eight miles north of the ground markers, and the Master Bomber could be heard clearly exhorting the crews to aim for these. A feature of Berlin operations had been the number of outlying communities finding themselves under attack, and on this night more than a hundred reported bombs falling around them. The part of the attack that hit the city inflicted moderate damage in residential districts, but no important industrial concerns were damaged. Many crews found themselves straying over heavily defended areas of the Reich on the way home, as it remained difficult to resist the jetstream wind, and over two-thirds of the seventy-two missing bombers were claimed by flak batteries, mostly in the Ruhr region. From now on, it would be left to the Mosquitos of 8 Group to maintain the pressure on the Capital, and this they would do until Russian troops fought their way into the city in April 1945.

It is interesting to take stock of the eight month period from August 1943 to March 1944, during which nineteen major operations were directed at Berlin. In his superb book, The Berlin Raids, Martin Middlebrook provides many statistics, which allow a clear picture of the fortunes of respective groups and squadrons to emerge. The 1 Group A-O-C, AVM Rice, believed fervently that the way to win was to deliver the maximum possible bomb tonnage to the enemy. He undertook trials to ascertain just how much a Lancaster could carry before its undercarriage showed signs of failure while taxying to the runway. The answer was around four hundred pounds more than that carried by 5 Group aircraft. This meant that 1 Group Lancasters were less able to reach the safer higher altitudes, and were less manoeuvrable in a combat situation. As a result 1 Group's rate of early returns was greater than 5 Group's, and it was noticed that 1 Group crews were guilty of jettisoning bombs over the sea, thus negating the point of loading them to the maximum. It is worth noting that four 1 Group squadrons featured in the top ten table of sorties dispatched, 460 and 101 Squadrons in first and second place respectively, while 103 and 100 Squadrons occupied sixth and seventh spot.

Although the Berlin offensive was now over, the winter campaign still had a week to run, and two more major operations for the crews to negotiate. The first was against Essen on the 26/27th, for which over seven hundred aircraft took off, 165 of them from 1 Group. The benefits of returning to a target within range of Oboe were made manifest by the destruction of over seventeen hundred houses, and the serious damage to forty-eight industrial buildings. Thus was continued the remarkable run of successes against this once elusive city since the introduction of Oboe to main force operations a year earlier. The defences were caught napping by the sudden switch to a Ruhr target, and only nine aircraft were lost.

The winter offensive was brought to a conclusion on the night of the 30/31st, when a standard maximum effort raid was planned for Nuremberg. A 5 Group-inspired route was offered for consideration, which would take the bomber stream on a long, straight leg from Belgium across Germany to a point about fifty miles north of Nuremberg, from where the final run-in to the target would begin. During a planning conference, the Lancaster Group A-O-Cs unanimously expressed a preference for this, rather than a more circuitous route as prepared by 8 Group, and 4 Group's AVM Roddy Carr was the lone dissenting voice. AVM Bennett, the Pathfinder A-O-C, blew a gasket and predicted a disaster, but his warning went unheeded, as did a report from a Met Flight Mosquito crew, which cast grave doubts on the accuracy of the cloud forecast. More than a few crews expected the operation to be scrubbed, but it was not to be, and no one could have predicted the extent to which the conditions would blight the forthcoming proceedings.

795 aircraft took off either side of 22.00 hours, among them 180 from 1 Group. They converged on the rendezvous point over the North Sea, before setting a south-easterly course for Charleroi in Belgium, and then an almost due easterly heading into Germany. Once at cruising altitude, the crews became aware of some unfamiliar meteorological characteristics, which left many of them feeling distinctly uneasy. Although relatively new, the moon cast an unusual brightness, and the visibility possessed a crystal clarity that enabled the crews to see the other aircraft in their part of the sky. The forecast high cloud failed to materialize, but formed instead beneath the bombers, to silhouette them like flies on a table cloth. As if this were not enough, condensation trails began to develop to further advertise their presence over hostile territory, and as the final insult, the jetstream winds, which had so adversely effected the Berlin raid a week earlier, were also evident, only this time from the south. These conditions and the route served to hand the bomber force on a plate to the night fighters, which were waiting at their control beacons close to the chosen route.

The carnage began at Charleroi, and from there to the target the track was clearly marked out by the burning wreckage of bombers on the ground. Over eighty were shot down before the target was even reached, and the jetstream wind was breaking up and dispersing the bomber stream to reduce still further the numbers available to deliver the attack. In every operation certain crews were designated as wind-finders, and it was their task to gauge the strength and direction of the wind, and pass that on by W/T to the raid controllers, who would broadcast the findings back to the whole force. In the event, the wind-finders found it difficult to believe what they were seeing, and modified the readings for fear of being disbelieved. In turn, the groups were disbelieving even of the modified readings, and modified them further before transmitting them back to the bomber stream. As a result navigators were working from wildly inaccurate data, and this led to numerous crews turning towards Nuremberg from a false position up to fifty miles north of where they believed themselves to be. Many of these were among more than a hundred who bombed Schweinfurt in error, and together with the fifty-two early returns and the losses already sustained, this dramatically reduced the numbers reaching the target to around 540 aircraft. In the face of heavy cloud cover, these failed to find the mark, and much of the bombing was wasted in open country.

A poignant and iconic photograph, taken at RAF Snaith before the disastrous Nuremberg raid. Squadron Peter Hill briefs crews of 51 Squadron. By the following dawn thirty five of these men would be dead, including S/L Hill. Seven others would be PoWs (Crown Copyright).

Nuremberg escaped lightly, but Bomber Command had suffered by far its heaviest defeat of the war, amounting to ninety-five aircraft, and others were written off in crashes at home, or with battle damage too severe to repair. The 1 Group casualty figure amounted to twenty-one failures to return, and it was a tragic ending to a long and bitterly fought first quarter of the year. 300 Squadron undertook just a single operation during the month, with three sorties and no losses.

April 1944

That which now lay before the crews was in marked contrast to what had been endured over the preceding months. The new priority was the Transportation Plan, the systematic dismantling by bombing of the French and Belgian railway networks in preparation for the forthcoming invasion, which, as already mentioned, had been initiated in early March by elements from 3, 4, 6 and 8 Groups. The availability now of the rest of the main force squadrons meant that the time had arrived for the campaign to get into full swing. In place of the long slog to distant German targets on dark, often dirty nights, shorter range trips to the occupied countries would become the order of the day in improving weather conditions. These operations would prove to be equally demanding in their way, however, and would require of the crews a greater commitment to accuracy, to avoid unnecessary civilian casualties. The main fly in the ointment was a pronouncement from on high, which decreed that most such operations were worthy of counting as just one-third of a sortie towards the completion of a tour, and until this flawed policy was rescinded, an air of discontent pervaded the bomber stations.

Despite the prohibitive losses over the winter, the Command was in remarkably fine fettle to meet its new challenge, and Harris was in the enviable position of being able to achieve that which had eluded his predecessor. This was, to attack multiple targets simultaneously, with forces large enough to make an impact, and he could now assign objectives to individual Groups, to Groups in tandem or to the Command as a whole, as dictated by operational requirements. Although pre-invasion considerations would always take priority, Harris's favoured policy of city-busting would never be entirely shelved, and whenever an opportunity presented itself, he would strike. 300 Squadron would begin its operational career on Lancasters under a new commanding officer, after W/C Kowalczyk was posted to HQ ADGB on the 1st after just ten weeks at the helm. He was to take up duties as a liaison officer with the 1st Polish Armoured Division, and was succeeded as commanding officer by W/C Pozyczka, who would remain in post for ten months. Two days later LL856 became the first operationally fit Lancaster to be taken on charge by the Poles, and the process of working up to operational status began.

W/C Teofil Pozyczka completed 36 operations during his first tour of duty in 301 Squadron from Sept. 1940 to June 1942. After spending almost two years as instructor in 18 OTU at Bramcote he was appointed CO of 300 Squadron in April 1944. Between April and Nov. 1944 he flew 19 sorties of his second tour. (PISM via WM)

The first major night of operations since Nuremberg came on the 9/10th, when elements of 3, 4, 6 and 8 Groups attacked the Lille-Delivrance goods station, while 225 aircraft from all Groups targeted the railway yards at Villeneuve-St-Georges in Paris. Both of the main operations were claimed as successful, the Lille force destroying over two thousand items of rolling stock, and seriously damaging buildings and track, but heavy casualties were inflicted upon French civilians at each location. It was a sobering start to the new phase of operations, which carried over into the following night, when five railway yards were attacked in France and Belgium. 130 Lancasters of 1 Group were assigned to those at Aulnoye, where the marking was carried out by Oboe Mosquitos. The attack resulted in damage to the engine shed and thirty locomotives, but 340 houses were also destroyed or damaged, and fourteen civilians lost their lives. On the night of the 11/12th over three hundred Lancasters from 1, 3 and 5 Groups provided the main force for an attack on railway installations at Aachen. Ninety-five 1 Group Lancasters took part in what became a highly destructive area raid that resulted in the deaths of over fifteen hundred people.

It was a week before the heavy brigade was in action again, and in the meantime, on the 14th, the Command officially became subject to the authority of Supreme Headquarters Allied Expeditionary Force (SHAEF), and would remain thus shackled until the Allied armies were sweeping towards the German frontier at the end of the summer. On the 15th 300 Squadron was declared operational on Lancasters with sixteen on charge and four in reserve. On the 18th 1 Group's Special Duties Flight, or SDF as it became known, was formed at Binbrook under the command of S/L Breakspear, an experienced flight commander from 100 Squadron. Its job would be to mark targets for the group, to provide it with a degree of autonomy, as was happening at 5 Group.

The crew of W/C Pozyczka (1st from right) beside Lancaster LM486 BH-C photographed at Faldingworth in April 1944. (PISM via WM)

The night of the 18/19th was devoted to attacks on four railway yards, for which 1 and 3 Groups were to act as the main force at Rouen. Among the 140 Lancasters of 1 Group were seven representing 300 Squadron on its maiden Lancaster operation. W/C Pozyczka led them away from Faldingworth at 22.02 in LM486, and carried with him Polish war correspondent Mr Kisielewski to record the night's events. The other crews on this momentous occasion were those of F/O Fedoronko, and F/Ss Markiewicz, Poludniak, Koziolek, Zoltanski and Nalepa. They all reached the target area to find clear conditions, and fires already beginning to spring up, which helped them to identify ground features. Red and green target indicators identified the aiming point, and W/C Pozyczka assessed that they were concentrated a fraction to the north of the southern end of the marshalling yards. He released his ten 1,000 and four 500 pounder medium capacity bombs onto them from 8,000 feet at 00.25, and the other squadron participants did likewise from 8,500 to 12,000 feet between 00.22 and 00.26. A number of crews reported hang-ups, but all returned safely to describe smoke rising to around 3,000 feet, and a successful first operation. Messages of congratulations were received on the 20th from AVM Izycki of the Polish Air Force Inspectorate, and from G/C Beill, the Polish liaison officer at Bomber Command HQ.

The first major raid on Cologne since its pounding during the Ruhr offensive was mounted on the night of the 20/21st, and involved a force of more than 350 Lancasters from 1, 3 and 6 Groups. 1 Group contributed a record 196 aircraft, of which seven were provided by 300 Squadron. W/C Pozyczka again led the way as they took off either side of midnight, when enemy intruders were known to be active, and crews responded to R/T warnings to be on the lookout. W4376 was at 21,000 feet over southern Belgium outbound, when the navigator became unwell, probably because of oxygen starvation, and F/S Markiewicz turned back at 01.35. He jettisoned the incendiary element of his bomb load, but retained his cookie and brought it home. The others found the target hidden by ten-tenths cloud, and W/C Pozyczka delivered his cookie and incendiaries from 23,000 feet on estimated position, backed up by a greenish light seen through the cloud. The others found skymarkers over the estimated position of the target, and they bombed from 20,000 to 21,000 feet between 02.07 and 02.10. Two minutes after bombing F/S Nalepa and crew spotted a twin-engine enemy aircraft eight hundred yards to starboard, which they evaded by corkscrewing, only to find a second one, identified as a JU88, two minutes later, manoeuvring into position above and behind. It closed to six hundred yards before firing a two-second burst, but it too was evaded by corkscrewing without the need for return fire. They all arrived home unable to offer an assessment of the outcome of the raid, but reconnaissance on the following day established that they had helped to inflict massive destruction on industrial and residential property, with railway installations and public buildings also featuring in the extensive catalogue of damage.

Two nights later Düsseldorf was selected to host a heavy attack, for which 596 aircraft from all but 5 Group were made ready. 1 Group detailed 178 Lancasters, of which seven were provided by 300 Squadron, and they got away from Faldingworth either side of 23.00, led again by W/C Pozyczka. On his way to the target the commanding officer watched an unidentified bomber being shot down by upward firing tracer near Charleroi in Belgium at 00.50. All of the 300 Squadron crews reached the target area to find clear skies and good visibility, with red and green target indicators cascading ahead of them as they approached. W/C Pozyczka bombed on a concentration of these from 24,000 feet at 01.25, and two minutes later observed a large orange explosion and a column of smoke rising to 15,000 feet. He saw a number of aircraft bomb decoy fires ten miles south of the target, and then on the way home, at 01.50 near Eindhoven, witnessed an unidentified aircraft catch fire and explode in the air. The other squadron crews bombed from 20,000 to 23,500 feet between 01.23 and 01.27, and returned safely with stories of their own about the intensity of the defences and the sight of crashing bombers. Reconnaissance confirmed that more than two thousand houses had been destroyed, mostly in northern districts, and local reports detailed fifty-six large industrial premises hit, seven of them completely wrecked. A message was received from the 1 Group A-O-C on the 23rd, congratulating the squadron on its excellent performance during its first three operations. AVM Rice added that he looked forward with the greatest confidence to the day when they would be up to full strength with their new equipment, to surpass the splendid record already achieved.

S/L Ludwik Kurowski."B" Flight Commander took part in 23 operations from July 1943 to April 1944 with 300 Squadron, but failed to return from his 24th sortie. (PISM via WM)

Southern Germany was the destination for more than nine hundred aircraft on the night of the 24/25th, as 637 headed for Karlsruhe and 260 others, all but ten of them from 5 Group, targeted Munich. 1 Group contributed 179 Lancasters, seven of which represented 300 Squadron, and they began departing Faldingworth at 22.09 led by S/L Kurowski. The outward journey was routed over Holland, and when twenty miles south of Eindhoven at 22,000 feet, LM487 was approached by an enemy night fighter, which made a number of attempts to manoeuvre into a favourable position astern. Ultimately, no combat took place, and the enemy aircraft was lost. Heavy cloud was encountered for a large part of the operation, some of it reaching up to 27,000 feet, and icing became a problem for many crews. The skies were clear by the time the target hove into sight, and it was identified by cascading green and red TIs. The squadron crews bombed from 21,000 to 23,500 feet between 00.41 and 00.48 in the face of moderate to intense heavy flak in barrage form, and explosions and fires were seen as they turned for home.

F/L Korepta and crew were severely afflicted by the conditions during the return flight, and lost the use of the guns in the rear turret after they iced up. A sudden loss of control had the Lancaster drop to 17,000 feet over eastern France, and the pilot ordered his crew to prepare to bale out, before he regained control as soon as LM487 emerged from the cloud. At 02.25 in the same region, believed to be ten miles north-east of Charleroi, another enemy fighter was encountered, which made six unsuccessful attempts to engage the Lancaster over a twenty-five-minute period, and managed just one burst of fire from four hundred yards astern. There was no damage and no claim, and the aircraft and crew arrived home safely. F/S Koziolek and crew reported stronger-than-forecast winds, and around a hundred searchlights, mostly in the south-western quarter of the city, co-operating effectively with the flak. They described scattered fires in the north-east of the target, and one large one resembling a figure of eight. This crew also encountered an enemy aircraft, at 02.30 near Compiegne, north-east of Paris, and well to the south-west of LM487's position, but it was another inconclusive engagement with no consequences. These were the fortunate ones, as two other 300 Squadron Lancasters failed to arrive home. LL855 was attacked by a night fighter while closing on the target, and exploded in the air south-east of Darmstadt without survivors from the crew of F/O Fedoronko. The fate of LM486 and the crew of S/L Kurowski has never been established, and it is likely that they went down over the sea. The observations of returning crews were confirmed by reconnaissance, which revealed that the strong wind had pushed the bombing into the northern part of Karlsruhe, but even so, over nine hundred houses were destroyed or seriously damaged.

Over nine hundred aircraft were involved in three major operations on the night of the 26/27th, the largest one to Essen being undertaken by almost five hundred aircraft, while more than two hundred each went to Schweinfurt and the railway yards at Villeneuve-St-Georges in Paris. Two of the raids were successful, but the 5 Group effort in southern Germany lacked accuracy and cost twenty-one Lancasters. 300 Squadron did not take part in operations on this night, and, in fact, would remain at home for the rest of the month. On the following night 322 Lancasters of 1, 3, 6 and 8 Groups set off for the long flight to the highly industrialized town of Friedrichshafen, on the northern shore of the Bodensee near the Swiss frontier. I Group dispatched 162 Lancasters, and they contributed to a highly concentrated and effective raid which, because of the relatively small size of the town, necessitated an attack in moonlight. An estimated 67% of the built-up area was left in ruins, while a number of factories sustained severe damage, and the destruction of a tank gearbox plant had a major effect on Germany's tank production. The night fighters arrived on the scene as the attack was in progress, and benefiting from the bright conditions, contributed to the loss of eighteen Lancasters in the target area and on the way home. The Squadron operated on four occasions during the month, dispatching twenty-eight sorties for the loss of two aircraft.

May 1944

The new month's operations began for the Command with attacks against six separate targets on the night of the 1/2nd. 300 Squadron would not operate at all during the first nine nights of May. The 3rd was Poland's National Day, and a well-attended concert was held in the station institute in the evening to commemorate the occasion. Parties were held in the respective messes afterwards, and all Polish crews were invited, including those under training at Hemswell and Blyton. The night of the 3/4th became one of high drama, when the target was a German army Panzer training camp and motor transport depot at Mailly-le-Camp, in the Aube region of north-central France. Its presence posed a potential threat to the Normandy landings now only a month away. The two phase operation by 1 and 5 Groups was ultimately highly successful, but communications difficulties led to delays in the bombing, which allowed enemy night fighters to infiltrate the circling bombers and shoot down forty-two Lancasters, twenty-eight of them from the 1 Group second phase.

A number of small scale operations occupied elements from the Group over the succeeding week, and seven coastal batteries were attacked in the Pas-de-Calais on the night of the 9/10th, to maintain the deception concerning the true location of the D-Day landings. 1 Group was assigned to targets at Merville and Mardyck, and all of its one hundred aircraft returned. Four railway yards and a coastal battery provided the objectives for five hundred aircraft on the 10/11th, the night which saw a return to operations for 300 Squadron. Six Lancasters departed Faldingworth shortly after 22.30 led by W/C Pozyczka, and they were to join up with fifty-four others from the group to attack a coastal battery near Dieppe. They reached the target area to find clear skies, good visibility, and concentrated Pathfinder marking, and they delivered their eleven 1,000 and four 500 pounders each from 11,000 feet between 00.01 and 00.09, before returning to report a trouble-free operation.

Three railway yards were among a variety of targets selected for attention on the following night, and 300 Squadron contributed eight Lancasters to the 1 Group raid at Hasselt in eastern Belgium. There were no senior pilots on duty as they got away from Faldingworth either side of 22.15, and made their way to the rendezvous point. They found the target under a thin veil of cloud and hidden by haze, and F/O Rozanski reported the Pathfinder marking to be late and poor. The Polish crews were each carrying ten 1,000 and four 500 pounders, and these were delivered from 10,000 to 12,000 feet either side of midnight. Enemy aircraft were spotted dropping flares, and one was seen to be communicating with the ground through coloured lights. Ultimately, the poor visibility persuaded the Master Bomber to send two-thirds of the crews home with their bombs, and reconnaissance established that those bombs dropped had missed the target. P/O Adler was delayed by head winds, so he joined the 3 and 8 Group attack on the railway yards at Louvain, further west towards Brussels. On return he reported picking up a spoof German transmission telling the bombers to return to base.

Minor operations then held sway until the night of the 19/20th, when five railway yards and two gun emplacements provided the main fare. Over a hundred Lancasters of 1 Group were detailed to carry out an attack on the marshalling yards at Orleans, for which 300 Squadron contributed six aircraft. F/S Nalepa led them away at 22.18 on a night of poor local weather conditions, which saw the Lancasters disappear into the cloud base at 1,500 feet. On board LL857 was a Polish war correspondent, Mr Piekarski. F/O Adler abandoned his sortie midway across the Channel at 23.42 after his Gee equipment failed, and, unusually for a Polish crew, he jettisoned his bombs into the sea, probably because of doubts about landing conditions at base. The others pressed on to reach the target, where they found small amounts of patchy cloud, but fairly good visibility, and the River Loire was easily identified. The aiming point was marked by cascading red and green target indicators, and the squadron crews delivered their mix of medium capacity (MC) and general purpose (GP) 1,000 and 500 pounders from 8,000 to 12,000 feet between 00.46 and 00.48. Returning crews reported concentrated bombing, large fires and explosions, and the glow of fires visible from eighty miles away. Reconnaissance confirmed the crews' impressions, that the operation had been highly successful.

The first major raid on Duisburg for a year was delivered by over five hundred Lancasters of 1, 3, 5 and 8 Groups on the night of the 21/22nd. 300 Squadron detailed eight Lancasters among a 1 Group record of 207, and they took off either side of 23.00 led by W/C Pozyczka. F/S Koziolek was accompanied by G/C Mason, the station commander at Faldingworth. They found the target hidden beneath ten-tenths cloud with tops at 10,000 feet, but release point flares guided the crews to the aiming point, although W/C Pozyczka reported aircraft approaching it from various directions while waiting for the flares to appear. Large numbers of searchlights lit up the cloud base, and heavy flak in barrage form was observed to burst through the cloud at between 18,000 and 25,000 feet throughout the attack. The commanding officer watched an air-fired rocket projectile travel horizontally below his aircraft at 21,000 feet, before it disappeared into the cloud. It was established later that 350 buildings had been destroyed in southern districts of the city, in return for the loss of a hefty twenty-nine aircraft.

Dortmund was similarly honoured with its first major raid for a year on the following night, when 6 Group substituted for 5 Group. Of over 370 aircraft taking part 183 were provided by 1 Group, 300 Squadron again contributing eight Lancasters. F/S Nalepa led them away at 22.40 in LL857, and all was well until they neared the enemy coast, when the port outer engine began to fail. The engine was shut down and the bomb load jettisoned into the sea, and the return to Faldingworth proceeded without further incident, until the flaps were lowered for final approach. At that point the port-inner engine cut, with the inevitable consequence of flinging the Lancaster into a steep bank to the left, which was unrecoverable. It crashed into the firing range on the edge of the airfield and burst into flames, killing the navigator and wireless operator instantly, and mortally wounding the flight engineer, who succumbed within hours. The other members of the crew were lucky to survive, and all sustained serious injury. F/S Poludniak abandoned his sortie over the North Sea, midway between the Lincolnshire coast and Den Helder, after his navigator became too ill to continue.

The others pushed on to the target, which they found under clear skies and in good visibility. Red, green and yellow target indicators could be seen burning on the ground, and the impression was of a very concentrated marking effort by the Pathfinders. An estimated three hundred searchlights were in operation, and medium to heavy barrage and predicted flak detonating at 17,000 to 22,000 feet made life uncomfortable while over the target. A number of aircraft were seen to bomb decoy fires west of the city, but they were the exception. Most of the others deposited their bombs into south-eastern districts, and a huge explosion was witnessed at 00.55, along with smoke rising to around 9,000 feet. The glow of fires was visible eighty miles into the return journey, but eighteen aircraft failed to enjoy a return after falling victim to the defences. LM487 was attacked by a night fighter on its way home over the Ruhr, and severely damaged, and F/O Adler was unable to maintain control. He ordered his crew to bale out, at which point the Lancaster broke up over Krefeld, and he was thrown clear as the only survivor. Among those losing their lives was the twenty-two-year old F/O Bergner DFM, who was on the third operation of his third tour. His first thirty sorties had been as a wireless operator with 304 Squadron, after which he was commissioned and retrained as a navigator before joining 300 Squadron for a second tour. Reconnaissance confirmed the success of the attack, which destroyed more than 850 houses and six industrial premises.

Two railway yards were the aiming points in Aachen on the night of the 24/25th, but the town and outlying communities also suffered at the hands of over four hundred aircraft from all but 5 Group. 300 Squadron was not called into action for this operation, but when it was repeated three nights later by elements of 1, 3 and 8 Groups, six Lancasters lined up for take-off at Faldingworth at 00.15 led by S/L Korepta. The aiming point was the Rothe Erde yards at the eastern end of the town, which had escaped terminal damage during the earlier raid, and special tactics were to be used by the main force crews. They were to approach the target area at 20,000 feet, and then descend to 10,000 to deliver their bombs onto ground markers if the conditions allowed, or release point flares if it was cloudy. In the event the skies were clear and the visibility good, and the crews had the luxury of TIs cascading in the air and a plentiful supply burning on the ground. The 300 Squadron crews delivered their eleven 1,000 and four 500 pounders each from 10,000 or 12,000 feet between 02.26 and 02.32, and many bursts were seen on and around the aiming point. Nine 1 Group aircraft failed to return, and among them was DV282, which was hit by flak outbound over south-east Holland at the start of the Ruhr flak defence zone, and exploded with great force. The wreckage fell around the town of Heusden, and there were no survivors from the eight-man freshman crew captained by the experienced F/S Koziolek, among which was an American, P/O Tapp, who had volunteered to join the Polish Air Force. Reconnaissance confirmed the success of the operation, which halted all though-traffic. The squadron operated six times during the month, and lost two aircraft from forty-two sorties.

Lancaster ED779 BH-L with the artwork of a nude girl named Lili sitting on a bomb. The aircraft was flown by 300 Squadron crews during 18 operations in summer 1944. (PISM via WM)

June 1944

The first few nights of June were dominated by preparations for the invasion, which was being delayed by bad weather. 1 Group joined others in maintaining the deception by sending 166 Lancasters to bomb coastal batteries in the Pas-de-Calais and a signals station at Berneval on the night of the 2/3rd. On the following night a battery at Wimereux was the target, but neither of these operations involved 300 Squadron. Its turn came in the early hours of the 5th, when five of its Lancasters took off to attack a coastal battery at Sangatte, ten miles south-west of Calais. They were safely airborne from Faldingworth by 02.00 in good weather conditions, but the target was found to be hidden by ten-tenths cloud. At briefing they had been instructed to bomb on target indicators if the target was clear, otherwise on a Gee fix, and F/Ss Fudali and Badowski picked out the faint red glow of markers beneath the clouds and aimed their eighteen 500 pounders accordingly from around 9,500 feet shortly before 03.30. The remaining three crews bombed on a Gee fix from 7,500 to 11,000 feet at the same time in the face of moderate and accurate flak. ED779 was hit over the target, and sustained significant damage to the port wing and main-plane, and the right side of the fuselage, but landed safely in the hands of P/O Burkiewicz and crew.

Over a thousand aircraft were made ready for operations on D-Day Eve, the 5/6th, to bomb ten batteries on the Normandy coast overlooking the landing grounds. 1 Group contributed 191 aircraft along with a further twenty-four ABC Lancasters from 101 Squadron, which would be engaged in special patrol duties. No direct reference was made at briefings to the invasion, but crews were given strict flight levels, and were instructed not to jettison bombs over the sea. 300 Squadron detailed six Lancasters to join in the attack on the Crisbecq site, north of the village of Saint-Marcouf and overlooking Omaha Beach, where American forces were about to land. F/O Rozanski was the senior pilot on duty, and he was first away from Faldingworth at 21.39 in good weather conditions. The Normandy coast was mostly covered by ten-tenths cloud, in the face of which the Special Duties Flight carried out skymarking for the 1 Group effort. The 300 Squadron crews aimed their eleven 1,000 and four 500 pounders each at the red glow of TIs through the cloud from 6,000 to 11,000 feet between 23.35 and 23.43, and returned home unable to offer any assessment of the results. Aircraft were taking off throughout the night, and those crews returning at low level in dawn's early light were rewarded with a glimpse of the armada ploughing its way sedately across the Channel below.

That night another thousand aircraft concentrated their efforts against road and rail communications in or near nine towns on the approaches to the beachhead. 1 Group sent ninety-seven aircraft, six of them from 300 Squadron, to attack a railway junction at Acheres, on the north-west outskirts of Paris. They were instructed at briefing to aim for the ground markers, but if conditions prevented them from doing so, they were to bring their bombs home. W/C Pozyczka led them away at 00.30, and they arrived in the target area to find complete cloud cover below the briefed bombing height of 9,000 feet. It seems that the 300 Squadron crews did not comply with instructions, and all but one bombed. W/C Pozyczka saw the red glow of the ground markers as he approached the target at 02.19, but dropped his bombs on a Gee fix from 8,000 feet at 02.23. On return he would complain that the operation was a complete failure because the Master Bomber had been unable to identify the aiming point, and had not called the crews down to below the 8,000-foot cloud base. F/S Badowski dropped to 7,000 feet, from where the TIs were clearly visible, and he took an excellent photograph as evidence. Others from the squadron bombed from 9,000

Lancaster LL807 BH-N which took part in 11 operations with 300 Squadron. The crew of F/L Rozanski flew all but one raid in this aircraft. (PISM via WM)

and 10,000 feet before the Master Bomber called a halt to proceedings, and only F/O Rozanski complied with his instructions.

Similar targets occupied large sections of the Command over the following two nights, before 1, 4, 6 and 8 Groups attacked airfields south of the battle area on the night of the 9/10th. A hundred 1 Group crews were briefed to attack the airfield at Flers on this night, for which 300 Squadron contributed seven Lancasters, led by F/O Rozanski. He was first away at 01.11, with instructions to bomb from 3,000 feet, or down as low as 1,500 feet if the conditions demanded. Visibility in the target area was good, and the airfield was identified visually or by red and green TIs. The crews delivered their eighteen 500 pounders from 2,000 to 6,000 feet between 03.18 and 03.27, and returned to report a successful operation carried out with no opposition. 300 Squadron remained at home on the following night, when the railway junction at Acheres was one of four railway targets in the bomb sights.

Elements from 1, 3, 4 and 8 Groups bombed four different railway yards on the following night, 300 Squadron briefing eight crews to attack the one at Evreux, a town midway between Paris and the Normandy beachhead. The newly-promoted F/L Rozanski was the senior pilot on duty as they prepared for take-off at 01.20, their numbers depleted after one of the Lancasters put a wheel off the runway in the dark, and became bogged down. This was to be another low-level attack, and the conditions in the target

The crew of F/L Rozanski (3rd from right) after return from an operation. Also standing: P/O Hahn (nav.) 3rd from left and F/O Bakun (B.A.) -4th from left. (PISM via WM)

area allowed most crews to identify the town and its marshalling yards visually, and if not, there were target indicators to guide them to the aiming point. The Polish crews bombed from 2,300 to 3,500 feet between 03.20 and 03.32, and a very large explosion was observed at 03.21, which was believed to be a train carrying petrol and oil. All crews returned safely to report other sizeable explosions at 03.23 and 03.27.

A new campaign against Germany's oil industry began on the night of the 12/13th at the hands of a 1 and 3 Group main force. The Nordstern synthetic oil refinery at Gelsenkirchen was the target, for which 300 Squadron contributed eight Lancasters to an overall heavy force of 286. They began taking off from Faldingworth at 23.16 led by F/L Rozanski, and they arrived over the target to find good conditions. The availability of an improved version of Oboe enabled the Pathfinders to mark the aiming point with great accuracy, and the Polish crews, each of which was carrying a 4,000lb cookie and sixteen assorted 500 pounders, aimed at strong concentrations of red and green ground markers. As always at this location, there was a fierce defence from searchlights and flak, with bursts seen as high as 22,000 feet. There were also night fighters in the vicinity, and some crews reported tracer and aircraft falling in flames and exploding on the ground both before and after bombing. The 300 Squadron contingent carried out their attacks from 19,500 to 25,000 feet between 01.06 and 01.12, and five of them returned home to report on a successful attack, which had left large fires burning and black smoke rising to 14,000 feet.

Seventeen Lancasters failed to return, ten of them from among the 193 dispatched by 1 Group, and there were three empty dispersals for the residents at RAF Faldingworth to contemplate on the following morning. LL807 was brought down by flak at the Dutch coast, probably from Texel, while outbound, and crashed into the Ijsselmeer with no survivors from the crew of F/L Rozanski. DV286 was on its way home when it was intercepted by a night fighter, and also crashed into the Ijsselmeer, killing F/S Rembecki and all but one of his crew. The bomb-aimer, P/O Morski, managed to drop through the escape hatch underneath him, and parachute to safety, and he was rescued by two Dutch fishermen, before being handed over to the Germans. JA683 was shot down by a night fighter, and crashed on the south-eastern fringe of the Ruhr, almost certainly after bombing, and only the rear gunner, Sgt Klucha, survived from the crew of F/O Burkiewicz. Sadly, after hiding for two days, he was found and murdered by civilians. Reconnaissance revealed that a large proportion of the bombs had fallen within the plant, bringing all production to a halt for several weeks, at a cost to the German war effort of a thousand tons of aviation fuel per day.

Six RAF crews were posted in to 300 Squadron on the 14th, and they would represent a stopgap measure to address the shortage of Polish crews currently restricting the squadron's development. On the following day five more would arrive to bring B Flight up to a strength of eleven crews, to operate alongside A Flight with its twelve Polish crews. The influx came from 101, 550, 576 and 626 Squadrons, along with others from 1 LFS. The first daylight operation since the departure of 2 Group a year earlier was mounted against E-Boats and other light marine craft at le Havre on the evening of the 14th. It was a two phase operation, in which a predominantly 1 Group force of 198 Lancasters took the first shift, followed by 3 Group at dusk. 300 Squadron provided seven Lancasters, including one piloted by P/O Jones RAF. F/L Rosiniuk was the senior pilot on duty as they took off shortly before 21.00, and they arrived in the target area under the protection of a fighter escort to find excellent conditions. They attacked from 20,000 feet between 22.40 and 22.46 in the face of intense light and heavy flak, and a number of BF110s were seen above and below flying straight and level. F/S Danieluk saw a Spitfire shot down by flak. The attack was entirely successful, and few if any craft remained to pose a threat to the Allied shipping supplying the beachhead.

1 Group contributed 101 aircraft to a similar operation against Boulogne twenty-four hours later, for which 300 Squadron briefed seven crews. W/C Pozyczka was the senior pilot on duty as the first Lancaster began to roll down the runway a few seconds after midnight, and two of the crews carrying the Polish red and white checkerboard emblem into war were British. ED382's sortie was over as soon as it began as a hydraulics failure prevented the undercarriage from retracting. W/O Nalepa dumped the bombs into the sea some miles out from Mablethorpe, before returning home. The others reached the target area under the umbrella of a fighter escort, and found the aiming point clearly visible and well marked below them. They each carried eleven 1,000 and four 500 pounders, which they delivered onto a concentration of red TIs from 14,000 to 18,000 feet between 22.48 and 22.56 in the face of a spirited flak response. Sticks of bombs were seen to fall all around the markers, and a large orange and a large white explosion were observed, along with smoke, which remained visible from the English coast. The operation was as effective as that on the previous night, although, on this occasion, there were many civilian casualties.

A second new campaign was opened by elements of 1, 4, 5, 6 and 8 Groups on the night of the 16/17th, when four flying bomb launching sites were accurately bombed in the Pas-de-Calais. These and V-1 storage sites would feature prominently over the next two months, alongside the Command's other responsibilities to the Transportation Plan, oil and tactical support for the land forces. Also on this night,

1 Group contributed a hundred Lancasters to a raid on the Ruhrchemie AG oil plant, also known as Sterkrade/Holten, in the city of Oberhausen. The attack was rendered generally ineffective by cloud, and thirty-one aircraft were lost, most of them Halifaxes. Railway targets dominated on the night of the 17/18th, when elements of 1, 3, and 4 Groups provided the main force at three separate locations. 300 Squadron contributed eight Lancasters, four from each flight, which set off either side of midnight for a double railway bridge at Aulnoye in north-eastern France, close to the Belgian border. They had been told at briefing to bomb on TIs from 8,000 feet, but when they arrived the ground was completely hidden by cloud dense enough to prevent any glow from the markers to penetrate. The Master Bomber decided to abandon the operation, but before the order was issued, P/O Jones caught a glimpse of a red glow, and dropped his eighteen 500 pounders onto it from 8,000 feet at 01.38. The others were sent home with their bombs, and all jettisoned their two long-delay-fused 500 pounders and brought the rest home.

5 Group entered the oil offensive on the night of the 21/22nd, when sending separate forces to Wesseling, near Cologne, and Scholven-Buer, north of Gelsenkirchen in the Ruhr, with Pathfinder support at the latter, and a sprinkling of 101 Squadron ABC Lancasters at both. Cloud prevented use of the normally highly effective 5 Group low-level visual marking method, and the Wesseling force was badly mauled by night fighters, losing thirty-seven aircraft, in return for modest damage to the plant. A V-Weapon site at Mimoyecques was the target for a 1 Group contingent by daylight on the 22nd, and that night, a second element attacked a railway junction at Reims in north-eastern France. 300 Squadron briefed a dozen crews for the latter, six from each flight, and all five of the officer pilots were RAF. They began taking off at 22.30, and climbed into bad weather, which persisted until they reached the Channel coast. The skies remained clear then until they approached the target, which was covered by a patch of cloud. The aiming point was identified by a solid concentration of yellow markers seen through gaps in the cloud, and these were bombed by the squadron crews from 8,000 to 11,000 feet between 00.45 and 00.50. Bursts were seen around the markers, but the cloud cover made it difficult to assess the outcome. Returning crews reported being unable to hear the Master Bomber, and many observed tracer and a number of unidentified aircraft falling in flames. P/O Arnold spoke of a large number of searchlights operating independently and in cones in the searchlight belt north of Paris on the way home, and suggested that it extended further than the current flak maps suggested. Reconnaissance revealed that the attack had been successful at a cost of four Lancasters, which all came down on French soil.

Three flying bomb sites in the Pas de Calais were selected for attention by daylight on the 24th, and among them was a constructional works at Les Hayons, for which 1 Group detailed a hundred Lancasters, ten of which belonged to 300 Squadron. They were again split evenly between A and B Flights, with all four of the officer pilots from the RAF. The senior officer on duty, however, was S/L Jezycki, the navigator in the crew of F/S Markiewicz, who led the take-offs at 16.10. The weather outbound and over the target was excellent, and a comforting escort of Spitfires protected them in and out. The aiming point was identified both visually and by red markers, and the squadron crews released their eighteen 500 pounders each from 10,000 to 11,000 feet between 17.39 and 17.44. They were able to see them burst on and around the aiming point, and returned home confident that they had fulfilled their brief. All crews commented on the absence of flak over the target, but F/S White and crew saw two aircraft seeming to be troubled by flak at Dieppe on the way home, and it is likely that EE124 was one of them. It arrived over Lincolnshire with both starboard engines feathered, and made a number of circuits of the airfield before making its approach to land. Sadly, F/S Badowski was unable to maintain control, and the Lancaster was seen to lose height rapidly before entering an unrecoverable spin and crashing onto farmland about two miles east of Faldingworth. There were no survivors, and the wreckage was completely consumed by fire.

Three more flying bomb sites were targeted on the following day, and 1 Group supported the attack on constructional works at Ligescourt with a hundred Lancasters, ten of them provided by 300 Squadron. Each flight detailed five crews, and the senior pilot on this occasion was S/L Misselbrook, who had arrived from 550 Squadron, and would return there in September. They were all safely airborne by 08.00, and had to contend with unfavourable weather in the form of low cloud and rain. The conditions improved as the aircraft made their way south to pick up the fighter escort, and by the time the target hove into sight, visibility was good. Bombing was carried out from 13,000 feet between 09.15 and 09.20, either visually or on a red target indicator said to be right on the aiming point. Returning crews described the bombing as very accurate in the absence of a flak defence, and the aiming point was plastered and soon became obscured by smoke. F/S Gorny was unable to contribute to the destruction after suffering a total hang-up, and he brought his entire load of eighteen 500 pounders home.

A busy night for 1 Group on the 27/28th involved attacks on flying bomb sites and railways, and the ninety-nine Lancasters bound for the flying bomb site at Chateau Bernapre included thirteen from 300 Squadron. There was a late take-off, beginning with F/S Zoltanski at 01.44, and the senior officer on duty was S/L Jezycki in the crew of F/S Markiewicz. Eight of the crews were Polish and five RAF, but the British effort was reduced when P/O Lintott had to turn back after his navigator reported being too ill to continue. Visibility in the target area was moderate, but yellow target indicators were clearly seen, although one crew thought them to be somewhat scattered. The bombs went down from 11,500 to 14,000 feet between 03.32 and 03.37, and many were seen to straddle the TIs. There was no opposition from flak or fighters over the target, but most crews commented on the abundance of searchlights on the way home, suggesting that the enemy was beefing up its protection of flying bomb-related targets.

A dozen 300 Squadron Lancasters were led away by F/S Zoltanski at 12.14 on the 29th, bound for a constructional works at Siracourt, twenty miles north-east of Abbeville. S/L Misselbrook was the senior pilot on duty among the six crews from each flight, as they headed south to pick up the rest of the force and the fighter escort. The outward flight was undertaken in cloudy conditions, but the target was clearly visible through gaps, and markers could be seen on the ground. Some crews described the marking as scattered, and this was confirmed when the Master Bomber, F/L Clarke of 7 Squadron, urged the crews to bomb one mile east of the TIs. Bombing took place from 12,000 to 14,000 feet either side of 14.00 in the face of accurate predicted flak, by which time the Master Bomber had been shot down. At 13.56 a Lancaster was seen by F/S Ostrowski and crew to be hit by flak in the fuselage and break in two, before spinning into the cloud. Only one parachute was seen to open. This sighting was confirmed by F/S Barton and crew, while F/S Markiewicz and his crew saw a Lancaster hit by flak at 13.59, this time a port engine fire leading to the port fuel tank blowing up and tearing off the wing. One parachute was seen to open, and a second crewman was observed to exit the aircraft without any evidence of a parachute. The descriptions and the location of the crash sites east and north-east of the target suggest the earlier victim to be the Master Bomber, and the later one a 12 Squadron Lancaster. F/L Clarke and one of his crew survived as PoWs, and four also survived from the 12 Squadron aircraft. The consensus of returning crews was of a successful operation, based on a large fire observed in the centre of the target, and black smoke rising to 4,000 feet.

On the last night of the month, 118 Lancasters of 1 Group were made ready for an attack on the marshalling yards at Vierzon, south of Orleans in north-central France. The Special Duties Flight was to carry out the marking for the main force element, which included thirteen Lancasters from 300 Squadron. W/C Pozyczka was the senior pilot on duty among seven Polish and six RAF crews as they departed Faldingworth in the minutes leading to 22.30 in low cloud, rain and icing conditions. As the force reached the Channel, F/L Rosiniuk began to experience communications problems, and turned back at 23.39, when at 10,000 feet a few miles out from Worthing on the Sussex coast. Crews had been told at briefing to aim for the ground markers, and to listen out for further instructions from the Master Bomber, and the reduction in cloud from the French coast made it a simple task. The SDF provided an excellent reference by marking the aiming point with great accuracy, and the main force exploited the opportunity to inflict heavy damage. Bombing was carried out by the 300 Squadron crews from 6,000 to 12,000 feet between 01.08 and 01.16, and they reported it to be concentrated around the aiming point. One rear gunner reported pink explosions still taking place when he was sixty miles into the return trip. Fourteen Lancasters failed to return, 12% of the force, and among these was ED814, which was on its way home when shot down by a night fighter at Beauvilliers, south-west of Paris and half way between the target and the coast. There were no survivors from the crew of F/S Fudali. This operation concluded the busiest month of the year for 300 Squadron, during which fifteen operations had been undertaken,

July 1944

Lancaster ED327 BH-R with a group of ground personnel at Faldingworth in June 1944. This aircraft belonged to the British "B" Flight with 300 Squadron and failed to return from Stettin on 29/30th August 1944. The entire crew of P/O Harry Lupton perished. (PISM via WM)

July would follow a similar pattern, and it began for 1 Group with raids on flying bomb sites at Domleger and Oisemont/Neuville on the 2nd. At Faldingworth ten crews were called to briefing at 08.30, five from each flight, and informed that they were to be part of a force of 125 Lancasters targeting the constructional works at Domleger, thirty miles south-east of Boulogne. The bomb-aimers were instructed to bomb visually and on target indicators in the expected fine weather conditions, and they were led away by P/O Robinson at 12.35. Veteran Lancaster W4376 lost the use of its port-inner engine at Gravesend on the Kent coast, but F/S White opted to press on and try to complete the relatively short range trip. They encountered ten-tenths cloud for most of the outward flight, but as they closed on the target, a large gap appeared, which afforded a clear view of the ground. Each Lancaster was carrying eleven 1,000 and four 500 pounders, and these were delivered by most crews from 14,000 feet either visually or on a red TI between 14.15 and 14.20. F/S White let his load go from 10,000 feet, and he returned safely with the others to report a concentrated and accurate attack.

Typical English summer rain caused the 3rd to be a total washout, and operations planned for that night were cancelled. Eight crews were briefed on the following day for an attack on the railway yards at Orleans, which was an important component in the enemy supply system. 1 Group provided 156 aircraft as the main force, and the 300 Squadron contingent took off shortly after 22.30, with S/L Misselbrook the senior pilot on duty. Conditions throughout the operation were good, and bright moonlight provided excellent visibility. The target was identified by red spot-fires and yellow TIs, and the Master Bomber instructed the crews to bomb the southerly red spot-fire. They delivered their eighteen 500 pounders each from 7,500 to 8,500 feet between 01.30 and 01.40 in the face of light flak from four batteries, and smoke was drifting across the target as they turned for home. F/L Rosiniuk and F/S Markiewicz each had an encounter with a night fighter, the former before bombing and the latter just after, and their gunners returned fire to drive the enemy off. A small fire on the ground seemed to confirm the claim by F/L Rosiniuk's gunners, that they had hit their assailant and probably destroyed it.

The next target for 1 Group was the railway yards at Dijon on the night of the 5/6th, for which a main force of 149 aircraft was made ready, along with five marker aircraft from the SDF. 300 Squadron detailed nine crews, five Polish and four RAF, and they were all safely airborne for east-central France by 21.31. The weather outbound was quite poor, but matters improved in the target area, and bombing took place in excellent visibility under bright moonlight. Assembly point flares were reported by some crews to be late, and the yellow TIs had burned out before the release point was reached, but they delivered their eight 1,000 and four 500 pounders each from 7,000 to 10,000 feet onto red spot-fires either side of 02.00, observing a one second overshoot as instructed by the Master Bomber. They all landed safely on the 5 Group airfield at East Kirkby because of poor weather conditions over Faldingworth. A V-Weapon site in the Foret de Croc was the target for a daylight attack on the evening of the 6th, for which 1 Group put up a hundred Lancasters, seven of them provided by 300 Squadron, led by W/C Pozyczka and S/L Misselbrook. They were airborne by 19.00, and reached the target to find adequate conditions for bombing, which was carried out from 17,000 to 19,000 feet shortly after 21.00, and all returned safely home to praise the work of the marker element and the Master Bomber.

The first major operations in direct support of the land forces took place on the evening of the 7th. 1 Group provided almost half of the force of over four hundred aircraft sent to bomb open ground between Caen and a number of fortified villages to the north, ahead of advancing British and Canadian forces. 300 Squadron contributed thirteen Lancasters, seven with Polish NCO crews, and six with RAF crews, four of them with officer pilots, and they departed Faldingworth either side of 20.00. The need for accuracy had been stressed at briefings because of the close proximity of Allied troops to the aiming points, and Master Bombers were on hand to direct the proceedings. As the Lancasters approached the Normandy coast the target and markers could already be seen in the excellent visibility under clear skies, and the eleven 1,000 and four 500 pounders each were released from 4,500 to 8,000 feet either side of 22.00. All crews returned safely to report an accurate and concentrated attack, and there was further praise for the efforts of the Pathfinders. P/O Robinson reported a Lancaster diving vertically into the sea, and another leaving the target area on fire and later ditching a few miles off the Normandy coast. The former was a 166 Squadron aircraft captained by a flight commander, from which none survived, and the latter was from 626 Squadron, and all but the two gunners were rescued. A message from the Second Army in Normandy awaited their arrival at debriefing, and it read, "The heavy bomber attack which took place this evening was a wonderfully impressive show. The Second Army would like to send its appreciation and thanks for the raid to all crews".

On the following day another message was received, this one from General Bernard Montgomery, which read; "Again the Allied armies in France would like to thank you personally, and all Bomber Command, for your magnificent co-operation last night. We know well that your main work lies further afield, and we applaud your continuous and sustained bombing of German war industries, and the effect this has on the German war effort, but we also know well that you are always ready to bring your mighty effort closer in when action is really needed, and to co-operate in our tactical battle. When you do this your actions are always decisive. Please tell your brave and gallant pilots how greatly the Allied armies admire and applaud their work. Thank you very much." General Dempsey added; "Your magnificent operation yesterday evening was the greatest assistance to us. The Second Army sends Bomber Command its thanks and congratulations."

After a hectic start to the month the 300 Squadron crews enjoyed a few nights off the Order of Battle, although elements from 1 Group returned to the railway yards at Vaires on the night of the 7/8th, and joined forces with 3 Group for what was an ineffective attack on a flying bomb site at Nucourt on the 10th. An important railway junction at Revigny in eastern France was assigned to 1 Group on the night of the 12/13th, for which a hundred Lancasters were to act as the main force for six SDF marker aircraft and one route marker. Six 300 Squadron crews were briefed for this operation, while seven others were told that they were to be part of a 100-strong force to attack a similar target at Tours in the north-west of the country. They were all airborne by 22.00, and headed south to the Channel coast in good weather conditions, which persisted all the way to Tours. The target was identified by red and green TIs, and the Master bomber called for the crews to aim for these. However, with smoke beginning to obscure ground detail, he gave instructions to later arrivals to bomb the eastern end of the smoke. The crews complied from 6,000 to 8,000 feet between 00.45 and 00.52, and all returned safely to report an excellent concentration of bombing, a number of large explosions and thick, black smoke.

Conditions for the Revigny-bound force had also been good until about fifty miles from the target, when thin layer cloud slid in, with tops at around 6,000 feet. F/S Stepien and crew were attacked by a BF110 while outbound at 6,000 feet over north-central France at 01.03. The gunners returned fire, and saw strikes on the cockpit, and they would later claim it as probably destroyed. Over the target there was five to eight-tenths cloud, and the presence of ground haze added to the difficulties for the SDF marker force. The Master Bomber, whose H2S had failed, was forced to make a dead reckoning run to the target, and, after dropping a green TI at the assembly point, called for those with reconnaissance flares to drop them, hoping to be able to identify the aiming point by their light. Neither the Master Bomber nor his deputy was able to identify the aiming point, despite searching for fifteen minutes, and he decided to send the crews home with their bombs. By this time all six of the 300 Squadron crews had bombed from 2,300 to 6,000 feet between 01.52 and 02.13, either on the green assembly point marker or the white reconnaissance flares. W/O Poludniak aimed at what he erroneously believed to be a red spot-fire, but as none had been dropped, it was more likely a burning Lancaster on the ground. He witnessed two Lancasters and three unidentified aircraft crashing in the target area, three shot down by night fighters, and two probably through a collision, as aircraft were approaching the aiming point on a variety of headings. F/S Stepien reported a collision astern of his aircraft at 3,000 feet at 01.56, and two large objects falling in flames after an initial explosion. F/S Sarachman came down to 3,000 feet, below the cloud base, from where he was able to pick out the marshalling yards and the town, and he dropped his bombs onto railway tracks by the light of flares. He heard no instructions from the Master Bomber, whose R/T signal was weak. At debriefing it was learned that half of the force had bombed, and that ten aircraft were missing. There was also eventually confirmation that a 103 Squadron Lancaster had, indeed, collided with one from 550 Squadron in the target area. A return to Revigny was rescheduled for the night of the 14/15th, when Pathfinder markers replaced those from the SDF. Haze prevented any bombing from taking place, and a further seven Lancasters were shot down for their trouble, including that of 550 Squadron's commanding officer, W/C Connolly.

Sgt Jozef Pialucha who flew 11 operations with 300 Squadron between June and Aug. 1944 before being posted to 1586 (Polish) Special Duty Flight at Brindisi, Italy. (GK)

The briefing of fourteen 300 Squadron crews took place at 01.30 on the 18th, in preparation for a massive operation in support of the ground forces trying to fight their way out of the Caen bridgehead under Operation Goodwood. 942 RAF aircraft were to bomb five fortified villages in concert with the American Army Air Force, 1 Group providing 125 Lancasters for the northern aiming point at Traorne, and seventy-six for the southern aiming point at Emieville, both just east of the town. P/O Hansell led the Anglo-Polish contingent away at 04.11, bound for the latter, and they initially encountered low cloud over England and haze at the coast. By the time they reached the target area, however, the sky was clear and visibility excellent. The attack opened at the northern aiming point in three-quarter light conditions, and the target indicators were easily identified and plastered with bombs, to the extent that the area was soon obscured by smoke and dust. It was full daylight by the time the second phase crews ran in to bomb at Emieville, and the 300 Squadron crews identified the aiming point by yellow TIs, ground detail and smoke. They delivered their loads of eleven 1,000 and four 500 pounders each from 7,000 to 8,000 feet between 06.01 and 06.09 in the face of moderate predicted flak, which dwindled in ferocity as the attack progressed.

P/O Jerzy Bregman in tropical uniform photographed after his commission in 1943. He was killed on his 28th sortie with 300 Squadron. (B. Marlow via RG)

JA922 was over the target at 06.05, when it was hit by predicted flak, which severed electrical connection to the bomb release gear and prevented the bombs from being dropped. It also caused major damage to the rear turret, which had been in the process of rotating as its occupant, F/S Zentar, searched for enemy fighters. It was forced beyond its normal limits and jammed, and the doors were ripped off, all but sucking F/S Zentar out into space without his parachute. He was held in place only by his feet, while his head and body dangled outside of the aircraft. The flight engineer, wireless operator and mid-upper gunner managed to prevent him from falling by hanging onto his clothing, but the stitches began to break as the strain took its toll. The flight engineer, Sgt Pialucha, climbed out to stand on a small ledge between the turret and the fuselage, and, hanging on with one hand, managed to loop a rope around the gunner and secure it to the turret seat. He then went back to his duties assisting the pilot in the cockpit, leaving his two colleagues to continue supporting the gunner. They made a safe landing at Tangmere on the Sussex coast, and F/S Zentar had to physically hold his head up to avoid it hitting the runway. For his gallantry, Sgt Pialucha was awarded a much-deserved CGM, and was the only Polish airman to be so decorated. *(Sadly, he would lose his life near Belgrade in Yugoslavia on the 1st of September, while serving with 1586 (Polish Special Duties) Squadron in support of partisan groups in Italy and eastern Europe.)* 6,800 tons of bombs had been delivered in these highly effective attacks on enemy ground forces, and of this figure, 5,000 tons was delivered by aircraft of the RAF.

That night 5 Group finally completed the job at Revigny, but at the huge cost of twenty-four Lancasters. While that operation was in progress, 1 Group was active over the oil refineries at Wesseling, near Cologne, and Scholven-Buer in the Ruhr. 300 Squadron detailed ten crews as part of an overall heavy force of 153 Lancasters assigned to the latter, and they were led away by P/O Arnold at 23.08. P/O Lintott turned back at 00.21, when half way into the North Sea crossing after his Gee failed, and he jettisoned his cookie and four delay-fused 500 pounders, but retained twelve other 500 pounders. Weather conditions were good throughout, and identification was made on cascading red target indicators. As always over an oil town, the searchlight and flak defence was intense, and many night fighters were seen. The bombing by the 300 Squadron crews took place from 19,000 to 21,000 feet between 01.26 and 01.32, and returning crews spoke of a highly concentrated and accurate attack, and an enormous explosion sending black smoke up to 15,000 feet. Four Lancasters failed to return, and among them was PB171, which went missing without trace with the crew of W/O Zoltanski, who were on the twenty-eighth operation of their tour. Both 1 Group operations on this night were successful, and each plant suffered loss of production, the Scholven plant completely so for an extended period.

After the war it was established that PB171 had been shot down over the North Sea on the way home by Lt Walter Briegleb, following an engagement at 11,000 feet some forty-five miles west-south-west of Den Helder. The navigator was twenty-one-year-old F/O Jerzy Bregman, who had escaped with his father from occupied Poland in 1940, after being granted a Romanian visa. Having made his way to England, he was accepted into the RAF in January 1941, training first as a pilot and then as a navigator in England, South Africa and Kenya, and was commissioned in December 1942. On hearing of his imminent posting to India, he applied for a transfer to the Polish Air Force so that he could fight against Germany, but was told he must complete his tour in India first. He was the only Pole in RAF bombers in India, where he served with 113 and 153 Squadrons, before returning to England at the end of 1943 and training on Lancasters. He was posted to 300 Squadron, and was responsible for writing up the squadron ORB from

Pictured on an earlier cross-country flight in April 1944, Lancaster LM488 BH-D failed to return from Kiel on the night of 23rd / 24th July 1944. Photo taken from Lancaster LL856 (PISM via WM)

April until his death, which occurred on his fifty-eighth operation. Also killed was a second pilot, F/L Ostaszewski, who was probably on board to gain operational experience.

The railway campaign continued on the night of the 20/21st, with an attack on railway yards and a triangular junction at Courtrai (Kortrijk) in Belgium, a town situated close to the border with France. Fifteen 300 Squadron crews were briefed to join forces with 287 others from 1, 5 and 8 Groups for the two-pronged attack, 1 Group providing ninety-four Lancasters for aiming point A, the yards. The eight Polish and seven RAF crews departed Faldingworth either side of midnight, and flew to the south coast over ten-tenths cloud, which dispersed over the sea, and by the time the target was reached the skies were clear and the vertical visibility was hampered only by thin haze. The aiming point was identified by red, green and yellow target indicators, and the bomb loads of eleven 1,000 and four 500 pounders each were aimed at either the greens or yellows according to the Master Bomber's instructions. The 300 Squadron crews attacked from 11,000 to 12,500 feet between 01.53 and 01.59, and all returned safely to report accurate bombing, little in the way of ground defences, but plenty of night fighter activity. F/S Gorny and crew saw an unidentified aircraft burst into flames and crash on the northern outskirts of the town, and, at 02.04, observed a Lancaster being hit by light flak and exploding in the air, sending burning fragments cascading downwards to litter the ground.

The first major raid on a German urban target for two months took place on the night of the 23/24th, when Kiel was the destination for a force of over six hundred aircraft, of which 189 were provided by 1 Group. Twelve 300 Squadron crews were briefed, six from each flight, and they were given the docks as their specific objective. W/C Pozyczka led them away at 22.50, and they had to climb through a thin layer of ten-tenths cloud, which persisted all the way to the target. Thanks to a RCM screen provided by 100 Group, the force appeared suddenly and with complete surprise in the target area, which was identified by red and green markers and a few green flares with red stars. The whole area was lit up by flak, bomb bursts and fires, but the initially intense heavy and light flak activity diminished as the attack progressed. The 300 Squadron crews bombed from 20,000 to 22,000 feet between 01.23 and 01.38, and all but one returned safely to report an accurate attack, which produced fires visible for up to a hundred miles into the return journey. F/L Rosiniuk and crew reported an aircraft being hit by flak and falling in two pieces over the target, and this proved to be one of just four aircraft failing to return. 300 Squadron's LM488 was hit by flak on approach to the target, and it seems that F/S Ostrowski sought somewhere to carry out a forced landing. On touching down on the eastern shore of the Dobersdorf Lake, east of Kiel, the bomb load exploded, and all on board were killed. Severe damage was inflicted upon the town and the docks area, which suffered its worst experience of the war to date, and all of the U-Boot yards were hit. Delayed-action bombs caused further problems for the emergency services, there was no running water for three days, or gas for cooking for three weeks, and the public transport system was paralysed for eight days. On the following night, the Command launched the first of three raids in five nights on Stuttgart. Over six hundred aircraft were involved, 120 of them from 1 Group, including twelve representing 300 Squadron. There were five crews from the Polish A Flight and seven from the RAF B Flight, and F/L Rosiniuk was the senior pilot on duty as they got away from Faldingworth from 21.29, and flew into cloud that persisted all the way to the target. P/O Hansell and crew were outbound over France at 10,000 feet at 01.10, when they encountered a twin-engine enemy aircraft with a yellow light in its nose. The mid-upper gunner, Sgt Lowbridge, opened fire, closely followed by the rear gunner, and the enemy aircraft immediately burst into flames, fell to the ground and exploded. For his actions Sgt Lowbridge received an immediate award of the DFM, the citation reading; *"One night in July 1944, Sgt Lowbridge was mid-upper gunner of an aircraft detailed to attack Stuttgart. En-route he sighted an enemy fighter. He gave his pilot clear and concise directions, which enabled him to manoeuvre the aircraft into an advantageous position. Sgt Lowbridge then opened fire, and with his first burst shot the fighter down in flames. On the return journey the aircraft was again attacked by another enemy fighter, but this gunner again cooperated well with his pilot, and the enemy aircraft was evaded. Sgt Lowbridge has invariably displayed great courage and determination, and his keenness and ability as an air gunner have been of a high order."* F/S Mioduchowski and crew were approached three time by an enemy fighter while outbound, and they responded with fire from all three turrets, which seemed to dissuade the enemy from engaging. The target was identified by green flares with yellow stars, and also by the red glow of fires beneath the cloud cover. The 300 Squadron crews were each carrying a 2,000 pounder and twelve J cluster bombs, which were dropped on release-point flares from 16,500 and 18,500 feet between 01.51 and 01.56. Returning crews were unable to provide a clear assessment of the results, but many bomb bursts were seen through occasional gaps in the cloud, and the glow of fires suggested a concentrated attack. Twenty-one aircraft failed to return, and among them were two belonging to 300 Squadron, both from B Flight, and the first RAF crews to be lost in 300 Squadron service. ND984 crashed at 02.15 north-west of Stuttgart on the way home, but P/O Harkin and crew all escaped with their lives to become PoWs.

LM178 was shot down by a night fighter about two miles north of St-Laurent-des-Bois in Central France, it is believed while outbound, and four members of the crew were killed. All three survivors sustained injuries, but evaded capture and were liberated in August. The pilot, P/O Robinson, ended up in a Paris hospital, where he was treated by a German doctor, while rear gunner, F/S Dunseith, was in hospital in le Mans. Navigator, F/O Clement Forman RCAF, a twenty-nine-year old former high school teacher from Windsor Ontario, found himself on this night floating down on the edge of the Foret de Marchenoir. On landing he buried his parachute and Mae West, and soon met up with F/S Dunseith, and they hid in the forest until dawn, when the rear-gunner decided to go in search of a doctor to treat his injuries. They agreed to meet up in the forest that night, and F/O Forman remained there all day waiting. His crew mate did not return, and it was only later that he learned he had been taken to hospital in le Mans. He realised he had to go on alone, and presented himself at a farm on the edge of the forest, where he was received by an elderly man and two elderly ladies. He was given food, after which he set off for Montoire during the night of the 25/26th, but lost his bearings, and stopped to rest his injured leg at about 03.00. Later he found a road running north-south, but almost ran into three men on bicycles with rifles slung over their shoulders, so he ducked out of sight again. At dawn on the 26th he reached a farm just south of St Leonard-en-Beauce, where he was fed and lent clothes for the duration of his stay. That night he moved on again, heading south, but making slow progress because of his injured leg and the hard-going across country. In the early afternoon of the 27th he reached another farm, where he was sheltered until the evening, when a young man of about eighteen arrived to take him to his own farm, where he stayed for two nights. The young man was in touch with the resistance, and late on the 29th he took F/O Forman to another house in the town of Oucques, where he was given food and clothes and accommodation for two more nights. At 06.00 on the 31st he was taken by car north on the road to Chateaudun, passing through Moisy, before turning east towards the Aigre river. Somewhere in that area he found himself in a school house with a transmitter, and he stayed there from 08.00 until 16.30, while arrangements for his continued journey were made. He arrived back in England on the 18th of August.

The second Stuttgart operation took place on the following night, for which a total of 550 aircraft were made ready, of which 108 of the Lancasters represented 1 Group. The Faldingworth contingent of eight got away shortly after 21.30 in good weather conditions, which would persist throughout the operation. PB252 was outbound over the Orleans region of France at 10,000 feet, when an enemy night fighter was spotted. A corkscrew manoeuvre was carried out and the fighter was lost. Shortly afterwards, while the bomb aimer, F/S Witrylak, was dispensing window, he caught site of another Lancaster bearing down on their position. There was a crash, which knocked him backwards, and tore the intercom lead from its socket. When he had recovered his senses and reconnected, he tried to jettison the bombs in accordance with a prior agreement with his captain in such an emergency. However, he believed later that the bomb doors had been damaged, and the bombs had remained on board. He heard the pilot call for the port-outer engine to be feathered, but as the aircraft was in a steep dive and apparently out of control, he opened the escape hatch and dived through. The pilot, F/S Danieluk, had given the order to bale out, but only F/S Witrylak and mid-upper gunner, W/O Wziatek, had time to comply before the Lancaster crashed, killing all still on board. The other aircraft involved was ND903 of 103 Squadron, from which there were no survivors.

Both men evaded capture, F/S Witrylak later reporting that it was about 01.00 when he baled out, and landed in a field, where he buried his parachute before walking in a north-westerly direction. At dawn he rested up in a field and remained there all day, before continuing on to reach the banks of the Loire, where he hid in bushes throughout the following day. On the evening of the 28th he approached a farmhouse, where he was given food and a civilian coat. He left a little later, swam the river, and then continued

Left: P/O Donal Richard Harkin who served in British "B" Flight with 300 Squadron. He was shot down and taken prisoner on his 10th sortie. (Harkin family via P. Sikora). Right: Sgt Martin Arthur Collis (A.B.) who successfully bailed out from burning Lancaster of P/O Harkin and was captured with the rest of the crew. (Collis family via P. Sikora)

walking until daylight, when he hid in a haystack for the whole of the 29th. After dark he approached another farmhouse, where he was fed, and told that the Germans had already searched the farm for evaders. There were apparently few Germans in the area, and he was told that he would receive help from any Frenchman he approached. That night he reached Josnes, and declared himself at another farm house, where he was invited to stay. The farmer contacted the Maquis, who gave instructions for him to go to Vendome, where he would be met. The farmer accompanied him by bicycle to Vendome on the 1st of August, but no one came for him, and after waiting for a considerable time, the farmer took him to his brother's house in Averdon. Here he was visited by a member of the Maquis, who took down his details, and told him he would return with an identity card. By the 13th the man had not returned, and F/S Witrylak cycled back towards Vendome, having heard that it had been taken by the Maquis. Passing through Selommes, he learned that the Americans had passed through a couple of hours earlier, and he set off in pursuit. He reached Villetrun at around 19.00, but found it under attack from Allied aircraft and turned back. He spent the night in a house in Selommes, and on the 14th was taken back to Villetrun by the Maquis, and put in touch with American forces.

The others arrived safely in the target area to find Stuttgart identified by red and green target indicators on the ground, and release-point green flares with yellow stars. They delivered their 2,000 pounder and twelve J cluster bombs each from 16,000 and 17,500 feet between 01.52 and 02.09, in accordance with instructions from the Master Bomber, and returned to report a concentrated attack, which produced explosions, fires and black smoke rising to 10,000 feet, and a glow visible from 150 miles away. W/O Laskowski and crew reported two aircraft in flames at 16,000 feet at 01.57, and descending towards the ground. PA161 developed a fuel system problem on the way home, which caused a leakage, and preparations were made for a ditching. In the event the fuel lasted, and F/S Barton was able to bring the Lancaster home.

Twelve 300 Squadron crews found themselves in the briefing room at 04.00 on the 28th, only to have the prospective operation cancelled. Eight of them were back at briefing at 19.00 to be told that the final raid on Stuttgart was to be mounted that night, and that they would be part of an overall force of 494 Lancasters from 1, 3, 5 and 8 Groups, of which 159 were provided by 1 Group. The 300 Squadron aircraft were airborne by 21.51, but ED327 suffered intercom failure shortly after crossing the Normandy coast at 12,000 feet, and F/O Wilson turned back at 23.57. F/L Rosiniuk was over central France at 17,000 feet at 00.18, and was about to turn port for the long leg to the target, when a FW190 opened fire from the starboard side. Both Lancaster gunners returned fire, and the enemy seemed to have been lost. Twenty-four minutes later and further east another, or possibly the same FW190 attacked from the port side, and was again driven off by return fire, this time not to be seen again. In fact, night fighters were out in force to take advantage of the moonlight conditions above the cloud, and they would score steadily all the way to the target. F/S Gorny and crew saw three aircraft go down from 18,000 feet, the first exploding in the air at 00.02, the second catching fire and diving vertically into the ground at 00.16, and the third exploding in the air at 01.10. This crew reached the target, which was identified by green cascading TIs and two release-point flares, and in the absence of any instructions from the Master Bomber, the cookie and eleven 500 pounders were released from 18,000 feet at 01.50 onto a red TI through eight-tenths cloud. The others from the squadron bombed from 16,000 to 18,000 feet between 01.49 and 02.01, and returned home safely to learn that thirty-nine aircraft had failed to make it back. A further twenty-two had been lost from a simultaneous raid on Hamburg, bringing the night's total casualty figure to sixty-one. There were no reports from Stuttgart, and it is difficult to assign damage to a specific operation, but it is known that the second raid was the most devastating of the three, and the centre of the city was now in ruins with more than eleven hundred of its residents killed.

There was another early morning briefing for ten 300 Squadron crews on the 30th, who were told that they were to be part of a force of almost seven hundred bombers attacking six enemy positions in the Villers Bocage-Caumont area ahead of advancing Allied forces. 1 Group was assigned aiming points E and F at Caumont, to which thirty-four and seventy Lancasters respectively were dispatched. The 300 Squadron contingent was led by W/C Pozyczka with S/L Misselbrook in support, and they took off shortly after 06.30 into ten-tenths cloud with tops at 5,000 feet. Those arriving at the French coast below the 3,000 foot cloud base were able to map-read their way to the target in excellent visibility, while the others heard the Master Bomber call them down. W/C Pozyczka identified the aiming point visually, by the contour of the woods on approach, and confirmed his position by red target indicators on the ground. He delivered his eighteen 500 pounders from 2,700 feet at 08.16, and watched them straddle the aiming point and send smoke rising to 2,500 feet. The other squadron participants bombed from 1,500 to 5,500 feet between 08.15 and 08.20, and returned safely to report a good Pathfinder performance and concentrated bombing.

The final operation of the squadron's busiest month of the war to date was directed at a flying bomb storage site in the Foret de Nieppe in north-eastern France, some thirty miles south-east of Calais. It was one of four storage or launching sites detailed for attention by a total of 202 aircraft from 1, 6 and 8 Groups. 1 Group provided ninety Lancasters, of which ten represented 300 Squadron, four from A Flight and six from B Flight, with F/L Monk the senior pilot on duty. They were all safely airborne by 21.52, and headed for the target in low cloud, which persisted all the way there and back. The aiming point was marked by red target indicators, the glow of which could be seen through the cloud, and the Master Bomber was on hand to direct the squadron's dropping of eighteen 500 pounders each. The squadron crews attacked from 12,000 feet between 23.31 and 23.37, and the consensus was of a successful operation. Sixteen operations undertaken by the squadron during the month had generated a record 159 sorties for the loss of five aircraft.

Left: W/O Zoltanski and crew failed to return from the 28th op of their tour, against the Scholven-Buer refinery in the Ruhr on 18 / 19th July. They had the misfortune to encounter Lt. Walter Briegleb and crew (right) and were shot down over the North Sea at 0220hrs. Briegleb survived the war with 25 victories in the night war (Harry Holmes).

August 1944

Of particular significance for the Polish personnel serving with Bomber Command was the Warsaw uprising by the Polish Home Army, which began on the 1st. Operationally, the first week of August was dominated by the campaign against flying bomb sites, and attacks would be mounted daily from the 1st to the 6th. Operations began for 300 Squadron, however, with participation by eleven of its crews in an attack on enemy naval vessels in the port of le Havre on the 2nd. Six crews from A Flight and five from B Flight took off shortly after 17.00, with S/L Misselbrook the senior pilot on duty. Weather conditions were good, and excellent visibility in the target area enabled the crews to identify the aiming point visually. They delivered their eleven 1,000 and four 500 pounders from 10,000 to 14,000 feet between 19.00 and 19.05 in accordance with instructions from the Master Bomber, and returned safely to report concentrated bombing, explosions and thick smoke.

The largest effort against flying bomb sites took place on the 3rd, when over eleven hundred aircraft were involved in attacks on three sites. 1 Group provided 180 Lancasters for the flying bomb store at Trossy-St-Maximin, among them eleven 300 Squadron Lancasters led again by S/L Misselbrook. They were all safely airborne shortly before noon, albeit in poor weather conditions, but matters improved during the outward flight, and visibility in the target area was good. The aiming point was identified by red and yellow TIs, and the squadron participants bombed on these from 11,000 to 13,000 feet between 14.16 and 14.18. F/L Rosiniuk was forced to take evasive action to avoid falling bombs, and then, while homebound north of Paris, watched a Lancaster being hit by flak at 14.34, catch fire and dive, before being hit again and exploding. It disappeared into cloud, and one parachute was seen to open. F/O Pope was on his bombing run when he observed a Lancaster four hundred yards ahead being struck by a bomb. The Lancaster turned upside down, and disappeared into the cloud, but a piece of its wing with an engine still attached came very close to colliding with Pope's ME847. Two parachutes were seen to open. S/L Misselbrook confirmed this incident and reported two other Lancasters falling victim to flak. Returning crews claimed a successful attack, which left the target covered by smoke.

While attacks on flying bomb sites continued on the 4th, 288 Lancasters of 1, 3 and 8 Groups set off to target oil storage depots at Bec-d'Ambes and Pauillac in the Gironde Estuary north of Bordeaux. Eleven 300 Squadron crews were assigned to the latter, and this would require them to fly their longest-yet daylight round-trip, deep into south-western France. The target sat on the west bank of the Gironde Estuary twenty-five miles north of Bordeaux, and would take almost five hours to reach. They departed Faldingworth either side of 13.30 led by W/C Pozyczka, and joined up with the rest of the bomber force as they flew south to the coast. It was here that they were joined by a fighter escort of Mosquitos provided by 100 Group, and this was the first of many occasions when these Serrate-equipped night fighter versions of the type would be employed as escorts. Weather conditions were good throughout, and the target was reached in excellent visibility at around 18.00. W/C Pozyczka delivered his nine 1,000 and three 500 pounders onto yellow TIs from 8,500 feet at 18.06, and observed an enormous fire with flames up to 2,000 feet and smoke rising to 10,000 feet. The other squadron crews bombed from 7,500 to 9,500 between 18.05 and 18.12, and all returned safely to echo the commanding officer's report of a successful operation.

Three hundred Lancasters of 1, 3 and 8 Groups returned to the region on the following afternoon to hit Pauillac again and two other oil storage depots on the Gironde River at Blaye and Bordeaux. Ten 300 Squadron Lancasters were assigned to the former, situated fifteen miles north of Bordeaux, and the senior pilot on duty was S/L Misselbrook, who had with him G/C Ogilvie-Forbes, the British station commander at Faldingworth. Take-off began at 14.10, in weather conditions which would remain ideal throughout the operation. The defences were non-existent as the target was reached shortly before 19.00, and the bombing was carried out in accordance with the Master Bomber's instructions from 6,000 to 8,500 feet between 18.55 and 19.07. The attack produced flames up to 1,000 feet and a mushroom of smoke rising to 5,000 feet as the bombers turned away. The umbrella of a 100 Group Mosquito escort kept the bombers safe from fighter attack, and not a single aircraft was lost from the three sites, all of which sustained serious damage.

On the evening of the 7th, over a thousand aircraft took off to bomb five enemy strong points facing Allied ground forces in the Caen area of Normandy. The attacks, which involved 204 Lancasters from 1 Group, including six from the SDF and eleven representing 300 Squadron, were carefully controlled by Master Bombers to try to avoid "friendly fire" incidents. W/C Pozyczka led them away at 21.19 in weather conditions ideal for bombing, and the target, some six miles south-east of Caen, was easily identifiable even without the markers, which were also clearly visible. W/C Pozyczka delivered his eleven 1,000 and three 500 pounders onto green TIs from 7,600 feet at 23.25, and he watched the markers being straddled and ultimately obliterated. F/S Walczyk was the only other from the squadron to bomb, doing so at the same time as his commanding officer, and, thereafter, the Master Bomber called a halt to proceedings because of the absence of viable markers.

The group was involved in attacks on oil and fuel storage dumps on the nights of the 8/9th and 9/10th, but 300 Squadron played no part. On the afternoon of the 9th the Polish air and ground crews gathered for an address by the Polish station commander about the latest situation in Poland, and the discussions between the Polish Prime Minister and the Soviet leader, Marshal Stalin. There was an early morning briefing for thirteen crews on the 10th, for an attack on railway tanker-wagons containing aviation fuel, that were gathered on sidings in the Paris suburb of Dugny. Take-off began at 09.16 with S/L Misselbrook the senior pilot on duty, and they headed south in good weather conditions which persisted all the way to the target. The rest of the 98-strong heavy force was picked up along the way, as was a fighter escort, and all from the squadron arrived safely in the target area to find moderate flak, but otherwise no opposition. The aiming point was identified visually and by yellow TIs, and bombing took place from 13,000 to 16,000 feet at 12.04. The attack was concentrated until smoke obscured the aiming point, and then it may have become a little scattered. Thick, black smoke had reached 5,000 feet as the Lancasters turned away, and all returned safely home to report a successful operation. The SDF operated for the final time on the 11th, when called upon to operate in a bombing rather than marking role against a railway target at Douay. The flight was ultimately disbanded without ceremony a few days later, with little recognition of its contribution to 1 Group's war effort.

The principal operation on the night of the 12/13th was an attack by all but 8 Group on Brunswick, to ascertain the ability of main force crews to identify and attack a target on the strength of H2S alone without Pathfinder marking. Supported by eighty Lancasters from 1 Group, it was not an entirely successful experiment, and while a proportion of the bombing did fall within the town, there was no concentration, and much of the effort was wasted on other towns and communities. Meanwhile, a second force of almost three hundred aircraft attempted to hit the Opel motor works at Rüsselsheim, but succeeded in inflicting only slight damage. Also that night, a modest number of Lancasters and Halifaxes bombed a German troop concentration near Falaise, twenty-two miles south-south-east of Caen. This was the town upon

Aerial photograph taken by a 300 Squadron crew during daylight raid on Le Culot Airfield on 15th Aug. 1944. (JC)

which the Third Canadian Division was advancing, and on the afternoon of the 14th, eight hundred aircraft took off to attack seven German positions. 300 Squadron contributed a dozen Lancasters, led by W/C Pozyczka with S/L Misselbrook in support. They took off either side of 13.30 in good weather conditions that persisted throughout the operation, and arrived in the target area to find the aiming point well-marked by red and green TIs. The squadron crews bombed from 2,500 to 4,000 feet between 15.28 and 15.41, and all but one returned to report concentrated bombing and black smoke rising up to 5,000 feet. DV278 failed to return after being shot down by flak after bombing, and crashing fifteen miles south-west of Falaise, killing F/L Rebinski and crew. Halfway through the raid some bombs fell among Canadian soldiers, and thirteen were killed, while fifty-three others were wounded. A number of Squadron commanders were apparently carpeted as a result of this "friendly fire" incident, for not adequately briefing their crews.

In preparation for his new night offensive against industrial Germany, Harris launched a thousand aircraft on the morning of the 15th to bomb nine night fighter airfields in Holland and Belgium. 1 Group sent a hundred Lancasters each to Volkel in Holland and le Culot in Belgium, and 300 Squadron supported the latter operation with thirteen Lancasters. They took off either side of 10.00 in excellent weather conditions which persisted all the way to the target. F/O Jones and crew got only as far as the Lincolnshire Fens east of Coningsby, before a short circuit in a power lead caused a fire in the wireless operator's station, and made it necessary to remove all fuses with a consequent loss of navigational equipment. The others reached the target, which they identified visually and by red target indicators, and delivered their eleven 1,000 and four 500 pounders from 15,000 to 18,000 feet between 12.01 and 12.04 in accordance with the Master Bomber's instructions. Bombs were seen to burst across the airfield and runways, and smoke soon began to obscure ground detail. PA160 was hit by heavy flak, which damaged the fuselage and port-outer engine, and evasive action had to be taken by F/O Pohoski to avoid being struck by bombs from above, which ultimately missed by twenty yards.

On the night of the 16/17th a 1 Group contingent of 137 aircraft joined others to form an overall force of 461 Lancasters to raid the Baltic port of Stettin for the first time since January. 300 Squadron had detailed ten aircraft and crews, but a misunderstanding led to three aircraft not receiving the required amount of fuel, and only seven took off for the operation. They were all airborne by 21.30, and flew out in clear conditions over the North Sea and Denmark, until cloud began to build up over the Baltic and northern Germany. Unfortunately for Stettin, it was largely free of cloud, and the aiming point was identified by red and green TIs, which the squadron crews bombarded with their 2,000 pounders and J cluster bombs from 17,000 to 19,000 feet between 01.07 and 01.14. They all returned safely to report concentrated bombing, huge red fires, explosions and much smoke, and this was confirmed by local reports, which catalogued fifteen hundred houses and twenty-nine industrial premises destroyed, and thirteen ships either sunk or seriously damaged in the harbour. A simultaneous raid on Kiel was moderately successful, and caused particular damage in the docks area.

Nine 300 Squadron crews were briefed during the morning of the 18th for an attack on an oil storage dump at Ghent-Terneuzen in Belgium, in concert with aircraft from 101 and 626 Squadrons. A total of thirty Lancasters was involved, and the Faldingworth element took off either side of midday in clear conditions, which held firm until the Dutch coast, where cloud built up to eight-tenths. The Master Bomber called the crews down to cloud-tops at around 8,000 feet at this point, and then to below the cloud base at 4,000 feet for the bombing run. This late instruction forced the bombers to make a circuit and approach for a second time, and not all of the 300 Squadron crews complied. The first three squadron participants to arrive bombed red TIs from 8,500 to 10,000 feet at 13.50, while the fourth released their eleven 1,000 and four 500 pounders from 6,000 feet at 13.56. The rest attacked from 3,000 to 4,000 feet at 13.58, and returned safely to report large fires and smoke obscuring the ground. That night Bremen suffered its most catastrophic raid of the war at the hands of 5 Group, in which over 8,600 apartment blocks were left gutted, and eighteen ships were sunk in the harbour.

Over four hundred Lancasters of 1, 3, 6 and 8 Groups set out to return to Rüsselsheim on the night of the 25/26th, and twelve provided by 300 Squadron were among 189 put up by 1 Group. S/L Misselbrook was the senior pilot on duty as they became airborne from Faldingworth by 20.30, and headed for the Normandy coast near Caen, before passing south of Paris and turning east to the target area. They flew out in patchy cloud, which had largely dissipated by the time they arrived in the searchlight belt west of Darmstadt, and turned north to approach the target from the south-east. The pathfinder marking was accurate, and the aiming point was clearly identified by red and green target indicators, upon which the squadron element delivered their cookies and incendiaries from 15,500 to 19,000 feet between 00.57 and 01.09. The attack was concentrated, and returning crews reported the glow of fires still visible eighty miles into the return trip. Local reports would later confirm that parts of the Opel factory were put out of action for several weeks, although most of the machine tools escaped damage, and production was not badly effected. Night fighters were out in force, and F/O Pohoski and crew observed a Lancaster being hit by tracer and catching fire, before two parachutes were seen to open. Fifteen aircraft failed to return, and two of these were from Faldingworth. JB561 is believed to have crashed in the target area, with no survivors from the crew of F/O Whyte. The flight engineer in this crew was F/S Jagiello of the Polish Air Force, and this was, therefore, the first mixed RAF/PAF crew to be lost. The location of the burials of F/O Hansell DFC and his crew in the Rheinberg Cemetery, suggests that LM172 crashed much closer to the Ruhr or the border with Holland, and occurred on the way home. On the following night elements of 1, 3 and 8 Groups provided the 372-strong heavy force for an attack on Kiel. 300 Squadron briefed ten crews, among which F/L Monk was the senior pilot. One aircraft was found to be unserviceable at the last

Above: Two views of the wreckage of LL947 BH-W which failed to return from Stettin on 29 / 30th August 1944. The aircraft suffered control problems and crashed in Sweden having been abandoned by the crew. F/O Jones and his crew survived and were interned (Harry Holmes).

Faldingworth, August 1944. Above: 300 Squadron crew beside Lancaster JB561 BH-B. This aircraft took part in 11 operations with Polish crews on board and was shot down on its 12th sortie with a British crew of "B" Flight. Below: Lancaster LM172 BH-Q of British "B" Flight. The crew of W/O Hugh White (probably posing in the front) flew six of eight operations of this aircraft with 300 Squadron. (PISM via WM)

Above: Apparently slightly retouched photograph of Lancaster PA163 BH-M at Faldingworth. This aircraft was shot down on her 6th operation with 300 Squadron. (JC). Below: Lancaster ED327 BH-R displaying artwork symbolising the coalition of allied countries and motto "Facta non Verba" (Deeds Not Words). (PISM via WM)

moment, leaving nine to take-off, and all were safely airborne by 20.25. ME847 lost the use of its port-outer engine almost immediatcly, F/O Pope jettisoning the bomb load off the Lincolnshire coast before returning home, where he overshot the end of the runway and ended up in a ditch, possibly after deliberately retracting the undercarriage in an attempt to slow down. The Lancaster was extensively damaged, but there were no crew casualties. The others continued on, and encountered a thin layer of stratus cloud during the outward flight, with patches over the target itself, but insufficient to hamper the marking process by the Pathfinders. The aiming point was clearly marked by red and green TIs, and the squadron crews delivered their cookies and incendiaries onto them from 15,000 to 19,000 feet between 23.07 and 23.19. Returning crews commented on the concentration of the bombing, and a long line of fire from south-west to north-east, as if following the layout of a street. The fires appeared to become a general conflagration as the raid progressed, and the glow of the burning town was visible for a hundred miles into the return journey. F/O Pohoski and crew described an unidentified aircraft bursting into flames at 23.21, and diving steeply to explode on the ground just north of the target. F/L Monk's crew reported a large orange explosion as they were leaving the target area at 23.39, and ten minutes later an aircraft was seen to fall into the sea. Local reports confirmed the effectiveness of the operation, which left widespread damage in the town centre and surrounding districts.

The final acts of the flying bomb campaign were played out on the 28th, and shortly afterwards, the Pas-de-Calais region fell into Allied hands. Stettin became the third German city to receive a second visit during the month, when attacked by almost four hundred aircraft from 1, 3, 6 and 8 Groups on the night of the 29/30th. 300 Squadrons dispatched eleven crews, led by W/C Pozyczka at 21.05, and they flew out in cloud, on a route which took them over northern Denmark and Sweden. To reach the target they had to run the gauntlet of flak and fighters, and not all made it through. F/O Davis had just passed over Viborg on the Jutland peninsular when he saw tracer, followed by a four-engine aircraft catching fire and exploding on the ground at 00.13. Ten minutes later F/O Pope observed a similar incident a few miles further east, and F/S Wasilczuk watched a burning aircraft dive steeply and explode on the ground at 00.42 in the same general area of north-eastern Denmark. Most arrived in the target area to find ten-tenths cloud, but there were gaps, and W/C Pozyczka was one who was able to pick out ground features to identify his position. The majority of crews relied on the red target indicators or their glow beneath the cloud to establish the location of the aiming point, and the 300 Squadron crews, who were carrying either a cookie and incendiaries or a 2,000 pounder and incendiaries, delivered their loads from 16,000 to 19,000 feet between 01.57 and 02.12. It was during the attack that F/L Monk observed a Pathfinder aircraft jettison a load of TIs, before exploding on the ground a mile or so north of the target at 02.05.

On return W/C Pozyczka reported being able to see the glow for many miles into the homeward flight, but complained that the route was too long and tiring for the pilots. W/O Warchal and crew were others to observe a Lancaster crashing after being coned by searchlights and hit by flak, but this occurred over the target. Others spoke of explosions and the glow of fires visible from the Swedish coast on the way home. Twenty-three Lancasters failed to make it back, and 300 Squadron was one of two from 1 Group to lose three aircraft. PA163 was almost certainly one of those observed to fall over Jutland. It was intercepted by a night fighter, exploded in the air, and crashed west of Aalestrup. The pilot, F/L Wasik, was thrown clear as the sole survivor, and he was helped by the Danish resistance to evade capture and return to the UK. His brief account is included in the Escape and Evasion reports at the end of the narrative section. Remarkably, this was his second evasion after being shot down, his first having occurred on the night of the 27/28th of April 1942, when he had been second pilot to P/O Fusinski during an operation to Cologne. LL947 crashed in Sweden at around 00.25, but not before the crew of F/O Jones had abandoned it to its fate. While in internment the crew reported that aileron problems outbound had made the Lancaster difficult to control, and it had been decided to make for Sweden rather than risk a hazardous return to England[3]. ED327 is presumed to have crashed into the Baltic, based on the recovery of a single member of the crew on Sweden's east coast. A local report catalogued over fifteen hundred houses and thirty-two industrial premises destroyed, and many more seriously damaged, and thirty-one thousand tonnes of shipping sunk or damaged in the harbour. The death toll on the ground exceeded a thousand people.

On the 31st, six hundred aircraft were dispatched to attack nine suspected V-2 storage sites in northern France, and six 300 Squadron crews were briefed for an attack on the one at St Riquier in company with forty-two others from the Group. They took off either side of 13.30, and flew out in four to seven-tenths cloud with tops at 13,000 feet. They arrived over the target to find heavy flak and inaccurate markers, which had either under or overshot the aiming point. F/O Davies dropped his eleven 1,000 and four 500 pounders visually from 12,000 feet at 15.30, as did three of his squadron colleagues, who were the first over the target, before anything was heard from the Master Bomber. W/O Barton heard the Master Bomber call for a two-hundred-yard undershoot, which he complied with at 15.38, the same time as F/S Wasilczuk released four of his 1,000 pounders manually on his third run across the target after experiencing bomb release problems. On the way home he jettisoned two more 1,000 pounders, and brought five home.

This was the final operation for B Flight, which was now disbanded and its crews posted to RAF units. As a result of the heavy losses sustained by the squadron in May and June, eight in all, the number of Polish crews on strength had fallen to fourteen, according to the weekly list of operational crews for 7th of July. Twelve new Polish crews were posted in from 18 O.T.U in July, and a further four in August, to

Left: F/L Waclaw Wasik was a lucky survivor who was shot down and evaded capture twice. This outstanding record is even more remarkable as he flew only four sorties with 300 Squadron and was shot down in 1942 and 1944. (PISM via WM) Right: F/S Michal Wasilczuk - Pre-war pilot of 51 Reconaissance Flight in Poland. Having spent two years in a Russian gulag after the September 1939 Campaign, he reached the UK and completed training as a bomber pilot. He took part in 32 bombing operations with 300 Squadron from Aug. to Dec. 1944 before taking up an instructor post in 10 OTU at Abingdon. (J. Wasilczuk)

[3] *An escape and evasion report is included in the appropriate section at the end of the narrative.*

bring the squadron up to full strength. However, an urgent need arose to provide crews for 1586 (Polish) Spccial Duties Flight in Brindisi, following extremely heavy losses sustained while conducting sorties to Poland in support of the Warsaw Uprising. As a result, ten crews were posted from 300 Squadron to Brindisi between the 14th and 25th of August, reducing the strength once more to eight Polish crews and eleven RAF. Now that the RAF element had departed, the squadron would face the coming month as a single flight unit with just six Polish crews on strength. Another busy month had seen the squadron operate fourteen times, launching 146 sorties for a new record loss of six aircraft.

The crew of F/O George R. Davies beside Lancaster LL798 BH-V after returning from a raid against a target in France (B. Marlow via RG).

September 1944

Another photograph of Lancaster ED327 BH-R (B. Marlow via RG).

Having returned to an all-Polish and one flight status, the new month would bring many fewer operations and sorties for 300 Squadron. Twelve new crews would join the squadron during September and October, but it would be December before there were sufficient to reform B Flight. For the Command as a whole, September would be devoted largely to clearing enemy resistance from the three French ports still unavailable to the Allies, but the first major activity of the month came on the 3rd, when over six hundred aircraft carried out heavy raids on six airfields in southern Holland. 1 Group targeted Gilze-Rijen and Eindhoven with ninety-nine and fifty-one Lancasters respectively, 300 Squadron providing three Lancaster for the former. They took off shortly before 16.00, and arrived in the target area to find good visibility and ground detail clear enough to bomb visually. They released their loads of eleven 1,000 and four 500 pounders from 11,500 to 13,000 feet between 17.29 and 17.33, and returned safely to report an accurate and concentrated attack.

The first of six raids on enemy strong points around le Havre took place on the 5th, and involved 348 aircraft, of which three Lancasters represented 300 Squadron. They took off either side of 16.30, and reached the target to find excellent conditions and the aiming point marked by red and green target indicators. All three from the squadron bombed within seconds of each other at 18.25 from 12,000 feet, and returned safely to report accurate marking and bombing. W/C Pozyczka and crew and two others from the squadron joined a force of 344 aircraft, tasked with continuing the assault on enemy positions around le Havre on the 6th, when conditions were again ideal for bombing. They took off at 17.31, and found the red and green target indicators to be short of the aiming point. The Master Bomber called for a one-mile overshoot, and the squadron crews complied from 7,000 feet in a six-minute slot from 19.20. W/C Pozyczka watched his bombs straddle the aiming point, and commented on return that most of the bombing had been concentrated on a wooded area close to the town. Weather conditions on the 8th were less favourable, with low cloud, and by the time that W/C Pozyczka and two others from the squadron reached the target area shortly after 09.00, the Master Bomber was calling a halt to proceedings and sending the crews home. 109 of the initial heavy force of 308 aircraft did bomb with indeterminate results, but the 300 Squadron element was not among them, jettisoning part of their bomb loads before returning home.

The operation over le Havre on the 9th was hampered by poor weather again, and this time the Master bomber sent the crews home without any bombing taking place. 300 Squadron had not taken part, but four crews were briefed for inclusion in the next attack, scheduled to take place on the evening of the 10th. The Polish station commander at Faldingworth, G/C Dabrowa, flew on this operation in the crew of W/O Sarachman, and they were first to take off at 17.14. The weather on this occasion was excellent for the 992 participating aircraft, whose crews had been briefed to attack eight different enemy strong-points. The Polish crews all identified the target visually, and delivered their bombs from 8,000 to 10,500 feet between 18.52 and 18.56, before returning home to report that the markers had been positioned slightly south of the aiming point, but this had not interfered with the concentrated bombing. The final operation against le Havre took place on the 11th, without participation by 300 Squadron, and shortly afterwards the German garrison surrendered to British forces.

Aerial photograph taken by a 300 Squadron crew during a daylight raid on Le Havre on 6th Sept. 1944. (JC)

The final major raid of the war on Frankfurt was delivered by elements of 1, 3 and 8 Groups on the night of the 12/13th, and was attended by 198 Lancasters from 1 Group, including three representing 300 Squadron. They were off the ground by 18.31 as part of an overall heavy force of 378 Lancasters, and headed towards southern Germany at the same time as a two-hundred-strong predominantly 5 Group force bound for Stuttgart. The weather was clear, enabling the Pathfinders to locate the target easily and deliver illuminator flares at 22.52, for the marker aircraft to follow up and drop red and green ground markers. The three Faldingworth crews delivered their cookies and incendiaries from 17,000 to 19,000 feet between 22.58 and 23.06, in the face of intense searchlight and flak activity and a night fighter presence, and returned home safely to report fires taking hold as they left the target area. This operation took place just twenty-four hours after a 5 Group attack on nearby Darmstadt, which had resulted in a firestorm, and the deaths of more than 12,000 people. Most of the Frankfurt firemen and rescue workers were still active there when the RAF arrived, and local reports confirmed that severe damage was caused in the city's western districts, where much of the industry was located. The Stuttgart raid was also highly destructive, and a firestorm afflicted one of the central districts.

The dismantling of Kiel continued on the night of the 15/16th at the hands of 4, 6 and 8 Groups, with a sprinkling of ABC Lancasters from 101 Squadron, and further heavy damage was inflicted on central districts and the port area. On the following night 1 and 8 Groups put two hundred Lancasters into the air, along with a force of Mosquitos, to bomb the airfields at Leeuwarden and Steenwijk in Holland and Hopsten and Rheine just across the frontier in Germany. The attacks were in support of Operation Market Garden, which was to be launched on the morning of the 17th. 300 Squadron detailed four Lancasters, which took off shortly before 21.30 bound for Hopsten, a fighter station situated near the Mittelland Canal west of Osnabrück. Weather conditions were good throughout, and no enemy night fighters were encountered, but the airfield was defended by light flak batteries. The aiming point was identified by red target indicators, and the Polish crews delivered their eighteen 500 pounders each from 17,000 feet between 23.21 and 23.28. On return two crews commented on an aircraft bombing on a red beacon, dropped to set the northern boundary of the bombing area, and this occurring before the TIs went down. Many bombs were also observed to straddle the markers, and the attack was deemed to be successful.

Boulogne was returned to Allied control after three thousand tons of bombs were dropped onto enemy positions on the morning of the 17th. 300 Squadron was not called into action for this operation, but, late in the afternoon, provided three Lancasters among 104 dispatched by the group to attack three coastal batteries and an ammunition dump on the Island of Walcheren in support of Operation Market Garden. They took off at 16.45 to join twenty-three others bound for the battery at Biggekerke, north-west of Flushing, and they were blessed with good weather conditions on the way out and over the target. They were able to identify the aiming point visually, and by target indicators, and they released their thirteen 1,000 and four 500 pounders each from 11,000 feet at 18.17, before returning home to report concentrated bombing, but nothing heard from the Master Bomber.

The first of a series of operations to liberate Calais took place on the late afternoon of the 20th, when over six hundred aircraft were assigned to enemy strong points around the port. 300 Squadron contributed four Lancasters, which took off at 15.38, and proceeded to the target in good weather conditions to find the aiming points clearly marked by red TIs. They bombed from between 2,500 and 8,000 feet in an eight-minute slot to 17.08, and reported a concentrated attack with a few overshoots. Before the second raid on Calais, 1 Group contributed a record 204 Lancasters to a 1, 3, 4 and 8 Group operation against the Ruhr town of Neuss on the night of the 23/24th. 300 Squadron again provided four Lancasters, which took off

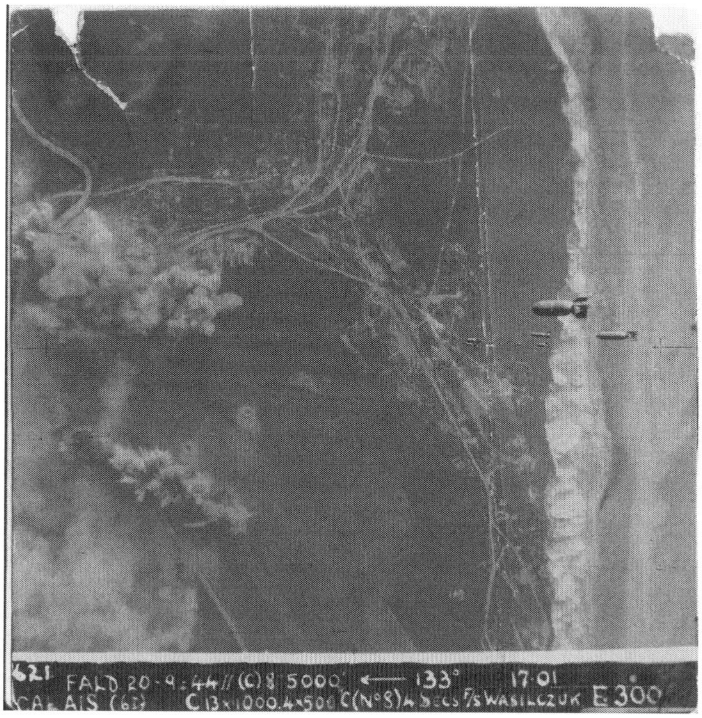

Aerial photographs taken by the crew of F/Sgt Wasilczuk during daylight raids on the German garrison at Calais on 20 Sept. 1944 (left) and 26 Sept. (right). Note the numerous craters made by falling bombs which demonstrate the intensity of the bombing operations. (J. Wasilczuk)

at 19.00, but, in contrast to recent favourable weather conditions, they encountered ten-tenths cloud with tops as high as 20,000 feet. The Pathfinder markers quickly disappeared into the cloud, and bombing had to take place on the glow, although crews in H2S-equipped Lancasters were able to establish their own position over the target. Despite the difficulties, sufficient bombs found their way into the town to destroy or seriously damage more than six hundred houses and public buildings. The Polish crews delivered their loads from 18,000 feet between 21.22 and 21.35, and returned safely unable to offer an assessment of results.

Cloud interfered with the second raid on Calais on the 24th, and some crews came below the cloud base to bomb from two thousand feet, suffering the consequences from the light flak. A massive force of more than eight hundred aircraft was sent back on the morning of the 25th, and among them were four Lancasters from Faldingworth. They took off shortly after 07.20, and arrived in the target area to find heavy cloud with a base at around 2,000 feet. Fewer than three hundred aircraft bombed before the Master Bomber called a halt to proceedings, and the 300 Squadron element was sent home. More than seven hundred aircraft were sent back on the following morning to attack four aiming points at Cap Gris Nez, and 300 Squadron supported the operation with four Lancasters. They took off at 10.30, and this time encountered favourable weather conditions, which allowed them to pick out the aiming point visually. There were also accurately laid target markers to aim at, and three of the squadron's crews delivered their loads from 6,000 to 10,000 feet between 12.02 and 12.09. W/O Stepien made three runs across the target, but his bombs failed to release, and he turned for home with his bombs still on board. Whatever the problem, he was able to jettison his load over the Channel, and return home to give his impressions of the operation. Further operations against enemy positions around Calais were mounted on the 27th and 28th, both supported by 1 Group but not 300 Squadron, and Canadian ground forces took control of the area shortly afterwards. The squadron took part in twelve operations during the month,

October 1944

After a very low key September, 300 Squadron would make a larger contribution to the war effort from this point on. A number of attempts had been made during September to bomb heavy gun emplacements on the island of Walcheren in the Scheldt Estuary, which were barring the approaches to the much-needed port of Antwerp. They proved to be difficult targets, and it was decided instead to breach the sea walls, and inundate the batteries, while also creating difficult terrain for the enemy to defend against ground forces. On the 3rd crews were briefed for an operation involving eight waves of thirty Lancasters each, which were to attack the sea walls at Westkapelle at fifteen minute intervals. 1 Group aircraft would be present in waves five to eight, with the five 300 Squadron participants in the final wave. They took off at 13.22, led by W/C Pozyczka, and reached the target area in good weather conditions to find that a breach had already been created by wave 5, and it was gradually becoming enlarged by subsequent bombing. The Faldingworth crews each carried a cookie, eight 1,000 pounders and a single delay-fused 500 pounder, and these were delivered visually onto the aiming point by four of them from 4,000 feet at 14.47. P/O Kapciuk bombed on his second run across the target at 15.02 from 6,000 feet, before returning home safely with the others to report accurate and concentrated bombing, a breach some five hundred yards wide, and water spreading towards the town, which was already partially flooded.

The night of the 5/6th, brought the first attack on Saarbrücken for two years, for which a force of over five hundred aircraft from 1, 3 and 8 Groups was made ready. This figure included a new 1 Group record to a single target of 239 Lancasters, of which nine were provided by 300 Squadron. The operation had been requested by the American Third Army, which was advancing towards the town, and the objective was to cut all enemy road and rail communications and thereby block supply routes. Take-off from Faldingworth was completed by 19.03, but three early returns soon reduced the squadron's effort. F/L Brogowski and crew abandoned their sortie in mid Channel south of Brighton at 20.45, after the failure of navigational equipment. At around the same time and just short of the French coast near Abbeville, F/L Janas's navigator became too ill to continue, and, finally, P/O Kapciuk turned back at 22.08 when west of Verdun in north-eastern France, and cited severe icing as the reason. The others pressed on to reach the target in clear skies and good visibility with just a little haze. The aiming point was identified by red target indicators, and the squadron element bombed from 15,000 to 16,000 feet between 22.32 and 22.40. It was too early in the proceedings to make an accurate assessment of results, but fires could be seen taking hold as they departed the target area, and these were still visible eighty miles into the return trip. The attack was massively successful, and resulted in the destruction of almost six thousand houses in what was now a frontier town, and it would not be necessary for the bombers to return.

A new Ruhr campaign began at Dortmund on the night of the 6/7th at the hands of 3, 6 and 8 Groups, and from this point on, an unprecedented weight of bombs would fall on Germany's urban centres. The frontier towns of Cleves and Emmerich were earmarked for destruction, to prevent their use by enemy forces as a staging post to threaten the Allied right flank following the failure of Operation Market Garden. Emmerich sat on the east bank of the Rhine, which formed the border with Holland, and it was assigned to elements of 1, 3 and 8 Groups, including nine Lancasters from 300 Squadron. They took off shortly after noon to rendezvous with the rest of the 340-strong force and pick up an escort of Spitfires, and flew to the target in conditions of eight to ten-tenths cloud as far as the Dutch coast. From then it began to thin, and eventually dissipated altogether, allowing the crews to follow the Rhine right into the town, where ground detail was easily identified. The 300 Squadron Lancasters all arrived in the target area with their cookie and incendiaries, and attacked from 11,000 feet between 14.20 and 14.25. The centre of the town was soon covered in flames with smoke rising to 10,000 feet, but the defences remained active, and F/L Janas and crew saw a Lancaster being hit by flak, and disintegrate in the air. The operation was highly effective, and left over 2,400 houses in a state of ruin.

300 Squadron remained at home over the next few days and nights, and on the morning of the 10th, all Polish personnel attended a high mass in the station Roman Catholic church to commemorate the victims of the Warsaw uprising, which had been brutally suppressed by the Germans after weeks of fierce fighting. The squadron returned to operations on the afternoon of the 11th, when 160 Lancasters and twenty Mosquitos of 1 and 8 Groups were sent to attack the Fort Frederik Hendrik gun battery at Breskens on the south bank of the Scheldt. 300 Squadron prepared six Lancasters, which took off either side of 15.15, and they arrived in the target area to find four to six-tenths cloud. This was not a problem, as the aiming point could still be identified visually and by Pathfinder target indicators. The Polish crews dropped their thirteen 1,000 and four 500 pounders each from 3,500 to 5,000 feet between 16.51 and 16.54, before dust and smoke obscured the ground and forced the raid to be abandoned after less than half of the crews had bombed.

Another interesting example of 300 Sqn artwork. "Madame 4x Hard to Get" adornes an unidentified Lancaster of the unit. Note the symbols of sorties completed are denoted by pints of beer rather than bombs. (PISM via WM)

W/O Stanislaw Sarachman who was shot down on his 19th sortie with 300 Squadron. (PISM via WM)

The new Ruhr offensive led inexorably to Operation Hurricane, a demonstration to the enemy of the overwhelming superiority of the Allied air forces ranged against it. At first light on the 14th over a thousand aircraft took off for Duisburg, among them 243 Lancasters of 1 Group, whose crews had been briefed for three aiming points, including the Thyssen Steel Works. 300 Squadron contributed eight crews, whose briefing had been at 04.00, and they began taking off shortly after 06.30. The outward flight was undertaken in cloudy conditions, but a large gap appeared, which enabled the crews to pick up the Rhine for a short period on approach to the target. Duisburg itself was largely hidden by cloud, but some of the 300 Squadron crews were able to identify the aiming point visually and by green TIs, and bombed from an average of 19,000 feet between 08.46 and 08.52. F/S Bury dropped his load on Homberg, an oil town on the north-western outskirts of Duisburg after failing to identify the primary. As always at this target the flak defence was intense, and F/S Wasilczuk and crew observed a Lancaster being hit by flak at 08.49, and dive in flames to explode on the ground in the docks area. Two minutes later they saw another Lancaster spinning to earth with its port wing all but shot away, and at 08.52 a third Lancaster blew up in the air about a mile ahead. In all, thirteen Lancasters and one Halifax failed to return, and among them was 300 Squadron's NF959, which contained the experienced crew of W/O Sarachman. It crashed some ten miles north-east of the target near Bottrop, after being hit by flak, and only the rear-gunner, W/O Brulinski, survived to be taken into captivity.

Five of the 300 Squadron crews taking part in this operation were on the Order of Battle for a return to the Ruhr city that night by a force of 1,005 aircraft, to press home the point about superiority. F/L Brogowski, F/Os Kolodziej and Pohoski, and F/Ss Bury and Wasilczuk and their crews were airborne again by 22.58, less than twelve hours after landing from the previous raid. Remarkably, these 2018 sorties in less than twenty-four hours were achieved without a contribution from 5 Group, which was active to devastating effect over Brunswick on this night. There should have been seven Lancasters departing Faldingworth for this operation, but one got bogged down while taxying, and prevented another from taking off. The flight out was undertaken in clear skies, and the target was visible through a layer of thin stratus cloud. The aiming point was identified by a concentration of red and green TIs, and the 300 Squadron crews bombed them from 19,000 to 20,000 feet between 01.38 and 01.43. Returning crews spoke of concentrated bombing and many fires with smoke rising, but also of an intense searchlight and flak defence. F/O Pohoski and crew reported a Lancaster being coned eight miles ahead at 01.33, and then going down in flames to crash, and an unidentified Pathfinder aircraft exploding in the air two miles north-west of the city two minutes later. Just seven aircraft failed to return from this operation, making a total of twenty-one over the two raids, during which nine thousand tons of bombs had been delivered in less than twenty-four hours.

The Independent Air Force, or "Lincolnshire Poachers", as 5 Group had been dubbed by 8 Group, was also absent from what the Command claimed was a successful raid by almost five hundred aircraft on Wilhelmshaven on the night of the 15/16th, for which 1 Group contributed seventy Lancasters. Just four 300 Squadron crews took part, and they departed Faldingworth in the early evening led by F/L Janas at 17.40. They flew out in good weather, but encountered sixth to eight-tenths cloud over the target, where red and green TIs marked the aiming point. They bombed from 14,000 to 18,000 feet between 19.48 and 19.51 in the face of intense but inaccurate flak, and returned safely home to report fires and smoke, but no real idea as to the effectiveness of the attack.

Two new crews, captained by F/L Wyganowski and Sgt Szczesny, arrived from 1 LFS on the 19th, to begin the process of bringing the squadron back up to strength. They were, of course, not among the seven crews called for briefing at 18.30, to be told that they would be part of a heavy force of 565 Lancasters of 1, 3, 6 and 8 Groups detailed for a two phase attack on Stuttgart that night. The two waves of bombers were to be separated by four-and-a-half hours, with the Polish crews assigned to the second one, and they lined up for take-off shortly before 21.30. F/S Plucinski put a wheel off the peri-track while taxiing in LL798, and blocked the path for F/L Janas in ME744, thus reducing the squadron's effort to five aircraft. This became four, when LM141 lost its port-outer engine two minutes after take-off, and then experienced problems with the starboard-outer while heading out to sea to dump the bombs. F/S Bury turned back immediately and jettisoned the load safe near the airfield before landing. The others pressed on to reach the target, which they found under ten-tenths cloud, and identified by means of the glow from target indicators. They bombed from 14,000 to 17,000 feet between 00.59 and 01.06, and W/O Bakinowski reported three large explosions, one at 00.58 and two within thirty seconds of each other at 00.59. NN718 lost the use of its rear turret through a hydraulics failure, and could not respond to the approach of an enemy night fighter over the target, but no engagement took place. It was established afterwards that the bombing had been scattered, but had, never the less, caused substantial damage in central and eastern districts.

What might be termed the "Hurricane" force moved on to Essen in the early evening of the 23rd, to continue the dismantling of this once proud industrial city. 1055 aircraft were detailed, of which eight belonged to 300 Squadron, and their crews settled in the briefing room at 13.40 to receive their instructions. Take-off was set for 16.30, and all got away safely, but the operation ended for F/O Kapciuk and crew when at 10,000 feet over Gainsborough, after the mid-upper gunner injured his middle finger in the breech block of one of his guns during the loading process, and was in too much pain to continue. The others pressed on to join up with the rest of the force over the North Sea, and reached the target in good visibility above a layer of ten-tenths cloud. The Pathfinders were using red and green flares, which appeared to be scattered over a wide area, and the crews selected concentrations to aim at as they drifted into the cloud tops. The 300 Squadron crews delivered their cookies and incendiaries from 19,000 to 20,000 feet between 19.31 and 19.49, and returned to report the glow of fires beneath the clouds, but no genuine sense as to the outcome of the raid. They also described moderate heavy barrage-form flak bursting at heights up to 22,000 feet, and bad weather and icing conditions during the return flight. More than 4,500 tons of mostly high explosive bombs were dropped, and a local report listed 607 buildings as destroyed and a further eight hundred seriously damaged.

Above: Faldingworth, March 1945. The crew of F/L Brogowski beside Lancaster PA261 BH-L. 5th from left – F/O Leon Dubicki (A.G.) (T. Dubicki). Left: F/O Leon Dubicki who took part in 36 operations with 300 Squadron from Aug. 1944 to March 1945. (T. Dubicki)

770 aircraft took off on the afternoon of the 25th, to attack the city by daylight, and this time seven 300 Squadron crews took part, including F/O Kapciuk with a replacement mid-upper gunner. They were airborne shortly after 13.00, and encountered poor weather conditions outbound and over the target, where all from the squadron arrived at around 15.40 to begin their bombing runs in good visibility above the cloud. They identified the aiming point by yellow target indicator flares as they disappeared into the cloud tops, and by red release point flares, and dropped their eleven 1,000 and four 500 pounders each from 17,000 to 20,000 feet. F/S Plucinski described an aircraft being hit by flak and exploding during its bombing run a thousand yards ahead, and pieces falling to the ground. The 300 Squadron contingent returned safely uncertain as to the effectiveness of their efforts, but a local report would eventually catalogue the destruction of more than eleven hundred buildings, and a death toll over the two raids of almost fifteen hundred people.

A series of massive attacks on Cologne began on the afternoon of the 28th, when 733 aircraft took off, among them eight Lancasters from 300 Squadron. They got away either side of 13.30, and this time encountered more favourable weather conditions outbound and over the target. The well-placed Pathfinder ground markers were mostly easily identified through gaps in the cloud, and the 300 squadron crews, each of which was carrying a cookie, five 1,000 and six 500 pounders, delivered their attacks from 16,500 to 20,500 feet between 15.58 and 16.18. They returned home safely to report fires taking hold as they turned away from the target area, and smoke rising to 10,000 feet. Local reports confirmed that both aiming points, one to the north-east of the city centre and the other to the south-west, were left devastated, and more than 2,200 blocks of flats were destroyed, along with many industrial premises and public buildings. There was also heavy damage in the harbour and to railway installations and power stations, and the number of Germans killed was put at 630.

The ordeal for Cologne was far from over, as a second assault, this time involving nine hundred aircraft, was mounted on the evening of the 30th. 300 Squadron detailed eight Lancasters, which took off shortly before 18.00, and enjoyed fair weather conditions outbound, but eight-tenths cloud over the aiming point. They identified the target by means of red, green and white flares, and dropped their loads from 16,000 to 19,000 feet between 21.02 and 21.18, F/L Brogowski observing an orange explosion at 21.08, and a cloud of black smoke rising to 12,000 feet south of the target. Moderate to intense heavy flak was encountered over the target, and LM632 sustained damage to its hydraulics system, which prevented the undercarriage from being deployed. F/O Kolodziej opted to land wheels-up on the emergency strip at Carnaby, which he accomplished without injury to the occupants, and at debriefing reported seeing an unidentified jet-propelled enemy aircraft. F/L Brogowski was the senior pilot on duty, when six 300 Squadron Lancasters returned to Cologne as part of an overall force of 493 aircraft on the evening of the 31st. They took off shortly after 18.00, and flew out in good weather, but found the target covered by cloud. Red, white and green release point flares identified the aiming point, and the Faldingworth contingent bombed on these from 16,000 to 19,000 feet between 21.02 and 21.15, before returning safely. Most of the bombing fell into southern districts of a city now descending into a state of total chaos, and many of the occupants had long-since fled. In between these attacks on Cologne, elements of 1, 3, 4 and 8 Groups carried out the penultimate attack on enemy positions on Walcheren on the 29th, and on the 31st, ground forces went in to eventually secure the island after a week of heavy fighting. The following four weeks were spent clearing mines from the estuary, and it was the end of December before the first convoy arrived at Antwerp. The squadron took part in thirteen operations during the month, and lost one aircraft from eighty-eight sorties.

A collection of air and ground crew pose with Lancaster ME470 BH-F towards the end of the war. The aircraft survived the conflict (Harry Holmes).

November 1944

Düsseldorf became the next victim of a huge Bomber Command attack, when over nine hundred aircraft were made ready on the 2nd, among them 252 Lancasters of 1 Group, including eight from 300 Squadron. The Faldingworth contingent took off either side of 16.30, and found favourable weather conditions both outbound and over the target. The aiming point was identified visually and by target indicators, and the 300 Squadron crews bombed from 17,000 to 19,000 feet between 19.18 and 19.30, before returning safely to report accurate and concentrated marking and bombing. They commented on fires taking hold as they turned away, and clouds of smoke drifting across the city. Two crews saw a four-engine aircraft dive straight down in flames to explode on the target, and others spoke of the fires visible from up to eighty miles into the return trip. The northern half of the city bore the brunt of the attack, which destroyed or seriously damaged five thousand houses and twenty-five industrial premises.

Two nights later it was the turn of Bochum to face the horrors of an assault by an awesomely powerful and now unstoppable RAF bomber force from 1, 4, 6 and 8 Groups. Among the 749 aircraft waiting to take off in the early evening were 235 Lancasters of 1 Group, including eleven with Polish crews. One of these developed rising temperatures in an engine, and was pulled out of the line, but the others all got away safely either side of 18.00, and headed into good weather conditions, which persisted all the way to the target. F/O Pohoski was the first from the squadron to arrive, and he found concentrated and plentiful Pathfinder ground markers to aim at. He let his cookie and incendiaries go from 17,000 feet at 19.41, and described many large fires already burning, and one particularly large area of fire on the north-western edge of the city producing dense smoke. This crew always paid particular attention to what was going on around them, and were the most detailed in their reports of aircraft falling. They saw an explosion some fifteen miles ahead at the same height, presumably on the way out, which they took to be a collision between two bombers, and they watched burning pieces falling into the sea. Another aircraft a mile away was hit by heavy flak, and was observed to impact the ground, and a third unidentified aircraft was seen on fire three miles away, falling into the clouds after firing a red cartridge.

The other 300 Squadron crews bombed from 17,000 to 18,000 feet between 19.42 and 19.54, and three of them found themselves under attack from enemy night fighters within minutes of turning for home. PD383 was the first, when at 19.42 an unidentified enemy aircraft approached from the starboard side and opened fire from three hundred yards. F/S Niemiec's mid-upper gunner returned fire, but no hits were claimed and the engagement ended. PA160 was attacked at 19.50 by a FW190, and F/S Wasilczuk took evasive action while his rear gunner returned fire. The enemy was not shaken off, and a chase ensued with fire back and forth as the Lancaster headed towards Mönchengladbach and the Dutch frontier just beyond. At 20.05 the enemy approached from the port quarter below, and, as it pulled up, the rear gunner fired into its belly, scoring hits, and claiming it as damaged. JA922 was also homebound at 19.58, when a BF110 was spotted to starboard and below, but two long bursts of fire from F/L Konarzewski's rear turret hit it in the nose, and it, too, was claimed as damaged. Bochum had wilted under a very heavy blow, which destroyed or seriously damaged four thousand buildings in central and industrial districts, and killed almost a thousand people in return for the loss of twenty-eight aircraft. The Halifax brigade took a beating on this night, losing twenty-three of their number, and the five missing Lancasters all belonged to 1 Group. This would be the final heavy raid on Bochum.

A force of seven hundred aircraft was prepared on the morning of the 6th to attack the town of Gelsenkirchen and its important Nordstern oil plant. 1 Group again put up over two hundred aircraft, of which ten Lancasters belonged to 300 Squadron, and they departed Faldingworth in two sections, seven before 11.30 and three at 12.14. There was five-tenths cloud over England, but this had increased to ten-tenths by the time the Dutch coast was reached. Fortunately, a large gap appeared over the target, and this enable crews to identify the town by the distinctive L-shaped docks to the north-west of the aiming point. Red and green TIs were also in evidence as the attack opened a few minutes earlier than planned, the former slightly misplaced but the latter accurate. However, haze made it difficult to distinguish the colours, and the Master Bomber's communications did not get through with clarity. At 14.01 crews were given the option of bombing on TIs, smoke or visually, and five minutes later they were told to bomb any built-up area in their sights. It was difficult to assess the results, but a column of thick, black smoke rising through the cloud tops at 10,000 feet suggested that the oil plant had been hit. Ground defences were formidable as the bombers traversed the Ruhr, but a fighter escort kept enemy aircraft at bay. The 300 Squadron crews bombed from 16,500 to 19,000 feet between 13.57 and 14.04, F/S Niemiec having to take evasive action to avoid bombs falling from above. This crew also commented on aircraft approaching the aiming point from a variety of headings and altitudes, and, thereby, creating a danger of collisions. LM141 was hit by flak over the target and damaged, and could not maintain sufficient height for the return flight across the North Sea. P/O Latkiewicz ordered his crew to bale out, which they did successfully close to the German/Dutch frontier, and all were taken prisoner.

On the morning of the 9th another 228 Lancasters from the group set out for the oil town of Wanne-Eickel, situated north-west of Gelsenkirchen, with Recklinghausen to the north, Herne to the east and Bochum to the south. 300 Squadron dispatched eleven aircraft, which were safely airborne by 08.00. They flew out in formation as far as 04°E in poor weather conditions of ten-tenths cloud with tops at 21,000 feet. There was no improvement in the target area, and the skymarkers soon disappeared from sight. No instructions were heard from the Master Bomber, and the Polish crews dropped their loads on e.t.a or a Gee fix from 19,500 to 22,000 feet between 10.42 and 10.50, and returned home to report an inconclusive and ultimately unsuccessful operation. Where the bombs actually fell was never determined, but few landed anywhere near the intended aiming point.

The group hoped for a better performance on the evening of the 11th, when it dispatched 183 Lancasters to the Hoesch Benzin plant at Dortmund, among them seven representing 300 Squadron. This was Poland's Independence Day, and all Polish personnel had attended a high mass in the station's Roman Catholic church in the morning. They were all safely airborne shortly after 16.00, but LL804 lost its port-inner engine soon after crossing the Lincolnshire coast, and F/S Rosochacki ordered the bombs to be jettisoned some miles out from Mablethorpe. The remainder pressed on in almost cloud-free conditions over the North Sea until the enemy coast was reached, where the cloud began to build to ten-tenths over the target. The conditions were hardly favourable for an accurate attack, but red target indicators were visible through the cloud, and the squadron element bombed on these from 17,000 to 20,000 feet in a three-minute slot from 19.01. They all returned safely to report slight heavy flak, the glow of fires and a number of large explosions, but it was not possible to make an accurate assessment. In fact, it had been a successful operation, which had caused substantial damage to the site, and spilled over into adjacent residential areas.

The 16th was devoted to the destruction of the three towns of Heinsberg, Jülich and Düren, which lay in a line from north-west to south-east behind enemy lines, north-east to east of Aachen. The last mentioned was assigned to 485 Lancasters of 1, 5 and 8 Groups, with Mosquito support, and ten Polish crews underwent briefing at Faldingworth at 10.00. They were in their aircraft ready for take-off shortly before

13.00, and soon encountered cloud, which built up over enemy territory to nine-tenths with a base at 10,000 feet. However, as the force approached to within about fifteen miles of the target it dissipated, to leave the town protected only by haze. Ground detail was easily identified, and the Pathfinder markers went down accurately to clearly identify the aiming point, until it was blotted out by the early stages of the bombing. The Master Bomber had to find new reference points for the bomb-aimers to keep the raid on track, and this he did successfully. The 300 Squadron crews attacked from 10,000 to 11,500 feet between 15.30 and 15.34, and all returned safely to report a highly effective attack which had sent smoke drifting upwards to 7,000 feet and beyond. Two crews described a four-engine aircraft disintegrating after being hit by flak, and a third reported a "scarecrow", which was believed by many crews to be an enemy flak shell designed to simulate an exploding bomber to weaken their resolve to press on. There is no evidence of such a flak shell being employed by the Germans, and one must conclude, therefore, that what looked like a bomber blowing up was, in fact, a bomber blowing up. Post-raid reconnaissance confirmed the effectiveness of the operation, which all but erased the town from the map, and left over 3,100 of its inhabitants dead.

The Group returned to Wanne-Eickel on the 18/19th, when all but two of its 253 participating Lancasters bombed as briefed and inflicted some fresh damage on the Krupp synthetic oil refinery. 300 Squadron did not take part, but eleven of its crews were briefed at 13.00 on the 21st to participate in a hive of activity involving 1,345 sorties against five main targets, and others in various support and minor operations. 1 Group's main effort was against the marshalling yards at Aschaffenburg, situated south-east of Frankfurt, for which 238 Lancasters were made ready. The Polish element departed Faldingworth either side of 15.45, and initially found good conditions, until cloud began to build from the French coast. By the time the target drew near the ground was completely obscured, and the Master Bomber instructed the crews to bomb on e.t.a or by H2S. Fortunately, most crews identified the target by the glow of TIs in the clouds, and bombing by the 300 Squadron participants took place from 7,000 to 14,000 feet between 19.17 and 19.21. They all returned safely to report the glow of fires reflected in the clouds, but no real clue as to the outcome of the raid. It was established later that it was the town itself, rather than the marshalling yards, that sustained the heaviest damage, with five hundred houses destroyed and fifteen hundred others seriously damaged.

As worthwhile targets became increasingly difficult to find, some seemingly strategically insignificant towns and cities began to find themselves in the bomb-sights. Freiburg was a minor railway centre, deep in south-western Germany close to the Swiss border, and until the night of the 27/28th, it had never been attacked by the RAF. Now that mobile Oboe stations were located in France, these hitherto inaccessible targets were now within range, and 1 Group prepared a new record of 292 Lancasters as part of an overall heavy force with 8 Group of 341 aircraft. 300 Squadron briefed thirteen crews, and they were all safely on their way before 16.30 led by W/C Pozyczka. Weather conditions were favourable throughout, and visibility over the target was good with just a little haze. The aiming point was identified by red and green TIs, and the squadron participants released their loads onto them from 12,500 to 14,000 feet between 20.00 and 20.13. Some were carrying a cookie, five 1,000 and seven 500 pounders, and others a cookie and incendiaries, and all returned safely to report explosions, fires and smoke. Photographs revealed that the railway yards had largely escaped damage, but, according to local reports, the twenty-five minute orgy of destruction had destroyed two thousand houses, and killed a similar number of people.

Lancaster LL804 BH-F being bombed up before the operation at Faldingworth, August 1944. This was the squadron's longest serving Lancaster and completed 70 sorties before being transferred to 1660 CU in March 1945. Due to her long operational service she was nicknamed "Grandma" by Polish crews. (JC)

The final operation of the month for 300 Squadron was against Dortmund by daylight on the 29th, for which fourteen Lancasters were made ready as part of a 1 Group force of 262 aircraft. They began taking off shortly after midday, and reached the target to find six to eight-tenths cloud and haze, and an intense flak defence. Bombing was carried out on skymarkers and visually in accordance with the Master Bomber's instructions, and the squadron element delivered their mixed loads of high explosives and incendiaries from 19,000 to 20,000 feet within three minutes of each other shortly after 15.00. NG269 was hit by heavy flak over the target, and P/O Kozuba-Kozubski had to feather his starboard-outer engine. He returned safely to report a Lancaster a thousand yards ahead going down with its starboard-outer engine on fire, and exploding on the ground. This was confirmed by another crew, and they had almost certainly witnessed the end of PB459 of 460 Squadron RAAF. There was general uncertainty at debriefing as to the accuracy of the attack, some crews reporting scattered bombing, while others thought it concentrated, but it was established later that further damage had been inflicted upon this much-bombed city.

One of the new crews taking part in this operation was that of F/O Kozicki, whose flight engineer was Sgt Henryk Drozdz. They were in LL804 BH-F, and it was with a degree of trepidation that Drozdz learned of the target for his maiden operation. After nine months of training, and almost three weeks on the

Sgt Henryk Drozdz (F.E.). He successfully completed his tour of 30 operations in the crew of F/L Kozicki from Nov. 1944 to April 1945. (G. Drozdz)

squadron, he was about to put into practice all that he had learned as a fully fledged member of a tightly-knit bomber crew, with all of the responsibility to his crew mates which that entailed. Not only that, in order to fulfil his brief, he was going to have to fly over the entire Ruhr and face its fearful defences. We will observe the final stages of the war partly, and uniquely, through his eyes, by means of the personal diary entries that charted his tour. They are included with the kind permission of his son, Gregory Drozdz.

"And so arrived the day of the Great Adventure—my first operational flight. My legs shook when I learned that today will be my first sortie. My God! How many fears, emotions and nerves, how many conjectures and dreams are bound up in this day. When I write this it is already in the past, but before that all the various emotions are so short-lived and elusive. My heart stopped when in the briefing room I saw on the map eight sinister letters of our destination—DORTMUND. It gave me a very unpleasant feeling—it meant we had to fly over the entire 'Ruhr' and this my first combat flight. What rotten luck! But I pay attention to the rest of the briefing and learn many important things—but will it all matter if bad luck will have its way? But I banish these thoughts from my mind—nothing matters but achieving the objective of my dreams. It is not easy, but we have to go. According to orders we fly in the aircraft 'F', the same that we flew our last cross-country flight. It is not a bad plane, powerful and fast Lancaster "F". It is a day flight and we take off at 12.05. It is a smooth take-off and it stirs up a variety of emotions before one says goodbye to the airfield and climbs to 2,000 feet. Soon after take-off there is assembly of the whole flight. It was a pretty sight; a swarm of planes under the leadership of 'Master Bombers'. They all fly merrily towards Germany. The weather is not bad but when you fly in formation you meet a lot of air pockets, which is very unpleasant."

"After we crossed the English coast I had a weird feeling—soon we will cross the French coast and so the coast of the Continent—my European home, abandoned several years before. My heart starts beating faster—there it is—the narrow strip of Europe, to which Poland belongs. I feel happy, I can't say why. It is good to be here—it seems a different world. The flock of 'crows' heavy with their load of bombs is moving forward—it must be a magnificent sight from the ground. Where are our friends—perhaps on the ground. Maybe Zenek raised his head up, opened his mouth and stared—it's our planes flying. Yes, they are our planes flying to avenge the wrong. And then the feelings change into fear and helplessness against the air power. Yes, how many such feelings I experienced myself during the memorable September 1939. The worst fear of the defenceless against the air raids. And now the roles have changed. Thanks be to God that I can now avenge this fear of thousands of children, mothers, elderly and other people. I remember it as if it happened today—in fact it is happening today, but to different people. Today we are the perpetrators of this tragedy—today yesterday's heroes and tyrants will howl with pain and fear under the bombing. In a moment we will send down repayment for September 1939, and for the nightmare five years of murderous German occupation, 14,000 pounds of bombs. On the way to our objective all the time artillery blazes away, here and there little black clouds pop up. Some of them so near they seem to touch the plane. It causes a lot of fear—you want to reach your target—you dodge to the left, then to the right—steady! steady! It's a veritable hell and ..."bombs gone!" Bang, bang—a second of relief, then duck to the left, nose-dive on full throttle, we are fleeing as quickly and as far as we can. And beneath us on the ground all is confusion and chaos—that's for September and Poland. For a long time artillery still blazes away trying to shoot someone down, but to no avail. In front of us an aircraft is trailing smoke, but it is too far to see what the trouble is, then it turns slowly left over France and disappears from sight. In time, as we get farther away from the target, the artillery subsides into silence. It is time to heave a sigh of relief. The bombs were dropped at 3.02 p.m. from the height of 20,000 feet, i.e. about 6½ kilometre."

"After crossing the battle front we start descending—over Belgium we are flying quite low, a mere 6,000 feet. Now we pass Antwerp on the right, the beautiful city seems to be dozing, unaware of the flight of the 'birds of prey'. We pass over the coastline, the white ribbon of the sea looks calm and friendly. So we are saying farewell to Europe, but we will be back soon, maybe even tomorrow. After two hours we reach our base. The weather is not good but everything is O.K. We have no trouble landing, I heave a sigh of relief, after all I was not on my own. "Happy landing" marks the end of my first combat mission. Modest pride and satisfaction fill my breast—from now on I am a combat airman, my destiny had been fulfilled—thanks be to God, let his will be done. We climb down from the plane in a happy mood, the "fed up" feeling of the last few days completely gone. In the log book I will write tomorrow: 'Dortmund operational flight'. I wish that this beginning is the happy start of my air force career. God's peace.

During the course of the month the squadron participated in nine operations, and dispatched ninety-five sorties for the loss of a single aircraft.

December 1944

The first operational activity of the new month for 300 Squadron came on the morning of the 3rd after a briefing for thirteen crews at 05.00. The target for 183 Lancasters of 1 and 8 Groups was the Urft Dam, situated near the town of Heimbach in the Eiffel region of Germany close to the frontier with Belgium. It was believed that the Germans might strategically release flood water to impede the advance of American forces, and it was decided to destroy the dam to remove it as a threat. They took off from Faldingworth either side of 07.45, and flew out in cloud as far as the Belgian coast. Here the skies cleared, only to fill with thick nine-tenths cloud again at the German border, obscuring all sight of the ground. The Master Bomber descended to 4,000 feet, but was still unable to identify the aiming point, and issued instructions shortly after 09.40 to abandon the operation. W/O Bakanacz and crew failed to pick up the message, and the bomb load was released on a Gee fix onto a small town on a railway line south of Heimbach at 09.52. All of the others complied with the order, and brought their bombs home. At debriefing F/L Wyganowski and crew reported seeing a Lancaster going down in flames and disappearing into cloud at a map reference that places it south-east of Liege. It was at 09.33 on the way out, and six parachutes were observed, identifying it as belonging to 582 Squadron. It was shot down by an enemy aircraft, and the mid-upper gunner was the sole fatality, while the rest of the crew landed safely in Allied-held territory.

Sgt Drozdz had the following to say on this operation. "They woke us up at 4 o'clock in the morning because of the mission. Today it is not so frightening—maybe there is less secrecy. What I heard during the briefing made me very happy. The target is one of the easiest—destruction of a dam, and it makes a picturesque and almost fairy-tale object. The weather is also 90% perfect. No wonder that during the briefing everyone is more talkative, the fact that there is no artillery over the target also helps to create good mood. I myself feel 100% better than yesterday. Today's sortie seems almost like a pleasure trip. We take off very early—at 7.45. The flight to the target is without any major incidents, but as always there are various emotions. Almost imperceptibly we arrive over the totally undefended target. Everything is going according to plan, but the weather is completely different from the 'Met' forecast. At 10,000 feet clouds completely cover the target. The whole fleet of 250 Lancasters begins to circle over the target—it looks quite funny. Silently, like flies, we go round looking for a 'hole'. All in vain, we have to go back... with the bombs. I feel like crying, having to go back with the bombs, but orders are orders; if you can't find the target you have to return with the bombs. So we are going back with long faces."

"We fly over Belgium and Brussels—somewhere down there must be Zenek who does not even imagine that somewhere above him at only 10,000 feet I am flying. But there is no time for thoughts and dreams. We pass Antwerp, Belgium, coastline, the Channel itself and then in addition it is icing over. We cross the Channel at 2,000 feet. To make matters worse every so often a group of three Dakotas come towards us. What the hell are they doing, I keep thinking, they are coming straight at us. Luckily we are higher. Russet-green English Channel seems angry and frothy, as if it wanted to swallow us. Brr, brr! It is cold and raining, the plane is tossed about. Thus we reach the English coast. Here we descend even lower, beneath the clouds, which are at about 200 feet. This flight, which started so happily, could almost end in tragedy. Flying at 100 feet fully loaded, being tossed about, is terrifying. And then the clouds, the rain, but we are flying on at the speed of 180 mph. In these poor conditions we near the airfield. In a moment the final chapter—landing with the bombs in this weather! Brr! But we follow the normal procedure; 'undercarriage down', 'flaps 20', 'flaps 30', RPM 2650. We approach from a distance, the visibility improved. Now we are in the 'funnels' full flaps, 2800 RPM. The pilot circles over the runway—power off! We land softly, even with bombs. The fear is gone. In this way ends this well-augured 'pleasure' flight. Its target—Urft Dam—was nearly the last in my air force career. But how can one compare 3 pages of writing with 4 hours 40 minutes flight full of pleasure, terror and near tragedy?"

The first large-scale 1 Group effort of the month involved 259 of its Lancasters as part of an overall force of 535 aircraft, the destination for which was Karlsruhe on the night of the 4/5th. 300 Squadron made ready thirteen Lancasters, which began to depart Faldingworth at 16.40, and headed into fair conditions, which alternated between clear and eight-tenths cloud all the way to the target. The early arrivals were met by large amounts of cloud over the city with a few gaps, and most had to rely on the glow of red and green target indicators or H2S to find the aiming point. However, the cloud was being blown eastwards, and later arrivals were able to identify ground detail and bomb visually. The Polish crews were carrying either a cookie and incendiaries or twelve 1,000 pounders, and these were released from 17,000 to 20,000 feet between 19.30 and 19.41. They all returned safely to report large fires and a glow visible up to 120 miles into the return flight, and the success of the operation would be confirmed later. Sgt Drozdz continues his story.

Faldingworth, summer 1945. An unidentified Polish Lancaster bearing intriguing artwork on its fuselage. Note the impressive tally of 58 operations flown and two swastikas, probably denoting destroyed German fighters. (Kuczera family via P. Hodyra).

"My third combat flight is to Karlsruhe. A lot of fear during the briefing and during the take-off. It is 16.45. 'B' for Betty climbs up at full throttle. Everything goes well—1,000, 2,000, 3,000 up to 12,000 feet and then 'straight level'. This is my first night mission, so I am quite curious to find out what it is like at night. Curiosity is coupled with quite a dose of fear—instinct of self-preservation in the face of death. The flight seems monotonous. From time to time I make some technical adjustments as we climb up to 20,000 feet. Sometimes we pass by another Lancaster, or one passes us by. We are not flying alone but part of a large group so we have to be careful. Ah! these combat flights! In truth Lancaster is like a whole eye—to the left, to the right, up and down, to the front and to the rear—there is no blind spot. Six people are looking, 12 pairs of eyes straining into the distance. Oh, now, Saarbrucken begins to shoot, but it does not matter because they shoot from the left. I have no time to stare as I am busy throwing so-called 'windows', i.e. silver papers which would look quite pretty on a Christmas tree. We are getting near the target. Artillery blasts away, in front of us and below through the clouds. There is a sea of fire—the target. Karlsruhe is burning. Markers on the left, markers on the right and we in the middle. Artillery is blasting, but no matter. We dive down, left, right, steady! and ... "bombs gone". Bang! bang! Have we been hit? No, it is only the bombs going down. They have gone. Now it is lighter, duck to the right, duck to the left, God save us! Artillery is blazing without a break, beneath us the fire is awful. It is light as day. It reminds me of Kurów, maybe you lose the taste for war. We are going back, here and there flashes and 'sausages' of bullets, nearly directly at us. Kindly 'Lanc' goes forward, we are descending, some 220 on speedometer, we are going quickly away from the target, but the fire glow remains the same, enormous, sinister patch of fire and light through the clouds. Even after an hour's time, while already over France, the glow of burning Karlsruhe was still visible. I haven't seen such sight so far. Even though the artillery was still blazing we got out. Now only the return. Again with God's help we return safely. No trouble with landing. After landing—surprise! 'B' Betty is waiting for me and ... throws herself into my arms. Somewhat disconcerted at this display of rather excessive show of devotion or love I try to be good and reply in similar manner. We return together to crew quarters in a happy mood as if from the altar. After changing we go for debriefing by the intelligence officer. Afterwards tasty egg finishes off the 6½ hour flight."

It was followed on the night of the 6/7th by the first of a concerted campaign against the synthetic oil refineries in eastern Germany. The target was a plant at Leuna, near Merseburg, west of Leipzig, and the operation was to be carried out by 475 Lancasters of 1, 3 and 8 Groups. 1 Group put up 294 aircraft, including fourteen from Faldingworth, which took off either side of 17.00 in cloudy conditions, which persisted for most of the way out. LL804 made it as far as Bedfordshire before turning back with Gee failure, but the others pressed on to encounter ten-tenths cloud over the target, and an intense flak defence. The initial ground marking by the Pathfinders soon proved to be ineffective in the conditions, and they quickly changed to skymarking, allowing the Polish crews to aim for the red flares with green stars as they ran across the aiming point at 17,000 to 20,000 feet between 20.45 and 20.50. NN718's rear turret was damaged by flak, but all returned home to report being unable to observe results. Post-raid reconnaissance provided the answers, and showed the plant to have sustained considerable damage. Henryk Drozdz wrote;

"The long winding course of today's flight fills us with dread. It is a little village and next to it is a large factory producing oil and motor fuels—Merseburg. This is today's target, a few miles to the west of Leipzig. During the briefing everyone is very quiet. Today's flight of 1,700 miles casts a gloom over the company. When I look at the faces they all look depressed, but here and there somebody tries to smile. Only to an outsider it may look like heroism or important event, but not here among the hundreds of people who will soon take off—for them it is not heroism, just duty and maybe fear or thrill. Here nobody is asking whether you are flying or not—we fly because this is an order. It is the second time I am flying in 'B' Betty (the mechanic in the ground crew is Adamski, a friend from France). We take off at 5 p.m. The whole flight is similar to the last one but the defence is different. As soon as we cross the German border there is artillery to the left and to the right—it does not augur well. This flight to the target seems to last ages, but I am occupied by throwing 'windows'. Eventually we are nearing the target. As usual battle course—full throttle and to the target. Ready, steady and the bombs are gone—it is 20.45 hours. The artillery fire intensifies left and right, then the searchlights start—we duck to the left, then down—my stomach is in my throat. But we escape. It causes a lot of fear and excitement, but now we are out of reach. We dropped the bombs on the red 'markers'. We are busy today, we fly for a long time over Germany and we have to look out for fighter planes. After leaving Germany the flight continues unhindered and we land safely—it is 1 a.m. So the whole flight lasted full 8 hours. This was my longest flight to date. How nice it is to climb down from the plane, heave a sigh of relief and say: one flight less to go and it was a hard one. In fact the briefing is the worst, but the return is pleasant, especially when you celebrate 'B' Betty with a drink of rum."

1 Group contributed over 260 Lancasters for the final heavy night raid of the war on Essen, which was mounted by over five hundred aircraft from 1, 4 and 8 Groups on the night of the 12/13th. 300 Squadron

Crews are briefed at Faldingworth before an operation. (PISM via WM)

briefed fourteen crews, and they took off either side of 16.30, and headed into cloud, which persisted most of the way to the target. Essen itself was under ten-tenths cloud, and the Pathfinders were a little late in opening the attack with release point flares, some of which, crews later complained, were igniting too high to be effective. The marking soon became concentrated, however, and the Faldingworth crews passed over the aiming point at 17,000 to 20,000 feet between 19.31 and 19.43. Flak over the target was moderate to intense, but none of the 300 Squadron aircraft was hit, although NG269 lost its port-inner engine as W/O Bakanacz and crew left the target, but they made it safely home on three. PB722 was approached twice from astern by an enemy night fighter at 19.43 and 19.54, but a burst of fire on each occasion from F/L Konarzewski's rear turret dissuaded it from pressing home an attack. Despite the already massive damage inflicted on this city since March 1943, there were still buildings standing, and almost seven hundred of them were destroyed on this night, while the Krupp works was among the war industry factories to be hit again.

"Third time lucky—at last we took off without a hitch, previous two flights were cancelled—boring... As I write about today's flight I notice an odd thing about myself. Fear which I felt before every flight gave way to pure emotion. I don't doubt it had a trace of fear in it, especially as the target for tonight's mission could evoke a feeling of dread: Essen. Although it means we have to fly over the Ruhr I am quite hopeful. We take off at 16.40. The same tactic as before. Our arrival over Ruhr is greeted by the faithful artillery, which cannot do anything in spite of doubling its efforts. We fly on without interruption. Nothing can stop us—it is not for my benefit—it is for the thousands or millions of children, women and old people who must be avenged. We can see 'markers' in the distance—battle course. Oh! tremble you Germans, the time of revenge is approaching. Hundreds, thousands of flashes and bullets, to the left and to the right they blaze away mercilessly, but will it stops us? No—battle course. Steady! — "Bombs gone". Oh! we dive down, God save us! To the left, to the right, then down, oh horror—how they blast. Now we are in the middle of exploding flashes—will we survive? Full throttle—that saves us. We are diving down, slowly the hell is behind us. We shake off feelings of fear and emotion, only the memory of having been in 'deep waters' remains. Here and there we see flashes but they don't matter, the worst is now over. We can still see in the distance Essen on fire. It had been on fire maybe a hundred times already and it is still not the end. Until the Teutonic arrogance is crushed Essen and all the German cities will burn every night with the fire of vengeance. Yesterday it was you, today it is us who rule the skies. Swift 'R' -Roger hurries home with double speed, he hurries because he is injured. A small piece of shrapnel entered the cabin next to me. Luckily it struck the hydraulic cable first so it did not cause too much damage."

Ludwigshafen was one of the cities associated with the important I G Farben chemicals company, and contained one factory in a northern suburb, and another in the nearby town of Oppau. Over three hundred Lancasters of 1, 6 and 8 Groups provided the main force for the raid on the 15th, of which a dozen were provided by 300 Squadron. They took off into clear skies either side of 15.00, and headed south to the Channel, where cloud began to build, only to disperse over France to offer promise of good vertical visibility over the target. This began to appear very unlikely as thick cloud developed only fifty miles short of the objective, but the front ended abruptly to leave the city clear. A strong tailwind caused the main force to arrive ahead of the Pathfinders, and while they orbited awaiting the first markers to go down, some crews saw decoy fires being lit to the north-north-west and south-west. The Polish crews identified the target by ground features and red TIs and green release point flares backed up by Gee, and passed over the aiming point at 18,000 feet between 18.28 and 18.36. They were each carrying a cookie, some with 1,000 pounders and others with incendiaries, and all were deposited squarely onto the markers to produce large fires, explosions and much smoke. All returned safely from what was an incident-free operation, and it was later confirmed to have been highly effective, halting production at both I.G Farben sites.

"I remember hearing it so many times: "Our bombers were over Ludwigshafen last night". They were and will be today as well. By an odd turn of events I will be one of them. I can hear this queer sound in my ears: Ludwigshafen. We take off at 2 p.m. as ordered no quibble about that, even the dodgy weather can't stop us. Like black crows the Lancasters start one after another. We climb higher and higher into the sky and on our wings: Vengeance. It is for Warsaw and Wawer and so many thousands of murdered people. Bang! bang! the bombs are going: one, two, all of them, it is now lighter. Artillery is blasting but it doesn't matter, we go left and right and then we fly on full throttle. We have done our duty. It is a hard duty involving fear, nervous tension and psychological exhaustion, but battle mission is crowned with the greatest happiness—safe return to base."

The old city of Ulm in southern Germany became the latest virgin target to attract the attention of Bomber Command, for which 1 Group prepared a main force element of 265 Lancasters. Two large lorry factories, Magirius Deutz and Kässbohrer, were of particular interest, and other useful industrial and military objectives would also be vulnerable in the event of an accurate attack. Fifteen 300 Squadron crews were called to briefing at 13.00, and they took off either side of 15.30 led by S/L Janas. The weather outbound did not offer favourable prospects for the attack, but, by the time the target drew near, the skies had cleared, only for a layer to slide in at the last minute to obscure the ground. The Pathfinders opened the attack with illuminating flares and red TIs at 19.24, but the TIs were soon lost in the clouds and became quickly extinguished as they landed in the deep snow. At 19.31 the Master Bomber instructed the crews to bomb on the well-concentrated skymarkers, and these were maintained throughout the attack. The 300 Squadron crews bombed from 10,000 to 13,000 feet between 19.31 and 19.44, and observed many large fires developing with explosions and black smoke. PD257 was attacked twice by night fighters after bombing, but the mid-upper gunner drove both off with return fire, on the second occasion hitting the assailant in the nose and watching it dive away trailing smoke. The wireless operator and rear gunner confirmed the damage claim, and F/S Jachacz brought the Lancaster safely home. Returning crews reported that the glow from the burning target could be seen for more than a hundred miles into the return journey, and local reports confirmed that the city had suffered a catastrophe. The main weight of the attack had fallen into the central districts before creeping back towards the west. A square kilometre was engulfed in flames, and over 80% of the city's buildings were damaged to some extent, this figure including twenty-nine industrial premises. Around seven hundred people lost their lives, but this number might well have been considerably higher, had a hurried evacuation of the inner city planned for the next day, not been suddenly and hurriedly brought forward.

"After the briefing the mood lightened. That's how one should start describing today's mission, since everybody is in good mood only if the target is easy. My dear God, it is easy to say that, but has any flight ever been easy? The same dangers, the same white death lies in wait on the tips of the wings. One small careless error, one small mistake and it is so very easy not to return. We take off at 15.35. It is hard to leave Mother Earth, but she is soon left below, only the altimeter needle jumps to 1,000, 2,000, 3,000 and so on up to 6,000 feet. The weather is reasonable so we can watch the ground, It is rather a monotonous picture, only sometimes a small castle here and there provides some diversity. I try to imagine what they are like inside. But I haven't got much time for such thoughts in my job of flight mechanic. The ground beneath us seems to move quickly in the opposite direction. On the right we pass Oxford and then Abingdon. Can you see me Pawciu? No, but I am sure you can hear the sinister drone of planes. After all there are 6,400 horse-power in each Lancaster—and look—there are hundreds of them. They are everywhere—above, below, in front, at the back, difficult to count, and they are all going in one direction: Ulm, small town with a large railway junction, our target for tonight. How lovely that sounds, and yet till quite recently it seemed like a film, an unattainable dream. And now, after all, I am "one of them". It sounds affected and yet true. Dreams do seem to come true. We are passing over the British coastline, then the sinister and always rough English Channel and we are over France. The tune of the Marseillaise seems to accompany us and swift 'T' for Telimena flies in the south-easterly direction. On and on, passing towns and villages, we are nearing our target. Whilst over the German territory I can watch the ground which is covered with snow. It is a beautiful sight of mountains and hills enveloped by this white shroud of snow. The earth seems to be asleep and oblivious, only the people are shaking with fear, I know the feeling, I have experienced it many times myself. Is it not the same? Of course, but the roles are reversed. Is it not wonderful to be able to repay the many sleepless nights?"

"In the distance I can see the red and green 'markers', little stars in the sky indicating the target. There are a lot of them. My blood runs cold, life seems to stop as if the world did not exist. Hundreds, thousands fires and flares of various colours seem to hypnotise. I stare at this hell on earth where dozens of fires already burn. It is light as day, the glow of fires grows bigger and swells to form a huge sea of fire. It is a marvellous sight, even the sporadic artillery fire cannot spoil it. Despite the weak defence we instinctively turn away from the target. Time over the target, even lasting only seconds, seems like hours. It is only an optical illusion for the glow of fire spreads far and wide. I don't know what was happening on the ground, but even after an hour you could still see burning Ulm. In spite of the long flight the way back seems three times shorter. We pass the Rhine for the second time and we are again over France. The war does not seem to exist here. Hundreds, thousands of lights twinkle below and above us, so at times I can't tell which is earth and which is sky. Doubtless down below the merry French drink red wine and make love in brothels. And if we were to turn left in southerly direction after an hour we would arrive in Lyon. It is an old town I know well. I am sure it is as illuminated now as it was then and ... making merry. But it is not for me to dream and speculate. My duties are to evaluate fuel, switch over fuel tanks (when over the target I don't do anything, only watch), make tea and other similar tasks, which I perform when we are in a safe environment. It shows that I am not flying as a passenger. You have to be more alert and watchful over enemy territory. Each centre of defence makes itself known, you have to find a way between them. There are flashes from left or right. German territory seems to be always restless. All the time you can see some light flashes. But we don't take any notice. We have to reach our objective—nobody is asking whether we return or not, you have to reach your target. Even if you wanted to cheat, the camera will tell the truth."

"At midnight hell breaks out in front of us. Oh! God, it is frightening to look. It seems impossible to find a way free from exploding bullets. They draw nearer ever more threatening, my legs shake. God save us!—an involuntary sigh from my soul. I haven't yet been in the middle of such hell. One moment more and the doors are open. "Bombs Gone!" From all sides flashes appear. 'R' for Roger, like a bison which has been hit, breaks away and speeds off to get away at all costs. The most important thing is that we have reached our target and completed our mission. Now all that remains is the return journey. It does not matter how we go back, it is more important that we leave the target safely. A moment of relaxation; below us to the rear something is burning, there are sporadic bursts. Automatically I check the instruments, everything is O.K.—we have enough fuel. I can say I am happy when we cross the British coast. You don't always come back from such hard mission, you have to have a bit of luck. It is only my 12th flight but it seems to me like a hundredth. It is a very long flight, luckily the time over the target lasts only a few seconds. Even after crossing the British coast it seems to me I have been flying for several hours. Oh! There it is at last; F.H. i.e. the base-airfield. I feel as if I am already in bed. But that is still far off—3 hours after 'Happy Landing'. All our planes returned safely. The mission is now behind us. As we fly over England we see plenty of fiery rings—these are the airfields, blinking kindly, inviting us in, but we are looking for our own. Aha! It is in front of us. We approach and report "White Lane 'R' for Roger has arrived" and ask permission to land. We circle twice and land safely. 5 hours 40 minutes in the air. Fairly short flight of 1,160 miles."

Fifteen 300 Squadron crews attended briefing at 13.00 on the 22nd to be told they would be attacking the Mosel marshalling yards at Coblenz that night as part of a 1 Group main force of 156 Lancasters. S/L Jarkowski's participation was cancelled before take-off, leaving the remaining fourteen to depart Faldingworth either side of 15.30. Conditions outbound were reasonable, if cloudy, but this had thinned to around four-tenths thin stratus in the target area, which allowed some restricted view of the ground. The aiming point was identified by both ground and skymarkers, and the Polish crews bombed from 18,500 to 20,000 feet between 18.51 and 19.00, without observing any outstanding results. NG269 and NN746 sustained flak damage, but arrived back safely over an England blighted by marginal conditions for landing. All aircraft from Faldingworth were diverted to stations equipped with FIDO, Bradwell Bay and Woodbridge receiving the majority of lodgers. It was somewhat fortuitous that all pilots had attended a demonstration of FIDO at Ludford Magna only two day earlier.

Sunset over Faldingworth. (H. Stawicki via W. Zmyslony)

The Nippes marshalling yards in Cologne was the target for a 1 Group main force of eighty-one Lancasters on the night of the 24/25th, but 300 Squadron sat this one out, and had, in fact, already settled in to observe what would be the final wartime Christmas. Representatives from all Groups were in action on Boxing Day, to attack German troop positions at St Vith, following their breakout in the Ardennes ten days earlier. A full programme of operations resumed thereafter, and 1 Group rounded out the year against oil and railway targets. Faldingworth remained off the Order of Battle until the 28th, when sixteen crews were called to briefing at 13.00 to be told that railway yards at Bonn was to be their objective. Situated a little to the south of Cologne, this represented a shallow penetration into Germany, and would be a relatively short trip. Take-off began at 15.30, with both flight commanders, S/Ls Janas and Jarkowski, on duty, and this was something of a rare event nowadays at 300 Squadron. They flew out over England and France in good weather, but encountered eight to ten-tenths cloud over the target, which they identified by means of red TIs with green stars. The bomb loads were a mixture of high explosives, some including a cookie and others a variety of designations of 1,000 and 500 pounders, but all were deposited squarely into the target area from an average of 16,000 feet between 18.43 and 18.48. All made a safe return to Faldingworth with little to report, and the Command claimed that most of the bombing had hit the yards. A local reports, however, claimed that the yards sustained little damage, and it was the city which bore the brunt of the attack.

On the 29th fourteen 300 Squadron crews prepared themselves for their final operation of the year as part of a 1 Group contribution of 239 Lancasters to a 6 and 8 Group overall heavy force of 324 of the type. Their target was the synthetic oil refinery at Scholven-Buer, on the northern outskirts of Gelsenkirchen, for which an Oboe marking plan had been prepared. The Polish crews were led away by S/L Janas at 15.13, and they arrived in the target area to find a thin layer of ten-tenths cloud, into which the Pathfinders delivered their initial red TIs at 18.54. The first bombs to fall set off a very large explosion, which caused a column of thick, black smoke to rise up through the clouds. The Pathfinders maintained the aiming point right up until the last main force aircraft turned away at 19.18, by which time the target lay under a mushroom of thick black smoke rising to 14,000 feet. The Polish crews bombed from 16,000 to 20,000 feet between 18.57 and 19.06, before returning home safely to report a successful outcome. Special mention was due to W/O Bakanacz and crew, whose PD387 lost its port-outer engine soon after take-off, but pressed on to complete the operation on three engines. Local reports confirmed that three hundred high explosive bombs had fallen into the oil plant, and more than three thousand others had hit other parts of the town, causing much industrial and residential damage.

"I am still tired after yesterday and I have to fly again today. What are they thinking—after all I have only just returned from holiday. I am still in holiday mood and they play the fool and order me to fly and you know where? To the Ruhr and Gelsenkirchen. My hair will turn grey if we have more such flights. Like yesterday the take off is at 3.15. We get on course without much trouble. Up to front line the flight is peaceful, but as we cross, emotions build up. Soon the artillery will start blasting. A few moments of peace and then fireworks! They shoot literally everywhere, but luckily not at us. That is what luck means and 'Roger' continues peacefully on the way. It is not far now to the target, but the artillery shoots like blazes. One plane veered from the course and they are shooting at it from all sides, the damned Krauts. The target is illuminated and the bombardment starts. Hundreds of planes converge on the target, but the artillery doesn't stop. If we leave here in one piece it will be really lucky. A few more seconds, which seem like eternity, and we are over the target. Veritable hell, thousands of flashes, glow of fires. We are blinded, but 'Roger' goes forward. I step on the gas, small dive—"bombs gone"—bang, bang. The speed increases: 190, 200, 220, but we are still in line of fire. Slowly we move away from this hell, the artillery does not seem to cause us damage. We get away safely, now only fighter planes threaten us, but they are not so frightening though in fact more menacing. We are returning along the edge of the Ruhr, and high above us we see condensation trails—German fighter planes. Brr, my blood runs cold, but luckily they are a lot higher and maybe they haven't seen us because they are flying in the opposite direction. We breathe a sigh of relief when we leave them behind—they haven't noticed us. On the left we pass Duisburg, but luckily it is quite far and the artillery doesn't reach us. It is peaceful—here and there red lights blink—they are navigation lights of other planes. We are approaching England. It seems to me that I know by heart how many lights there are at Uxbridge airfield. I saw the same identical picture yesterday, but today there was an additional element—fear of the Ruhr. You never know when the artillery will strike. You are flying along and suddenly a ring of bullets explodes. You have nowhere to escape, everywhere flashes appear. I don't know if I can describe it all. Usually I record the events after the mission, maybe on the second or third day and then the emotion is gone, only the memory remains. And this is not the same as the actual emotions felt over the target 'Happy Landing' ends this almost 6 hours lasting mission. Although short it was full of various emotions which will always be remembered. And if one day somebody mentions Gelsenkirchen my blood will run cold and I will change the subject."

On New Year's Eve, the Group sent 130 Lancasters to attack the railway yards at Osterfeld, and achieved moderate success in what was the final operation of a successful year. 300 Squadron stayed at home to leave the month's tally standing at 125 sorties from nine operations and no losses. Henryk Drozdz has the last word on 1944. "It so happened, and it was rather fortunate, that there are no flights tonight. I can't imagine why anyone would want to fly on New Year's Eve, after all the Germans also want to have a holiday. And so, as there is no flight, we are planning to go to a dancing party in the camp. Dance itself doesn't matter—it is the same as hundreds others—the important thing is to keep the tradition of New Year's Eve celebrations. Tradition which remains whatever the circumstances.

January 1945

Despite the unmistakable scent of victory wafting in from the Continent, much remained to be done before the proud, resolute and resourceful enemy finally laid down his arms. Although stretched beyond their capability to protect all corners of the Reich, the defenders were still able, on occasions, to take a heavy toll of Bomber Command aircraft. The Luftwaffe did itself no favours when launching its ill-conceived and ultimately ill-fated Operation Bodenplatte at first light on New Year's Morning. The intention to destroy large numbers of Allied aircraft on the ground at the recently liberated airfields in France, Holland and Belgium was only modestly realized, and in return, the day fighter force lost around 250 aircraft. More importantly, a large proportion of the pilots were killed, wounded or taken prisoner, and this was a setback from which the Tagjagd would never fully recover.

1 Group opened its account on the night of the 2/3rd, when a new record of 296 of its Lancasters joined forces with others from 3, 6 and 8 Groups to form a heavy force of 514 aircraft. 300 Squadron was able to offer a new record of eighteen Lancasters, and their destination was Nuremberg, the target for the Command's heaviest defeat of the war eight months earlier. They began departing Faldingworth shortly after 15.00, with S/L Janas the senior pilot on duty, and they climbed into cloud, which would cover most of the route across France to the target. PD383 dropped out very early on with intercom failure, and F/S Niemiec jettisoned part of his bomb load in the North Sea before returning home. Fortunately for the others, the cloud dissipated as the force approached Nuremberg, and the Pathfinders were able to identify the built-up area. Tailwinds had put them slightly ahead of schedule, and the attack opened early with red and green target indicators going down over the marshalling yards in the city centre. The 300 Squadron crews arrived to find excellent visibility, backed up by illuminating flares, and they bombed on the red TIs from 16,500 to 18,000 feet in accordance with the Master Bomber's instructions. By the time that the last Polish crew turned away from the target at 19.40, the central and eastern districts were becoming a mass of flames, the glow from which was visible from up to two hundred miles into the return flight. Only five aircraft were initially unaccounted for, and among them was 300 Squadron's PB823, which contained the crew of S/L Janas. The Lancaster exploded over north-eastern France, close to the frontiers with Belgium, Luxembourg and Germany, and there were no survivors. The fact that a violent explosion took place suggests that it was outbound with a full bomb load when it was hit,

S/L Brunon Janas was the ATA pilot who delivered the first Wellington to 300 Squadron in October 1940. From Aug. 1941 to July 1942 he completed his first tour of duty in 301 Squadron. In October 1944 he was posted to 300 Squadron but failed to return from the 10th operation of his second tour. (PISM via WM)

and probably fell victim to one of the batteries in the flak belt guarding the approaches to Germany's southern cities. However, some sources suggest that it was shot down by the ace Martin Becker of IV/NJG.6. At Nuremberg the tables had been turned, and the birthplace of Nazism wilted under a massively accurate attack, which left over 4,600 houses and apartment blocks in ruins, and destroyed a further two thousand preserved medieval houses, while industrial districts and railway areas also sustained heavy damage.

"Always ahead of time we race to the briefing room to satisfy our curiosity—where to today? The answer is short and simple—Nuremberg. The briefing becomes noisy and I do not like either the turmoil or the target. It is the home town of Alfred Rosenberg, the author of racial ideology of Nazism, and besides the prognosis is not good for tonight. 96 planes did not come back from the last sortie to that city. According to the briefing the flight should be easy—they always see everything as easy (from the ground). We take off at 15.10 hours. 3,000 revolutions plus 14 booster and we lazily leave Mother Earth who always seems to want to keep us with her. Nothing is happening as we reach the French coast. Constant hum of the engines makes you sleepy and you could fall asleep if you did not have to watch the clocks and other instruments. We are flying at 6,000 feet, but the clouds are very low—less than a hundred metres above the ground. This shroud envelops the earth and keeps us apart. We are flying above the clouds and suddenly we see a tower. It must be the tower of Reims Cathedral."

"It is a wonderful sight—all you can see is this slender spire like God's finger pointing the way. After crossing the front line it is completely dark, so we increase our vigilance in case of eventual attack by fighter planes. It is quiet in spite of us flying over enemy territory. The earth is sleeping. Underneath we can see white patches of snow. It is winter below us—Brr, and here in the plane at 19,000 it is warm and cosy but for the nervous tension, when I think of the target—Nuremberg. How long do we have to wait before we see the long-awaited markings, i.e. the red and green lights on parachutes, that indicate the target for dropping the bombs. We are in the second wave, there are others in front of us, maybe they will start some fires so that it will be light. My legs are shaking, there are searchlights in front of us. Beautiful silver-white cone of 10 searchlights is lying in wait for the audacious. It does not last long though and I don't know why this sinister cone of light goes out. Thank God for that. But that was just the beginning, the prelude, now the main performance. Artillery blasts away but gradually grows weaker. Now one after another come the Lancasters. It is light as daytime, not a single cloud in the sky. Underneath us the city appears. This is something I will never forget—the whole city of Nuremberg lies under our feet with its thousands of streets and alleyways. We can see everything—every street and block of houses. We cross the river—left turn—"keep it steady" shouts the bomb-aimer. Centre of the city and the bombs are gone. I try to see the result of the bombing, but a huge pall of smoke and fire begins to envelop the whole city. Quickly we leave the target, we are turning right and now I can still see the target. It is a splendid view—I have never seen the like of it before—it is magnificent. Oh, something is not right. Behind us something is on fire and goes down—probably one of the planes, now another one already past the target. I can see it clearly breaking up into 4 pieces and falling down. This is not good, shivers go down my spine and automatically I check my engines. Luckily everything is in order and this has a calming effect."

"We are going full speed ahead, the further the safer. Below us to the right something else is burning, but we are going ahead. Flying at the speed of 200 while slightly descending is good tactics as far as fuel goes. I am still elated by the sight of the target which is still aflame and of the ground itself which is clearly visible with its mountains, snow, houses and other buildings. I am certain every Kraut's skin creeps at the sound of the formidable armada. But this is no time for reflections and meditations. I have a lot of tasks to perform, this and that, "give me the hammer", "get the sandwiches" etc. I have no trouble keeping the log. After ten sorties I acquired some practise and knowledge of the subject, which you will not get in any school. As I just said this is mine and the whole crew's 10th battle flight. Only 10th, which is just one third of what we have to do, but still a lot. My dear God, 10 sorties are not many in number but quite a lot in quality. And now we take our leave of the continent and arrive in England. It seems to me that we have done it a hundred times. The same identical route and therefore part of the flight. Maybe the least interesting but equally important as every other moment of flight. And maybe, as when over the target, most dangerous. There is still the Channel and even when over the base itself. There are quite a few airports around here and all the aircraft are returning."

"And now we are over the base. Having reported our arrival we fly in a circle and at this moment it seems that over Wickenby something in the air caught fire. It is a huge fire which breaks up and falls down in big trails. Could it be that some planes collided? I become more watchful to what goes on around me. One more circle and "prepare to land". The longed-for "power off"—moment of waiting and then we feel mother earth beneath our feet. We land and disperse. We learn that in fact two planes collided over Wickenby. In the interrogation room we learn that one plane has not yet returned and is "missing". This is 'T' for Telimena. I feel sad when I see Halinka crying in the interrogation room. It was her sister's fiancé, Captain Janas, who flew in that plane. Their wedding was to take place in two weeks' time. He probably did not come back."

Faldingworth, late 1944. Enigmatic artwork on Polish Lancaster, probably PB730 BH-R for Roger. (G. Drozdz)

In the early hours of the 5th, ninety-eight Lancasters from 1 Group joined others from 5 Group to carry out what became a controversial attack on the French town of Royan. This was in response to a request from Free French forces, which were laying siege to the town on their way through to Bordeaux. Fourteen 300 Squadron crews underwent briefing at 23.00, and the first Lancaster took off at 02.10. Take-offs continued until shortly after 02.30, when PB722 and PB730 each put a wheel off the peri-track and had to be withdrawn. This delayed the final four aircraft, which eventually got away between 02.50 and 02.58. S/L Jarkowski was the senior pilot on duty as they headed for the Channel to encounter thickening cloud, which persisted for most of the outward flight. Over the target itself there was no cloud below bombing altitude, and the Pathfinder illuminator flares allowed the crews to identify the coastline and the built-up area of the town. The aiming point was marked with red and green TIs, which were maintained by backers-up, and the subsequent bombing was accurate and concentrated. The Polish crews attacked from 8,000 to 10,000 feet between 05.29 and 05.38, and all returned safely from an incident-free operation. Many of the residents had declined an offer by the German garrison commander to evacuate the area, and they suffered terrible consequences under the weight of over fifteen hundred tons of bombs. In the event, the French did not take the town, and it was mid April before the garrison finally surrendered.

On the night of the 5/6th, Hanover received its first major raid since the series in the autumn of 1943. 163 Lancasters from 1 Group joined elements from 4, 6 and 8 Groups to destroy almost five hundred apartment blocks. 300 Squadron sat this one out, but fifteen crews were called to briefing at 13.00 on the 6th to learn that they were to be part of a 1 and 3 Group attack on the marshalling yards at Neuss, situated on the west bank of the Rhine opposite Düsseldorf. This was one of two operations on the night involving 1 Group aircraft, the other being against Hanau in concert with elements of 4, 6 and 8 Groups. The original plan had detailed fifty-four 1 Group Lancasters, but difficulties in bombing-up reduced the figure to thirty-three, and only thirteen could be made ready in time at Faldingworth. F/L Brogowski led them away at 15.37, and they climbed into cloud, which dissipated for a time before building again to ten-tenths over the target. The Pathfinders opened proceedings with red TIs at 18.39, but these quickly disappeared into the cloud tops, forcing them to employ release point flares, which were laid in a compact line running roughly north to south. The Polish crews ran across the aiming point at 18,000 to 20,000 feet, and were well on their way home by 19.00 to report what they believed was a scattered attack. This was confirmed later, when it was established that some bombs had fallen into the railway yards, but many more had hit the town, destroying or seriously damaging almost eighteen hundred buildings.

The final raid of the war on Munich came at the hands of an all-Lancaster force of over six hundred aircraft from 1, 3, 5, 6 and 8 Groups on the night of 7/8th, of which 235 were provided by 1 Group. Thirteen 300 Squadron crews presented themselves for briefing, and they took off either side of 18.30 before climbing into patchy cloud that persisted all the way to the French coast. Once over land again the cloud built and thinned again, producing icing conditions, but at the target there was complete cover. F/O Kirkilewicz and crew failed to get that far, after the rear gunner became too ill to continue when over north-eastern France. Stronger than forecast winds had driven the bomber stream to the target ahead of schedule, and some doglegging and orbiting took place before the first Pathfinder markers went down precisely at the allotted time. The early marking was sparse, and the TIs soon disappeared into the cloud tops at 12,000 feet. It was 22.33 before any concentration of markers was available, by which time many crews had already bombed. The Faldingworth contingent was over the aiming point at 16,000 to 20,000 feet between 22.25 to 22.42, and all returned safely with little to report, other than the glow of fires for up to forty miles into the homeward flight, and one crew observed an unidentified aircraft dive into the clouds on fire. F/L Zarebski landed NG269 at Woodbridge after completing the entire round trip with the starboard undercarriage in the down position. This concluded a busy first week of the new year.

"Immediately after the morning Mass there are rumours that there will be battle. It would not be surprising if it wasn't for this last incident with Captain Janas. I am sure he himself decided to dive down over the target. It was unfortunate, I shall miss him, also Wrusio who had been a good friend. That's life, you are alive today and in a few hours you can remain "there"—on the other side of the Channel, forever. It is difficult to believe that yesterday we were together, talking, and today the thought that I will never see them again. It is awful and very painful. But enough of my sentiments. 'Briefing'—a word that electrifies like a powerful magic wand. A few guesses and there it is—Munich. That's all that is missing from this series of 8-hour flights. You could go to Warsaw and back in that time. It promises to be a record-breaking mission. The whole weight of the plane 66,326 pounds. The weight of the bombs 10,400 pounds. Fuel 2,104 gallons. Judging by the flight-path it will be the longest flight. We take off somewhat late, at 18.20, which forces me to pay more attention to both sides. In today's mission 600 planes take part, of which 200 started an hour before us to commence the job, and our 400 planes will finish it. It means we are going to cause Hitler some trouble, or heaven forbid he will cause us grief. But there is no point in being afraid."

"We fly to the target only just above the clouds. It costs us a bit of tension and nerves. The tension rises as we get nearer to the target. There is a lot of artillery fire, but no need to fear the searchlights as the cloud cover is complete. As we approach the target over which the 'markers' are now lit, the cold which made me shiver is slowly disappearing. I don't know why today there is a lack of emotion, only a slight fear. We arrive over the red and green markers. Bombs gone! 22.30—right on time and then a sharp turn right. In comparison with Nuremberg today there is no spectacle. We depart the target. Oh! the show begins, artillery blasts with full might, the number of flashes and lights swiftly increase. I can observe the target being away from it. In fact there is nothing special and as we get farther away from the target, the tiredness increases. We have been in the air for 4½ hours and that is only half the time. I can hardly bear it—I have a headache, and I feel generally tired and fed up. But that's not an excuse, you have to watch the fuel, as the flight is a long one, estimated at 9 hours. The clouds and foul weather cause the speedometer to freeze and we have to increase the revolutions, and that causes more fuel use, and so you have to be more careful and watchful. The constant height of 8,000 feet and higher changes this flight into some very heavy and endless dream. Additionally I am beginning to feel sick—that's all I need. But I hold out and the sight of the airfield brings my suffering to the end. After landing I feel as if I was taken down from the cross. I haven't yet had such a flight—a record 8 hours 50 minutes in the air. Coastal Command! shout the landing crews. All our planes have returned thank God, but 15 others are missing. I go to bed completely drained physically and mentally."

In his diary for the 9th of January Sgt Drozdz wrote; "Snow in England is rather rare. Rain yes, it rains every day, but snow makes an appearance perhaps once a year in these parts. Like today. It is beautiful, white. The world looks quite different. Enveloped in white shroud it looks magical, and it is a dry and fairly sunny day. Almost like Polish winter of my memories and dreams. And even the unattractive landscape of Lincolnshire Plain can seem beautiful in this innocent white attire. What would I have given if this present time was the winter of 1936-37. I remember the holiday trip to Zakopane. I will never forget it and today it seems like a dream."

After Munich there was little to occupy the crews of 1 Group until mid month, when 245 of its Lancasters joined forces with elements of 5, 6 and 8 Groups on the night of the 14/15th for a return to the oil refinery at Leuna. The attack was to be conducted in two phases separated by three hours, with 5 Group, as always, taking the early shift. 300 Squadron detailed fifteen Lancasters and crews, but two of these would be cancelled before take-off. The first Lancaster lifted off from Faldingworth at 19.04, and the last at 19.23, and they climbed into varying amounts of cloud, which dissipated completely east of the Rhine. The target seemed to be covered by a thin layer of ten-tenths cloud, which may have been thick mist, but the glow of fires from the earlier 5 Group raid identified it, and the Pathfinders delivered illuminator flares at 23.54, followed by red and green TIs. The glow of these could be clearly seen, but ground detail was obscured, and the Master Bomber and deputy were hesitant in declaring the aiming point. Bombing began before the Master Bomber issued instructions to aim at release point flares, and the Polish crews complied with this from 20,000 to 22,000 feet between 00.01 and 00.05. All but one returned safely, unsure as to the effectiveness of the operation, but some commented on a huge explosion and three large columns of black smoke. PA160 hit the ground on approach to Faldingworth in the hands of F/O Kozuba-Kozubski, and five members of the crew sustained injury. After the war Albert Speer would describe this operation as one of the most damaging attacks of the war on Germany's synthetic oil industry.

"We did not go yesterday because of the weather, but today we have to fly. But where? Merseburg—old and familiar town or rather target. We were there once before, but obviously with little effect, because today we again have to attack German refineries. If it goes well it will be a pretty fire. Although the flight itself fills me with dread, because it belongs to the 'Coastal Command' series, familiarity comes into its own. If it was my 5th flight I would probably be more afraid, but as it was my 12th I take it in my stride, even though artillery is sure to blaze. 2,154 of fuel with the total weight of 65,900 pounds. We take off at 19.05 (it is bad to take off at night). The best take-offs are in daytime, then you gradually get used to the fading light. After "set course" we fly familiar route and nothing is happening as we reach the German border. Of course you have to be careful, the plane is tossing us about from time to time, but this is all normal and has happened before."

Two nights later 232 Lancasters from the group joined elements of 6 and 8 Groups to attack the Braunkohle-Benzin synthetic oil plant at Zeitz-Tröglitz, situated south-west of Leipzig. 300 Squadron detailed thirteen Lancasters, but two were cancelled before take-off, which took place either side of 18.00. LL804 lost its starboard-outer engine immediately after leaving the ground, and F/O Rudakowski had to extinguish the resultant fire and dump his bomb load before returning safely. The others pushed on in cloudy conditions, which persisted for a time until thinning, and dissipating completely from 6° East. The entire force arrived at the target approximately six minutes early, and found only haze to impair the visibility. Despite this the crews were able to pick out ground detail and assess for themselves the accuracy of the marking. The Master Bomber ordered the crews to begin bombing at 22.09, and the illumination and marking maintained the aiming point throughout. The 300 Squadron crews bombed from 17,000 to 19,000 feet between 22.13 and 22.21, and all but one returned safely to report a series of explosions, and one particularly impressive one at 22.19, with a large pall of smoke rising to 15,000 feet. PD257 was one of ten Lancasters failing to return and crashed near Kleinfurra, south-south-east of Nordhausen, and some sixty miles north-west of the target. W/O Bakinowski and three of his crew survived in enemy hands, but three others died in the wreckage. It was established later that the operation had caused substantial damage to the northern half of the plant.

"Please imagine my feelings during today's sortie which for me will be number 13. The operation starts one hour late and even then it is not certain that we will take off—we wait for two hours sitting in the aircraft. Then at 17.50 we take off. Heavy dark clouds are waiting threateningly for us. It is a hard climb, the machines are heavy after all—66,000 pounds. Merlins 22 are roaring but we continue to climb. We are surrounded by milky clouds which is quite unnerving, green lights are flickering at the ends of the wings—navigation lights. It goes on for quite a while, it is so unpleasant in the clouds, especially as 350 planes took off at the same time. We really need some good luck. We are climbing higher and higher—11,000! Feeling of relief as it gets lighter. It is fantastic—we are skimming over the top of the clouds—then again we plunge into them but only for a moment and then we see beautiful blue sky at sunset. It is difficult to believe that 10,000 feet below us there is fog and clouds and generally bad weather and here it is so glorious. In a short while we are leaving these cloud 'mountains' and changing course towards Zeitz—in the region of Leipzig which is heavily defended, the same as Merseburg. In spite of the fact that our target is almost the same as Merseburg, the nature of our sortie is quite different—total surprise. Today the return journey does not lead through France as before—all the time we will fly over Germany, the Ruhr and Holland — over the Ijsselmeer to the north of Amsterdam. My dear God, it is all part of our

Above: Probably the most recognised Polish Lancaster LL804 BH-F with artwork of a woman in a glass of champagne and symbols of first (bombs) and second (glasses) tours of duty with 300 Squadron. (PISM via WM) Below: The same Lancaster with added symbols of third tour of duty (skulls) photographed at the end of February 1945 at Faldingworth. F/L Korczak-Krzeczowski is standing beside the aircraft. (JC)

thirteenth sortie—let's hope we will return. It seems to me that the whole flight leads over dangerous territory—either searchlights or anti-aircraft guns let you know that it is not X country."

"It is now 10 o'clock at night, the flight seems to have gone on forever and there are still 15 minutes to go before we reach our target. Looking down all you can see is snow covered ground, hardly any houses or signs of human habitation, you can count them on your fingers. The Krauts must be sleeping unaware that we are bringing them presents. Aha, we have reached our target, there are flares and hell breaks loose again. It is the same as last time, even worse, as hundreds of searchlights light up the sky. I think we will have fun and I am getting my parachute ready just in case. This time we seem to be flying faster to our target. I strain my eyes but it does not help, my knees are shaking slightly. There seems to be thousands of fireworks, sparklers and lights going—it seems like daylight—the damned searchlights make a ring round our target. Please God save us from this hell, it is terrifying. We are getting closer and closer. Thousands, millions of flashes and lights—to the left and right—the searchlights are everywhere. The whole aircraft is lit up, we choose a path. "Bomb door open" sounds in the earphones. Another moment and then dry crack of jettisoning bombs: one, two, three and so on—total weight 9,700 pounds. When they are all down not only our plane is lighter, but our spirits too. It is still light as in daytime, the artillery fire is still going on but we are leaving the target area. For the 13th time I am marvelling at the view. This is perhaps the one and only, similar to Nuremburg, sight. You can see everything, fires everywhere as if after a hundred lightning strikes."

"Oh! Now there is a huge blast, a mere two minutes after our bombs fell (it is now 22.18 hours). Left turn and we are past the target but still almost at the same height. Slowly losing height we are approaching a 'gate' between two heavily defended objects: Osnabrück and Münster. Again this time our Wladzio is infallible—it is his good navigation that allows us to squeeze silently between these two spots bristling with gun barrels. Now only shore defences remain in the 'bag of fear'. Silently, silently we are edging forward. Moment of relief when under our feet blue-black mass of the North Sea smiles ominously. This is not as threatening as the thousands of bullets and shrapnels lying in wait for our lives. Still a few hundred miles over the blue-black depths of the North Sea bristling with menacing waves and in the distance lights of our safe haven—England. This flight is quite different—this is not the usual monotonous return. It is quite wonderful. After safe landing I can look back on it as a beautiful and exhilarating flight with thousands of dangers but now behind us. But?... Not everyone was so lucky—ensign Bakinowski does not come back. His fate is shared by Sasin, friend of Bolek. Then 'Jacek' with his 'E' Easy lands in the field, the plane is smashed but the crew escape alive, although Antoś Jackowski is badly injured. It seems today's sortie was not that easy, maybe we were just lucky that our 13th mission did not end in a crash. For Bakinowski it was his 26th sortie. As far as I remember many crews did not return. Can you believe that you will never see them again. They were not my close friends, but it is still strange, especially as it seems they had a premonition about this flight—Bolek's friend said goodbye to him—he never did this before other flights. God how dismal it seems! He flew 26 sorties and always returned and today it was different. That's flying—you return a hundred times and on the hundred and first you land in Abraham's bosom. Poor Jacek was badly bruised and was taken to hospital."

A synthetic oil plant in Duisburg was targeted by elements of 1, 3 and 8 Groups on the night of the 22/23rd, when 300 Squadron stayed at home, and the nearby Thyssen steel works was also hit be five hundred high explosive bombs. On the night of the 28/29th, six hundred aircraft were detailed from 1, 4, 6 and 8 Groups to attack two targets in Stuttgart and Kornwestheim, a town less than three miles away. The aiming point at the latter was the railway yards, and this operation was to take place three hours before the second wave targeted the Zuffenhausen district in the north of Stuttgart, wherein lay the Hirth aero-engine factory, which may have been the specific objective. 300 Squadron briefed four crews, who took off either side of 20.00 with F/L Zarebski the senior pilot on duty. P/O Janczur abandoned his sortie with Gee failure while over central Belgium, and returned home. Cloud had built up during the outward flight, and completely covered the target area as the force arrived. The Pathfinders were about three minutes late, and some crews had already bombed by then. Release-point flares were dropped at 23.30, and, although sparse and scattered at first, they became more numerous as the raid developed. The bombing never achieved concentration, although there was a good coverage of the target area, and four large explosions were observed between 23.28 and 23.42. F/S Plucinski bombed from 20,000 feet at 23.31, and W/O Ilnicki followed up eight minutes later from 18,000 feet, and both returned safely. PB846 was shot down by a night fighter, and crashed south-east of the target, almost certainly after bombing. F/L Zarebski and two of his crew lost their lives, and the four survivors were taken into captivity. The bombing fell mainly into the city's northern and western districts, and did not achieve the desired outcome, while the Kornwestheim attack inflicted severe damage, though a decoy site also attracted some bomb loads. The squadron undertook just seven operations during the month, and flew eighty-four sorties for the loss of three aircraft.

Lancaster PD379 BH-S photographed at Faldingworth after the war. Note white serial numbers painted under the wings. (PISM via WM)

February 1945

W/C Boleslaw Jarkowski flew his first tour of duty as observer in 305 Squadron. Having trained as a pilot he was posted to 300 Squadron. From Dec. 1944 to April 1945 he took part in 12 operations. In February 1945 he became CO of 300 Squadron (P. Sikora)

The weather conditions at the start of February were not ideal for marking and bombing, and complete cloud cover over many targets would lead to a number of failures. The new month's account opened at Ludwigshafen on the night of the 1/2nd, for which 1, 6 and 8 Groups prepared a heavy force of 382 Lancasters. 1 Group's contribution was 277 aircraft, of which thirteen belonged to 300 Squadron, and they became airborne from Faldingworth either side of 16.00. PD379 suffered the failure of its port-outer engine at 2,500 feet over the station, and F/L Kapciuk jettisoned most of his bomb load before returning home. The others pressed on in scattered cloud, which dispersed to leave clear skies over the Channel and France, but built up again to nine-tenths as the target drew near. The Pathfinders opened the attack punctually at 19.11 with red TIs, which the crews could see burning in the city's built-up area as they prepared to run across the aiming point. Unfortunately, the cloud directly above the target obscured them, and the Pathfinders reverted to skymarking, which produced scattered bombing. The Polish crews delivered their mixed loads of a cookie and incendiaries from 15,000 to 17,000 feet between 21.19 and 21.28, and all returned safely with varying reports of explosions and black smoke, the glow of fires, fires visible for a hundred miles, and bombing undershooting. Local reports provided a picture of bombs falling in many parts of the city, and destroying or seriously damaging nine hundred houses and the railway yards.

"After a longish break back to battle. This time it is a known target—Ludwigshafen. I won't describe this mission in detail as before due to lack of time. We took off at 16.15. The flight was quite hard and lasted 6 hours 40 minutes. Everything was fine, it finished with a "happy landing" at 22.55. In fact you could write a lot about it, but would it reflect the emotions and moods and the whole flight—probably not, although 'R' Roger could say quite a lot. Again another chapter in this great book of the life of a good chap. Maybe colourless on paper but in fact so attractive and colourful in emotions."

300 Squadron swapped commanding officers for the final time during the war on the 2nd, when S/L Jarkowski was promoted to succeed W/C Pozyczka, who was posted to liaison duties. This allowed F/L Brogowski to step up in rank to assume the role of flight commander. That night the Command carried out the first and only large raid of the war on Wiesbaden, a city roughly twenty miles to the west of Frankfurt. A heavy force of 495 Lancasters drawn from 1, 3, 6 and 8 Groups contained 233 aircraft of 1

Faldingworth, 20th May 1945. Lancaster NG265 BH-V for Victory and the crew of S/L Wierzbowski. Left to Right: 1st Sgt Koltonowski (A.G.), 2nd Sgt Soltys (A.G.), 3rd Sgt Krzewinski (W.Op.), 4th S/L Wierzbowski (pilot), 5th Sgt Stawicki (F.E.), 7th F/S Blicharski (B.A.) and 8th F/S Franczak (nav.). (Cz. Blicharski via W. Zmyslony)

Group, of which twelve represented 300 Squadron. They began to depart Faldingworth shortly before 21.00, and reached the French coast to find cloud building to ten-tenths, and this remained the case all the way to the target, where the tops reached 20,000 feet. Lighter than forecast winds delayed the start of the raid, and all efforts by the Pathfinders to provide adequate marking failed, forcing the majority of crews to bomb on a Gee fix or H2S. The 300 Squadron crews delivered their cookie and incendiaries each from 18,000 to 24,000 feet between 23.40 and 23.55, and all but one returned safely, although F/L Wierzbowski landed at Fiskerton in error. ME744 was hit by flak over the target, and exploded in the air before crashing into a wooded area in the city's north-eastern suburbs. The rear gunner, Sgt Masiorski, was thrown clear as the sole survivor from the crew of F/L Kapciuk, and he became a PoW. It was the crew's twenty-eighth operation.

On the following afternoon a 1 Group main force of 164 aircraft was made ready to attack the Prosper Coking plant at Bottrop. 300 Squadron briefed nine crews, and they took off in a ten-minute slot from 16.20 to find favourable weather conditions and mostly clear skies all the way to the target. The Pathfinder element opened the attack punctually with red TIs at 19.26, and the main force crews were able to confirm visually that these and the later green TIs were concentrated right on the aiming-point. The Polish crews were each carrying a cookie and sixteen 500 pounders, which all but one delivered from 16,000 to 19,000 feet between 19.33 and 19.39. F/S Jachacz had lost the use of his Gee equipment over France, which had delayed him by sixteen minutes, but, to his credit, this setback did not persuade him to turn back. He eventually bombed from 18,000 feet at 19.52, before returning safely. At debriefing F/S Szczesny reported having to take violent evasive action to avoid bombs falling from above while he was waiting for his photo-flash to burst. A local report confirmed the accuracy of the raid and the resultant severe damage to the plant.

"So what if one of the stars dies when the whole squadron again dashes on track". These words taken from a song are a kind of gospel-order. Some people perish and others take their place to continue the fight to the last breath in spite of threats and deaths. And so we fly. The Ruhr—Bottrop—that's the target for tonight. We fly in 'H' for How. If somebody were to ask me what impression today's flight left on me I would say it is difficult to have a worse experience than to find yourself in hell. And hell on earth it certainly was. Thousands of searchlights, illuminations, fires and... Lancasters magnifying this hell every minute. I haven't yet seen this number of searchlights, in spite of experiencing similar emotions fifteen times. Every flight has something different, something more that is unforgettable, and if in the future someone mentions Bottrop my blood will run cold and... I will be pleased—for Warsaw."

Crews were called to briefing on the 5th to learn that Leipzig was to be their destination. "Probable flight to Leipzig. We know this course and the heaviest defence imaginable. The whole briefing costs us a lot of nerves—we simply don't like the area of Leipzig—it is very unpleasant there. Many of us had anxious moments before the flight was cancelled. You can't imagine the relief and shouts of joy of everyone when we heard this magic word: "cancelled"."

The frontier towns of Goch and Cleves were earmarked for destruction on the night of the 7/8th, in preparation for the impending crossing into Germany of the British XXX Corps. The latter was assigned to a 1 Group force of 250 aircraft, of which thirteen were to be provided by 300 Squadron. In the event only nine took off, and a fourteen-minute delay between the final two departures at 19.21 and 19.35 suggests that, perhaps, one or more had put a wheel off the peri-track, leading to the scrubbing of four sorties, although the ORB makes no mention of such an incident. W/C Jarkowski was taking the opportunity to lead his squadron into battle for the first time since assuming command. The weather conditions outbound were excellent, with clear skies to within twelve miles of the target, when seven-tenths cloud bubbled up with tops at around 7,000 feet. The Master Bomber called the crews down to 5,000 feet, from where those who complied with his instructions had a clear view of the perfectly-illuminated and well-marked aiming point. Not all bothered to descend through the cloud, however, and the bombing heights of the Polish crews ranged from 4,500 to 13,000 feet. They were each carrying a cookie and sixteen 500 pounders, which they deposited on the unfortunate town between 22.00 and 22.10, and when the bombing was over, little of it remained standing. Fortunately, most of the civilian population had evacuated the area by this time, and casualties were probably few.

"8th February, 1945 —Faldingworth-Hinckley. Six long weeks of waiting, planning etc. came to an end. Today is the happy day when one, dressed in one's best clothes, starts on his journey. "Goodbye" War, "Goodbye" squadron, "Goodbye" lifeless desert for whole six days. It is strange: six long weeks, tiring, sometimes boring and claustrophobic, and then six beautiful days of holiday. The sun rises early and shines all day with happiness and contentment. I am greeted very warmly in Hinckley, (Leicestershire), where I meet my friend Pawcio."

A two-phase attack was planned for the following night against the synthetic oil refinery at Politz, situated north of Stettin in Germany's north-eastern corner. *(This location is often confused with Pölitz, a town in the Schleswig-Holstein region of Germany at the western end of the Baltic.)* 5 Group was scheduled to open proceedings employing its low level marking method, with 1 Group following up with 184 aircraft two hours later with a Pathfinder element. 300 Squadron dispatched a dozen Lancasters from Faldingworth either side of 19.30, led by S/L Jan Brogowski, and they climbed into ten-tenths cloud that persisted as far as the German coast. Thereafter, the skies cleared, and at the target there was only patchy cloud above the bomber stream with a base at around 15,000 feet. The crews had been able to identify the target from as far away as seventy miles by the fires burning from the 5 Group attack, and the Pathfinders arrived bang on schedule to provide illuminating flares and salvoes of red and green TIs. The deputy Master Bomber was heard to call the Master Bomber, and get no response, after which he took control of the attack himself. The 300 Squadron crews ran across the aiming point at 12,000 to 15,000 feet between 23.15 and 23.25, and returned safely to report many explosions and smoke rising to well over 8,000 feet as they turned away. A massive explosion at 23.17 lit up the whole target area and the surrounding countryside for some distance, and was described as among the largest explosions ever witnessed. The plant was put out of action completely, and would produce no further oil for what remained of the war. AVM "Bobby" Blucke became the new A-O-C 1 Group on the 12th, succeeding AVM Rice, who would be posted to HQ 7 Group on the 21st.

"13th February, 1945 — Hinckley. And so it came to pass what nobody expected: fourth partition of Poland by... their Allies. It was announced today, quite plainly and bluntly, after the conference of the Big Three in Yalta, that the Soviet Union takes one third of Polish territory and Polish eastern frontier runs along so-called 'Curzon Line'. And so we have a 'Free' Poland with Committee of Lublin—they really did for us, our allies—England and the United States. Damn them all! Especially Churchill who misled Roosevelt and surrendered to Stalin. Yes, that's how matters stand, and we still fight for "your freedom and ours". My blood boils that we live in such times and have such poor allies. This is the reward for our 5 year constant battle against Germany. Rich reward, thanks! Mr. Churchill."

The Churchill inspired series of raids on Germany's eastern cities under Operation Thunderclap began at Dresden on the night of the 13/14th, in another two phase assault to be opened by 5 Group. A layer of cloud hampered the marking and bombing, but 244 Lancasters delivered over eight hundred tons of bombs into the beautiful and historic city, and started fires burning. 1 Group contributed 260 Lancasters to a force of 529 of the type drawn also from 3, 6 and 8 Groups, which was scheduled to arrive at the target three hours after 5 Group. 300 Squadron briefed thirteen crews, the participation of one of which was cancelled before take-off. They began departing Faldingworth at 21.30, and last but one away at 21.47 was PA185 with the crew of W/O Mykietyn. While still climbing out at 21.59, this Lancaster collided with NF932 of 550 Squadron, and both aircraft exploded, before crashing three miles south-west of Wragby with no survivors. The others pressed on, and could see the burning city twenty minutes before reaching it. By this time the skies had cleared, although a large bank of cloud hovered close by to the east. It was clear that the main weight of the 5 Group attack had fallen into an area south of the Elbe, and between the marshalling yards and the 1 Group aiming point. Illuminating and marking was hardly necessary, but was carried out anyway, and the Polish crews bombed from 17,000 to 20,000 feet between 01.32 and 01.42, and all returned safely to report fires visible up to eighty miles into the return trip.

The second phase of this now controversial operation had delivered a further eighteen hundred tons of bombs onto the city and upon its hapless population, which had been swelled by a massive influx of refugees fleeing from the eastern front. The same chain of events was unleashed, that had devastated parts of Hamburg in July 1943, and the ensuing firestorm engulfed a large area of the city. Initial estimates of the death toll were hysterically high, but a figure of twenty-five thousand has now been settled upon. This operation has been seized-upon by anti-war campaigners, and used as a bludgeon to attack Harris as a war criminal, and much misinformation has been spread to support this view, particularly in Germany. Firstly, a firestorm was a meteorological phenomenon, which occasionally occurred when a variety of circumstances coincided, and it was an event which could not be planned. Secondly, survivors claim that Allied aircraft flew low over the city to strafe the streets and open spaces where people were sheltering. RAF bomber crews had one intention at this stage of the war, to do the job, and get out as quickly as possible. They had strict routes and timings to govern their activities, and although a very small number liked to return at low level to avoid flak hotspots, this normally occurred over more familiar terrain in western Germany and the Occupied Countries. It is highly unlikely that any would risk diving to roof-top height to shoot at civilians when so deep inside Germany. Thirdly, the American bombers arrived later that morning, and they were protected by escort fighters, which were better suited to strafing, but there is no direct evidence that they did so, and no fingers are pointed in their direction. Fourthly, Harris was not interested in bombing Dresden, and had to be almost bullied by Portal to comply with Churchill's wishes. It should also be remembered, that shortly after this operation, with peacetime elections to consider, and in an act of betrayal, Churchill distanced himself from the area bombing policy, which he had championed, and all-but accused Harris of terror bombing.

"14th February, 1945 — Hinckley – Faldingworth. So it was that my holiday which started so well, ended dismally because of the political situation. And that's not all. After returning to camp I learned that the previous day there was a crash beyond the airfield. W/O Mikietyn and his crew were killed. Olek Jameliniec was also killed. We were together on the flight mechanics course. Such a jolly chap. It was terrible—immediately after take off for a mission they collided with another plane, and fully loaded. I can imagine their death when the plane exploded. That's our fate, but for what?—half a Poland. I feel like crying, I wish the earth would swallow me up. Or to be somewhere in the middle of Africa so that I would not witness all that is happening here. Forget this tragic reality. Sleep Olek in the dark grave, may you dream of the whole Poland and your Janów."

Twenty-four hours after Dresden, Operation Thunderclap moved on to Chemnitz, where a similar two phase operation was planned. 202 Lancasters of 1 Group were made ready, among them ten by 300 Squadron, and they would be part of an overall heavy force of 499 aircraft drawn also from 3, 4, 6 and 8 Groups. They began taking off from Faldingworth at 20.11, with W/C Jarkowski the senior pilot on duty, supported by S/L Brogowski. F/L Wierzbowski turned back at 22.30, when at 8,000 feet about sixty miles north-east of Paris, after his navigator became ill. The others carried on, and what, initially, had been good weather conditions, deteriorated steadily as the target drew near, and the crews were met with ten-tenths cloud over Chemnitz with tops as high as 18,000 feet in places. The Master Bomber called for markers at 00.25, but these did not materialize, and at 00.29 he instructed crews to bomb on Gee and H2S. The 300 Squadron crews bombed from 16,000 to 20,000 feet between 00.32 and 00.39, and all returned safely. Sparse marking did eventually take place, but it could not rescue what became a scattered and largely ineffective raid. At debriefing F/S Szczesny and crew reported bombing Kaiserslautern as an alternative target, after the navigator and rear gunner became ill.

Left: Faldingworth, 20th February 1945. W/C Pozyczka receives his DSO. (PISM). Right: S/L Jan Konarzewski "B" Flight Commander. He flew his first two operations on Battles with 300 Squadron in 1940. Later he was posted back to Faldingworth and completed another 13 sorties on Lancasters before being killed on the 16th operation of his tour of duty. (PISM via WM)

On the 20th W/C Pozyczka was presented with the DSO by the A-O-C 1 Group during the morning parade. In the afternoon fifteen crews were briefed for an operation that night, involving 271 Lancasters of 1 Group and 243 from 3, 6 and 8 Groups, the target for which was the southern half of Dortmund. They were all safely airborne by 22.05, with S/L Konarzewski the senior pilot on duty. Initially clear skies were replaced by increasing amounts of cloud, until the bomber stream was flying above ten-tenths low stratus from 5° East. There was eight-tenths cloud over the target, which the Pathfinders marked punctually and accurately with red TIs, backed up later with greens. There were also skymarkers from the start of the attack, but these were spread back along the line of approach for some fourteen miles, and never achieved concentration. The early bombing was concentrated on the glow of the TIs through the cloud, but as it thickened and the glow became harder to pick out, the attack became more scattered. The 300 Squadron crews bombed from 17,000 to 21,000 feet between 01.02 and 01.19, and all but one returned to report the glow of fires covering an extensive area, a few explosions, but generally a scattered attack for which it was not possible to make an accurate assessment. Bomber Command claimed that the aim of this operation was achieved, but administration within the city had broken down completely, and there were no local reports to confirm or deny this. PB722 was one of fourteen Lancasters lost on what was the penultimate heavy raid of the war on this city, and blew up over Bergisch Gladbach after being hit by flak. The location of the crash on the southern fringe of the Ruhr suggests that S/L Konarzewski and crew were homebound

Sgt Tadeusz Picho (W.Op.) from the crew of S/L Konarzewski. He was shot down and taken prisoner on his fifth operation with 300 Squadron. (Picho family via P. Sikora)

on their way towards Belgium when the end came. The pilot and navigator, Sgt Modrany, lost their lives, while their crew mates parachuted into the arms of their captors.

"After more than two weeks break today we again board 'R' for Roger. Today's course and target are familiar—Dortmund. Henryk, do you remember your first sortie? Of course—it was Dortmund on 29th November, 1944. A long way and many changes and experiences and today the 16th flight in all and second to Dortmund. I push these thoughts away for the first and last time as I press the ignition lever forward: 3,000 revolutions plus 14 booster to go faster and farther to banish these thoughts. Whatever happens we trust in God. We take off late but the visibility is good so the flight is not tiring. Somehow the flight is different than the first one—then it was daytime, today we are surrounded by night. It is a beautiful moonlit night. Wrr-wrr... monotonous and menacing sound in my ears. Four Merlins like four night birds of prey rumble this wonderful tune of confidence and power. There are thousands, millions of stars and hundreds of these rapacious birds of prey are flying to Dortmund for a feast. "Bombs gone". We spend only a short time over the target. It looks the same as before: light as day, below us red explosions of 4,000lb bombs and we are above that. The night 'birds of prey' are returning, but not all of them. Below us and to the rear I see a Lancaster on fire. It is eerie—it's breaking up and falling—it could not hold on, maybe it is one of ours? We are returning by moonlight, here and there above us we see white streaks—it's the night fighter planes, you have to be vigilant. The three hours of return flight pass quickly. Let us land safely without further thrills. Mother England greets us with thousands of lights. Here and there friendly beacons blink. We descend to 4,000 feet. The ground can be clearly seen, we pass several airfields, till at last familiar letter 'F.H.' – Faldingworth. We land, but not everyone is so fortunate. Lieutenant Konarzewski with Lieutenant's Janczur's crew did not come back. One crew less. I feel sad for them—they shared my billet. I am especially sorry for 'Grandad' Jakimowicz, he could easily have been my father, such a fine chap. May they rest in peace! It is all for "your freedom and ours".

Elements of 1, 6 and 8 Groups returned to the Ruhr on the following night to carry out what would be the final raid of the war on Duisburg. 1 Group contributed 245 Lancasters to the overall heavy force of 362, and among them were thirteen representing 300 Squadron. They departed Faldingworth either side of 20.00, and climbed into relatively clear skies, which remained so across Belgium until shortly before the target was reached. A thin layer of stratus slid in at 15,000 to 16,000 feet to cover the target, but was seen to be moving north. Inaccurately forecast winds delayed the arrival of the main force by a few minutes, and by the time they began to fly across the aiming point, the initial red markers, which had gone down at 22.56, had disappeared into the cloud. No further reds were seen until 23.08, and the green back-up TIs were too sparse to provide an accurate indication of the target area. The early bombing was seen to undershoot as far back as Krefeld to the south-west, but as the cloud drifted away, the bombing became more concentrated. The Polish crews delivered their cookies and 500 pounders or incendiaries from 15,000 to 20,000 feet between 23.00 and 23.18, and all returned safely to report undershooting, explosions, streets outlined in flames, and fires visible for sixty miles into the return trip. There was no local report, but it was established that the operation had been highly destructive.

"Today again we have to fly even though we haven't had enough rest. Some perish and don't come back, others replace them—like us who are still alive. During the briefing they change our easy target for Duisburg. It is still in the Ruhr basin but nearer. It is just my luck that if it is easy flight we don't go, but when it is the Ruhr it is always us, but it's God's will, sometimes you may not return from an easy mission. We fly in 'R'. Similar to yesterday visibility is good and we have the moon at the back. As usual the Ruhr is belching fire, but this is only a repeat of yesterday's flight. Today we are flying a little higher and maybe faster for we have the wind helping us. Normal procedure on landing. We land at 1.25 - 5½ hours. Shorter than yesterday, and all the planes landed in home nest. Another 1,140 miles added to the long track going east—to Poland. How many more thousands of miles one will have to travel to land at Okęcie?"

The original intention on the 21st had been to attack Pforzheim, a town to the north-west of Stuttgart, which was believed to be a manufacturing base for precision instruments, as well as being a railway hub. In the event the target had been changed to Duisburg, but this was only a temporary reprieve, and 367 Lancasters of 1, 6 and 8 Groups were made ready during the course of the 23rd for an operation that night. This would be the first and only major raid of the war on this location. 300 Squadron contributed fifteen aircraft to the 1 Group total of 258, and they began to take-off at 16.00, with W/C Jarkowski the senior pilot on duty. They climbed away into ten-tenths low cloud, which persisted until the French coast, when it began to break up, and the target was reached under clear skies. The first red TIs went down at 19.54, followed by illuminating flares and salvoes of mixed red and green TIs, which were seen in the excellent visibility to be accurate and concentrated. The 300 Squadron crews bombed from medium level, 7,000 to 10,000 feet, between 20.00 and 20.06, contributing to the eighteen hundred tons of bombs delivered onto the target in a twenty-two-minute orgy of destruction. As they turned away, they left behind a sea of flames, which was captured for posterity by a Film Unit Lancaster. It would later be established that 17,600 people lost their lives in the inferno, the third highest death toll of the war from a Bomber Command raid, and that approximately 83% of the town's built-up area had ben reduced to rubble. Among the ten missing Lancasters were two belonging to 300 Squadron. NG266 was shot down by a night fighter and crashed into the north-eastern outskirts of the town near the River Enz, and there were no survivors from the crew of F/L Filipek. PA161 also fell victim to a night fighter, and crashed near Sindelfingen, south-east of the target and south-west of Stuttgart, after bombing. F/S Jachacz and three of his crew survived to be taken prisoner, but three others lost their lives.

"22nd February, 1945 — Faldingworth. After the last hard two days came a break, It was especially pleasant and desirable, for a Polish concert party arrived to give us three shows. So we all go to see the revue. Whole two hours of good jokes, songs, and a chance to hear mother tongue from the stage. That's the most important thing—a piece of Polish stage and the performance of the old stager Tadeusz Olsza complete the enjoyment. His name is very familiar. I kept hearing it thousands of times looking through Warsaw papers. I can't remember whether it was 'Warsaw Barber' or 'Qui Pro Quo', anyway a well known small theatre and this laughing Olsza. I leave the show with the sensation of some Warsaw stage—

my vivid imagination lets me enjoy the wide world of dreams rather than the claustrophobic cauldron of toxic reality. Art and music—two powerful forces ruling our human souls."

"24th February, 1945 — Faldingworth. So called 'lemonade'—a word most pleasing to the ears, it simply means no mission. What can be better than the certainty of a good night's sleep? Let others face the dangers. In the afternoon, taking advantage of 'no war', we go to Lincoln to a football match between 'Polish Airforce eleven' and the town of Lincoln team. Feverishly we root and cheer for 'our' team, maybe it helped them to achieve a 2—2 draw against a good and well playing English team. The Poles scored the first goal, but the English quickly equalised, then it was 2—1 to England and the Poles equalised in some style. And this was the final score. The Polish team played quite well, but they lacked cohesion and team-work. Our left-winger Olympian Wodarz distinguished himself, also Bojar from our squadron."

Thirteen 300 Squadron Lancasters took off for Neuss shortly before 09.00 on the 28th, as part of a 1 Group force of 248 aircraft. The entire force was recalled before it had crossed the coast, because of a swifter than anticipated advance into the area of Allied ground forces. Eleven operations during the month had generated 133 sorties at a cost of five aircraft.

Faldingworth, 1945. Lancaster SW279 BH-E ready for take-off on her next operation. (PISM via WM)

March 1945

Mannheim was selected to host the first major operation of the new month, and what would prove to be its final heavy raid of the war. Briefings took place early on the 1st, and fourteen Lancasters from 300 Squadron took off either side of noon to join up with 234 others from the group. Elements from 6 and 8 Groups brought the overall force to 478 aircraft, which encountered ten-tenths cloud from the French coast to the target. The main force maintained a good formation during the outward leg, but arrived a few minutes late, by which time the Master Bomber had asked the marker force to orbit. Blue smoke-puff skymarkers went down at 15.03, and crews bombed on these in accordance with the Master Bomber's instructions. The Polish crews delivered their cookies and incendiaries from 17,000 to 19,000 feet between 15.03 and 15.10, and all returned home safely, unable to offer any assessment of the attack. SW279 arrived back with an incendiary bomb lodged in its port wing fuel tank, which, fortunately, had been empty when the incident occurred.

An aerial photograph of the centre of Cologne being bombed by the crew of F/L Kolodziej in Lancaster LM632 BH-O on 2nd March 1945. (JC)

Cologne was likewise bombed for the last time on the morning of the 2nd in a two-phase operation. The first phase involved seven hundred aircraft, 244 of them from 1 Group, including thirteen belonging to 300 Squadron. They began taking off at 07.05, led by S/L Brogowski, and encountered varying amounts of cloud during the outward leg, until about twenty miles from the target, when the skies began to clear. Visibility over the target was perfect, and the crews in the spearhead had no difficulty in visually identifying the aiming points near the cathedral and Hohenzollern bridge. Smoke began to drift across the city as the raid developed, and obscured the red and green TIs, forcing the Master Bomber, whose transmissions were not picked up by every crew, to give instructions to bomb at the centre of the upwind smoke. The Polish crews released their loads from 16,500 to 18,000 feet between 10.00 and 10.05, before setting off home to report a concentrated and destructive attack. The flak defence was described as moderate, and it claimed two 300 Squadron Lancasters. PB854 crashed into the suburbs, killing F/L Kirkilewicz and his crew, and NG501 also fell within the city, with the loss of F/L Wyganowski and all but one of his crew. It is believed that the flight engineer, Sgt Filek, managed to bale out, but was murdered by German civilians. The second phase of the operation was to have been carried out by 155 Lancasters of 3 Group, but only a handful bombed after the failure of a G-H station in England. Never-the-less, the much bombed city was left in a state of paralysis, and was taken by American forces four days later.

W/O Andrzej Gorski took part in 16 bombing operations between Feb. and Apr. 1945 (A. Gorski)

F/L Kozicki and crew stayed on the ground on this day. “Second battle mission and our crew is forced to wait and laze about, I don’t know why. Today it is a day flight to Cologne. It seems an easy one, but as always “you cannot make an omelette without breaking eggs”—two crews don’t come back. The crew of Lieut. Kirkilewicz with mechanic Norberg, also Wieckowski and Lieut. Wyganowski and with him Jacek Filek, always reliable and jolly chap. I will miss him the most, as we spent quite a lot of both happy and sad times together. The best times were those spent in Romania and France. So Jacek, it was not meant for us to see Poland together. Such bare, laconic words. “Killed in action”. May you rest in peace and may God let you see heaven. Sleep my friend in the dark grave and dream of Poland—dear Jacek.”

One of the 300 Squadron crews taking part in this operation was captained by W/O Andrzej Gorski, and they were flying in NN746, BH-N for Nan. The following is an edited version of his account of the operation.

“We were to bomb a railway station. During the briefing the intelligence officer mentioned that a thousand 88 and 105mm guns had been amassed to form the target’s flak defences. That didn’t really cheer us up! We took off early in the morning and flew in perfect weather. Visibility was excellent in a crystal clear blue sky adorned with occasional white cumulus, which indicated a cold front. Starting from the gathering point at Reading, I could see the endless stream of bombers flowing over the North Sea towards the Dutch coast and Germany. Our escort consisted of long-range Mustangs to meet us near the target. I didn’t see enemy fighters, but they must have been present, as I observed spots in the bomber stream where aircraft tightened up their formation to have a better chance of fending off the attackers. Approaching Cologne we saw its Gothic cathedral dominating the view of the city. The flak intensified, and the close-by explosions rocked our N-Nan, making it harder for me to keep it on course. I located the approximate position of my target and made a turn. The railway station was covered with dense smoke and couldn’t be seen. Only the cathedral’s steeple was visible. Therefore, I decided to use it as an aiming point. I told Fabrycy, my bomb-aimer, to unload right past it. The station was located some one hundred metres away. Bombs always dropped in sequence, and their explosions formed a line on the ground. While flying on the right course, this would give a good chance to hit our target. I risked striking the cathedral only to achieve my objective, to land some bombs on the railway station.”

"During the bombing run my aircraft was tossed around by flak bursts. Just then, somebody reported a gaping hole in the port wing. It was right where the third tank was located (by then empty), and I didn't think much about it. After welcomed "bombs gone", and about three minutes for taking pictures, I put my Lancaster on a course straight for home in a shallow dive. I wanted to get out of the AA artillery range as quickly as possible, turn off the oxygen and have a smoke. I passed by one of our unit's planes, which had lost its upper gun turret. The gunner was in the hole and waved to us gaily. I met him later on during debriefing, and, to this day, I don't understand how nothing happened to him. While we were having our usual treat of grog, tea and sandwiches, he was still finding pieces of shrapnel in his battledress. I took one for a souvenir. The weather continued to hold, so it was all pilot-navigation. Approaching the coast I invited my navigator Jan Sierbien to the cockpit for a smoke, where he could enjoy a beautiful view. A navigator couldn't see anything from his post. I identified the coast crossing point and relaxed, as, once over the sea, we were out of danger of enemy attack. The rest of the trip was uneventful, and we made an easy landing. After taxiing to the dispersal pan and switching off engines, I sent my upper gunner, Zbyszek Torka, to investigate the port wing damage. As I was sitting in my seat resting and meditating about our mission, I was astounded to see him taking out of the ripped tank an incendiary with broken fins. I yelled at him to keep it as a souvenir. Wanting to get off the wing, he dropped it into the hands of one of the ground crew, who, in turn, threw it on the grass, where it started to burn."

On the night of the 3/4th the Luftwaffe mounted its highly successful Operation Gisella, in which around two hundred aircraft carried out intruder sorties as bombers returned from Kamen, the Dortmund-Ems Canal, various support and minor operations and training flights. Twenty Bomber Command aircraft were brought down in this manner, as was a JU88 responsible for the loss of a 460 squadron Lancaster. It strafed a car, killing a member of the Royal Observer Corps, before itself colliding with telephone wires and crashing with fatal consequences for its crew. (Bomber Command Losses, 1945, Bill Chorley.) 300 Squadron did not operate on this night, and carried out no night training, so was exempt from the attentions of the enemy.

Having failed to inflict a telling blow on Chemnitz on the night after Dresden, over seven hundred aircraft were made ready to return on the night of the 5/6th. 1 Group put up 239 Lancasters for this operation, of which thirteen were provided by 300 Squadron. S/L Brogowski was again the senior pilot on duty as they departed Faldingworth either side of 17.00. Sgt Gorski was forced to abandon his sortie after NN746 lost its port-outer engine while climbing out over the station. The others flew out in cloud of varying amounts over England and the Channel, which became ten-tenths over eastern France and Germany. F/S Schlichtinger became the second from the squadron to turn back, after his H2S and air position indicator (a.p.i.) failed over the Channel. The others pressed on, and saw the first release point flares go down at 21.42. They were plentiful and well-grouped, but quickly disappeared into cloud, and there was a period between 21.55 and 21.58 when no TIs were visible. The Master Bomber's transmissions were indistinct because of static, but he instructed the crews to bomb on the glow visible beneath the clouds. The 300 Squadron crews bombed from 15,000 to 18,000 feet between 21.45 and 21.56, and all returned unable to offer an accurate assessment of the outcome. F/S Plucinski landed PD362 at Wigsley with a port-inner engine fire and a shortage of fuel.

Henryk Drozdz wrote; "I am writing this after it happened. It all started with the modest name of the German town of Chemnitz. That was how it looked when I entered the briefing room. However, in time modest Chemnitz was suitably adorned and embellished—it only needed 9,500 pounds of battle freight which we were to deliver. And here again I must remark that if you wanted to write something about every average flight you would need a lot of time and paper, so I will limit myself to just a few facts, which will throw some light on what was achieved today. We took off at 17.10 fully laden with 66,300 pounds. The flight to target was uneventful, only here and there artillery fire. At 21.50 hours we arrived at our target. The hottest point of the flight, full of various dangers and unforgettable experiences and emotions. The return flight again without any major incidents. The enemy of night flights—sleep—nearly overcame me completely, also the radio was tormenting us. There were moments during the return flight when I thought I should have jumped out over France. The whole sortie lasted 9 hours 10 minutes—it was the longest flight of my life and the most tiring. After landing safely I thought I would pass away and as long as I live I will not forget this most unpleasant flight of my career. Even the sleep afterwards was exhausting—I pray that this was the last flight of the 'Coastal Command' series."

The eastern town of Dessau, situated seventy-five miles south-west of Berlin and thirty-five miles north of the recently attacked Leuna (Merseburg), had, up to this point, not received a visit from Bomber Command. It was the birthplace of the Junkers aviation company, and home to a large aircraft factory, as well as having inland docks and railway installations. 526 aircraft of 1, 3, 6 and 8 Groups were made

Faldingworth, May 1945. F/S Marian Matejski in the cockpit of Lancaster ME470 BH-F with symbols of 22 bombing and 8 supply-dropping operations and the individual artwork of a girl with a bomb on a crescent moon. (PISM via WM)

Faldingworth, Spring 1945. F/S Gorski with crew posing in Mae Wests among the group of ground personnel in front of their Lancaster NN746 BH-N. Left to Right: 1st – W/O Golicz (A.G.), 3rd – Sgt F/S Sobczak (F.E.), 6th – F/S Gorski (pilot) holding helmet, 9th – W/O Torka (A.G.), 10th - F/O Fabrycy (B.A.), 11th - W/O Pietrzak (W.Op.), 12th - F/O Sierbien (nav.) (A. Gorski)

ready during the course of the 7th, 243 of them provided by 1 Group, of which thirteen belonged to 300 Squadron. S/L Brogowski was the senior pilot on duty as they departed Faldingworth in a fifteen minute slot from 17.07, and made their way to the French coast in ten-tenths cloud. It thinned somewhat as the force approached the German frontier, and remained so until thickening again to eight-tenths at the target. PA233 was attacked four times by a single-engine enemy fighter while passing between Cologne and the southern edge of the Ruhr at 10,000 feet, and, having lost the use of the mid-upper and rear turrets, W/O Warchal dropped the bombs live at 20.32 onto a last-resort target before returning home. Illuminating flares were released over the target at 21.56, followed by red and green TIs, which were quickly lost from sight. The Master Bomber called for skymarking, which appeared to be concentrated, and the main force crews bombed on these. The 300 Squadron crews were over the aiming point at 12,000 to 15,000 feet between 21.58 and 22.10, and delivered their cookies and incendiaries in accordance with the Master Bomber's instructions. All returned safely home to report concentrated bombing and the glow of many fires beneath the clouds. Post-raid analysis confirmed a highly effective operation, which had caused extensive damage in central, residential and industrial districts. One 1 Group crew claimed an enemy jet fighter as destroyed.

The following is W/O Gorski's account of this operation. "As usual, it started with the briefing. The intelligence officer droned on about something to do with the strategic importance of the target, but not very convincingly, and it was clear that he was struggling. From what I heard, Dessau had no important industry. The marshalling yards, supporting the withdrawal of the German army ahead of the Soviet offensive, was a sensitive point, and was our target. Reportedly, the town was jammed with German refugees. At one point I stood up and interrupted, saying, that I was not a butcher and I would drop my bombs off target. At this, our CO, W/Cdr Jarkowski, told me that he had not heard what I just said, probably hoping I would withdraw my statement, so the incident could be avoided. But a few others stood up as well in my support, and refused to take part in the mission. Such an ultimatum had Jarkowski come to the front and give us a little speech. He spoke about the deteriorating relationship between the Polish and British governments, our role as an air force at that time, and gave us half an hour to rethink our decision. It is important to explain here, that, although independent, the Polish Air Force was under the "Kings Regulations", which gave each pilot the great privilege to refuse the flight. Other crew members had no such privilege, and their refusal would result in their being court-martialled."

"Jarkowski left the briefing room and we were given further details about bombs, fuses, etc. F/Lt Kot described our route, its major points, bomb run, and four-minute 'window' in which our squadron was to unload. The raid was divided into several four-minute bomb runs with four-minute intervals between waves of bombers. The planned separation of waves served its purpose. The objective was to prevent congestion over the target to minimize collisions. That was the theory. In reality, to avoid flak or thunderstorms, pilots habitually chose their own routes and altitudes. The navigators had to cope with wind velocities (W/V), usually different from those reported by the Group, and often made more than four-minute errors. Everybody tried to co-ordinate their times over the target more or less as briefed. Nobody wanted to be caught alone by the concentrated anti-aircraft fire over the target. It happened to quite few. When our CO came back, there were no flight refusals among the pilots. Before take off, my navigator reported both "Gee" box and the radar out of order. But since were to take off and fly the first leg in daylight, I decided to go. I was planning to keep with the bomber stream, hoping that my navigator would be able to get a precise wind force and direction reading, which was needed for dead reckoning."

"Over the continent the weather deteriorated rapidly. I flew at 18,000 feet between two layers of various clouds. At some point our aircraft started to ice up and I lost speed. I tried to fly 2,000 feet higher, and then descended to 16,000, which was a much better choice. The ice fell off the wings. Perhaps an hour later we saw the target. It was illuminated with hundreds of searchlight, which reminded me of knights' lances pointing straight to the sky and declaring upcoming danger. The black shapes of Lancasters reflected against the clouds above. They created dimness over the target, what with the lack of flak barrage, suggested we could expect fighter attacks. This tactic was called *Wilde Sau*, or 'Wild Bore'. No Focke-Wulfs were around me, but at instant, the whole of my crew started to bellow over the intercom. I told them to shut up and realized that two Lancasters were boring at us in a dive. My rear gunner, Roman Golicz, reported the third one closing up on us dangerously. To avoid a mid-air collision I had to dive. I ordered the crew to keep quite and I asked Golicz to report positions of those three Lancasters. One of them had a speed advantage and was passing us in his nearly vertical dive. When its wingtip passed a few feet off the Golicz's turret I decided to pull up. We must have been doing close to 400 knots as the speedometer raced past the red mark set at 320 knots or so. At this speed and fully loaded I was afraid to use flaps to reduce the speed, as it was very possible to loose both wings. I ordered the flight engineer 'power off' and I lowered the landing gear. I started to pull up only when the aircraft slowed down to 320 knots, with a help of a trimmer. I lost 8,000 feet but I had the plane at level flight and in one piece. Then it was the bomb-aimer's turn to fly the bomber. During the bombing run I kept the course according to Jan Fabrycy's corrections: left-left-steady- left-steady- right-steady..."

"Suddenly I was astounded to see an FW190, whose starboard wingtip was right under our fuselage. We were flying exactly the same course with similar speeds. I could clearly see the pilot's profile, starring closely at his instrument panel. He didn't see me, as most likely being a day fighter pilot (Wilde Sau) he wasn't experienced in night flying. Excited, I wanted to shoot him down, but none of our gunners could depress the guns enough to be able to shoot. The FW190 was simply too close. I had to be extremely careful, not lose the course or collide with the German at the same time. The only one who could have a shot at him was Fabrycy. But he was at the bombsight and his turret was empty. If I told him to climb back to his guns (it wasn't easy with all this flying gear on us) the Focke Wulf would have been gone and our bombs off target. When I heard Fabrycy's 'Bombs gone', the German plane disappeared.

Relieved after preceding tense moments I took what I thought to be a homebound course. To avoid icing I took a southerly course intending to turn west later hoping to find better visibility. After about half an hour, the navigator reported that he lost his navigation. I upbraided myself for having decided to fly my "N for Nan" deprived of its radio navigational aids. I chose the most economical speed and altitude and turned in an approximate direction of Switzerland. I reason that I would be able to use its lights on the horizon as a reference point for my flight home. I was very happy to recognize identification codes of few lighthouses on the British coast. We landed at our base one-hour after everybody else. When we finally showed up for debriefing - always preceded by grog and sandwiches – our crew was listed as missing. This flight lasted over ten hours, and it was my longest. When together with my wife I visited my ex CO, Bolek Jarkowski in Jacksonville in Florida, he recalled the briefing, which by then I vaguely remembered. To Bolek who was a career officer it was the most trying event in his military career."

Two major operations were mounted on the following night, the larger against Hamburg by a predominantly Halifax main force, while Kassel was raided for the first time since its ordeal by firestorm in October 1943 by a 1 Group main force of 235 aircraft, of which fourteen were provided by 300 Squadron. W/C Jarkowski led them off at 17.31 for what would be the final heavy raid on this city, and they headed into heavy cloud, which persisted along the circuitous route across northern France into Belgium and north of the Ruhr, where it began to thin. Once past the Ruhr the force turned south-east and the cloud began to increase again to eight to ten-tenths thin stratus over the target. The attack opened on time with both sky and ground marking, and the main force crews were able to see the red and green markers through the cloud. All but one of the Polish crews bombed from 19,000 to 22,000 feet between 21.30 and 21.45, but F/L Kozicki lost the use of his starboard-outer engine, intercom and rear turret while outbound, and arrived late and low to bomb from 14,000 feet at 21.54 on a Gee fix. According to Sgt Drozdz, as recorded in the following paragraph, they probably bombed Coesfeld, a town situated between the Dutch frontier and Münster. Returning crews described a concentrated and successful operation, with many fires, explosions and smoke. Local reports confirm much damage in western districts, but as in most German towns and cities by this stage of the war, administration had broken down and official reporting was largely abandoned.

"Happy Birthday to you, Happy Birthday to you!", — sang to me my birthday nymphs of good fortune and beauty. Today is the 25th anniversary of the day my mother brought me into this world. Maybe it sounds a bit poetic, but the reality remains the same—everyday, eventful, dangerous—magnificent. Battle flights are the most tragic but also most admirable element. It is not about killing people, or about revenge, what matters is the Fight. Fight to victorious conclusion. Where there is war there must be fighting. That is just what we are doing—fighting regardless of any obstacles or different emotions. For instance today—my birthday—there is a moment of uncertainty—could it also be the day of my death? But we must not think like that, we have to fly. Fly far away—hundreds of miles to Kassel. One after another the planes take off like bats. More and more wings in the sky. It looks ominous but there is peace in the soul. Just as in past ages Polish hussars rustled their wings when getting ready for battle, so now it is the same. Grim faces and utter composure, everyone knows what to do when the time of battle comes. One after another the night predators fly. I don't know whether there is anything more fabulous and splendid than battle flight. It is only a few hours which sometimes seem like a lifetime. Sometimes they are the last hours of one's life. But luckily one comes back, like today—in spite of one engine failing. We were not over the correct target i.e. Kassel, because we were unable to climb to the required height, our bombs fell on some small town, probably Coesfeld, that was the order. With luck and God's help we return home on 3 engines and land safely. And so I have summarised my 'birthday' flight—apart from the proverbial excitement there was maybe some other, more elusive element."

An all-time record was set on the 11th, when 1,079 aircraft, including 240 from 1 Group, took off in the late morning to bomb Essen for the final time. S/L Brogowski was the senior pilot on duty as the fourteen 300 Squadron Lancasters lifted off from Faldingworth either side of noon, and headed into ten-tenths cloud, which persisted all the way to the target and back. Visibility above the cloud was excellent, and the crews watched the first blue smoke-puff skymarkers go down at 14.58, before bombing in accordance with the running commentary instruction from the Master Bomber. The Polish crews were over the aiming point at 16,000 to 19,000 feet between 15.00 and 15.06, and all returned safely with reports of brown and black smoke rising through the clouds, and the glow of fires still visible a hundred miles into the return trip.

"This is the 20th sortie to Essen. God! Daylight flight over the Ruhr! We take off at 11.55—nearly noon. Only 12,600 pounds of bombs. I will not dwell on our feelings ahead of the flight, enough to say that during the briefing it was very quiet, everyone had the gloomy look of someone under the sentence of death. The chronic fear of the Ruhr disappeared during the flight over France and even over the Ruhr itself. It was lucky for us that the whole area was covered with clouds. When we are nearing the target here and there plumes of smoke jump out of the clouds—artillery. It looks extremely unpleasant. The intensity increases the nearer we get to the target, my legs begin to shake as usual. Small plumes of blue smoke indicate point of aim. Height of emotion over the target, it seems like the end, planes on all sides left, right, in front, above—there seems no way out. Plumes of smoke shoot up like mushrooms after rainfall. Another moment, which seems like the longest time over the target, and then full throttle and away. Now the firing stopped and it is safe. I have time to have a look at what is happening. Actually it is just a swarm of planes. Temporary congestion on the turn and then the long flight home. 1,000 planes took part and Essen went up in smoke."

A little over twenty-four hours later, 1,108 aircraft departed their stations in the early afternoon, for the final raid of the war on Dortmund, and this new record would stand to the end of hostilities. 1 Group put up 243 Lancasters for this operation, of which sixteen were provided by Faldingworth. They began taking off shortly after 13.00 led by W/C Jarkowski, and the Polish station commander, G/C Robert Beill, hitched a ride with F/S Szczesny in PD379. The skies were clear as far a Reading, at which point cloud began to build, and the target was hidden by ten-tenths strato-cumulus with tops at around 5,000 feet. Marking began punctually at 16.27, and, although the ground markers could not be seen, blue and green smoke-puff skymarkers were plentiful, and the Master bomber maintained a running commentary throughout the attack to ensure concentration. The 300 Squadron contingent bombed from 16,000 to 19,000 feet between 16.30 and 16.37, and returned safely to report a two-mile-diameter mushroom of black smoke spiralling up through the clouds to 8,000 feet, and still visible from a hundred miles away. A record 4,800 tons of bombes had rained down into mainly central and southern districts, and all production in the factories of this once-proud city ceased.

"Go round again". Today again day flight to the Ruhr—Dortmund. 1,000 planes and us in 'R' – Roger. The same load and almost the same experiences, but today our crew will gain honorary citizenship of the City of Dortmund, if we return, because according to tradition, three flights to the same target entitle the crew to honorary citizenship. We all know that and even the artillery doesn't frighten us, but as it happens there was no artillery over the target. So the mission was accomplished with ease, but there was lack of the experiences for which we were prepared. So the flight seemed like 'cross country', short and comfortable, and after the return a glass of rum and cigarettes await and good food—enough to make flying worthwhile. Another flight added to the tally and one less operational trip. Thanks be to God who protects us. Or maybe it is our destiny, which I firmly believe. All the planes returned."

1 Group continued its involvement in the oil offensive by attacking two Ruhr Benzol producers on the night of the 13/14th. Seventy-five Lancasters were involved at the Erin plant at Herne, while eighty others targeted the Dahlbusch site at Gelsenkirchen. 300 Squadron supported the latter with eleven aircraft, which took off either side of 17.45, and headed for the enemy coast, where the skies were clear and

The artwork on the nose of Lancaster PB705 BH-B depicts a woodpecker pecking the bomb bearing Hitler's face and symbols of 49 missions flown. This particular artwork refers to the crew of Sgt Jozef Bus, who usually flew this aircraft. He is seated by the cockpit window with F.E. Sgt Tadeusz Dzieciol is on the left. Note: the Polish word "dzieciol" means "woodpecker" in English. (PISM via WM)

remained so for the attack. PB705 lost its starboard-outer engine immediately after take-off, and F/S Bus decided to abandon the sortie at 16.25 when at 9,500 feet between Cambridge and Sudbury, when it was realised that the mid-upper and rear turrets were also not working. As always over the Ruhr, industrial haze lay between the target and the bomb-aimers high above, but the first red TIs were seen to cascade at 20.41, and, thereafter, the aiming point was accurately maintained. The crews were unable to pick out ground detail, but Gee and H2S confirmed their position over the aiming point, and the Polish crews each delivered a cookie and sixteen 500 pounders from 15,000 to 16,000 feet between 20.42 and 20.45. They all returned safely, some to report a huge red explosion at 20.46, followed by black smoke, and fires visible well into the return journey. Photo-reconnaissance confirmed the effectiveness of the operation, which was achieved for the loss of a single Lancaster.

"Unlucky 13", I try to avoid this number, but I could not do it today. We have to fly third time in a row. Tonight's target is Gelsenkirchen. In spite of the fact that the last two flights confirmed German decline and weakness of the defence of the Ruhr, today's 'trip' invokes a feeling of foreboding. Perhaps it is the thought that it is '13th' and one has to fly to Gelsenkirchen where there was always artillery fire. I was there once before and I did not like it. The flight itself goes without serious incidents. But it is not the same as yesterday—German artillery is still there and not asleep. The same picture of hundreds and thousands of fires on all levels, but in spite of the number 13 luck is with us. A few successful dodges, full throttle, and the worst moment is in the past. Even the time over the target is not as bad as that just before, when you have time for fear, but when the bomb-aimer shouts "bombs gone", then you feel light hearted, ready for a cup of tea and safe landing at base."

Two nights later over two hundred 1 Group Lancasters were involved in a raid on the Deurag oil refinery at Misburg on the outskirts of Hanover. Ten 300 Squadron crews were briefed, and they were all safely airborne by 17.32. Apart from cloud over the Channel, the skies were clear all the way to the target, and the visibility was sufficiently good for the crews to identify it visually by the light from illuminating flares. The attack began on time with red TIs, followed by accurate salvoes of mixed red and greens. The Master Bomber called in the main force at 21.12, and almost immediately the target became engulfed in flames, the smoke from which rose quickly to 10,000 feet. The Polish crews passed over the aiming point at 17,000 to 19,000 feet between 21.15 and 21.21, and all returned home without incident to report a massive red explosion at 21.16 followed by black smoke, and there was much appreciation for the work done by the Pathfinders. There was some disappointment when photo-reconnaissance revealed that much of the bombing had fallen south of the target.

"One day's break and another flight. I took the opportunity to make my Easter confession. No wonder that I have a good feeling about today's flight, although the target is nothing special, one that I know already—Misburg. It is difficult to describe the flight in a few words. As every flight it is full of familiar emotions—slight pride at the start and return and composure over the Channel towards the target. Almost 6 hours of staring in all directions. The climax is the target itself, beautifully illuminated with millions of lights and fires. After short moments of excitement over the target, short breath before dropping the bombs and then just one thought—to return home safely. I must mention one curious fact: to our crew there has never been any difference whether flying to target or coming back, we never relax our guard and sometimes we are even more careful on return journey, maybe to this fact we owe our good luck and fast approach to 30 flights—the final point of battle career."

Faldingworth, spring 1945. Lancaster PB705 BH-B for Bus. F/S Jozef Bus, whose name was taken as the nickname of the aircraft, is standing 2nd from right. (PISM via WM)

Nuremberg was visited for the last time on the night of the 16/17th by a force of 230 Lancasters from 1 Group, with Pathfinder Lancasters and Mosquitos to provide the marking. 300 Squadron contributed eleven aircraft, with W/C Jarkowski the senior pilot on duty. They got away from Faldingworth shortly after 17.30, and headed into patchy cloud, which became ten-tenths over enemy territory until thinning to four to six-tenths in the target area. Enemy night fighters were active during the outward flight, and they would be largely responsible for the loss of twenty-four 1 Group Lancasters, but none of the Faldingworth element reported contact before reaching the target. An unexpectedly strong tail wind drove some aircraft to the target ahead of schedule, and a proportion of these bombed before the first markers went down. The Pathfinders delivered illuminator flares bang on schedule at 21.24, followed by single red TIs and salvoes of greens, and the Master bomber kept the bombing on track throughout. All but one of the 300 Squadron participants bombed from 16,000 to 20,500 feet between 21.26 and 21.34, and returned home without incident to report a concentrated attack, and fires visible more than a hundred miles into the return trip. F/S Bus and crew found themselves under attack from a night fighter during the bombing run, and had to take violent evasive action, which cost them altitude, and they ultimately bombed from 14,000 feet. Heavy damage was caused in southern and south-western districts, with a number of areas of fire, and more than five hundred people were killed. It was a bad night for the group, to which all of the missing aircraft belonged, and, in human terms, the losses amounted to ninety-four men killed, thirty-eight in captivity and one evader.

"I don't know if it is good or bad but today we fly again. 'R' – Roger seems to be untiring when it comes to flying. Personally I am quite pleased about it in line with the motto: "What is due to hang will not drown". And so today we are going to visit Nuremburg for the second time. To tell the truth it is possibly the worst target to bomb, because of the number of night fighters in that area. We take off at 5.40. The way to the target is not especially dangerous and 'windows' partially protect the line of 230 aircraft. We arrive over the target a little early, so we fly around which is very dangerous. When the target is on fire and thousands of flames and plumes of smoke fill the air between the ground and our flight path 17,000 feet and higher, it is time for us. It feels like a jump into an abyss or hell. It is light as day, here and there a plane, and underneath us a sea of fire and smoke. The city is clearly visible, we are over the centre of it. Artillery guns blast away, another moment, bomb-aimer shouts and the plane is tossed up—have we been hit? —no, it is the bombs going down. These are only short moments, but can there be anything more wonderful? No human eye could see nor memory retain these moments. Sometimes it is only hair-breadth and one plunges to earth—left, right and duck. I can find no words to describe the action. Action of moments and minutes involving thousands of human beings, where the stronger win. This time we belong to them and return safely to our base in Faldingworth. As could be foreseen many planes did not return from this sortie, as usual in the case of Nuremberg. This time 36 planes were lost. Thanks be to God we were not one of them."

Hanau had been attacked on a number of occasions during the war, but never in large numbers until the night of the 18/19th, when it was the destination for 230 Lancasters of 1 Group, in company with Lancasters and Mosquitos of 8 Group. Situated on the Rhine twenty-five miles east of Frankfurt, it had spent much of its existence as a garrison town, and contained railway installations. 300 Squadron briefed thirteen crews, and they began departing Faldingworth at 00.35. There were varying amounts of cloud for most of the outward journey, but the skies cleared for the final leg, and the approaching main force crews saw the first illuminator flares go down five minutes before the scheduled opening of the attack. Immediately thereafter, both sky and ground markers were delivered onto the aiming point, and despite the haze, the crews could clearly see how accurate they were. The Polish crews bombed from 10,000 to 12,000 feet between 04.31 and 04.39, and flew home without incident to report a successful outcome, and the glow of fires visible well into the return journey. Local reports put the level of destruction at 2,240 houses and fifty industrial premises, with damage to all of the municipal, public and historical buildings, while around two thousand people were killed.

An operation to Bremen in the morning of the 21st involved a hundred Lancasters from 1 Group, although none from 300 Squadron, and they attacked in fine conditions to produce accurate and concentrated bombing. It was after midnight on the 22nd when 117 Lancasters from 1 Group began leaving their stations for Bochum to attack the Bruchstrasse Benzol plant, situated south of the city centre. S/L Brogowski led the fourteen 300 Squadron participants, and they took off either side of 01.00 to encounter small amounts of cloud until the French coast, when the skies became clear and remained so for the duration of the attack. PA220 lost its port-outer engine at 03.25 when over the Franco-Belgian border south of Charleroi, and F/S Kalinowski decided to turn back. PD383 was approaching the target with a dead starboard-outer engine, and when the port-outer also began to lose revolutions, F/S Niemiec decided it was time give up. He dropped his bombs from 11,000 feet onto a built-up area on the southern edge of the Ruhr between Krefeld and Mönchengladbach at 04.20, and made it safely home. Meanwhile at Bochum, the ground markers had fallen accurately into an area between the aiming point and the marshalling yards to the south, and the Pathfinders maintained a concentration of markers throughout. The 300 Squadron crews were over the target at 17,000 to 18,000 feet between 04.15 and 04 22, and at debriefing described many fires and smoke rising to 8,000 feet, and the glow from the burning target still visible eighty miles into the return trip. F/L Kozuba-Kozubski and crew reached the target, but NG269 suffered an electrical problem, which prevented the bombs from releasing. Part of the bomb load was jettisoned, and the remainder was dropped on Solingen, south-east of Düsseldorf on the southern edge of the Ruhr at 04.25.

"After nearly a week's rest due to the weather, today tradition was revived that we are a combat wing and not just 'coastal command'. This time the target for bombing mission of 'Mr. Harris' is Bochum. The usual cheerless prognosis for this evening, as this is the well-known Ruhr area, and in addition the late start, at 1.10 at night, define in advance the quality of the flight. In Bochum itself and in that area generally there is always a lot of gun-fire, the defence never sleeps, but in comparison with other targets it is bearable, maybe because it is my 25th flight and I don't react as strongly as before. We arrive over the target at 4.15, and then we start the return journey. As much as the flight to the target was quite uninteresting, the return flight was one of the most beautiful. Can there be anything more beautiful than flying at sunrise? Everything is waking up, and we, like fishermen or huntsmen, are coming back from night hunt. I will never forget this flight above the tops of the clouds. Yes, it really was wonderful and when you fly like that you can't think of anything, danger doesn't exist, only this marvellous dream, beyond human imagination."

Hildesheim was one of a number of Germany's cities to escape attention almost until the end of hostilities, but when its one and only raid came on the afternoon of the 22nd, it did so with terrifying fury at the hands of a 1, 6 and 8 Group heavy force of 220 aircraft. 3,300 apartment blocks were destroyed or seriously damaged, the cathedral and many other public buildings were reduced to rubble, while over sixteen hundred people were killed. 300 Squadron sat this one out having operated during the early morning of this day. 97 Lancasters from the group joined others from 5 Group on the morning of the 23rd to target a bridge at Bremen. Four of the 1 Group element were tasked with windowing, and the remainder with bombing. Thirteen crews from 300 Squadron attended briefing, and S/L Brogowski was the senior pilot on duty as they took off either side of 07.00 into weather conditions described as perfect with excellent visibility. PD361 suffered the failure of its starboard-outer engine as it approached Hull, and Sgt Wojtowicz jettisoned the bomb load over the sea before turning back. PB705 developed a similar problem, and had just crossed the Dutch/German frontier at 14,000 feet at 09.30 when the starboard-inner engine also began to smoke. F/S Bus dropped the bombs onto the town of Nordhorn, and abandoned the sortie. The others reached the target to find a smoke screen in operation, but the prevailing wind kept the aiming point clear. The 5 Group element was to have opened the attack, but arrived a little late, and the first bombs were delivered by the 1 Group spearhead. The 300 Squadron crews identified the aiming point visually, and bombed from 16,000 to 18,000 feet between 10.00 and 10.06. The attack was confined to the immediate target area, where a number of direct hits were observed before smoke obscured ground detail. The flak defence was accurate, and three Faldingworth crews returned with slight damage.

Above: The cartoon cow and the inscription "Pardon me Boys, I am infallible. Iza" pictured on Lancaster ME546 BH-I for Iza. This aircraft managed to take part in 8 operations before the war ended and was flown mostly by the crew of F/S Karpinski. (PISM via WM) Below: The crew of Sgt Jozef Bus (2nd from left) posing in the front of their Lancaster at Faldingworth in the spring of 1945. (Bus family)

The following account is by W/O Gorski. "The object of our attack was a bridge on the Weser River. Northern Germany was under a cold front and visibility was fantastic. Our planned route included a few doglegs. It was done mostly to keep Germans uncertain as to what was the target for our raid, and foil their air defences. At that phase of the war, we had our own escorts, which normally were more numerous than the German fighters sent to attack us. Sometimes we met our Mustangs at certain gathering points where they would fly some 10,000 feet above us, so as not to be tied to our formations. No planes attacked us. Approaching Bremen we flew unmolested as if on parade. Flak stayed quiet, but the city was partially obscured by smoke screens laid on by the city defences. I started my bomb run as the first or second in line to unload. Head to head and some 100 feet on my right flew another Lancaster from one of the British squadrons. About five miles before the target the flak opened up. The first few explosions quickly grew into one giant ball of black smoke with an approximate radius of one mile, and dappled with bright red spots, indicating consecutive detonations. I thought it would be impossible to fly unscathed through that cloud of explosions and I almost panicked, as I was going straight into the middle of it. I was too close to fly under or over it, and making a sudden turn meant missing the target."

"With extreme tension, I decided to hold my course. As soon as I flew into the red-dotted black mass I could hear explosions over the drone of the engines. Shrapnel drummed staccato-like on the fuselage. The Lancaster on my right disappeared. Seconds later I flew out of that mess and into bright sunshine, and I quickly assessed the damage. The inner starboard engine had lost its spinner, but the engine kept running. My side of the windshield was cracked and all of it was blackened so that I could hardly see through it. It impaired my forward vision, and on several occasions I made sudden turns avoiding "phantom" planes that didn't exist. We dropped our bombs, and I took the shortest course for home. Some time later, having left Bremen far behind us, a battery took four very accurate shots at us. The first one exploded right in front of us, the third under the fuselage and the fourth way behind the rear turret. Not even ten minutes later, I saw ahead of us a Me262 flying some 2,000 feet below. It was the first time I had seen one in real life. I put my Lancaster into a shallow dive to give my gunners a chance to take a shot at him. Before they could try their lack with the jet plane, it dived away. Most likely it was out of ammo or had insufficient fuel; otherwise we would had been easy prey for him. That day over Bremen I experienced the most intense AA barrage. Those who followed a few minutes after me, though it to be normal, which told me that its intensity must have lessened quite a bit by then."

As Allied forces began their crossing of the Rhine on the 24th, the Command continued its attacks on oil related targets. The Harpenerweg oil plant at Dortmund was the objective for the afternoon of the 24th, for which 1 Group provided eighty Lancasters, with other aircraft in support from 6 and 8 Groups, but 300 Squadron remained at home. In the early hours of the 25th, crews from 1, 6 and 8 Groups were briefed for what would be the final operation of the war against Hanover. 1 Group contributed 151 Lancasters, including ten belonging to 300 Squadron, and flying with S/L Brogowski was the Polish Bomber Command liaison officer, G/C Dudzinski. There was complete cloud cover as they took off shortly before 07.00 and headed for the exit point at Wainfleet. The skies cleared for the first half of the North Sea crossing, until the cloud built again over the Continent. Fortunately, the cloud dispersed completely before the target was reached, and excellent conditions again prevailed. The crews were able to identify the built-up areas, marshalling yards and the river without difficulty, but also had red TIs to aim at until smoke obscured them from view. At that point the Master Bomber instructed them to bomb on the smoke as directed by him, and a pall rose up to 14,000 feet by the time the force turned away. The Polish crews bombed from 17,000 to 18,000 feet between 09.46 and 09.48, and all returned safely to report a successful attack.

Sgt Drozdz: "Aaaa!" I yawned a couple of times and yelled at the top of my voice that I want to sleep, when Chief Dworniczek was waking us up at 4 a.m. for a mission. But of course I got up, it was something new to get up at daybreak, actually it was still dark, which made it even more exciting. I must admit that it was rather fun to take off so early in the morning, at 6.45. And so began our normal working day. The sun was already warm auguring a fine day. Today's target—Hanover—doesn't look very promising, but at least it's daylight. Even the course of the flight is different—we are just going over the North Sea. This flight, like the one before, looks fabulous—long line of Lancasters raises one's spirits. Although we are passing groups of returning Liberators, their formations seem to be somewhat thinned out, but maybe it just looks like that to me. On the way we plunge into clouds, which is not very nice because of the large number of planes at the same height. But everything turns out all right when we cross the coastline. The clouds have gone so I can observe the ground. Beneath us is Holland—poor country completely flooded. Before Münster we make a turn east and start on our last but one 'leg'. Since the weather and visibility are excellent I observe the ground with interest. In spite of the fact that we are flying quite high traces of front line and battles are plainly visible. I can even see some multi-coloured flecks in front of us, which turned out to be landing area for paratroopers. Hundreds of blue, red and white spots on the carpet of green present a pretty picture. But we pass all that and enter our final leg."

"We make a turn over the River Weser. But this idyll of peace and landscape-watching doesn't last long. We are at the back of the line and the beginning of it approaches the target. It is confirmed by artillery fire. The time to target seems like hours. The file of 'crows' moves closer together like sheep in the face of wolves. We are safe however from the fighter planes, for our Mustangs cover us completely. A few more minutes to the target and suddenly in front of us a sudden flash! What's that? Aha, someone was hit. In front of us left side of fuselage with two engines bursts into fire and smoke, turns left and spirals down. My God! They didn't even have the time to bale out. Everything can be plainly seen. Artillery is going mad—they blast like hell. "Turn right, Janiu!" Oh, in front of us another plane goes down. "Janiu!" Keep more to the right, because on the left it is all smoke, and on the right you can see a town. "Attention! Steady, bombs gone!" yells the bomb-aimer. "Janiu!" Turn right for they are blasting away here, another moment—yes, it's better and safer now, I thought that this devil above us will drop his whole load on us. What a flight! 'Cruising power' that's 2,100 revolutions plus 1 booster, we are descending and chasing the bunch. Now I have time to look back on target—it is enveloped in clouds of smoke and is on fire. We fly on and pass Minden which is the target of another flight—the planes are approaching it and dropping bombs. I have a chance to see it as a spectator—fairly safely. It looks magnificent, maybe the artillery fire is weaker, but the 'show' is just as good. The return journey follows the same course. The same flooded Holland, deserted towns and villages—awful. We land safely just after noon—12.20."

In the early hours of the 27th 1 Group briefed 225 crews for an operation against the town of Paderborn, situated to the north-east of the Ruhr, and in the path of advancing American ground forces. 300 Squadron contributed a dozen Lancasters, which were led away from Faldingworth by W/C Jarkowski at 15.05. Cloud began to build at the Dutch coast, and was ten-tenths by the time the target was reached shortly before 17.30. The Master Bomber was heard to call for blue smoke-puff skymarkers at 17.25, but none was seen until five minutes later, forcing those in the vanguard of the main force to orbit. Once the marking began it was maintained, and the bombing proceeded in accordance with the Master Bomber's instructions. The 300 Squadron crews passed over the aiming point at an average of 17,000 feet between 17.32 and 17.36, and, as they turned away, smoke was beginning to billow up through the cloud tops to 10,000 feet.

"Today again another sortie or 'campaign' as it became generally known in the squadron. Since 'R' is on holiday being overhauled we go in 'O – boy'. Today's flight and target don't appear too sinister. Small town but large railway junction in central Germany—Paderborn—that's today's target. We take off quite early—at 15.15 as we assumed, though for once the assumption and information about the target was fairly accurate. Of course there was some shooting over the target, but it was not proper defence. The whole flight lasted only 4 hours 35 minutes, so it was one of the shortest and least significant. But it was still one flight less to go. Only 8 remained, for now the full tally is 35 flights."

On the 31st the group prepared two hundred Lancasters as part of an overall 1, 6 and 8 Group force of 461 heavy aircraft to target the Blohm & Voss U-Boot yards at Hamburg, where the new Type XXI vessel was under construction. 300 Squadron briefed ten crews, who departed Faldingworth shortly after 06.30, with S/L Brogowski the senior pilot on duty, and G/C Beill flying with F/S Zapasnik. There were varying amounts of cloud during the outward leg, but complete cover over north-western Germany, and as the crews closed in on the target at 08.30, they were warned by the Master Bomber to expect smoke-puff skymarkers. These first appeared at 08.43, and although sparse in the early stages, the Pathfinders maintained the aiming point by backing them up in plentiful numbers, and the bombing proceeded according to the Master Bomber's instructions. The Polish crews attacked from 17,000 to 18,000 feet between 08.46 and 08.50, and returned home safely but uncertain as to the outcome of the operation. Local reports spoke of considerable and widespread damage to housing, factories, energy supplies and communications in southern districts and across the Elbe in Harburg.

G/C Robert Beill. CO of 305 Squadron from Aug. 1941 to Apr. 1942. In 1942/1943 he was commander of RAF Hemswell. Later he assumed the post of Polish Liaison Officer in Bomber Command and, from April 1944, commander of RAF Faldingworth. (PISM via WM)

"I don't know how many times we have to get up so early to fly a sortie. It is quite absurd to rise at 4 a.m. The 'small' room provides an explanation—Hamburg. It is still quite dark as we start up the planes. We take off at 6.30, so quite early. Everything is going well. We don't even notice it is Holy Saturday. "My God" I sigh but orders are orders. Even the whole Bomber Command does not notice the clouds, you have to fly and fly. As it turned out the target was completely covered by clouds, which was good in one way, but then we won't be able to see the target. As usual over the target my legs start to shake, so it is this time, and Hamburg itself adds extra menace. Actually it does not look too bad with the cloud cover, but the rotters take their bearings. We are nearing the target, hails of bullets appear with frenzied speed, there are more and more of them all around us, it gets black. To break the dreadful silence I shout to the bomb-aimer to throw more 'windows'. Doors to the bomb bay are open, the bombs have gone. One toss, then the second—what is this, this is not normal—there should only be one toss. Artillery guns are blasting like the devil, only a moment more—my God, to the left to the right. Rear gunner Władek says he has been hit. We don't believe him at first since he is very calm about it."

"We leave the target area, the guns can't reach us. There is time to talk to Władek who reports that shrapnel struck the turret and his knee. I want to run to the tail to help him, but he says he is O.K., there is no blood. The tension among the crew is rising, but Władek assures us that he is all right. We are fast moving away from the target. The layer of cloud over Hamburg grows bigger from the heat—Hamburg must be aflame, pity we can't see it. I check carefully all the instruments and the whole aircraft to make sure everything is in order. The plane is flying home—no matter that its tail was hit, we will get there with God's help. Last round above the airfield and we are preparing to land. Mother Earth folds us to her breast happily once more. We jump quickly down from the plane, indeed only the turret has been shattered, and Władek gives each one of us a piece of the shrapnel. He is lucky because the shrapnel first struck the frame, bounced off the guns and only then hit Władek's knee, tearing the flying suit and causing a bruise. Had the shrapnel travelled a few more metres and struck the fuel tank we would not be coming back. Of the 400 aircraft 11 did not return."

Thus was concluded the busiest month of the war for 300 Squadron in terms of sorties, which reached a magnificent 201 from sixteen operations for the loss of two aircraft.

Two air-to-air photos of PA308 BH-K. The underwing serials suggest these were taken after the end of the war (Harry Holmes).

April 1945

April would prove to be the final month of the bombing war for the heavy brigade, and operations began for 1 Group on the 3rd, with a daylight attack on what was believed to be a military barracks near the town of Nordhausen. Located a hundred miles west of Leipzig and ninety miles south-east of Hanover, it was, in fact, a camp for forced workers at the underground secret weapons factory, which had been established after Peenemünde. 210 Lancasters were made ready, including fourteen at Faldingworth, which took off either side of 13.30 and headed into five to seven-tenths cloud, which would thicken to ten-tenths by the time the target was reached. The aircraft flew out in formation, which held well until approaching the target at 16.02, when the Master Bomber called for them to descend to below the cloud base at 8,500 feet. They had reached the cloud tops at around 10,000 feet when the Master Bomber amended his instructions and told them to climb again. The cohesion of the formation was lost as a result, and even though an attempt was made during the run-in to tighten up for the sake of concentration, this was not achieved. To make matters worse, the smoke-puff skymarkers burst in the clouds and could not be seen, and the Master Bomber was forced to instruct the crews to "bomb on best navigational aids". The 300 Squadron participants were over the aiming point at 13,000 to 14,000 feet between 16.12 and 16.19, and returned safely without being able assess the results. One Lancaster did bomb from beneath the clouds, and reported two small fires, one in the north-west of the town, and the other in the south-west near the marshalling yards, but the impression was of an unsuccessful operation.

"So the festivities (Easter) are now over. As usual a lot of preparations and noise and today again we are a bomber squadron. The flight to Nordhausen—a large railway junction in central Germany. For quite a long time we have been looking for these junctions, which in fact is not so bad, because they are usually less defended. Although this is true, still out of 200 planes 3 have not come back. The target itself was relatively weakly defended, but there were a lot of fighters. Personally I haven't seen any and without any incidents 'O – boy' completed our 29th mission, this would have been our last but one flight—Boy oh boy!" 5 Group would carry out an operation on the following day, which would be successful, but would cause heavy casualties among the friendly foreign nationals in the hastily constructed wooden barracks.

"4th April, 1945 — Faldingworth. Old 'Rogers' i.e. my crew are getting ready for a holiday. It is fortunate—now we are going on holiday and afterwards we will fly our 6 missions, which at worst should take 3 weeks, and then holiday again—this time for 10 days, after completing our full complement. But... that moment is still far, far away, and there are still 6 chances that we may not return—isn't it maybe too much? Immediately before setting off on holiday I learned from today's orders that the President of Poland awarded the Military Cross of Valour to our crew, and so to me as well. This longed-for moment finally arrived, though it should have come a month ago. And haven't you dreamt about it Henryk? 'Valour in Action'. It is an odd thing that everything I have ever dreamt about is coming true."

On the night of the 4/5th a 1 Group force of 238 Lancasters teamed up with an 8 Group element to attack the Wintershall oil refinery at Lützkendorf, another site, like Leuna, near Merseburg, west of Leipzig. 300 Squadron briefed twelve crews, but two were withdrawn before take-off because of aircraft unserviceability. The remainder got away safely by 21.30, but a lengthy forming-up process meant that it took almost four-and-a-half hours to reach the target area. Despite varying amounts of cloud over the Continent, the skies were found to be quite clear, with only haze to compromise the otherwise perfect visibility. The first Pathfinder ground markers went down at 01.25, and were easily identified by the crews flying at up to 15,000 feet above. The Polish element bombed from between 12,000 and 15,000 feet between 01.28 an 01.35, and returned to comment that the attack seemed to be concentrated on the markers. A large red explosion was observed at 01.30, followed by much smoke, and the glow of fires could be seen from a hundred miles away. Photo-reconnaissance revealed that the plant had not been decisively damaged, but an attack by 5 Group on the night of the 8/9th would bring an end to all production at the site.

300 Squadron now enjoyed a few nights at home following its most intense period of operations since forming in July 1940. In fact, the entire group was stood down until the night of the 9/10, when 256 Lancasters were made ready to carry out a raid on Kiel in concert with 335 others from 3 and 8 Groups. 300 Squadron briefed sixteen crews, but that captained by F/S Szczesny was withdrawn after the senior intelligence officer informed the commanding officer that they had already completed their tour of operations. The remaining fifteen took off either side of 20.00 led by S/L Brogowski, and they flew out in largely clear conditions, which persisted over the target. The illuminator flares went down on time, enabling the crews to visually identify the fjord and harbour, and red TIs marked out the two aiming points. The Faldingworth contingent delivered their cookie and sixteen 500 pounders each from 14,000 to 20,000 feet between 22.31 and 22.41, and all but one returned safely to report concentrated bombing, and fires visible up to 150 miles away. Photo-reconnaissance confirmed that the attack had inflicted severe damage on the Deutsche Werke U-Boot yards, capsized the surface raider Admiral Scheer, and damaged the Admiral Hipper and the Emden. Only three Lancasters failed to return, and among them was LM632, which was hit by flak over the target and crashed into the sea, killing S/L Rudakowski and his crew. S/L Rudakowski rank was actually "acting", since his promotion and elevation to B Flight commander on the 22nd of March.

On the night of the 10/11th a 1 Group main force of 253 Lancasters was sent to the town of Plauen, close to the Czech frontier and fifty miles south-west of Chemnitz. The target was the railway yards in the northern half of the town, but the attack would inevitably cause substantial destruction in adjacent districts, and render it effectively an area raid. Fifteen 300 Squadron Lancasters took off, led away by W/C Jarkowski at 18.29, and they undertook the long outward journey under clear skies that persisted all the way. The crews were able to identify the river and built-up area as they approached, and Pathfinder illuminator flares went down on time right across the town. These were followed at 23.04 by red TIs, which were backed up three minutes later by greens, and the Polish crews bombed from 16,000 to 19,500 feet between 23.08 and 23.19. The markers were soon obliterated, and the Master Bomber instructed the crews to bomb on the smoke, which was billowing up to 10,000 feet. Explosions and fires could be seen well into the return trip, and photo-reconnaissance confirmed that the railway yards in the northern half of the town had been hit, and 51% of the town's built-up area destroyed. NN746 lost its starboard-outer engine over north-eastern France on the way home, but Sgt Gorski and crew brought it safely back.

"13th April, 1945 — Faldingworth. I still haven't "recovered" from the holiday and the loss of my friend Olek and I learned from today's papers of the death of the American President, Franklin Delano Roosevelt. It was really unexpected not just for me but for the whole world. His deputy, Truman, became automatically the new President of the United States. Besides those two facts there was a third one—personally the most important—for while on holiday we "executed" 3 battle missions. It looks really funny, but during our holiday 'Bomber Command' i.e. Mister 'Bomber' Harris, reduced the first operation tour to 33 flights, therefore for our crew there remained only 4 flights to complete the course. Three flights mean a lot to us—the danger was reduced by half—thanks be to God."

The final area raid on a city target was directed at Potsdam by elements of 1, 3 and 8 Groups on the night of the 14/15th, and this would be the first time since March 1944 that RAF heavy bombers had conducted an operation within the Berlin defence zone. 1 Group contributed 215 Lancasters to this operation, while twenty-four from 576 Squadron carried out a spoof raid on Cuxhaven as a diversion. 300 Squadron dispatched fifteen aircraft, which were all safely off the ground by 18.28, each carrying a cookie and ten 500 pounders. They climbed into fairly heavy cloud, which persisted until east of the Rhine, when it began to disperse and disappear altogether. The marking commenced on time, six minutes before "H" hour, with illuminating flares and red TIs, and the early crews were able to identify the built-up area and surrounding lakes. Some of the initial markers were a little scattered, but the Master Bomber kept a firm grip on proceedings, and ensured that the bombing was aimed at the most accurate ones. The Polish crews bombed from 18,000 to 20,000 feet between 22.50 and 22.57, and on return reported fires and smoke covering the entire target area. Sgt Gorski and crew also mentioned having to take evasive action during the bombing run to avoid a collision with another Lancaster. Severe damage occurred in the city, where military barracks and railway installations had been the main objective, and it has been suggested, although not confirmed, that as many as five thousand people lost their lives. Some of the bombing also spilled over into northern and eastern districts of Berlin itself.

"When we entered the briefing room our hair stood on end for the flag marking today's target was pinned to... Potsdam. Nothing less than the capital of the Third Reich—Berlin. Was it the realisation of my dreams; to bomb the capital of Germany? It was, and nothing short of cancellation would change it. There was no cancellation and we take off at 18.15. The flight as far as Frankfurt was peaceful, then there was change—searchlights, flares and occasional artillery fire. The weather isn't too good—it is fairly cloudy, which increases the risk of collision, so you have to be more watchful. My heart is hammering at the thought of nearing the target. Yes, the 'pathfinders' illuminated the target and unleashed hell. It takes place on the ground and in the air. Hundreds of searchlights, flares and smokes. The 'markers' went down—there are masses of little red stars, now the planes one after another arrive over the target. The passing moments seem like hours and we are still not over the target. The speed is 170 miles and it seems to me like snail's pace. Artillery is ever nearer, I get up from my seat and draw my parachute closer—my one hope of salvation. My legs shake, the searchlights have found us, but we duck slightly and fly on. Not long now, artillery blasts all the time, thousands of flashes all around us, and on the ground exploding 'cookies'. We are near, we can see the target—the city—quite clearly. The artillery is going mad, the plane is tossed about, but we can see all the streets of the city as if it was daylight. Another moment, the artillery fires straight at us—we won't escape. A plane on the right, another on the left—Attention! — artillery from the right, another second—God— "bomb doors open". Now we are over the centre of the city—steady—"bombs gone" — a strong toss of the plane... and we dive down on full throttle. 19,500, 19,000, 18,000... we descend safely, artillery still blasts but not so accurately. We are saved, but don't drop our guard of the plane on our right, Janiu, reports that a Lancaster passed by us very near. We enter the clouds which is dangerous but unavoidable at this height. We leave the clouds and make haste for home. After landing safely at the base we share our experiences and emotions. It is the same after every flight and we have completed 30 of them. If the rules hadn't changed it would mean the end of our allocation, but now we still have 3 flights left. My dream of bombing Berlin is now past history."

Over nine hundred aircraft were prepared to take part in a lunchtime attack on the island of Heligoland on the 18th, for which 1 Group contributed a record 311 Lancasters, including seventeen representing 300 Squadron, led by W/C Jarkowski. Two aiming points had been assigned to the force, and the first, aiming point B, the docks and U-Boot pens on the southern end of the Island, were the preserve of 1 Group. The

Faldingworth contingent took off either side of 10.30, and they flew out in perfect weather conditions of clear skies and excellent visibility. Between the final turning point and the target a layer of cloud slid in to obscure it, but by the time the leading aircraft reached the Island the cloud had gone. The deputy Master Bomber was heard to say that he was unable to mark the aiming point, but this did not matter as the first bombs fell a minute ahead of schedule. So concentrated was the bombing, that any markers would have been obliterated before the bulk of the force arrived, and the Master Bomber directed the bombing from port to starboard of the smoke to ensure a complete coverage of the southern half of the island. The Polish crews delivered their twelve 1,000 and four 500 pounders each from 17,000 to 19,000 feet between 12.49 and 12.55, and the whole area erupted under the bombardment. A massive explosion occurred in the docks area at 12.47, followed by a column of black smoke rising to a 1,000 feet, and this was clearly from an oil fire. A few minutes later the northern half received similar treatment, and many crews noted a huge explosion, believed to be from an ammunition dump. As the massive force retreated it left behind it a heavily cratered and scarred surface that resembled a moonscape.

"At 4 a.m. reveille for a battle mission. Personally I like these early starts for I love day-time flights, they are not so boring. Briefing room reveals the target—Heligoland. It is not such enticing flight on account of thousands of gun barrels and hundreds of fighter planes. It was like that last time in 1941. It is a long time ago, but still it is a big "unknown" and somewhat sinister. Loaded like camels we drive to the planes, but we don't board them straightaway as we have a bit of time. After doing my 'inspection' I board the plane (always the first on and last after the flight) that is my function. The weather is absolutely magnificent. Here and there you can hear the engines being started. The crew are about to board the plane when Major Rogalski (from Intelligence) arrives and tells us to get off. We don't understand what is going on because we can hear other engines working, but he says that for our crew the flights are finished, because 'Bomber Command' reduced the total number of flights to 30. The news was greeted with enthusiasm—no more flying. After a while the planes get ready to take off—we wave them goodbye, they know why we are not going. We wish them "very happy landing" and "many, many happy returns", as it was for us. For the last time I get off the plane, solemnly kiss 'R - Roger' and we depart for a glass of rum. Long live our bit of luck and... God's help! As it happened all the planes returned from this mission, there was no artillery or fighter planes and the small island next to Heligoland itself sank."

As the British XXX Corps prepared to enter Bremen, 767 aircraft from 1, 3, 6 and 8 Groups were sent to attack its south-eastern suburbs on the 22nd. 1 Group put up 271 Lancasters, including fourteen belonging to 300 Squadron, and they took off shortly after 15.30 to encounter generally cloudy conditions which persisted all of the way to the target. PB730 turned back at 17.00 with a dead port-outer engine. The rest pressed on, listening out for the Master Bomber as they approached the target area. Conditions over the aiming point were far from ideal, with cloud almost completely obscuring the ground, and dust and smoke from the first-wave bombing adding to the problem. The deputy Master Bomber concluded that further marking was impossible, and at 18.11 the raid was halted after 195 aircraft had bombed. The entire 1 and 6 Group elements were sent home, and the 300 Squadron crews jettisoned their loads into the sea.

The 25th brought the final offensive operations by the heavy squadrons, and the day's activities began in the morning with an attack by 1, 5 and 8 Groups on the SS barracks at Hitler's Eaglesnest retreat at Berchtesgaden in the Bavarian mountains. 1 Group contributed 247 Lancasters, including fourteen provided by 300 Squadron, led by W/C Jarkowski. He was first away from Faldingworth at 05.20, and had with him as second pilot, F/S Suwala, whose maiden operation was to have been against Bremen, but had been cancelled before take-off. The route out was cloud free, and the conditions over the target were perfect for precision bombing, but the marking was not proceeding according to plan. As the leading wave approached the target, no marking had taken place, and the wave leader overshot the final turning point by two-and-a-half minutes, before making a wide orbit to get back on track. Unfortunately, this split up the formation, and aircraft began approaching the aiming point on a variety of headings. At 19.41 the deputy Master Bomber was heard to say that he was unable to mark the target, and at 09.45 the Master Bomber instructed the crews to bomb visually. However, a minute later a red TI went down accurately, although no instructions were given in relation to this. The Polish crews, like most, bombed visually, doing so from 16,500 to 19,000 feet between 09.49 and 09.58, and the consensus was of a successful operation. W/C Jarkowski bombed on his second pass, having failed to identify the aiming point on his first. PD383 was hit by flak over the target, and F/L Witkowski pulled off an outstanding emergency landing at Juvincourt airfield in north-eastern France.

Offensive operations had now ended for 1 Group, and the remaining two weeks of war would see it involved in humanitarian duties. The first flights under Operation Exodus, to ferry PoWs back home, took place on the 27th, when forty-six Lancasters were sent to Brussels. Bad weather intervened, however, and only twenty-two sorties were successful, bringing home 503 men. On the following day forty aircraft brought back another 901 former PoWs. 300 Squadron dispatched ten Lancasters, but they were ordered not to land on the Continent, and were recalled to base. NN718 was damaged by hitting the surface of the sea, and was landed by F/L Adamowski on airfield A58, and abandoned there. He and his crew were ferried home as passengers. On the 29th 145 Lancasters from the Group took part in Operation Manna, and successfully carried out food drops to the starving Dutch people still under enemy occupation. Sgts Gierejkiewicz and Gryglewicz and their crews represented 300 Squadron in this magnificent humanitarian work. 269 aircraft returned on the 30th, including twelve from 300 Squadron, and the efforts to feed the Dutch continued on each day thereafter, except for the 6th of May, up to and including the 8th, the day on which the war in Europe officially came to an end. Operations to repatriate former PoWs continued throughout the month of May. April's operational tally for 300 Squadron amounted to 114 sorties from eight operations and the loss of a single aircraft.

Above: Lancaster BH-V takes part in the last combat sortie of 300 Squadron crews. The target was Hitler`s Headquarters at Berchtesgaden on 25th April 1945. (H. Stawicki via W. Zmyslony). Below: Aerial photograph taken during the last operation by the crew of F/L Pruszynski in Lancaster SW279 BH-E. (JC).

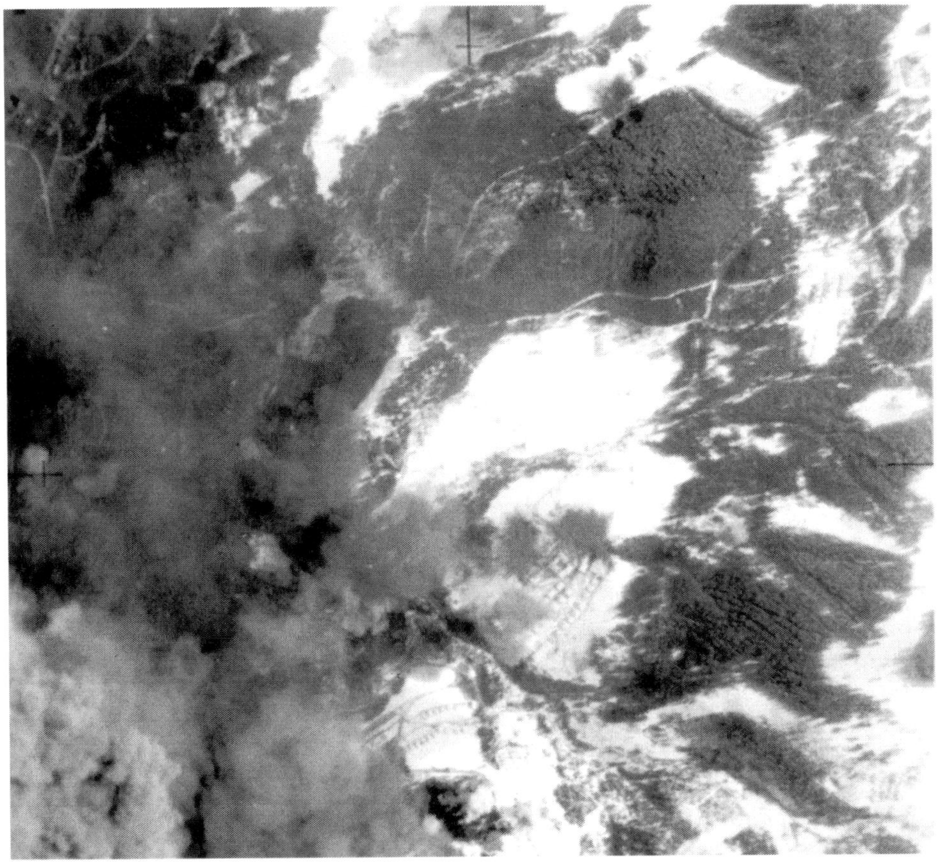

Above: Faldingworth, April/May 1945. One of 300 Squadron Lancasters taking part in Operation Manna, ME546 BH-I, being loaded with supplies. Below left: A picture of a bell boy carrying a bomb inscribed with letter "O" adorns the nose of Lancaster LM632 BH-O "Oh, Boy!" The aircraft was lost with her entire crew on its 51st operation with 300 Squadron. (PISM via WM). Below right: ACM Sir Norman Bottomley, who in September 1945 followed ACM Sir Arthur Harris as C-in-C Bomber Command, during the inspection of 300 Squadron at Faldingworth. Note the Polish pilot badge on his uniform. (PISM)

A Final Word from Greg Korcz

The celebration of the fifth anniversary of the formation of 300 Squadron took place on the 1st of July. The A-O-C 1 Group, AVM Blucke, was among the invited quests together with the commander of the Polish Air Force, AVM Izycki. During the official part of the celebration many aircrew were awarded with Polish and British decorations. Another change in command of the squadron took place on the 17th of August with the departure of W/C Jarkowski and the appointment of W/C Sulinski.

The entire second part of 1945 was spent by 300 Squadron predominantly on training flights and delivering supplies and medical supplies to the continent. Polish crews participated also in various air operations: Wastage, (the dumping of unnecessary bombs in the North Sea), Post Mortem, (exercises to assess the efficiency of the German radar and flak systems), and Dodge, (the transporting of allied troops from the Mediterranean area to the UK). One of these flights ended in a tragedy on the 5th of November, when PD383 disappeared without trace on the way from Italy to the UK, with the crew of F/S Warcholek and twenty British soldiers.

The beginning of 1946 was also not incident-free, and engine failure caused F/S Robaszewski to force-land NG269 near Normanby le Wold in Lincolnshire during training flight on the night of the 7/8th of January. Four of the crew, including the pilot, were killed, and the other two sustained injuries. Nearly a month later, on the 4th of February, another tragedy took place, when, despite adverse weather conditions, PA269 took off for a training flight with W/C Sulinski at the controls. An hour into the flight they encountered a very violent electrical storm, and it seems that the Lancaster was struck by a thunderbolt and plunged out of control to the ground near Wigston Magna in Leicestershire, killing all on the board. On 22th of February W/C Jarkowski was again appointed to the command of 300 Squadron. For the remainder of the year the Polish crews spent their time on training flights and day-to-day duties. On the 11th of November the squadron was inspected by the commander-in-chief of Bomber Command, ACM Sir Norman Bottomley. That day brought the official confirmation of the disbandment of the Squadron. During the ceremony the final air parade of 300 Squadron Lancasters was observed by invited guests. It was the official farewell to the gallant Polish crews. Shortly afterwards the remaining Polish personnel at Faldingworth began to depart the station, while the Lancasters were delivered to maintenance units to be struck off charge and ultimately broken up.

On the 2nd of January 1947 the Air Ministry officially approved the disbandment of 300 Squadron. This was the end for the first Polish squadron to have been formed in Britain, and which had fought gallantly and indefatigably against Germany together with its British and Commonwealth comrades until the very end of the hostilities. The squadron had the distinction of carrying out the most operations on Wellingtons in 1 Group, and the most sorties.

During the entire service of 300 Squadron, 408 Polish and twenty-four British and Commonwealth aircrew members lost their lives on operations, the highest figure among all Polish squadrons in the UK. They did not consider themselves to be heroes, but simply tried to do their best to fulfil the responsibilities placed upon them. They risked their lives each night when flying on operations, and they paid the ultimate price for it. It is the price of freedom, and their sacrifice should not be forgotten.

Escape and Evasion Reports

The following is the report of the observer, F/O Taras. "At 18.40 hours on 7 Nov 41 we left Hemswell to bomb Mannheim. *(The report actually states Munich in error).* We dropped our bombs on the target at 21.15 hours. As we neared Calais on the return journey, we ran into the light of about 40-50 searchlights. They switched off for a moment and then switched on again accompanied by heavy fire from flak, probably 35 and 75mm. The second hit got the petrol tank and the engine stopped. We baled out. The crew were: Sgt Nowakowski, first pilot, (believed PoW), P/O Radwanski, (second pilot), Sgt Kudelko, W/Op (in German hands), Sgt Iwanowicz, air gunner, (believed in enemy hands), Sgt Chrzanowski, rear gunner, (told he was at St Hippolyte).

I landed in the country near Calais, but there was a very strong wind and my parachute opened late, so that I broke some bones in my foot. I hid my parachute and made inland. For the next 48 hours I moved only at night, and hid during the day, but owing to my damaged foot progress was very slow. On the 10 Nov I spoke to a boy and told him who I was. He told me to wait, returning within an hour with his father and a wheelbarrow. I was taken to a farm behind a big house, where I was kept for six days. The owner of the house gave me civilian clothes and money. While I was there a priest came to the house and brought a French identity card for me. On 16 Nov my friend and his daughter took me to le Pont sans Pareil, where we took a train to Lille. There the daughter bought a ticket to Dole. I was four days on the way. Without maps and with a bad foot I thought it would be hard to cross the demarcation line. I went to a church, where I stayed eight hours. While I was there I tried to persuade the priest to help me, but he was afraid of the Gestapo. I had to leave the church when it was closed for the night, and that evening took a train to Belfort.

20 Nov Nancy. As I considered this town dangerous owing to controls, I left for Nancy, arriving there at 18.00. I went to sleep in the waiting room. At 01.00 hrs a German sergeant came in and asked for my papers. I said "Je ne comprends pas," and the German took me to the station master. I told the latter I had arrived late, and owing to the blackout was waiting until morning before trying to find my family. I showed him my identity card, but he knew I was not French, so I told him I was Polish. He then told the German that I was waiting for a train to Charleville. The German went away, and I went to the Prefecture de Police. There I found the Chef de Division, and, as he was wearing French medals, I told him my whole story. He advised me to stay in a small hotel near the Prefecture for the night, and to make for Besancon in the morning. He also told me that when I reached unoccupied France, I was not to say that I was RAF, but to say that I was an escaper from a German camp.

I spent the night in a small hotel, where I was given a meal, although I had no food card. I had been living on fruit. Next morning I took the train to Besancon. There I was taken to a house. In the evening a man arrived with a lorry. He had been in the French Air Force in the last war. He took me to a small farm near the Line of Demarcation, where I spent two nights. On 25 Nov he drove me to the Line of Demarcation near a wood. I went on alone through this small wood for about two kilometres, and saw Chamblay on my right. I walked on to Vaudrey, some eight kilometres further. There I went to the Gendarmerie, where I said I was an escaper from a German camp. They gave me a bus ticket to Lons-le Saunier, and a train ticket to Lyons, and told me to report to the Polish Demobilisation Camp.

Above: 300 Squadron Lancasters photographed during the squadron's last flight over Lincolnshire on 11th November 1946. (JC). Below: Another picture of formation of Polish Lancasters in their farewell fly past with Polish and British flags in the foreground. (Jacukiewicz family)

On arriving at Lyon I contacted a man, who arranged for me to go to the Spanish frontier, but as I knew I could not cross the Pyrenees by foot, I went to Marseilles, where I went to the English hospital, now used by Poles. I reached there on 2 Dec and stayed until 21 Feb. On 20 Dec I visited the US Consul, but he would not help. Later I went to Perpignan, but as the town was full of Gestapo, I returned to Marseilles. In Jan 42 I was introduced to an organisation, and from then my story corresponds with that of Major Challoner." F/O Taras eventually reached Gibraltar, departing there on the 27th of April 1942, and arriving in Liverpool on the 8th of May 1942.

The following is the report of P/O Radwanski, second pilot in the above crew. "I came down at 00.50 hours in the country near le Beau Marais. I remained in hiding for two days near a farm where the German Kommandatur was. I did not contact anyone there, and on 10 Nov I decided to get away from the coast. I started off due south across country, holding my line by the compass I had with me. My route led me through Coulogne and Les Attacques (where there were many Germans) to le Pont sans Pareil. I travelled by night as I still wore my uniform. There was a German guard on the canal bridge at this place, so I spent the night in hiding near a very big sugar refinery between the railway line and the canal. I remained in hiding the next day until I saw a French boy near a farm. This boy took me to his father at the farm. In exchange for £2 he gave me 260 Francs. Next night he took me across the canal by boat at about 19.00 hours. I was told by these people that 2 hours before I reached the farm another RAF man had been captured. This was our W/Op.

I continued across country by compass through Tournehem, Bonngues to Lumbres, which I reached at 06.00 hours next morning. I hid near Lumbres till 17.00 hours, then went across country to Clery, where I found a guard at the crossroads. I called at a house nearby, where the people gave me food and showed me the way to Fauquembergues. I met little traffic at night apart from a few military patrols. I carried on through Fruges to Anvin. On the way I tried to find some place to sleep, but all barns etc. were locked up. At Anvin I saw a girl at a big house near the railway station and asked her for help. She seemed afraid and went away, but in a short time her father appeared and took me to his house, where I stayed a day and a night. There I was given food, money and some civilian clothes. On 13 Nov this man and myself went by bicycle to St Pol. I was given a ticket to Amiens via Arras. Instead of taking the train from Arras, however, I walked through Bapaume to Albert and then to Clery, which I reached at 14.00 hours on the 14 Nov.

At Clery I found four branches of the Somme, the last of which I could not cross. I went to a farm nearby and asked for help, and that night the man took me to the bank of the Somme, where he broke loose his neighbour's boat and ferried me across. The canal beyond, I crossed quite easily at a mill, and carried on to Roye, which I reached at 06.00 hours. At the station there I heard workers talking in Polish and spoke to them. They took me with them in the workers' train, and one of them came right on with me to Compiegne, where I got a train to Paris at 10.00 hours. In Paris I stayed with a friend for about 3 weeks. While there I was given a French identity card and demobilisation card.

On 6 Dec I took a train to Poitiers, and from there took a bus to Gencay. On the bus I was spoken to by a Frenchman, who then realised that I was not French. As two German soldiers were sitting the other side of me, I gave the Frenchman a hint of my identity, and he stopped talking. On arrival at Gencay he brought the driver of the bus, and asked him to take me on to St Secondin, where the bus was garaged. At St Secondin I stayed in a sort of hotel for a night. Next morning at 11.00 hours the driver came and said the

German patrols were drinking in his house, and that I could walk through the barrier which was now unguarded. I did so with five Belgians. I gave the driver 200 Francs, which he was unwilling to take. I walked on to Montmorillon, and there went to an hotel, where I spent the night and was given food, though I had no food card.

Next morning I got a train at 05.10 hours for Lyons, intending to try to find friends there, but left next day for Marsailles, as I was stopped twice for my identity card and considered it rather dangerous. I lived six days in an hotel, but was unable to contact help and left on 16 Dec for Annemasse. There I stayed in an hotel until 02.00 hours, when I left for Geneva on foot. I had no difficulty on the way, though I went very slowly to avoid running into the many policemen along the route. I reached Geneva at 06.00 hours and went to the British Consulate. I remained in Geneva till March 42, by which time I had arranged a rendezvous with a Frenchman across the frontier. I had obtained a rather poor French identity card, and met him on the frontier. He took me to a house nearby for the night. Next day we took a train to Annemasse. While walking along the street we were stopped by French civil police and arrested. We were taken to the Commissariat Speciel and interrogated. We were then sent to Lyons and thence to Aix-en-Provence to the Special Intelligence Service of the French Air Force. There I was interrogated by a man who said he had been in England and knew all about aircraft aerodromes, etc. He was very friendly, but I told him nothing.

I was then sent to the barracks of the 156 Colonial Infantry Regiment, where I remained for six days. From 06.00 to 20.00 hours I was kept in the guardroom, and then shut up in a room on the second floor for the night. While I was in the guardroom a French officer used to come and chat to me. He spoke perfect English, and at first I though he was trying to pump me, but on the sixth day he told me I was to be sent to St Hippolyte and advised me to escape. I had already mapped out a route out of the barracks, and he described the route from the barracks to Marseilles. I had got the officer to buy me a knife, and that night I unscrewed the window of my room, crossed to the roof of the next house, which was a single-storey building, and then climbed down by means of scaffolding left by painters. I found no difficulty in getting out of the barracks as there was no guard. I made my way to Marseilles, which I reached on 23 Mar. There I contacted an organisation, and was sent to Toulouse on 27 Mar. From there I went to Banyuls on 2 Apr, and crossed the Pyrenees with five Polish soldiers. We took a train to Barcelona, where I stayed 11 days. I went on to Madrid, and thence to Gibraltar. I remained six days there, and left on 27Apr for the United Kingdom."

Sgt A Malecki, wireless operator in Z1276 captained by F/O Fusinski. "We left Hemswell at 22.00 on 27 Apr 42 to bomb Cologne. We were shot down before we reached there by three Messerschmitt 110s. The aircraft was set well-alight, so we baled out. I landed on a hillside somewhere near Givet. I spent a day and a night in the district, hiding most of the time. On 30 Apr in the afternoon, I met a man working in the fields. I told him who I was, and asked him for food and clothes, which he said he would bring that evening. I waited till 21.00 hours, but he did not come, I therefore decided to make south on my own, and that night I crossed the River Meuse just south of Givet by an old boat, which I found on the bank. I marched south by compass for five days, mainly through woods, till I found myself on the road just east of Charleville. During this time I had lived mostly on Horlicks tablets and chocolate. At this point I was arrested by a gendarme, whose attention was attracted to me by my unshaven and unkempt appearance. He did not search me, but locked me in an upstairs room in a house. I had with me a small saw, with which I managed to cut out the lock after about three hours work, and left the house safely.

I walked all that night and came to some farms in the morning. I saw some German soldiers at the first, and tried the second one, thinking they would not be there also. The people gave me a jacket, shoes and some food. They warned me not to go near Reims, as the Germans were on the look-out, having found five parachutes near Charleville. They advised me to cross the Line of the Zone Interdite near Vouziers. I therefore carried on south, mainly on side roads, for several days until I reached the River Aisnes at Vouziers. The bridge there had a German sentry at both ends, so I swam the river and continued south to Suippes. There I got some food at a house, where I was told that the US Consul was leaving Lyon because of trouble over the seizure of Madagascar. I therefore determined to make for Switzerland instead. I am not quite sure how long this took me. I lived on what little food I got from people I met and what I could pick up myself, such as an occasional chicken. I very seldom called at houses. The route I followed was Bar-le-Duc, Lamarche, Bourbonnes-les-Bains, Vesoul, Villersexel, Clerval and Maiche. The latter town was within 10 kms of the Franco-Swiss frontier. I tried to cross the frontier several times at different points in this district, but owing to the size of the river and the presence of Germans at all possible crossing places, I had to give up the attempt, and I turned back towards the demarcation line, which I managed to cross just below Arbois, near Poligny, on 21May.

As I had now been walking for over three weeks, I was very tired, so I called at a farm and asked them to help. When they heard I was Polish they passed me on to a Yugoslav at another farm. I told him I was making for Lyons, and he wrote out my particulars, including that I was RAF, and advised me to go to Lons-le-Saunier to the Commissariat Speciel, who would help me. When I reached there I was kept for three days, but as my Yugoslav friend had put down that I was RAF, they would not help me, but sent me to Lyons by car. I was taken to a café, where I was met by a civilian, who gave me some food, then took me to a building full of gendarmes. In a room there he put a number of questions to me such as; is food scarce in England? Is there any petrol shortage? In answer to the latter question I told him that when I went on leave, if there was no good railway route, my S/Ldr sent me by aircraft. This man then suggested that I should go back to England, and write him regular accounts about the situation there. He seemed especially interested in the US Army. He said he would make arrangements about censorship. If I did not agree, he said I would be interned. I asked him to give me time to think, so he said he would bring me a form to sign. When he walked out of the door I followed immediately behind him, and as he turned right, I turned left down a corridor. I walked out and passed the guard, and took to my heels. I was able to get in touch with people in the district, who arranged for my passage back to the UK."

An addendum to this report recorded on the 13th of July 1942 reads as follows. "At Lyons I went to the US Consulate, and was sent from there by the organisation to Marseilles, where I met F/O Krawczyk and Sgt Polesinski. After a day in Marseilles we were taken to Nimes (2 days) and then on to Toulouse. From there Sgt Polesinski and I were sent on our own to report at a hotel in Osseja. At Osseja we were stopped by a police patrol, who took us with them to their station. We were put in a room and told to wait. They took our papers and food, and locked it in the next room. We were then left alone, and immediately broke into the next room, recovered our papers and food and left the building. We hid in bushes on the outskirts of Osseja till nightfall, when we went to the hotel we had been told of. There we found a guide who took us to a farm near the border, where we found F/O Krawczyk and six others. We crossed the Pyrenees and took a train to Barcelona and then to Gibraltar."

Another evader from this aircraft was the second pilot, P/O Wasik. What follows, however, is his account of his second escape and evasion adventure, which began on the 29th of August 1944. "We left Faldingworth on 29 Aug 44 at 21.11 in a Lancaster aircraft, but before we reached our target, we were attacked by enemy aircraft. Our aircraft exploded in the air. I was thrown clear and landed in the water about two miles from Alstrup (Denmark) early on 30th Aug. I sank my parachute and harness in the water, and managed to swim ashore. I later hid my Mae West. On reaching shore I was exhausted, and went to sleep in a rowing boat until sunrise. I then went to a church, but there was no one there, so I stayed in the churchyard all day. I then approached a farmer, who gave me food, but he was afraid, and said he would have to telephone the police. I went to the stable and stayed there a while. In the middle of the night I walked into the village, and contacted a man who gave me civilian clothes and a bicycle, and directed me to the village of Ranum. On arrival at Ranum I got in touch with a man who sent me to Aalborg. A few miles out of Aalborg I contacted a member of an underground organisation, and stayed there until 2nd Sep. I was then sent to the village of Praestbro, where I stayed until 8 Sep. On 8 Sep I went to Saeby, stayed one night, and then crossed the sea to Varberg in Sweden. I reported to the police, who kept me in Varberg for two days, and then sent me to a civilian Polish refugee camp at Florsberg, near Sodenhamn, where I stayed until 22 Sep. On 23rd Sep I managed to contact the British Legation in Stockholm, who took care of me. I left Sweden by air on 27 Sep.

The entire crew of F/O Jones baled out over Sweden during the same operation as above, and a number of the crew provided the following reports. Sgt Whitworth, rear gunner. "We took off from Faldingworth at 20.00 on 29 Aug 44 in a Lancaster aircraft. I baled out at 01.00 hours on 30 Aug, and landed in a wood between Halmstad and Laholm on the west coast of Sweden. Before taking off we agreed to state that we had been on a training flight, and I therefore destroyed my parachute, harness, Mae West and escape purse. I had fractured my foot on landing, but managed to reach a farm. I woke the inhabitants, and they took me to another house, where I met Sgt McFarlane. We remained there until the arrival of the Swedish military authorities. We were then taken by car to a hospital in Halmstad. On 31 Aug we were joined by Sgt Tovey and Sgt Hendry. On 1 Sep we were taken by train to Falun. We arrived on 2 Sep, and remained there until 30 Oct. On that day I left with Sgt McFarlane for Stockholm. We returned to the UK by air on 7 Nov."

Sgt McFarlane. Mid-upper gunner. "I baled out at 01.00 hours on 30 Aug, and landed between Halmstad and Laholm. I buried my parachute, harness and Mae West and destroyed my purse. I walked till I reached a house, and remained there until the Swedish military authorities arrived. While at the house I was joined by Sgt Whitworth, and from this point my story is as related by him.

F/Sgt Tovey RAAF. Bomb-aimer. I baled out at 01.00 hours on 30 Aug, and landed near the village of Skogaby, a few miles north of Laholm. I destroyed my money, and slept the night in my parachute. Next morning I buried the remainder of my equipment and walked to Skogaby. Here I got in touch with the son of the schoolmaster, and later a Swedish military car arrived with Sgt Hendry, our navigator. We were taken to the military HQ at Halmstad, and from there to the hospital. From this point my story is the same as Sgt Whitworth's.

Key Facts about 300 Squadron

Stations

BRAMCOTE	01.07.40. to 22.08.40.
SWINDERBY	22.08.40. to 18.07.41.
HEMSWELL	18.07.41. to 18.05.42.
INGHAM	18.05.42. to 31.01.43.
HEMSWELL	31.01.43. to 22.06.43.
INGHAM	22.06.43. to 01.03.44.
FALDINGWORTH	01.03.44. to 28.12.46.

Aircraft Operated

BATTLE	01.07.40. to 11.40.
WELLINGTON IC	11.40. to 09.41.
WELLINGTON IV	09.41. to 01.43.
WELLINGTON III	01.43. to 04.43.
WELLINGTON X	04.43. to 03.44.
LANCASTER I/III	03.04.44. to 10.46.

Commanding Officers

WING COMMANDER K P LEWIS (British adviser)	
WING COMMANDER W MAKOWSKI	01.07.40. to 18.07.41.
WING COMMANDER S CWYNAR	19.07.41. to 27.01.42.
WING COMMANDER R SULINSKI	27.01.42. to 09.07.42.
WING COMMANDER W DUKSZTO	09.07.42. to 31.10.42.
WING COMMANDER A KROPINSKI	31.10.42. to 04.05.43.
WING COMMANDER M KUCHARSKI	04.05.43. to 18.11.43.
WING COMMANDER K KUZIAN	18.11.43. to 18.01.44.
WING COMMANDER A KOWALCZYK	18.01.44. to 01.04.44.
WING COMMANDER T POZYCZKA	01.04.44. to 02.02.45.
WING COMMANDER B JARKOWSKI	02.02.45. to 17.09.45.
WING COMMANDER R SULINSKI	17.09.45. to 04.02.46.
WING COMMANDER B JARKOWSKI	22.02.46. to 02.01.47.

Flight Commanders

A Flight

SQUADRON LEADER S CWYNAR	01.07.40. to 27.07.40.
FLIGHT LIEUTENANT S KRYNSKI	28.07.40. to 29.12.40.
SQUADRON LEADER R SULINSKI	30.12.40. to 27.01.42.
SQUADRON LEADER M WOLANSKI	28.01.42. to 01.09.42.
SQUADRON LEADER F WESOLOWSKI	01.09.42. to 30.01.43.
SQUADRON LEADER K KONOPASEK	30.01.43. to 02.04.43.
SQUADRON LEADER W ROGALSKI	02.04.43. to 19.07.43.
SQUADRON LEADER W CHRZANOWSKI	19.07.43. to 04.06.44.
SQUADRON LEADER J JEZYCKI	05.06.44. to 06.11.44.
SQUADRON LEADER B JANAS	06.11.44. to 02.01.45.
SQUADRON LEADER J BROGOWSKI	03.01.45. to 10.04.45.
SQUADRON LEADER M KOSTUCH	11.04.45. to 02.01.47.

B Flight

SQUADRON LEADER M PRONASZKO	01.07.40. to 27.07.40.
FLIGHT LIEUTENANT R SULINSKI	28.07.40. to 29.12.40.
SQUADRON LEADER S CWYNAR	30.12.40. to 09.07.41.
FLIGHT LIEUTENANT W CICHOWSKI	09.07.41. to 07.08.41.
SQUADRON LEADER J MICHALOWSKI	09.08.41. to 26.10.41.
SQUADRON LEADER W DUKSZTO	26.10.41. to 31.07.42.
SQUADRON LEADER T JASINSKI	07.08.42. to 01.10.42.
SQUADRON LEADER M KUCHARSKI	01.10.42. to 01.12.42.
SQUADRON LEADER B BILINSKI	01.12.42. to 18.06.43.
SQUADRON LEADER K KUZIAN	19.06.43. to 18.11.43.
SQUADRON LEADER A KOWALCZYK	18.11.43. to 17.01.44.
SQUADRON LEADER T POZYCZKA	19.01.44. to 01.04.44.
SQUADRON LEADER L KUROWSKI	02.04.44. to 25.04.44.
SQUADRON LEADER E KOREPTA	25.04.44. to 04.06.44.
SQUADRON LEADER T D MISSELBROOK	12.06.44. to 02.09.44.
SQUADRON LEADER B JARKOWSKI	28.11.44. to 02.02.45.
SQUADRON LEADER J KONARZEWSKI	03.02.45. to 21.02.45.
FLIGHT LIEUTENANT H RUDAKOWSKI	22.02.45. to 10.04.45.
SQUADRON LEADER T WIERZBOWSKI	11.04.45. to 30.04.46.
SQUADRON LEADER J KWAPNIEWSKI	01.05.46. to 02.01.47.

Operational Record

OPERATIONS	SORTIES	AIRCRAFT LOSSES	% LOSSES
468	3684	77	2.1

CATEGORY OF OPERATIONS

BOMBING	MINING
363	105

FAIREY BATTLE

OPERATIONS	SORTIES	AIRCRAFT LOSSES	% LOSSES
7	47	0	0.0

All bombing

VICKERS WELLINGTON

OPERATIONS	SORTIES	AIRCRAFT LOSSES	% LOSSES
323	2421	47	1.9

CATEGORY OF OPERATIONS

BOMBING	MINING
218	105

LANCASTERS

OPERATIONS	SORTIES	AIRCRAFT LOSSES	% LOSSES
138	1216	30	2.5

All bombing.

Roll of Honour

† 13/14.10.1940 – F/O Jan Gebicki, pilot (76605)
† 13/14.10.1940 – Sgt Tadeusz Egierski, observer (780113)
† 13/14.10.1940 – Sgt Edward Morawa, wireless operator/air gunner (780251)

† 29.10.1940 – Sgt Gerhard Goebel, pilot, (780040)
† 29.10.1940 – F/O Stanislaw Firley-Bielanski, observer (76828)
† 29.10.1940 – Sgt Tadeusz Szmajdowicz, wireless operator/air gunner (780068)

† 28/29.12.1940 – F/L Stefan Krynski, pilot (76611)
† 28/29.12.1940 – Sgt Henryk Wegrzyn, air gunner (781192)

† 11/12.06.1941 – Sgt Zygmunt Chowanski, wireless operator (780821)

† 18/19.06.1941 – Sgt Wladyslaw Paleniczek, pilot (780554)
† 18/19.06.1941 – Sgt Jerzy Domanski, pilot (780419)
† 18/19.06.1941 – Sgt Walenty Sieczka, air gunner, (781405)
† 18/19.06.1941 – Sgt Piotr Bankowski, air gunner (780554)

† 03/04.07.1941 – F/O Kazimierz Kula, pilot, (76652)
† 03/04.07.1941 – Sgt Jan Mieczkowski, wireless operator (780649)
† 03/04.07.1941 – Sgt Wladyslaw Urbanowicz, air gunner (780254)
† 03/04.07.1941 – Sgt Otto Herman, air gunner (780041)

† 25/26.07.1941 – Sgt Mieczyslaw Sloma, pilot (780434)
† 25/26.07.1941 – P/O Wladyslaw Jakimowicz, pilot (P-0483)
† 25/26.07.1941 – P/O Tadeusz Srzednicki, observer (P-0331)
† 25/26.07.1941 – Sgt Andrzej Horak, wireless operator (793746)
† 25/26.07.1941 – Sgt Feliks Zemmler, air gunner (780217)

† 06/07.08.1941 – F/L Wladyslaw Cichowski, pilot (76667)
† 06/07.08.1941 – F/O Stanislaw Jasinski, pilot (P-0624)
† 06/07.08.1941 – F/O Tadeusz Chrostowski, observer (76663)
† 06/07.08.1941 – Sgt Feliks Jezierski, wireless operator (780326)
† 06/07.08.1941 – Sgt Czeslaw Szczukowski, air gunner (781514)
† 06/07.08.1941 – F/O Edward Jura, air gunner (P-0671)

† 18/19.08.1941 – Sgt Kazimierz Ceglinski, pilot (784720)
† 18/19.08.1941 – Sgt Stanislaw Kuropatwa, pilot (782286)

† 15/16.01.1942 – F/O Jan Bak, pilot (76826)
† 15/16.01.1942 – Sgt Franciszek Chylewski, pilot (792071)
† 15/16.01.1942 – F/O Waclaw Mosiewicz, observer (P-1156)
† 15/16.01.1942 – Sgt Pawel Krenzel, wireless operator (780831)
† 15/16.01.1942 – Sgt Marian Lagodzinski, air gunner (784658)
† 15/16.01.1942 – P/O Stefan Berdys, air gunner (P-1541)

† 06/07.02.1942 – P/O Wojciech Veit, pilot (P-1630)
† 06/07.02.1942 – F/S Czeslaw Bialy, wireless operator (792267)
† 06/07.02.1942 – Sgt Stefan Niczewski, air gunner (784833)

† 06/07.02.1942 – Sgt Zygmunt Sadurski, air gunner (784033)

† 26/27.03.1942 – Sgt Mieczyslaw Slabikowski, air gunner (781592)

† 26/27.03.1942 – F/O Bogumil Zelazinski, pilot (76733)
† 26/27.03.1942 – P/O Boleslaw Uszpolewicz, pilot (P-1629)
† 26/27.03.1942 – F/O Franciszek Jakubowski, observer (P-1001)
† 26/27.03.1942 – Sgt Jerzy Kwiecinski, wireless operator (780881)
† 26/27.03.1942 – Sgt Teofil Niemeczek, air gunner (792834)
† 26/27.03.1942 – Sgt Wladyslaw Stachurski, air gunner (793106)

† 12/13.04.1942 – Sgt Wladyslaw Zalejko, pilot (780146)
† 12/13.04.1942 – F/O Piotr Pajer, observer (P-1336)
† 12/13.04.1942 – Sgt Konrad Lubojanski, wireless operator (781601)
† 12/13.04.1942 – Sgt Jozef Balucki, air gunner (793597)
† 12/13.04.1942 – Sgt Wladyslaw Strzelczyk, air gunner (784864)

† 17/18.04.1942 – F/O Jozef Kusmierz, pilot (P-0751)
† 17/18.04.1942 – F/O Jan Urbaniak, pilot (P-0523)
† 17/18.04.1942 – F/O Jan Orsza-Matysek, observer (P-1441)
† 17/18.04.1942 – Sgt Jan Orlewski, wireless operator (793829)
† 17/18.04.1942 – Sgt Franciszek Bay, air gunner (792075)
† 17/18.04.1942 – Sgt Aleksander Hupalo, air gunner (782753)

† 03/04.05.1942 – F/L Waclaw Wolski, pilot (P-0144)
† 03/04.05.1942 – F/O Norbert Lewald-Jezierski, observer (76827)
† 03/04.05.1942 – Sgt Zygmunt Samulski, wireless operator (782441)
† 03/04.05.1942 – F/S Boguslaw Nowicki, air gunner (781399)
† 03/04.05.1942 – Sgt Jozef Erdt, air gunner (780726)

† 08/09.06.1942 – F/O Franciszek Malec, pilot (P-0308)
† 08/09.06.1942 – F/L Marian Michalowski, pilot (P-0313)
† 08/09.06.1942 – F/O Aleksander Paszkowski, observer (P-1436)
† 08/09.06.1942 – Sgt Julian Keryluk, wireless operator (793014)
† 08/09.06.1942 – Sgt Leon Zalewski, air gunner (793239)
† 08/09.06.1942 – Sgt Edmund Polak, air gunner (794249)

† 19/20.06.1942 – F/O Jozef Tomaszewski, pilot (P-0340)
† 19/20.06.1942 – Sgt Jan Kropacz, pilot (783089)
† 19/20.06.1942 – F/O Konrad Jezewski, observer (76726)
† 19/20.06.1942 – Sgt Stanislaw Mielcarek, wireless operator (780902)
† 19/20.06.1942 – Sgt Stanislaw Kaczmarczyk, air gunner (794213)
† 19/20.06.1942 – Sgt Kazimierz Blaszczak, air gunner (783942)

† 19/20.06.1942 – Sgt Czeslaw Dziekonski, pilot (780037)

† 19/20.06.1942 – Sgt Ludwik Michalski, pilot (783148)
† 19/20.06.1942 – F/O Eugeniusz Lech, observer (P-1433)
† 19/20.06.1942 – Sgt Stanislaw Wardynski, wireless operator (792219)
† 19/20.06.1942 – F/O Kazimierz Szyszkowski, air gunner (P-0439)
† 19/20.06.1942 – P/O Stefan Neulinger, air gunner (P-1664)

† 08/09.07.1942 – Sgt Jan Rawski, bomb aimer (792938)

† 25/26.07.1942 – Sgt Stanislaw Janek, air gunner (794580)

† 26/27.07.1942 – P/O Boleslaw Boguszewski, air gunner (P-1853)

† 22.08.1942 – Sgt Izydor Konderak, pilot (782574)
† 04/05.09.1942 – Sgt Leon Szychowiak, pilot (793835)
† 04/05.09.1942 – F/O Adam Szpak, navigator (P-0135)
† 04/05.09.1942 – Sgt Tadeusz Kowalak, wireless operator (792828)
† 04/05.09.1942 – Sgt Jozef Jakubiec, air gunner (794222)
† 04/05.09.1942 – Sgt Zygfryd Blachowski, air gunner (781526)

† 10/11.09.1942 – F/O Stanislaw Waszkiewicz, pilot (76615)
† 10/11.09.1942 – F/O Jerzy Wierzbicki, navigator (P-1047)
† 10/11.09.1942 – Sgt Edward Zakielarz, wireless operator (784108)
† 10/11.09.1942 – Sgt Borys Sawczuk, air gunner (781411)
† 10/11.09.1942 – Sgt Jan Horoch, air gunner (794285)

† 13/14.10.1942 – F/L Jozef Wojcik, pilot (76650)
† 13/14.10.1942 – Sgt Ryszard Brych, pilot (783077)
† 13/14.10.1942 – P/O Stanislaw Janas, navigator (P-1847)
† 13/14.10.1942 – Sgt Zenon Wilczynski, wireless operator (781183)
† 13/14.10.1942 – Sgt Wojciech Peczkowski, air gunner (793713)
† 13/14.10.1942 – Sgt Jerzy Lagonski, air gunner (783106)

† 15/16.10.1942 – Sgt Czeslaw Szymen, pilot (784051)
† 15/16.10.1942 – F/O Piotr Sobolewski, navigator (P-1256)
† 15/16.10.1942 – Sgt Stanislaw Piątek, wireless operator (784660)
† 15/16.10.1942 – Sgt Michal Mielnik, air gunner (793975)
† 15/16.10.1942 – Sgt Lech Bialy, air gunner (794993)

† 03/04.11.1942 – P/O Ireneusz Sawicki, pilot (P-1620)
† 03/04.11.1942 – F/O Walenty Zubrycki, navigator (P-0230)
† 03/04.11.1942 – Sgt Zenobiusz Kozlowski, bomb aimer (792679)
† 03/04.11.1942 – Sgt Mieczyslaw Osciak, wireless operator (784659)
† 03/04.11.1942 – Sgt Janusz Treutler, air gunner (793743)

† 08/09.11.1942 – F/O Lubomir Borowicz, navigator (P-0586)
† 08/09.11.1942 – Sgt Zygmunt Rausinski, wireless operator (794046)
† 08/09.11.1942 – Sgt Jan Cieszynski-Nalecz, air gunner (794200)

† 25.11.1942 – Sgt Czeslaw Gebaczka, air gunner (784359)

† 03/04.12.1942 – Sgt Jozef Furmaniak, pilot (780860)
† 03/04.12.1942 – F/O Stanislaw Cichowicz, navigator (P-1301)
† 03/04.12.1942 – Sgt Zdzislaw Derulski, wireless operator (793486)
† 03/04.12.1942 – Sgt Boleslaw Sapko, air gunner (781680)
† 03/04.12.1942 – Sgt Adam Kozakiewicz, air gunner (703029)

† 14/15.01.1943 – Sgt Stanislaw Gosiewski, pilot (792204)
† 14/15.01.1943 – P/O Stefan Zukotynski, navigator (P-1982)
† 14/15.01.1943 – Sgt Henryk Imiolek, bomb aimer (781370)
† 14/15.01.1943 – Sgt Jerzy Burda, air gunner (793667)
† 14/15.01.1943 – Sgt Jozef Jednaki, air gunner (793701)

† 03/04.02.1943 – Sgt Wladyslaw Sowa, pilot (784778)
† 03/04.02.1943 – P/O Tadeusz Malicki, navigator (P-1848)
† 03/04.02.1943 – Sgt Jakub Mierzwa, wireless operator (794086)
† 03/04.02.1943 – Sgt Waclaw Wydzierzecki, air gunner (792781)
† 03/04.02.1943 – Sgt Teodor Ogrodnik, air gunner (794666)

† 03/04.02.1943 – Sgt Walerian Zielinski, pilot (782744)
† 03/04.02.1943 – Sgt Pawel Marciniszyn, pilot (782886)
† 03/04.02.1943 – F/O Stefan Kalina, navigator (P-0765)
† 03/04.02.1943 – Sgt Feliks Lazowski, bomb aimer (780109)
† 03/04.02.1943 – Sgt Jozef Matelowski, wireless operator (783855)
† 03/04.02.1943 – Sgt Zenon Sienkiewicz, air gunner (793327)

† 20.02.1943 – W/O Edward Szafran, pilot (783434)
† 20.02.1943 – Sgt Julian Kramarz, bomb aimer (780580)
† 20.02.1943 – Sgt Stanislaw Kaminski, air gunner (783767)

† 05/06.03.1943 – S/L Jan Jankowski, navigator (P-0053)

† 13/14.03.1943 – Sgt Tadeusz Kuzminski, pilot (783169)
† 13/14.03.1943 – F/S Karol Kramarczyk, navigator (780226)
† 13/14.03.1943 – Sgt Stanislaw Napora, wireless operator (782742)
† 13/14.03.1943 – Sgt Atanazy Papkow, air gunner (703539)
† 13/14.03.1943 – Sgt Franciszek Polom, air gunner (794726)

† 08/09.04.1943 – P/O Stefan Tomicki, pilot (P-1916)
† 08/09.04.1943 – Sgt Stanislaw Slusarski, pilot (792051)
† 08/09.04.1943 – F/O Jan Rudek, navigator (P-2021)
† 08/09.04.1943 – Sgt Tadeusz Kniazycki, bomb aimer (780782)
† 08/09.04.1943 – Sgt Wladyslaw Marczuk, wireless operator (794308)
† 08/09.04.1943 – Sgt Stanislaw Stepien, air gunner (792832)

† 22/23.04.1943 – F/L Eugeniusz Przysiecki, pilot (76635)
† 22/23.04.1943 – Sgt Janusz Belina-Prazmowski, navigator (784001)
† 22/23.04.1943 – Sgt Czeslaw Krelowski, bomb aimer (794182)
† 22/23.04.1943 – Sgt Ireneusz Debowski, wireless operator (781264)
† 22/23.04.1943 – Sgt Tadeusz Szeremeta, air gunner (703599)

† 12/13.05.1943 – Sgt Stanislaw Werner, pilot (782668)
† 12/13.05.1943 – F/O Rudolf Tabaczynski, navigator (P-0368)
† 12/13.05.1943 – Sgt Henryk Szymanowicz, bomb aimer (794517)
† 12/13.05.1943 – Sgt Henryk Lercel, wireless operator (794322)
† 12/13.05.1943 – F/S Mieczyslaw Galas, air gunner (784113)

† 23/24.05.1943 – F/O Henryk Piatkowski, pilot (P-1733)
† 23/24.05.1943 – F/O Witold Jankowski, navigator (P-2017)
† 23/24.05.1943 – P/O Henryk Lewicki, bomb aimer (P-0967)
† 23/24.05.1943 – Sgt Czeslaw Ratajczyk, wireless operator (783028)
† 23/24.05.1943 – Sgt Eugeniusz Kulikowski, air gunner (703387)

† 21.06.1943 – F/L Fabian Pokorniewski, pilot (P-0086)
† 21.06.1943 – F/O Zbigniew Kretkowski, navigator (P-1834)
† 21.06.1943 – Sgt Henryk Czarkowski, bomb aimer (794403)
† 21.06.1943 – Sgt Tadeusz Szczurzynski, wireless operator (784796)
† 21.06.1943 – Sgt Bernard Kot, air gunner (704008)

† 21/22.06.1943 – Sgt Mieczyslaw Bronicki, pilot (780940)
† 21/22.06.1943 – Sgt Mieczyslaw Glass, navigator (794632)
† 21/22.06.1943 – Sgt Stanislaw Nogacki, bomb aimer (784506)
† 21/22.06.1943 – Sgt Stefan Jama, wireless operator (794546)
† 21/22.06.1943 – Sgt Jan Lezuch air gunner (704315)

† 21/22.06.1943 – F/S Mikolaj Bialobrowka, pilot (782554)
† 21/22.06.1943 – P/O Jozef Blajda, navigator (P-2014)
† 21/22.06.1943 – Sgt Jan Ciuchcinski, bomb aimer (781076)
† 21/22.06.1943 – Sgt Jerzy Trzebuchowski, wireless operator (794311)
† 21/22.06.1943 – Sgt Roman Jacennik, air gunner (703492)

† 24/25.06.1943 – Sgt Stanislaw Jawoszek, pilot (784058)
† 24/25.06.1943 – F/O Karol Obrycki, navigator (P-0916)
† 24/25.06.1943 – Sgt Eugeniusz Bartosiak, bomb aimer (781725)
† 24/25.06.1943 – Sgt Franciszek Skoskiewicz, wireless operator (781577)
† 24/25.06.1943 – Sgt Sergiusz Jacewicz, air gunner (784500)

† 24/25.06.1943 – Sgt Antoni Bielski, navigator (794235)
† 24/25.06.1943 – Sgt Jan Bijowski, bomb aimer (781203)
† 24/25.06.1943 – Sgt Kazimierz Zarniewski, wireless operator (794425)

† 28/29.06.1943 – F/S Marian Kleinschmidt, pilot (782266)
† 28/29.06.1943 – F/O Stefan Boguslawski, navigator (P-1976)
† 28/29.06.1943 – Sgt Piotr Mazgaj, bomb aimer (794544)
† 28/29.06.1943 – Sgt Maksymilian Cieslik, wireless operator (781969)
† 28/29.06.1943 – Sgt Tadeusz Knebloch, air gunner (793149)

† 25/26.07.1943 – Sgt Edmund Garczynski, pilot (782805)
† 25/26.07.1943 – Sgt Stanislaw Skwarek, wireless operator (793899)
† 25/26.07.1943 – Sgt Stanislaw Galiczyn, air gunner (783260)

† 02/03.08.1943 – F/O Witold Smyk, pilot (P-0846)
† 02/03.08.1943 – F/O Tadeusz Skalisz, navigator (P-2113)

† 15/16.08.1943 – F/O Jozef Roubo, navigator (P-1838)
† 15/16.08.1943 – Sgt Jozef Martyniec, wireless operator (794865)
† 15/16.08.1943 – Sgt Henryk Blazejewski, air gunner (704195)

† 30/31.08.1943 – F/L Leon Osmialowski, pilot (P-0111)
† 30/31.08.1943 – F/L Aleksander Steininger, navigator (P-1026)
† 30/31.08.1943 – P/O Stanislaw Swiech, bomb aimer (P-2051)
† 30/31.08.1943 – Sgt Jozef Zabal, wireless operator (794044)
† 30/31.08.1943 – Sgt Franciszek Buda, air gunner (780664)

† 07/08.10.1943 – S/L Stanislaw Morawski, pilot (P-1326)
† 07/08.10.1943 – F/O Antoni Moskwa, navigator (P-1767)
† 07/08.10.1943 – F/S Edward Gastol, bomb aimer (793471)
† 07/08.10.1943 – F/S Wladyslaw Kordys, wireless operator (782530)
† 07/08.10.1943 – Sgt Roman Zukowski, air gunner (792392)

† 11/12.11.1943 – F/L Edward Korecki, navigator (P-0216)
† 11/12.11.1943 – F/S Henryk Winiarczyk, wireless operator (794338)

† 19.12.1943 – F/O Jan Ochedzan, pilot (P-1729)
† 19.12.1943 – Sgt Feliks Bluj, bomb aimer (794721)

† 20/21.02.1944 – F/S Wladyslaw Kabacinski, pilot (792027)
† 20/21.02.1944 – Sgt Zygmunt Grzesiak, navigator (703718)
† 20/21.02.1944 – Sgt Ferdynand Pitka, bomb aimer (794958)
† 20/21.02.1944 – Sgt Alfons Stankiewicz, wireless operator (703164)
† 20/21.02.1944 – Sgt Witold Plonczynski, air gunner (794959)

† 07/08.03.1944 – F/O Zdzislaw Ingling, pilot (P-0983)
† 07/08.03.1944 – P/O Kazimierz Lenartowicz, navigator (P-2280)
† 07/08.03.1944 – P/O Henryk Jarnicki, bomb aimer (P-2250)
† 07/08.03.1944 – Sgt Boleslaw Kot, flight engineer (794211)
† 07/08.03.1944 – Sgt Gustaw Liskiewicz, wireless operator (782035)
† 07/08.03.1944 – Sgt Boleslaw Machulak, air gunner (703158)
† 07/08.03.1944 – Sgt Aleksander Loksza, air gunner (703437)

† 24/25.04.1944 – S/L Ludwik Kurowski, pilot (P-0819)
† 24/25.04.1944 – F/O Zbigniew Woch, navigator (P-1780)
† 24/25.04.1944 – F/S Wladyslaw Karalun, bomb aimer (794454)
† 24/25.04.1944 – Sgt Wladyslaw Pruss, flight engineer (793556)
† 24/25.04.1944 – F/S Karol Kysiak, wireless operator (703157)
† 24/25.04.1944 – F/S Michal Wijtyk, air gunner (784189)
† 24/25.04.1944 – F/S Jozef Walecki, air gunner (704024)

† 24/25.04.1944 – F/O Aleksander Fedoronko, pilot (P-1083)
† 24/25.04.1944 – F/O Wladyslaw Jasinski, navigator (P-2264)

† 24/25.04.1944 – F/S Edmund Pogodzinski, bomb aimer (784557)
† 24/25.04.1944 – F/S Kazimierz Wodo, flight engineer (782600)
† 24/25.04.1944 – Sgt Zenon Rozycki, wireless operator (703225)
† 24/25.04.1944 – F/S Janusz Dudziak, air gunner (704196)
† 24/25.04.1944 – F/S Jan Jagiello, air gunner (704596)

† 22/23.05.1944 – F/S Jan Bychowski, navigator (709544)
† 22/23.05.1944 – Sgt Czeslaw Rybinski, flight engineer (780062)
† 22/23.05.1944 – Sgt Antoni Leszkowicz, wireless operator (704444)

† 22/23.05.1944 – F/O Mieczyslaw Bergner, navigator (P-2097)
† 22/23.05.1944 – F/S Stanislaw Chabrowski, bomb aimer (784982)
† 22/23.05.1944 – Sgt Kazimierz Kozanecki, flight engineer (780049)
† 22/23.05.1944 – Sgt Kazimierz Jankowiak, wireless operator (704437)
† 22/23.05.1944 – Sgt Leon Winkel, air gunner (792294)
† 22/23.05.1944 – Sgt Kazimierz Nawratil, air gunner (703889)

† 27/28.05.1944 – F/S Jerzy Koziolek, pilot (780879)
† 27/28.05.1944 – F/O Witold Osika, pilot (P-2320)
† 27/28.05.1944 – F/O William Tapp, navigator (P-2330)
† 27/28.05.1944 – Sgt Bernard Jankowski, bomb aimer (783084)
† 27/28.05.1944 – Sgt Marian Myszor, flight engineer (780604)
† 27/28.05.1944 – F/O Wladyslaw Szymanski, wireless operator (P-2263)
† 27/28.05.1944 – F/S Ludwik Maciejewski, air gunner (780896)
† 27/28.05.1944 – Sgt Jan Duchaczek, air gunner (704723)

† 12/13.06.1944 – F/L Jerzy Rozanski, pilot (P-1818)
† 12/13.06.1944 – P/O Mieczyslaw Hahn, navigator (P-2408)
† 12/13.06.1944 – F/O Waclaw Bakun, bomb aimer (P-2251)
† 12/13.06.1944 – Sgt Mieczyslaw Szeliga, flight engineer (782001)
† 12/13.06.1944 – Sgt Albin Pacula, wireless operator (704493)
† 12/13.06.1944 – F/S Marian Wroblewski-Jastrzebiec, air gunner (704824)
† 12/13.06.1944 – F/S Rajmund Barzdo, air gunner (704838)

† 12/13.06.1944 – F/S Franciszek Rembecki, pilot (793887)
† 12/13.06.1944 – P/O Isaak Feil, navigator (P-2485)
† 12/13.06.1944 – Sgt Feliks Bladowski, flight engineer (780153)
† 12/13.06.1944 – F/S Jan Bokros wireless operator (794816)
† 12/13.06.1944 – Sgt Stanislaw Miszturak air gunner (704821)
† 12/13.06.1944 – Sgt Wladyslaw Leppert air gunner (794154)

† 12/13.06.1944 – F/O Henryk Burkiewicz, pilot (P-2197)
† 12/13.06.1944 – P/O Eugeniusz Jozefowicz, navigator (P-2412)
† 12/13.06.1944 – P/O Kazimierz Andruszkiewicz, bomb aimer (P-2482)
† 12/13.06.1944 – Sgt Edward Porowski, flight engineer (784462)
† 12/13.06.1944 – Sgt Jan Sumiga, wireless operator (793195)
† 12/13.06.1944 – F/S Michal Golec, air gunner (782730)
† 12/13.06.1944 – F/S Lucjan Klucha, air gunner (704558)

† 24.06.1944 – F/S Zygmunt Badowski, pilot (793747)
† 24.06.1944 – P/O Andrzej Groblicki, navigator (P-2406)
† 24.06.1944 – F/S Jozef Staniewski, bomb aimer (782318)
† 24.06.1944 – Sgt Tadeusz Popowicz, flight engineer (7782374)
† 24.06.1944 – F/S Edmund Kosznik, wireless operator (780477)
† 24.06.1944 – F/S Wladyslaw Stec, air gunner (794733)
† 24.06.1944 – W/O Andrzej Madejowski, air gunner (781538)

† 30.06/01.07.1944 – F/S Wladyslaw Fudali, pilot (783291)
† 30.06/01.07.1944 – F/O Boleslaw Cwojdzinski, navigator (P-2400)
† 30.06/01.07.1944 – F/O Zygmunt Ziembinski, bomb aimer (P-2248)
† 30.06/01.07.1944 – Sgt Jozef Bukowski, flight engineer (793205)
† 30.06/01.07.1944 – Sgt Ignacy Malecki, wireless operator (703117)
† 30.06/01.07.1944 – F/S Klemens Lechnicki, air gunner (703050)
† 30.06/01.07.1944 – Sgt Kazimierz Bogusz, air gunner (782542)

† 18/19.07.1944 – W/O Jozef Zoltanski, pilot (793879)
† 18/19.07.1944 – F/L Stanislaw Ostaszewski, pilot (P-0445)
† 18/19.07.1944 – F/O Jerzy Bregman, navigator (P-2527)
† 18/19.07.1944 – F/S Fryderyk Janicki, bomb aimer (794451)
† 18/19.07.1944 – F/S Stanislaw Szychowski, flight engineer (780364)
† 18/19.07.1944 – F/S Ignacy Ratajczak, wireless operator (703975)
† 18/19.07.1944 – F/S Stanislaw Mamak, air gunner (703439)
† 18/19.07.1944 – W/O Stefan Stysiak, air gunner (783132)

† 23/24.07.1944 – F/S Antoni Ostrowski, pilot (794545)
† 23/24.07.1944 – P/O Eugeniusz Horwacki, navigator (P-2410)
† 23/24.07.1944 – F/L Mieczyslaw Ostrowski, bomb aimer (P-2119)
† 23/24.07.1944 – W/O Jozef Tomiec, flight engineer (780750)
† 23/24.07.1944 – Sgt Bogdan Grudzinski, wireless operator (794849)
† 23/24.07.1944 – F/S Jan Zatloukal, air gunner (783237)
† 23/24.07.1944 – F/S Stanislaw Rymaszewski, air gunner (704796)

† 24/25.07.1944 – F/O James Irving Duguid RCAF, bomb aimer (J.29676)
† 24/25.07.1944 – Sgt Ernest Leonard Morter RAF, flight engineer (7800371)
† 24/25.07.1944 – Sgt Leslie Trevor Page RAF, wireless operator (1581304)
† 24/25.07.1944 – F/S James Rheubottom RCAF, air gunner (R.196199)

† 25/26.07.1944 – F/S Jan Danieluk, pilot (780992)
† 25/26.07.1944 – F/O Kazimierz Galat, navigator (P-2404)
† 25/26.07.1944 – Sgt Jan Kabulski, flight engineer (781380)
† 25/26.07.1944 – F/S Albrecht Pagiela, wireless operator (794835)
† 25/26.07.1944 – F/S Henryk Czyżyk, air gunner (794365)

† 14.08.1944 – F/L Longin Rebinski, pilot (P-1999)
† 14.08.1944 – F/S Zbigniew Migaszewski, navigator (794716)
† 14.08.1944 – F/L Henryk Trawinski, bomb aimer (P-0853)
† 14.08.1944 – Sgt Stanislaw Bujnowski, flight engineer (784014)

† 14.08.1944 – Sgt Franciszek Wojtulewicz, wireless operator (705050)
† 14.08.1944 – P/O Stanislaw Czabanski, air gunner (P-2579)
† 14.08.1944 – Sgt Stanislaw Grabowski, air gunner (706050)

† 25/26.08.1944 – P/O Gordon Gambley Whyte RAF, pilot (175620)
† 25/26.08.1944 – Sgt Albert Clayworth RAF, navigator (1621688)
† 25/26.08.1944 – Sgt Maurice John Robertson RAF, bomb aimer (1397798)
† 25/26.08.1944 – F/S Wladyslaw Jagiello, flight engineer (780009)
† 25/26.08.1944 – Sgt Billie Sellars RAF, wireless operator (2206501)
† 25/26.08.1944 – Sgt John Herbert Moule RAF, air gunner (1853428)
† 25/26.08.1944 – Sgt Charles William Taylor RAF, air gunner (1880883)

† 25/26.08.1944 – F/O Richard Neville Hansell RAF, pilot (173340)
† 25/26.08.1944 – Sgt Randolph James Hayden RAF, navigator (913140)
† 25/26.08.1944 – F/S Arthur Norman Taylor RAF, bomb aimer (1537765)
† 25/26.08.1944 – Sgt John Letts RAF, flight engineer (1592026)
† 25/26.08.1944 – Sgt Walter Herbert Slater RAF, wireless operator (1428062)
† 25/26.08.1944 – Sgt Harold Oxspring Lowbridge RAF, air gunner (1860066)
† 25/26.08.1944 – Sgt Paul Peters RCAF, air gunner (R.256474)

† 29/30.08.1944 – F/O Marian Pretkiewicz, navigator (P-2152)
† 29/30.08.1944 – F/S Jozef Rutkiewicz, bomb aimer (794048)
† 29/30.08.1944 – Sgt Walerian Cent, flight engineer (792743)
† 29/30.08.1944 – F/S Jan Stolowski, wireless operator (793774)
† 29/30.08.1944 – F/S Jan Madracki, air gunner (784157)
† 29/30.08.1944 – F/S Zdzislaw Kardasiewicz, air gunner (704610)

† 29/30.08.1944 – P/O Harry Lupton RAF, pilot (179649)
† 29/30.08.1944 – F/S Kenneth James Jewell RAF, navigator (1401468)
† 29/30.08.1944 – Sgt Donald John Kelsall Baron RAF, bomb aimer (1389866)
† 29/30.08.1944 – Sgt John Bryce Hamilton RAF, flight engineer (1825268)
† 29/30.08.1944 – W/O Frederick William White RAAF,wireless operator (Aus.410758)
† 29/30.08.1944 – F/S Ivor Charles Vaughan RAF, air gunner (1389416)
† 29/30.08.1944 – Sgt Stanley Sutton Barnett RAF, air gunner (1584724)

† 14.10.1944 – W/O Stanislaw Sarachman, pilot (793177)
† 14.10.1944 – F/L Zbigniew Osuchowski, navigator (P-0266)
† 14.10.1944 – F/O Henryk Swiniarski, bomb aimer (P-2429)
† 14.10.1944 – F/S Czeslaw Marona, flight engineer (780079)
† 14.10.1944 – W/O Jerzy Perun, wireless operator (783189)
† 14.10.1944 – F/S Stanislaw Swiecicki-Stecki, air gunner (703444)

† 02/03.01.1945 – S/L Brunon Janas, pilot (P-1093)
† 02/03.01.1945 – Sgt Brunon Omiotek, navigator (704450)
† 02/03.01.1945 – W/O Jan Banys, bomb aimer (780229)
† 02/03.01.1945 – Sgt Maksymilian Wrus, flight engineer (781108)
† 02/03.01.1945 – Sgt Stefan Zielinski, wireless operator (705532)
† 02/03.01.1945 – F/S Walenty Heine, air gunner (784105)

† 02/03.01.1945 – Sgt Romuald Drozdowicz, air gunner (706719)

† 16/17.01.1945 – P/O Franciszek Matuszewski, bomb aimer (P-2722)
† 16/17.01.1945 – Sgt Mikolaj Piotrowski, wireless operator (794471)
† 16/17.01.1945 – Sgt Antoni Smoczkiewicz, air gunner (706697)

† 28/29.01.1945 – F/L Zbigniew Zarebski, pilot (P-0845)
† 28/29.01.1945 – P/O Romuald Paszkowski, navigator (P-2377)
† 28/29.01.1945 – Sgt Kazimierz Cymbala, air gunner (706584)

† 02/03.02.1945 – F/L Zdzislaw Kapciuk, pilot (P-2575)
† 02/03.02.1945 – Sgt Roman Reder, navigator (704322)
† 02/03.02.1945 – P/O Jan Branszted, bomb aimer (P-2721)
† 02/03.02.1945 – Sgt Bronislaw Wilk, flight engineer (780026)
† 02/03.02.1945 – Sgt Feliks Jurewicz, wireless operator (705695)
† 02/03.02.1945 – F/O Zygmunt Modro, air gunner (P-2150)

† 13/14.02.1945 – W/O Marian Mykietyn, pilot (792387
† 13/14.02.1945 – W/O Jozef Placzek, navigator (781228)
† 13/14.02.1945 – F/S Mieczyslaw Ogorzal, bomb aimer (704316)
† 13/14.02.1945 – Sgt Aleksander Jameliniec, flight engineer (704208)
† 13/14.02.1945 – Sgt Antoni Kaczmarz, wireless operator (705446)
† 13/14.02.1945 – Sgt Lucjan Goldowski, air gunner (706613)
† 13/14.02.1945 – F/S Boleslaw Nizinski, air gunner (704013)

† 20/21.02.1945 – S/L Jan Konarzewski, pilot (76636)
† 20/21.02.1945 – Sgt Stanislaw Modrany, navigator (704308)

† 23/24.02.1945 – F/L Adam Filipek, pilot (P-2648)
† 23/24.02.1945 – P/O Fedynand Magierowski, navigator (P-2792)
† 23/24.02.1945 – P/O Mieczyslaw Ziegenhirte, bomb aimer (P-2830)
† 23/24.02.1945 – Sgt Jozef Mrozek, flight engineer (782865)
† 23/24.02.1945 – F/S Czeslaw Kowalski, wireless operator (705573)
† 23/24.02.1945 – Sgt Wladyslaw Sadowinski, air gunner (706687)
† 23/24.02.1945 – Sgt Sabin Trzepiota, air gunner (706704)

† 23/24.02.1945 – P/O Jozef Barcikowski, navigator (P-2626)
† 23/24.02.1945 – Sgt Rudolf Lisak, wireless operator (705022)
† 23/24.02.1945 – Sgt Jerzy Stokarski, air gunner (706549)

† 02.03.1945 – F/L Mikolaj Kirkilewicz, pilot (P-1940)
† 02.03.1945 – F/O Adam Nieszkodny, navigator (P-2266)
† 02.03.1945 – Sgt Edward Szymanski, bomb aimer (704046)
† 02.03.1945 – Sgt Norbert Wieckowski, flight engineer (793480)
† 02.03.1945 – Sgt Mikolaj Kulik, wireless operator (706482)
† 02.03.1945 – Sgt Jozef Mrozinski, air gunner (705668)
† 02.03.1945 – Sgt Stanislaw Cwenar, air gunner (706851)

† 02.03.1945 – F/L Wladyslaw Wyganowski, pilot (P-0847)

† 02.03.1945 – Sgt Edmund Kulikowski, navigator (704443)
† 02.03.1945 – P/O Jozef Babiarz, bomb aimer (P-2732)
† 02.03.1945 – Sgt Jacek Filek, flight engineer (780727)
† 02.03.1945 – F/S Jan Horobiowski, wireless operator (705005)
† 02.03.1945 – F/S Stefan Chetnicki, air gunner (704989)
† 02.03.1945 – F/S Boleslaw Filipiak, air gunner (705000)

† 09/10.04.1945 – S/L Henryk Rudakowski, pilot (P-1770)
† 09/10.04.1945 – P/O Stefan Kucharski, navigator (P-2905)
† 09/10.04.1945 – F/S Jerzy Stebnicki, bomb aimer (709547)
† 09/10.04.1945 – Sgt Stefan Krasinski, flight engineer (794858)
† 09/10.04.1945 – F/S Waclaw Gold, wireless operator (705003)
† 09/10.04.1945 – Sgt Jozef Parol, air gunner (706726)
† 09/10.04.1945 – Sgt Zygmunt Szymanski, air gunner (706817)

† 05.11.1945 – F/S Bronislaw Warcholek, pilot (704745)
† 05.11.1945 – F/S Wladyslaw Szumski, navigator (704962)
† 05.11.1945 – F/S Bernard Nowak, bomb aimer (794948)
† 05.11.1945 – F/S Piotr Skibinski, flight engineer (793281)
† 05.11.1945 – F/S Zdzislaw Pietrzak, wireless operator (706646)
† 05.11.1945 – F/S Michal Antoszczyszyn, air gunner (703020)

† 08.11.1946 – F/S Wladyslaw Robaszewski, pilot (792391)
† 08.11.1946 – F/O Witold Brodzikowski navigator (P-2506)
† 08.11.1946 – W/O Roman Rozga, bomb aimer (782342)
† 08.11.1946 – F/S Stanislaw Kordys, air gunner (704802)

† 04.02.1946 – W/C Romuald Sulinski, pilot (76647)
† 04.02.1946 – F/O Wladyslaw Jedrzejczyk, navigator (P-2516)
† 04.02.1946 – W/O Michal Szwandt, bomb aimer (794532)
† 04.02.1946 – F/S Feliks Mikula, flight engineer (783490)
† 04.02.1946 – W/O Waclaw Brzezinski, wireless operator (793023)
† 04.02.1946 – F/O Czeslaw Sulgut, air gunner (P-2930)

Aircraft Histories

BATTLE.	From July 1940 to October 1940.
L5317 BH-T	To RCAF 18.12.40.
L5318 BH-L	To RCAF 16.12.40.
L5353 BH-O/V	To RCAF 26.2.41.
L5356 BH-R	Crashed in Nottinghamshire while training 29.10.40.
L5365	From 234Sqn. To RCAF 18.12.40.
L5425 BH-B	To RAAF 15.1.41.
L5426 BH-L/W	To RCAF 5.2.41.
L5427 BH-E/K	To RCAF 13.5.41.
L5429 BH-V	To 304Sqn.
L5490 BH-F	To RCAF 28.11.40.
L5492 BH-M	To RCAF 18.12.40.
L5499 BH-M/Y	Crashed in Nottinghamshire on return from Calais 13.10.40.
L5529 BH-N/V	To RAAF 15.1.41.
L5530 BH-A	To RCAF 13.5.41.
L5532 BH-K/T	To 103Sqn.
L5537	To RCAF 26.2.41.
L5567 BH-V/S	To RCAF 5.2.41.
N2127 BH-H	To RCAF 16.12.40.
N2147 BH-Q	To RCAF 11.12.40.
N2241 BH-G	To RCAF 11.12.40.
P2309 BH-J	To RCAF 5.2.41.
R7402	To SAAF 20.3.42.
WELLINGTON.	From October 1940 to March 1944.
L7789 BH-G	From 9Sqn. To 18 OTU and back. To 305Sqn.
L7817 BH-P	To 149Sqn.
L7873 BH-R/F	To 99Sqn.
P9228 BH-Y	From 9Sqn via RAE. To 22 OTU and back. To 5GpTF
R1035 BH-A	Crashed on approach to Swinderby on return from Antwerp 28.12.40.
R1061 BH-J	To 103Sqn.
R1178 BH-L	Ditched off Norfolk coast on return from Hamburg 26.7.41.
R1184 BH-B	FTR Cologne 10/11.7.41.
R1211 BH-T	To 21 OTU.
R1273 BH-H	Crashed almost immediately after take-off from Langham when bound for Berlin 23.3.41.
R1327 BH-W	To 18 OTU.
R1344 BH-L	To 103Sqn.
R1347 BH-D	To 103Sqn.
R1510 BH-H	Crashed at Hemswell while training 24.9.41.
R1610 BH-O	Crashed almost immediately after take-off from Hemswell while training 7.5.42.
R1617 BH-S	To 103Sqn.
R1620 BH-M	To 104 OTU.

R1640 BH-A	Ditched in North Sea on return from Bremen 29/30.6.41.
R1641 BH-Z	Crashed almost immediately after take-off from Hemswell when bound for Duisburg 18.8.41.
R1642 BH-X	FTR Bremen 3/4.7.41.
R1705 BH-U	FTR Mannheim 7/8.11.41.
R1715 BH-S/P	To 104 OTU.
R1725 BH-B/V/Q	FTR Essen 8/9.6.42.
R1795 BH-X/Y	From 458Sqn. To 104 OTU.
R3212 BH-V	From 149Sqn. To 18 OTU.
T2574 BH-F/R	To 150Sqn.
T2608 BH-Q	To 21 OTU.
T2623 BH-K	To 21 OTU.
T2719 BH-M	Crashed on take-off from Langham when bound for Berlin 23.3.41.
T2836 BH-S	
T2886 BH-U	To 18 OTU.
W5665 BH-M	FTR Bremen 18/19.6.41.
W5666 BH-H	FTR Düsseldorf 11/12.6.41.
X3175 BH-L	To 150Sqn.
X3283 BH-M	From 150Sqn. To 1481Flt.
X3459 BH-B	From 150Sqn. To 1481Flt.
X3548 BH-N	From 150Sqn. To 83 OTU.
X9639 BH-E	FTR Hamburg 25/26.7.41.
X9676 BH-M	FTR Frankfurt 6/7.8.41.
X9815	To 150Sqn.
X9829	To 304Sqn.
Z1183 BH-J	From 458Sqn. FTR Hamburg 3/4.5.42.
Z1204 BH-V	From 301Sqn. FTR Bremen (301Sqn crew) 2/3.7.42.
Z1213 BH-H	FTR Essen 12/13.4.42.
Z1215 BH-E	To 301Sqn and back via 458Sqn. FTR Emden 19/20.6.42.
Z1220 BH-X/U	To 301Sqn.
Z1244 BH-R/E/B	SOC 14.7.44.
Z1245 BH-P	From 142Sqn. To 305Sqn.
Z1250 BH-N/K	FTR Kiel 13/14.10.42.
Z1255	From 301Sqn. Returned to 301Sqn.
Z1256 BH-Z/A	FTR Emden 19/20.6.42.
Z1258 BH-N	From 301Sqn. FTR Düsseldorf 10/11.9.42.
Z1264 BH-D	To A&AEE and back.
Z1265 BH-K	Crashed in Nottinghamshire on return from Hamburg 15/16.1.42.
Z1266 BH-J	To 142Sqn.
Z1267 BH-P	FTR Hamburg 17/18.4.42.
Z1268 BH-Q/T	To 18 OTU.
Z1269 BH-L	FTR Essen 26/27.3.42.
Z1270 BH-T	FTR Hamburg 26/27.7.42.
Z1271 BH-A	FTR Mannheim 7/8.11.41.
Z1275 BH-W	To 104 OTU.
Z1276 BH-Z/W	FTR Cologne 27/28.4.42.

Z1278	From 460Sqn. To 305Sqn.
Z1279 BH-Z/X	From 458Sqn. To 305Sqn.
Z1282 BH-F	Crashed while trying to land at Exeter on return from Brest 7.2.42.
Z1286 BH-P	From 142Sqn. To 301Sqn.
Z1288 BH-N	From 460Sqn. To 305Sqn.
Z1291 BH-F	From 458Sqn. Ditched in North Sea on return from Bremen 4.6.42.
Z1318 BH-L	From 18 OTU. To 301Sqn.
Z1320 BH-K	From 458Sqn. FTR Bremen 4/5.9.42.
Z1326 BH-B	Ditched in North Sea on return from Bremen 3.7.42.
Z1332 BH-D	To 104 OTU.
Z1343 BH-L	From 460Sqn. FTR from mining sortie 8/9.11.42.
Z1382 BH-V	To 104 OTU.
Z1387 BH-Q	FTR Lorient 14/15.1.43.
Z1398 BH-L/B/J	To 301Sqn.
Z1400 BH-K	From 460Sqn. To 104 OTU.
Z1401 BH-O	From 460Sqn. FTR Mannheim 6/7.12.42.
Z1407 BH-Z	To 104 OTU.
Z1409 BH-A	FTR Osnabrück 17/18.8.42.
Z1415 BH-X/E	To 305Sqn.
Z1419 BH-Z/V	From 142Sqn. To 305Sqn.
Z1421 BH-V	FTR from mining sortie 3/4.11.42.
Z1465 BH-S	To 104 OTU.
Z1475 BH-X	FTR Cologne 15/16.10.42.
Z1488 BH-W	FTR Frankfurt 24/25.8.42.
Z1489 BH-J	Ditched in North Sea on return from Wilhelmshaven 9.7.42.
Z1490 BH-C	From 301Sqn. To 305Sqn.
Z1495 BH-J	From 460Sqn. FTR from intruder sortie to Essen 25.11.42.
Z1661 BH-Z	From 150Sqn. To 82 OTU.
Z8833 BH-B	To 150Sqn.
BJ581 BH-L	From 142Sqn. To 23 OTU.
BJ609 BH-W	From 199Sqn. Crash-landed in Lincolnshire while training 8.4.43.
BJ972 BH-S	From 150Sqn. To CGS.
BK150 BH-Q	From 199Sqn. FTR Essen 5/6.3.43.
BK196 BH-D	From 150Sqn. To 15 OTU.
BK236 BH-P	From 142Sqn. To CGS.
BK267 BH-O/W	From 150Sqn. To 148Sqn.
BK303 BH-Q	From 142Sqn. FTR from mining sortie 3/4.2.43.
BK305 BH-E	From 142Sqn. Crashed in Lincolnshire during air test 20.2.43.
BK354	To 199Sqn.
BK356 BH-G	To 30 OTU.
BK443 BH-V	To 30 OTU.
BK511 BH-X	From 150Sqn. FTR Hamburg 3/4.2.43.
BK516 BH-K	From 142Sqn. FTR from mining sortie 13/14.3.43.
HE147 BH-C	To 18 OTU.
HE148 BH-T	FTR Duisburg 8/9.4.43.
HE289 BH-A	To 18 OTU.

HE291 BH-V FTR from mining sortie 22/23.4.43.
HE295 BH-P FTR Duisburg 12/13.5.43.
HE327 BH-S FTR Krefeld 21/22.6.43.
HE373 BH-E From 16 OTU. To 11 OTU.
HE381 BH-X From 30 OTU. To 23 OTU.
HE420 BH-T/R To 18 OTU.
HE447 BH-Z/Y To 18 OTU.
HE464 BH-J/F From 30 OTU. To 166Sqn.
HE701 BH-U To 23 OTU.
HE749 BH-O To 166Sqn.
HE768 BH-B/N FTR from mining sortie 15/16.8.43.
HE769 BH-B To 12 OTU.
HE805 BH-C/W To 1481Flt.
HE807 BH-O Force-landed in Nottinghamshire when bound for Hamburg 3.8.43.
HE813 BH-E/L From 305Sqn. To 12 OTU.
HE869 BH-D To 11 OTU.
HE985 BH-C/W FTR Krefeld 21/22.6.43.
HF480 BH-V To 11 OTU.
HF487 BH-S From 199Sqn. To 11 OTU.
HF490 BH-O From 305Sqn. FTR from mining sortie 7/8.10.43.
HF590 BH-X From 199Sqn. Crashed on landing at Ingham on return from mining sortie 8.10.43.
HF591 BH-B From 199Sqn. Crashed in Lincolnshire during air-test 21.6.43.
HF598 BH-E/M From 199Sqn. Crashed in Lincolnshire during an air-test 19.12.43.
HF605 BH-P FTR Hamburg 2/3.8.43.
HF606 BH-C FTR Wuppertal 24/25.6.43.
HZ259 To 199Sqn.
HZ373 BH-A To 11 OTU.
HZ374 BH-K FTR Dortmund 23/24.5.43.
HZ375 BH-Q/N To 11 OTU.
HZ376 BH-G FTR Wuppertal 24/25.6.43.
HZ438 BH-J FTR Cologne 28/29.6.43.
HZ439 BH-V To 18 OTU.
HZ484 From 466Sqn. To 432Sqn.
HZ486 BH-Z From 466Sqn. FTR Essen 25/26.7.43.
JA116 BH-Q FTR Mönchengladbach 30/31.8.43.
JA117 BH-F FTR from mining sortie 20/21.2.44.
JA129 BH-T From 166Sqn. To 1481Flt.
JA451 BH-J From 432Sqn. To 16 OTU.
LN242 BH-L/D To 12 OTU.
LN297 BH-T/P To 11 OTU.
LN298 BH-B To 11 OTU.
LN299 BH-G To 11 OTU.
LN390 BH-C From 305Sqn. To 18 OTU.
LN391 BH-P From 305Sqn. To 16 OTU.
LN393 BH-A FTR from mining sortie 11/12.11.43.

LN507 BH-K To 16 OTU.
LN508 BH-U Crash-landed at Southam in Warwickshire when bound for mining sortie off St Nazaire 7.11.43.
LN544 BH-O To 26 OTU.
LN552 BH-D From 166Sqn via 1481Flt. To 82 OTU.
LN553 BH-W From 166Sqn via 1481Flt. To 16 OTU.
LN555 BH-Z To 14 OTU.
LN600 BH-L/E To 14 OTU.
LN697 BH-U To 14 OTU.
LN707 BH-R Crashed on landing at Ingham on return from mining sortie 15.1.44.
LP230 To 16 OTU.

LANCASTER. From April 1944.
L7541 From 550Sqn. To 1LFS.
R5866 From 1LFS. To 1LFS.
W4241 From 1LFS. No operations. To 1LFS.
W4376 BH-A/O From 166Sqn. To 1LFS.
W4821 From 103Sqn via 1656CU & 1LFS. To 1LFS.
DV165 From 1667CU. Training only. To 1LFS.
DV278 BH-A From 625Sqn. FTR Falaise 14.8.44.
DV282 BH-I/P FTR Aachen 27/28.5.44.
DV286 BH-C From 44Sqn. FTR Gelsenkirchen 12/13.6.44.
ED327 BH-H/R From 166Sqn. FTR Stettin 29/30.8.44.
ED382 BH-H From 625Sqn. To 1LFS.
ED749 BH-S From 100Sqn. To 1LFS.
ED779 BH-L From 57Sqn. To 1LFS.
ED814 BH-N From 625Sqn. FTR Vierzon 30.6/1.7.44.
EE124 BH-M From 50Sqn. Crashed in Faldingworth circuit on return from a flying bomb site at les Hayons 24.6.44.
HK541 To 75Sqn.
JA683 BH-S From 460Sqn. FTR Gelsenkirchen 12/13.6.44.
JA922 BH-J From 626Sqn. To 1LFS.
JB559 From 626Sqn. To 12Sqn.
JB561 BH-B From 12Sqn. FTR Rüsselsheim 25/26.8.44.
JB646 BH-T From 626Sqn. To 1656CU.
JB661 From 7Sqn. To 626Sqn.
LL798 BH-V From 626Sqn. To 1LFS.
LL804 BH-F From 115Sqn. To 1660CU.
LL807 BH-N/K FTR Gelsenkirchen 12/13.6.44.
LL855 BH-G FTR Karlsruhe 24/25.4.44.
LL856 BH-E/O/E To 6LFS.
LL857 BH-B Crashed while landing at Faldingworth following early return from Dortmund 23.5.44.
LL947 BH-W FTR Stettin 29/30.8.44.
LL959 To 625Sqn.
LM141 BH-D From 460Sqn. FTR Gelsenkirchen 6.11.44.

LM160	From 186Sqn. To 626Sqn.
LM172 BH-Q	FTR Rüsselsheim 25/26.8.44.
LM178 BH-U	FTR Stuttgart 24/25.7.44.
LM486 BH-C	FTR Karlsruhe 24/25.4.44.
LM487 BH-J	FTR Dortmund 22/23.5.44.
LM488 BH-D	FTR Kiel 23/24.7.44.
LM632 BH-O	From 626Sqn. FTR Kiel 9/10.4.45.
ME470 BH-F	
ME546 BH-I	
ME549 BH-M	
ME594 BH-B	From 625Sqn. Crashed while landing Faldingworth during training 23.7.44.
ME648 BH-A	From 100Sqn. To 166Sqn.
ME671 BH-B	From 103Sqn. To 576Sqn.
ME744 BH-P/V/P	From 460Sqn. FTR Wiesbaden 2/3.2.45.
ME780	To 625Sqn.
ME847 BH-Z	From 101Sqn. To 15Sqn.
ND861	From 460Sqn. To 103Sqn.
ND863	From 460Sqn. To 625Sqn.
ND984 BH-P	FTR Stuttgart 24/25.7.44.
NF925	To 12Sqn.
NF959 BH-R	FTR Duisburg 14.10.44.
NG265 BH-V	
NG266 BH-L	FTR Pforzheim 23/24.2.45.
NG269 BH-G/K	
NG283 BH-W	
NG501 BH-U	FTR Cologne 2.3.45.
NN718 BH-A	From 514Sqn. Force-landed at Brussels-Melsbroek airfield in Belgium during Operation Exodus.
NN746 BH-N	
NN748 BH-G	To 625Sqn.
PA160 BH-E	Crashed on approach to Faldingworth on return from Leuna 15.1.45.
PA161 BH-X	FTR Pforzheim 23/24.2.45.
PA163 BH-M	FTR Stettin 29/30.8.44.
PA185 BH-W	Collided with NF932 (550Sqn) when bound for Dresden 13.2.45.
PA220 BH-P	
PA233 BH-J	
PA261 BH-L	
PA262 BH-X	
PA269 BH-U	
PA308 BH-K	
PB171 BH-K	FTR Scholven-Buer 18/19.7.44.
PB252 BH-M	FTR Stuttgart 25/26.7.44.
PB705 BH-B	
PB722 BH-J	FTR Dortmund 20/21.2.45.
PB730 BH-R	
PB823 BH-T	FTR Nuremberg 2/3.1.45.

PB846 BH-K	From 12Sqn. FTR Stuttgart 28/29.1.45.
PB854 BH-I	FTR Cologne 2.3.45.
PD204	From 625Sqn. Returned to 625Sqn.
PD207	To 12Sqn.
PD257 BH-U	FTR Zeitz 16/17.1.45.
PD270	From 12Sqn.
PD361 BH-H	From 12Sqn.
PD379 BH-S	
PD383 BH-Z	
PD387 BH-D	
RF242 BH-T	
RF262 BH-R	From 101Sqn.
SW279 BH-E	From 626 Sqn.

Printed in Great Britain
by Amazon

33755894R00172